BEST WINES!

BEST WINES!

GOLD MEDAL WINNERS
FROM THE LEADING
COMPETITIONS WORLDWIDE

Edited by Gail Bradney
Research by Corliss Block

A PRINT PROJECT BOOK

The Print Project, Bearsville, NY 12409
© 1996 by Lowell Miller and Gail Bradney
All rights reserved. First Edition 1996
Printed in the United States of America

ISSN 1088-8608
ISBN 0-9651750-0-6

BEST WINES! can be purchased for educational,
business, or sales promotional use. For information
please write to:

> The Print Project
> P.O. Box 703
> Bearsville, NY 12409

Distributed to the book trade by:

> Independent Publishers Group
> 814 North Franklin Street
> Chicago, IL 60610
> (312) 337-0747

Contents

Acknowledgments   vii
Introduction   ix

PART I   Essays to Sip Wine By

1 Why "New World" Wines?   3
2 Competitions and Judges: Are They "Blind"?   7
3 About the Gold Medal Wine Listings   11
4 Tasting Wine: Do I Detect Cigarbox Aromas?   15
5 Storing Wine: My "Cellar" Lies Next to My Clorox   17
6 Avoiding a Bottle Gone Bad   19
7 Here's to Your Health!   21

PART II   A Reference Guide to Winespeak

8 Wine Varietals and Types: What's Blank de Blank?   27
9 Wine Language: Who Writes This Stuff?   47

PART III   The Gold Medal Winners

10 **Red Wines**
    Cabernet Franc   71
    Cabernet Sauvignon   73
    Italian Varietals   98
    Merlot   103
    Native American Reds   116
    Other Reds   117
    Petite Sirah   122
    Pinot Noir   125
    Red Blends   135
    Syrah/Shiraz   147
    Zinfandel   155

11 **White Wines**
    Chardonnay   169
    Chenin Blanc   197
    Gewürztraminer   200
    Other Whites   203

Riesling   210
Sauvignon Blanc   215
Sémillon   224
White Blends   226
White Zinfandel   229

12 **Rosés**   233

13 **Sparkling Wines**
Blanc de Noirs   237
Brut   239
Other Sparkling Wines   244

14 **Sweet/Dessert/Fortified Wines**
Icewine   249
Muscat   252
Other Sweet Wines   255
Port   264
Sherry   267

Appendices
1. Key to Competition Abbreviations   268
2. The Best of BEST WINES!   271
3. Mail-Order Wine Shopping   274
4. The Other Gold Medal Winners   279

Indices
1. Wines by Type and Region   285
2. Wines by Winery and Region   294

Acknowledgments

There are many people whose hard work, encouragement, and support contributed greatly to the completion of this project.

I first want to thank all the wineries who made the effort to provide tasting notes, suggestions, and other useful information that transformed this book from an idea into a reality. There are too many individuals to name who offered advice and guidance, but four who took extra time with me in telephone conversations, faxes, and letters at the crucial early stage of the book were: Axel Borg, head librarian at the University of California at Davis's Viticulture and Oenology Department; Darrell Corti, of Corti Brothers in Sacramento; Dr. James Crum, president of the Pacific Rim International Wine Competition; and Warren Mason, president of Sydney International Wine Competition.

Corliss Block walked into the project when it was merely a half-finished database, an incomplete mailing list, and a heap of disorganized papers. Her resiliency, energy, common sense, wonderful humor, good spirits, and tenacious research skills enabled the book to take shape. In spite of the fact that her job description changed daily—whether it was making five hundred phone calls to wineries, licking five hundred stamps, or sending five hundred faxes—she never complained. I'm deeply grateful for her contributions, and hope that she'll soon be able to get back to her Barbie-doll conceptual art and Imelda thrift shop enterprises.

Without computer wizard Mark Bernard, I would still be in a dark basement room somewhere typing in the index by hand. Mark was able to grasp the concept of bringing vast amounts of information into user-friendly formats, and setting up complicated computerized organizing/formatting systems in such a way that my literary mind didn't have to fret. He maintained excellent cheer even after his third foray into the innards of our computer to recover information I had "lost." At the end stages of the book he put in ungodly hours to help us meet our deadline, and I cannot thank him enough for all of the foresight, expertise, and patience he brought to the process.

Thanks also to Michael Beames, whose persistence in tracking down difficult-to-obtain information from Australian and New Zealand wineries was something to behold.

Beatrice Videz, our Spanish translator and South American liaison, provided the missing link for the Argentinean and Chilean wine producers in the book, and I am grateful to her as well.

Sara Beames was helpful in the book's physical production, but more than that, her friendship and support were invaluable throughout.

Susan Sewall deserves much thanks for her generosity and guidance, and for being such a wonderful role model in our bookmaking and marketing.

Producer Lowell Miller was an editor's dream come true. He provided a solid foundation for a rather ambitious first edition with his excellent business sense, creative vision, and unfaltering confidence, then let me have at it. Having such a mentor and partner taught me a great deal, and I'm full of respect and gratitude for his brilliance, generosity, and good spirits.

Finally, thanks to my friends and family who gave up expecting me to return their calls, and especially to my young son Finn, who learned to use the fax machine before he could write his name.

G.B.

Introduction

We're not wine experts. We're normal people; we love books, conversation, and sunny vacations. And, of course . . . we love a good bottle of wine. What we *hate* is spending our hard-earned money on something that tastes like vinegar. There are few more wonderful pleasures than a glass of well-made wine, and this book is the result of our quest to find that pleasure time after time—but without having to know everything there is to know about wine (because there's in fact a *lot* to know if you really want to know everything).

Lately, we're happy to report, all of our friends think we're the greatest grape mavens around. They corner us near one of our town's wine shops and make us pick out a wine to bring to a dinner party. Or they call us up and pry us for a scoop on sparkling wine to serve at their parents' golden wedding anniversary. Even people we don't know are calling us now, friends of friends, friends of friends of friends. It's really a triumph: the owner of the best restaurant in town called us in to help revise his (already quite excellent) wine list.

Without getting too deeply educated, we've figured out a way to buy a great bottle of wine every time. We don't pore through wine mags and scour oenologists' tomes for tips on what to buy. Too often we've found that one person's opinion—be it a friend, a wine merchant, or a revered wine writer—is just that, one person's opinion, and it isn't the same as ours. We've also learned from wine shop owners that certain wines reviewed in certain well-known wine magazines are promoted with advertising money: the same winery that rates a 90 just happens to be running full-page ads for the next four editions.

But, we thought, what if you could buy only wines that were given the highest award at a prestigious competition, where an entire panel of judges was made up of wine experts, and *where the identity of the wines awarded gold medals was not known at the time of judging?* Then you would truly have a reliable and objective way of knowing that the bottle you were about to buy was "best." This may be the lazyperson's path to enlightenment, but the result is unbeatable. *The experts do all the work for you.*

Every wine in **BEST WINES!** was awarded one or more gold medals in a prestigious regional, national, or international wine competition. But don't think because a wine won a gold medal that it's unquestionably great. It depends on the competition. We researched the field and found that there are hundreds of wine competitions. Some are relatively new and unknown, others are tainted by local or regional politics and commercial bias, and still others do not have reputations for using top judges or impeccable standards of judging. The twenty-four national and international competitions from which we obtained our initial list of gold medal wines are those that all top wineries recognize as the most competitive and honorable (these are the ones they clammer to enter). There are some excellent and well-regarded competitions that we did not choose, but we had to stop somewhere, so our source of gold medal winners came from a list of *twenty-four top competitions* from around the world. (For the Top 24 list, see Chapter 2.) If one of the wine winners was also awarded a gold from a competition outside of our Top 24, we listed the name of that competition as well.

As it turns out, many of the really great wines in our book won multiple awards. Think of it: *at different places, at different times, with different judges, these same wines won golds.* They were always judged "blind," meaning that other than knowing it was a Cabernet Sauvignon, say, and perhaps knowing its price range (some of the competitions group wines by price as well as by type), the judges knew little else about the wine they were evaluating, and independently found themselves reaching a consensus on its merit. How can anyone argue with that?

We didn't argue. Instead, we started this project by trying some of these gold medal winners. Without fail, the wines were excellent. And then we started getting adventurous. We had gotten into the habit of buying the same old wines over and over again, simply because we knew they were good. Now we could choose a wine by type, say Pinot Noir, but instead of buying that same old French burgundy (made from the Pinot Noir grape), we could buy one from Oregon or New Zealand, or could pick up a Chardonnay from Canada, Chile, or Australia. Suddenly a whole new world opened up, but it was risk-free. Our newfound wine-drinking experiences were always satisfying, and often absolutely *symphonic*. Not only could we try new wines from different wineries and winemaking regions, but we could choose ones in the price range we wanted.

There are so many wineries and so many wines produced on this planet that we decided for the first edition of the book to focus on "New World" wines. In winespeak, New World refers to wines that are produced anywhere but Europe. We've found that people who mostly drink French wine, for example, have a fairly good knowledge of that country's wines and wine producers, usually based on a loyal reading of one of the renowned wine gurus or periodicals, but may not have a clue about top-class bottles produced in California or Australia, for example. In addition, German and Spanish wines do not have a substantial hold in the American market, while New World regions such as Chile and Oregon are becoming commonplace in wine shops all over the country.

The book is divided into three parts. Part I is full of fun and useful information that every wine lover will want to know, such as practical suggestions for tasting and storing wine, the latest information about wine and health, and guidelines for using this book.

Part II is a user-friendly reference section comprising a chapter on the wine varietals and types included in the book, and a chapter alphabetically listing the jibberish that makes up wine language so you'll be able to translate tasting notes from winespeak into understandable English.

Part III is an easy-to-use reference you can take along to the wine shop that lists the wines by **broad category** (white wines or sparkling wines, say) and then more specifically by **varietal or type** (Sémillon or Blanc de Noirs, to use the above example). Additionally, the wines are listed by **price,** so that you can find exactly what you want for the price you're willing to pay.

But the name and price of a wine are often not enough to go on, so we obtained tasting notes on each of the gold medal winners, either from the winemakers themselves, from the judges, or sometimes from well-known professional wine writers, and included them in the listings to give consumers some sense of what's in the bottle before they buy it. *These* are usually one person's opinion, so read them more as a guide than as gospel. Also, since the winemakers love to heap praise upon their own wines, you'll notice that the wine descriptions in the listings are full of superlatives. However, these *are* superlative wines, so we allowed them to ring their own bell.

We want this book to be useful to experts and novices alike. Above all, we hope this will be the beginning for you, as it was for us, of a new way to be adventuresome and confident at the same time on your next foray through the wine aisles. Have fun!

Gail Bradney
Woodstock, New York

PART I

Essays to Sip Wine By

Chapter 1

WHY "NEW WORLD" WINES?

The world is changing. The balance of power is changing. The mouse's roar now reverberates globally, as once-developing nations begin to threaten the dominance of their Big Brothers in whole sectors of the world economy.

The same can be said of the wine world. Not too long ago a "fine wine" was inevitably synonymous with "French or Italian." If you wanted to impress your friends, a bottle of European wine costing upwards of thirty dollars would be the ticket.

But now high-quality non-European wines (known in the industry as *New World* wines) sit in unmarked glasses next to their European cousins at prestigious international wine competitions, and judges, not knowing which wines come from which countries, award the New World wines gold medals in equal numbers to their Old World counterparts.

This should surprise no one. After all, if you were to imagine ideal climates suitable for the sometimes cranky and contrary wine grape, and then marked all the regions on a globe encompassing those climates, you'd find that there are two narrow bands—one circling the Northern Hemisphere, one running through the Southern Hemisphere—that include many more countries than Germany, Spain, Portugal, France, and Italy (the so-called Old World). You'd find the United States, Canada, and Lebanon in the northern band; Australia, New Zealand, Argentina, Chile, and South Africa in the southern band. There are other wine-producing regions, of course, but the above-mentioned countries are what wine folks these days generally mean when they say "New World."

And we chose to focus on wines of the New World countries because, well, we're Americans, and we traditionally root for growth and change. We've been having a lot of fun sampling gold-medal-winning wines from "exotic" world regions—exotic in wine terms, at least. We've gotten to the point where it's almost taboo to buy a French Côte du Rhône, say, when a

California "Rhône Ranger" is just as delightful (and usually cheaper). A top Australian Chardonnay effortlessly holds its own next to its French counterpart. When we got to trying less-familiar (for us) types, such as Italian wines or dessert wines, we discovered some California Italian-style reds that were *bellissimo* as well as some *wunderbar* Canadian icewines.

We're not snubbing European wine and wineries. We've just decided, as many wine writers and publications have, that it's time to give the rest of the winemaking world more attention and recognition. The last twenty years have seen remarkable revolutions in the New World wine industry.

Some oenophiles say that the main difference between Old World and New World wines is that, generally speaking of course, European wineries focus on traditional methods of growing and making wine, while their New World counterparts are more invested in science—employing modern techniques in grape-growing and winemaking processes. Most of the best New World wines have found a way to marry the two approaches.

Here's a brief sketch of the New World winemaking regions represented among the gold medal winners in Part III.

Argentina The *world's largest producer of wine* by volume, Argentina is just now emerging as a potential competitor in the world of fine wine. Wine has been grown here since the mid-sixteenth century, when Jesuits recognized the ideal climatic conditions and introduced grapevines to the region. Most Argentine wine is "for the people," but a few forward-thinking wineries are beginning to make high-quality wines that they can export to the rest of the world. Economic instability has been a great factor in retarding the country's significant and largely untapped potential, but this is starting to change, as the gold-medal winners in this book will attest to.

Australia This country has had a remarkable impact on the wine world. A few years ago one might have said, "Australian wines—huh?" But now they are as visible in wine stores as many European bottles, and are certainly as admired.

What we learned while writing this book is that wine has actually been around in Australia for a long time. Anglo-Saxons of the First Fleet carried vines off the boat and planted them in Australia in 1788. As a result, many Aussie vineyards have something their California counterparts lack: old vines. And as conventional wisdom would have it, old vines make better wines even though they yield less grapes, because those fewer grapes possess *more concentrated flavor.*

With its Mediterranean climate, Australia has the potential to grow many varieties well—and does. Top-flight Chardonnays, Rieslings, Shiraz (as the Syrah grape is called in Australia), and Cabernets are among the excellent wines produced here. Also, Australia has a wine-drinking culture—twice as much wine per capita is consumed than in England, and three times as much per person as in the United States. Our friend Michael, a good old Adelaide bloke who helped us with much of the Australian research, says that when you open a refrigerator in his country, there's often a box of "cask wine," which is wine inside a plastic bag inside a box that has a spigot. Aussies have this accessible wine in tall glasses starting at midday, sort of like soda pop in America.

Canada Three quarters of the wine produced in Canada is grown in southern Ontario, mostly in the Niagara Peninsula. Surrounded on two sides by lakes Erie and Ontario, this viticultural region is warmed by the balmy breezes that blow off the lakes. Further, a bluff that was once the shore of an Ice Age lake protects the vineyards below from radical changes by encouraging onshore winds and minimizing frost damage. In addition to world-class Chardonnay, Riesling, and some of the Bordeaux reds such as Cabernet Sauvignon and Merlot, it turns out that Canada has a uniquely wonderful climate for icewine. This is a luscious dessert wine made from frozen grapes, and Canada's icewines beat most competitors from every other country in the world that attempts to produce them.

Chile Only Italy and France export more wine to the United States than Chile. With increasing U.S. and Australian investment, Chilean wineries are entering the world market at a sprint. Chile is unique in that it is the only region of the world free of phylloxera and downy mildew—the deadly crud that wipes out millions of dollars in grape crops every year. This gift frees Chilean wineries from the cost of spraying or grafting vines onto phylloxera-resistant rootstock. They can concentrate their money and efforts into other areas of the production, made easier still by dry summers, which produce exceptionally healthy fruit. Known for inexpensive, uncomplicated, everyday wines, Chile also makes gold-medal-caliber wines of great complexity, such as Cabernet Sauvignons, that are still a bargain compared with those of California.

Lebanon It's impossible to think of Lebanon as a wine-producing country without considering the devastating impact of the wars that have ravaged, and continue to ravage, the country. The vineyards there have not been immune to the destruction, particularly since Beirut is only twenty-five miles from the Bekaa Valley, where much of Lebanon's wine is produced. Lebanon is one of the oldest sites of wine production in the world; consider the Temple of Bacchus, built in the middle of the second century! French influence is still apparent today, as most of the vineyards are planted with classic French varieties. If the strife ever stops in Lebanon, it has the potential to become a prime player in the fine-wine game, since its Mediterranean climate is ideally suited for winemaking with minimal fuss.

New Zealand Even though grapevines were planted more than 150 years ago in New Zealand by missionaries (ever notice how it's the pious guys who always want to sling one back?), it's only been in the past twenty years or so that the wines of this cool, maritime island have achieved their present reputation for high quality. New Zealand gets lots of rain, and its mountainous terrain results in many individual microclimates that are suitable for one variety, while a vineyard nearby would have disastrous results with that same grape. (Perhaps this is a country for intellectual viticulturalists, since they have to determine their ideal grape type microclimate by microclimate.) When New Zealand's Sauvignon Blancs achieved international acclaim a few years back, the wineries got busy. The country's Müller-Thurgau (a German white variety that is well suited to New Zealand's climate) and Chardonnay are also in the running for worldwide admiration. Most of its 112,000 vineyard acres are planted with white varieties.

South Africa Everyone is well aware of the political storms that wracked South Africa over the past two or three decades. Now that relative calm has descended, South Africa can get back to being a player in the wine world. Ports and madeira-type fortified wines have had a long tradition in that country. But the wineries—especially those in the Cape—are bidding for a fresh start, and they're making one with wonderful red-wine blends, Pinotage (a specialty red-wine grape of the Cape), Shiraz, and especially Chenin Blanc and other white wines. Keep your eyes open for more South African wines at the corner wine shop in the coming years.

United States Wine is made in virtually every state, but the states that have made a dent in the wider market are: California; the northwest states of Oregon, Washington, and to a lesser degree Idaho; New York; and Texas. These are the regions that grow vinifera grapes, which are the most important species of the genus *Vitis,* include around forty of the most famous and familiar grape types, and are what most of the world's wines are made of. Every great wine that comes to mind is produced in these U.S. regions, of a caliber that equals and often surpasses Old World counterparts.

In Virginia (remember Thomas Jefferson's struggles with French grapevines?) and Massachusetts, vinifera grape wines are also produced, but on a vastly smaller scale.

Then there are states in other U.S. areas such as the Midwest that grow native American varieties—grapes that will grow in climates unsuitable for fussy *Vitis vinifera.* We've included a few of these because they've received gold medals at well-known competitions that have "Native American" as a category. Besides, it's downright interesting and admirable to see a winery in a place like Florida that wisely realized they couldn't compete with the French, so they went back to their own grape, which thrives in hot, humid conditions, and then took their winemaking seriously.

Chapter 2

COMPETITIONS AND JUDGES
Are They "Blind"?

Let's talk about competitions. One of us grew up in southern Illinois, where every summer at the Morgan County Fair twenty pubescent girls who had grown up on pork sausage, biscuits, and Tater Tots competed for the coveted title of Morgan County Pork Queen. Most of them were excellent candidates for the title, and we used to sneak in and watch the festivities from under the bleachers, breathing in the rich aromas of horse and cow manure, dusty leather boots, and ripe blue jeans. Now the question is, if there are twenty candidates, and one wins the crown, is she in fact the *best Pork Queen* to be found in Morgan County? Well, farm politics did play a role, and beauty and talent were not always the deciding factors. In fact, as far as we could tell, beauty and talent seemed to have almost *no importance* here.

Not so in the world of reputable wine competitions. Why? Because the best competitions require that the wines be judged "blind." This means that wines are poured into identical glasses and lined up in front of the judges, whose only information about the wines they are about to sample are *wine type,* sometimes the *vintage,* and sometimes the *price range.* (After all, a wine that is made to be consumed immediately will have very different qualities from one that's a keeper. The same is often—*but not always*—true of inexpensive versus pricy wines.) In this sense, wines that are awarded gold medals in blind competitions have been judged in the most objective and reliable manner possible. There's no commercial influence; there's only the expertise of the judges to wonder about.

So what about the judges? Depending on the competition, the judging panels will comprise professional wine writers, professional wine tasters and critics, prominent wine-industry people, and often winemakers themselves. These are people whose business it is to know wine: how to taste wines, how to judge wines, how to compare wines. We researched the field and came up with twenty-four very reputable, well-known, prestigious competitions—our

"Top 24"—from around the world, where only the most qualified judges are asked to participate. (See Top 24 Competitions, below.)

Because these experts are vastly better equipped than we are to make judgments about what constitutes a gold medal wine, we've left the decision making up to them. After all, we don't want to have to do any work or research to find the best wines, and we no longer trust just one person's opinion—we've been disappointed too many times. If a panel of these expert judges all agree that Wine X surpasses 158 others in its category, we'll believe them.

What about the downside of competitions? Well, believe it or not, there are some. Some wine snobs claim that the best wines never get entered. There's some truth in this. Consider, for example, a world-famous winery, the kind that produces tiny amounts of high-priced wines that have been purchased before they're even bottled. Their reputation reverberates throughout the world. Their stock is perpetually sold out. They don't need the advertising, so they're not likely to enter a competition.

And yet, if one were to name the great wineries of, say, California, 98 percent of these great producers will also have gold medal wines in their portfolios. Because let's face it, *awards sell wines,* as one Napa Valley winemaker told us. And awards are fun besides. One competition—the Orange County Fair—solves this "snob" problem by purchasing and entering the wines themselves. All California wines available in Orange County are entered by the competition organizers, and no fee for entering is charged. It's the only competition we know of that operates this way. Interestingly, we only came across one Orange County Fair gold medal winner who makes it their policy *not* to enter competitions.

Another argument goes like this: if you have a delicious but quirky wine with a lot of character competing against friendly, easy-to-understand wines in its category, what are the chances that the oddball wine is going to get the gold? Well, the wine world works the same as the movie world in one sense. We're film buffs as well as wine lovers, and we've noticed that great independent films that are truly original and innovative rarely win Academy Awards. Someone is bound not to like this kind of movie, so it gets the thumbs down. Yet sometimes there are surprises and the underdogs win against all odds, so you never know.

But the comparison ends there, because many of the movies that win Academy Awards do so because of the politics of the mass-media empire. A high-earner for the movie biz is much more likely to win than a low earner from a director who hasn't yet paid his or her dues. Not so with reputable wine competitions. As mentioned, *there is no possibility of commercial bias or corruption in a blind tasting.*

Still another criticism attacks the recent proliferation of wine competitions. This point is valid. If there are hundreds of wine competitions one can enter, starting at the local country club and moving up to the international arena, a wine is bound to win an award, maybe even a gold, *somewhere.* So how can you trust that "gold" really means "best"? We agree with this criticism, which is why we took special care to include only the *best* to make up our Top 24 Competitions, from which we obtained the names of our gold medal winners. There are some other fine competitions we could have included, but we'll save those for next edition. For now, know that the wine competitions we used for the Top 24 are regarded as *the best and most reliable competitions* by wine industry professionals.

In the case of less-known areas of the New World, like South Africa and Argentina, we sometimes allowed gold medal wines from competitions other than our original twenty-four—*on the condition that these were also blind tastings*—in order to have more wines represented from those regions.

Apart from the above handful, every wine in Part III won a gold at one of the Top 24, and many won at several of them. In other words, these multiple-gold winners were judged each time to be best by entirely different experts in different places and at different times. *We feel that this alone is proof of the fairness and objectivity of wine competitions.*

Since these multiple-gold-medal wines are the undisputed top winners, there's little chance that you won't love them. We call the wines that won three or more golds from the Top 24 Competitions "The Best of BEST WINES!" and they're listed in Appendix 2.

Wine competitions that are conducted blind all work basically the same way. The differences lie in the number of wines entered, the number of judges, the qualifications for entry, the categories judged, the number of golds awarded, etc. Most competitions charge fees. Some competitions, like California State Fair, have been around forever (the first event was held way back in 1854). The San Francisco International Wine Competition had 2,200 entries, but only awarded 70 golds. Sydney International Wine Competition serves food during the tastings, and judges are required to sample each type of wine alongside a dish that is supposed to complement it. Some of the judges like this novel approach; others feel the food gets in the way of the wines.

Finally, are all golds equal? Theoretically, if there are only eight wines in a particular category, the single gold medal winner in that category is as deserving as the sole gold medalist that competed in a field of ninety-nine. And in fact, there are many categories where no medals are awarded at all. So, yes, all golds should be equal. However, it is human nature to be more impressed by a wine that is only one of three gold medalists in a category exceeding one hundred entries. We don't know the logic of this, but we are certainly prone to the bias ourselves.

What we do know is that every gold medal wine we've tried from our Top 24 pool of competitions, whether it won one or more than one gold, has been delicious, stupendous, and sometimes out of this world.

Listed on the following page are the two dozen wine competitions from which we obtained our list of gold medal winners for this edition. A complete listing of all the competitions that awarded golds to the wines in Part III can be found in Appendix 1.

Top 24 Competitions

International
1995 Challenge International du Vin
1995 International Wine and Spirit Competition
1995 Intervin International
1995 New World International
1995 Pacific Rim International Wine Competition
1995 San Francisco Fair International Wine Competition
1995 Selections Mondiales
1996 Sydney International Wine Competition
1994 Vinitaly

USA/Canada
1995 California State Fair Wine Competition
1995 Dallas Morning News Wine Competition
1995 Farmers Fair of Riverside Wine Competition
1995 Los Angeles County Fair Wine Competition
1995 Northwest Enographic Wine Festival Awards
1995 Orange County Fair Wine Competition
1995 Oregon State Fair Professional Wine Awards
1995 Reno West Coast Wine Competition
1995 Tri-Cities Northwest Wine Festival
1995 San Diego National Wine Competition
1995 Western Washington Fair Wine Judging

Australia/New Zealand
1995 Air New Zealand Wine Awards
1996 Royal Melbourne Wine Show
1995 Royal Sydney Wine Show
1995 National Wine Show of Australia, Canberra

Chapter 3

ABOUT THE GOLD MEDAL WINE LISTINGS

Every wine competition publishes a list of their gold, silver, and bronze medal winners. Usually these are small booklets that merely list the names of the winning wines. Very few of these results booklets include details such as price, and almost none of them have tasting descriptions.

Since the world of wine can be somewhat daunting, we felt the more information we could provide about the gold medal winners, the better. After all, knowing that a wine won a gold isn't going to help much at the wine shop when you discover that it's ten dollars more a bottle than you were wanting to pay. Or if you love Chardonnay, but hate oaky ones, you could be in for a surprise, depending on the vinification methods used. In other words, we felt that listing only the name of a gold medal wine wasn't adequate for a truly informative and helpful guidebook.

Depending on one's level of expertise, there are any number of infobites "necessary" to the understanding of a particular wine. Connoisseurs at the highest echelon want to know the ins and outs of the entire growing and harvesting season: how many days of rainfall, temperature at harvest time, and so on; they demand exact residual sugar levels of the wine by volume down to the hundredth percent, as well as alcohol and pH. The list goes on.

We asked ourselves what *we* would want to know, besides the name and vintage of the wine. And that's how we came upon the format for the gold medal wine listings in Part III. Below is a brief rundown of the various elements of the wine listings.

Category The wines are grouped by broad categories, which correspond to the chapter names in Part III (Red Wines, White Wines, and so on). The most obvious reason for doing this is that wine shops are organized in this same manner.

Type/Varietal We've further grouped the wines in each category according to type (Red Blends, for instance) or varietal (such as Cabernet Sauvignon). We found this to be useful in many ways. For instance, we're red wine lovers, and seeing all of our options for reds got us out there trying ones we normally wouldn't have chosen—or wouldn't have known to choose. We also found ourselves trying the same wine varietal from different regions, of different price ranges, to get a sense of the spectrum of possibilities for, say, Syrahs. It's a fun way to educate yourself about wine and expand your wine-drinking parameters without taking a lot of risk in terms of quality. For more information on what the wine types and varietals are, see Chapter 8.

Price Range After category and type/varietal, wines are grouped by the price range they fall into. These are guides (see Suggested Retail, below) that will give the shopper a rough idea of what to expect at the cash register. If you never want to pay more than ten dollars for a bottle of wine, you'll know which listing sections to thumb through. If only wine shops were organized this way! Incidentally, some types of wine are always more expensive than others. For example, a Cabernet Sauvignon will be more expensive than a Gamay Beaujolais nearly every time; they're entirely different wines made for two different kinds of drinking experiences. Don't let price be your measure of quality. We've found ten-dollar bottles that are every bit as pleasing as wines twice their price. But some exquisite and pricy wines just can't be topped. We save these for the most special occasions, and savor every sip. (For a quick reference to *all wines fifteen dollars and under,* see the boldface listings in the Indices.)

Winery and Wine The gold medal wines are listed alphabetically by winery. One winery might produce several different Chardonnays, say, for each vintage. One might be a "reserve," another might include the name of a special vineyard from which the grapes were selected, and still another might just bear the name of the appellation from which it came. So at the wine shop you'll be faced with three different 1993 Chardonnays, and you'll have to *read the label carefully* to ensure that you're purchasing the gold medal winner. We've tried to include enough information in the name of each winning wine to clarify any confusion.

Availability There's no scientific way to determine if a wine listed in the book will be at your local wine shop. Too many factors are involved. Our original concept was to list the number of cases produced so that consumers could get a relative sense of a wine's availability. However, many of the wineries we contacted refused to provide this information. Perhaps they fear that a *small* case production would deter would-be buyers; or conversely, they assume that revealing a *large* case production would compromise the value of their wine. In any event, the initials **NP** after "Availability" stand for "not provided."

To determine how easy it will be to locate a wine, we had to take into consideration both how many cases were produced and when the wine was released. **Very Good** means that you should have no problem finding this wine in a decent wine shop, or that your wine merchant shouldn't have any trouble finding it for you if the shop doesn't have any in stock. **Good** means that your chances of finding the wine are above average if not downright rosy. And **Limited** means either that the wine was made in a small quantity to begin with, and thus is not widely available and never was, or that the quantity produced by the winery together with the time that has passed since its release adds up to less opportunity to find the wine easily. If you see a "limited" wine at your wine shop or on a restaurant wine list, by all means snatch it up.

Some wineries told us that their wines were "sold out." We did a little investigating and discovered that "sold out" for a winery means that *they* no longer have any in stock. However, *their distributors do, restaurants do, mail-order houses do* (for a listing of mail-order wine vendors, see Appendix 3), *and your wine shop might too.* We found this so often to be true that we began ignoring the wineries that told us they were sold out, unless, of course, the amount of wine they produced was microscopic to begin with.

Wines that cannot be purchased in the United States have **Outside USA** written after "Availability." These fall into two categories. The first one is wines that can be *purchased in Canada, but not the United States.* In these instances, the retail price is listed in approximate Canadian dollars (determined by the exchange rate at press time). The other group consists of wines that are not yet available in the United States, but soon will be. Certain New Zealand wineries, for example, are very close to finding U.S. importers, and may have done so by press time. *The retail price for these wines is listed in the currency of its country of origin.*

Suggested Retail Price Take these dollar amounts with a large grain of salt. Even in our little town of Woodstock, New York, we've found the same wine to be three different prices in the three local wine shops. The suggested retail prices we list were provided by the wineries themselves. This is the price they sell their wines for in their tasting rooms. However, let the buyer beware. We discovered, for example, a Cabernet Sauvignon listed as $4.99 that won a gold at Orange County over many other wines that were more than twice its price. Impressed, we rushed out to purchase a bottle of this little upstart. It was $6.99! Still a good price, but not the unbelievable bargain we supposed it to be. Further, restaurants get large markups for their wines, so don't even dream that a ten-dollar gold medal winner will be close to that when you're dining out.

Golds For a description of the significance of gold medals and the competitions who awarded them, see Chapter 2. Some wines won three or more golds from our "Top 24 Competitions" (listed at the end of Chapter 2). We call these "The Best of BEST WINES!" and you'll find them in Appendix 2. Although all the wines in the book won at least one gold from our Top 24, many also won golds in other competitions, and these "additional" gold medals are included.

Tasting Notes Obtaining descriptions of eight-hundred-plus wines was no easy task. But as it turns out, most winemakers release tasting notes when their wines are bottled. Sometimes these read like scientific data sheets, revealing every process, temperature, and percentage of mineral in the precious stuff. On the other end of the spectrum are the ones whose "descriptions" are anything but illuminating: "A delightful picnic wine."

More often, though, the winemakers take great care to reveal color, aroma and flavor components, body, finish, acidity, tannins, and so on. (For more on tasting wine and the components that make up tasting notes, see Chapter 4.) Winemakers frequently relay other useful information, such as ideal food complements and how long the wines should be cellared. We tried to pass on as much of this information as we had room for.

Unfortunately, the world of winespeak is atangle with strange ways of putting things, and with the exception of the odd tasting notes from a winemaker who actually made the effort to be original and literary, you'll find that the wine descriptions all begin to sound the same after a while. (Indeed, one small California winery we spoke with said they had to buy reference books and glean from other wine writers to learn "the language" so that their wine descriptions would *sound like everyone else's*. We wish they hadn't!) However, if you understand the lingo, you'll also discover that the tasting notes can be quite useful. (See Chapter 9 for a handy reference to wine language.)

In cases where it was difficult to obtain descriptions, we tried to give the reader *something* to go by. And there were some wineries that never provided us with *any* information, or sent information that was incomplete or incorrect, despite repeated letters, calls, and faxes. We didn't want to leave these gold medal winners out entirely, so they are listed in Appendix 4, "The Other Gold Medal Winners," with minimal accompanying information.

Special Awards Special awards are trophies or extra recognition bestowed upon a wine, and are considered a higher honor still than gold medal status. Incidentally, **Double Gold** means that *every* judge at that competition who evaluated the wine gave it a gold.

Chapter 4

TASTING WINE
Do I Detect Cigarbox Aromas?

One of our mothers recently related a story of dinner at the in-laws' where a quite expensive and well-known California wine was solemnly presented at the table. The air was thick with expectation. She tasted it and of course performed the obligatory oohs and ahhs, but privately told us that it "wasn't any great shakes for the price." She also regularly sends us newsletter clippings from the quality wine shop near her home, where she's scrawled notes in the margin like, "I've never detected cigarbox aromas in my life! And what's this grassy peapod nose all about?"

She's not alone. We too wonder at times where all *these layers upon layers* of flavors and aromas are coming from, the *chewy mouth feels*, and of course the *finishes that linger on and on*. So we did some research to find out how we could have an expansive, melodic sensory experience like the ones all the famous wine writers seemed to be having.

It turns out that to properly taste wine, you must understand two basic concepts. The first is that most of what we perceive as taste is really more closely related to smell. And the second is that to fully appreciate a glass of wine, you have to *think*.

On the first point, we'll skip good manners and hand you the bald truth: a dachshund is actually better equipped to pick up all the subtleties found in a glass of wine than we are. The reason for this is that dogs and other animals have much more acute olfactory sensors than do people. If you don't agree that flavor is dependent on smell, remember how you used to hold your nose as a child to gulp down something like awful-tasting medicine. Or how when your nose is stuffed up from a cold, you can't taste much of anything, so generally don't eat as much.

Our olfactory receptors allow us to experience around ten thousand different aromas—that's quite a lot, still, and nothing to sniff at. These receptors are found in the nose but also in the retronasal passage, which is at the back of the mouth. Our mouth, on the other hand, can distinguish but four kinds of taste: sweetness, on the tip of the tongue; saltiness, a little further back on the sides; sourness, on the sides even further back; and bitterness, near the back center of the tongue.

With the end of the biology part of this discussion, it's time to get to the nitty-gritty: how to taste wine.

First, you want to liberate as many aroma molecules as you can to maximize your total taste and smell experience. This you do by swirling the wine in the glass (didn't you always wonder why the heck you were doing this in front of your friends when selected as the table's "taster" by a sadistic wine steward?). Do this under your nose so you can sniff in the aromas.

Next, take a sip and "whistle in" some air along with it to direct the vapors to that waiting retronasal passage. While the wine is in your mouth, you can "chew it," as some tasters do, or at least make sure it touches all of your tongue, and then let it slide gently down your throat. (Professional tasters spit the wine out. But not us. We want to *drink* the stuff.)

Now we come to the second point, which is the thinking part of the equation. At least one thing humans have over canines, fortunately, is the ability to analyze the whole experience and put our sensations into language. Think about the first associations that came to mind when you smelled the wine. These are the famous bouquets and aromas you'll find in the tasting notes in Part III.

As for what happened "on the palate," as wine writers like to call the sensations inside the mouth, here's where the more cerebral stuff enters in. Saltiness isn't really a factor with wine. Sourness is experienced as acidity— a measure of how "zingy" the wine is. Sweetness is self-explanatory. And bitterness is something you shouldn't taste at all if you're drinking good wine.

But besides these, there are also other qualities to consider. One expert calls the mouth more of a "measurer," which is an apt description. Inside the mouth you can evaluate what the wine feels like: how heavy it feels (weight/body), how astringent or puckery it makes your mouth from the tannins, how long the characteristics linger after you've swallowed (length). You also might consider how much punch the alcohol delivers, and in the case of sparkling wines, how the mousse, or bubbles, feel on your tongue.

Most important is the balance of all these elements. When you consider all of the above, which ones seem to be overwhelming? A really fabulous wine will have great complexity—which has the same meaning when referring to wine as when referring to people. Its many traits should be in near-perfect harmony. (For more details about specific qualities of wine and explanations of common wine-tasting terminology, see Chapter 9.)

Finally, take notes if you're so inclined. Or do what we inevitably do: lean back in your chair, have some more sips, and say, "Uh, gee, I like this!"

Chapter 5

STORING WINES
My "Cellar" Lies Next to My Clorox

If the old adage "a man's home is his castle" were literally true, none of us would have a wine-storing problem. All castles come with underground wine cellars that are vibration-free, dark, damp, and kept at a steady 55 degrees F. These are usually next to the subterranean torture chamber.

Unfortunately or not, the rest of us have to make do with apartments or houses. One of our friends told us that his "cellar" is in his pantry where he keeps laundry detergent, canned goods, and dusty fondue sets and woks (does anyone use woks anymore?). There's nothing wrong with his arrangement since his pantry is in the back of his house next to an outside wall, is usually dark, has no heat source, and stays a fairly constant 68 degrees F.

Naturally, wherever you have enthusiasts, you're bound to find extremists. Wine cellars can run the gamut from exorbitantly priced refrigeratorlike cabinets that regulate temperature and humidity, to custom-designed insulated rooms, to closets. For our purposes, here and throughout the book, we'll use "cellar" to mean wherever you choose to store your wine.

The first thing to know about cellaring wine is that sometimes it's unnecessary and even unwise. Many wines are made to be consumed young, and if a wine is cellared past its prime, you're in for a rude surprise. (See "aging" in Chapter 9.) Concentrated, rich, full-bodied wines age better than light-bodied wines, and reds are generally more age worthy than whites, although it depends greatly on the type of wine and on any number of other factors, such as the particular vintage, the winemaking process, and so on.

But if you have bottles that are keepers, remember the following four simple rules and you shouldn't end up with unpleasant results.

1. Keep wines at a constant temperature not exceeding 70 degrees F. More important than the actual temperature is the *constancy* of that temperature. Changes in temperature should occur slowly; wild swings are undesirable.

Remember that wine is a living substance inside the bottle, where the water, acids, alcohol, and tannins are interacting to evolve into perfect balance and hopefully to cause the maximum flavor, aroma, and body to emerge from the fruits. Winemakers spend their careers creating wines that will undergo this process gracefully. Your role is to allow the elements to do so with the least stress, and that means *constancy*.

The cooler your cellar, the slower the evolution inside the bottle. Anything between 55 and 70 degrees F is fine (although at 55 degrees, your wine may live longer than you do). Try adapting part of your basement, a closet, a large cupboard, or even under a stairwell. Be sure that no heat sources are nearby, and this includes the top of a refrigerator, a water pipe, and especially a furnace or radiator.

Incidentally, white wines are more fragile and more sensitive to higher temperatures than reds. Never let a white wine get above 70 degrees F.

2. Keep wines in the dark. Light—especially direct sunlight—is not good for wine. In stylish living magazines it's not uncommon to see photos of wines stacked on beautiful wooden racks atop a sunny kitchen counter. Not a good idea: the critters inside those bottles will be squirming, and you'll end up with something undrinkable.

3. Keep wines in a humid place. Basically the reason for this is so that the corks will not dry out. If they do, oxygen will get inside the bottle and your wine will turn to vinegar. (This is the same rationale behind storing bottles on their sides; contact with the wine keeps the corks moist—and expanded.) Humidity above 50 percent is essential, and 70 to 75 percent is ideal.

4. Keep wines in a place that is vibration-free. Don't put your wine rack above a washing machine or in a garage/wood shop. The sediments will get all stirred up and upset the delicate balancing act that's happening inside the bottle.

Chapter 6

AVOIDING A BOTTLE GONE BAD

One advantage of writing a book about gold medal wines is that we don't have to write a chapter on wine flaws. For the most part, the unpleasant characteristics one might find in a bottle as a result of poor winemaking or bottling won't even be a factor here. ("Corkiness," however, a wet-cardboard aroma caused by a bad cork, is something that happens with even the best wines. But since you won't find out about it until you open the bottle, there's no way to avoid it.)

What *is* important to know, however, is how to spot a bottle that's gone bad as a result of *irresponsible storage or transportation.* Read Chapter 5, on cellaring wine, and you'll see that temperature changes, especially extreme changes, are hazardous to a wine's health. Think about it: even within the United States wines have to travel thousands of miles from coast to coast, and may change hands a half-dozen times or more by the time they reach the shelves in your wine shop. Now think about a South African, New Zealand, or Chilean bottle that's trying to get to Milwaukee intact and you begin to see the enormity of the problem.

Theoretically, wines should be cushioned every step of the way inside air-conditioned containers that keep them at a stable temperature, whether they're floating through the Panama Canal in August or trucking toward Poughkeepsie in December.

Since we know this doesn't always happen, there are three things the consumer can look for to see if he or she is about to purchase a "bad" bottle.

1. Look for signs of seepage around the rim of the bottle. This is usually a sign that the wine has undergone extremely high temperatures in transit or in storage. Wine expands when exposed to heat—especially wines made in the Old World style that have not undergone a lot of modern intervention such as filtering in order to stabilize them. Naturally, the expanding wine inside the bottle puts pressure on the cork, so wine is able to seep out over the rim of the bottle as the cork gives way. We have heard that most wine merchants do not bother to wipe down all their bottles, so giving the rim a good look will clue you in to a gold medal winner that's turned brass.

*2. **Look for a slightly popped-up cork.*** A wine that has been exposed to either freezing or high temperatures during storage or transit will have a cork that is not flush with the rim. You'll be able to see this through the lead or plastic that caps the top of the bottle. Again, this is caused from pressure inside the bottle from a wine that has expanded, and it's bad news.

*3. **Look for excessive air space beneath the cork.*** Most wineries these days fill the bottles to within 1/8 inch of the cork. If you can see more air space than that, there's a good chance that the cork has not done its job of stopping up the bottle. Evaporation or seepage has taken place, which can only mean one thing: the wine has come into contact with its enemy, oxygen.

Chapter 7

HERE'S TO YOUR HEALTH!

Doesn't it seem that the things you *most* love to eat and drink sooner or later turn out to be bad for you? Not so with wine, we're glad to report. In fact, independent studies conducted around the world over the last thirty years, and continuing up until press time, suggest that consuming moderate amounts of wine, defined as one to three glasses per day, has been found to be beneficial in more ways than it was ever dreamed.

We don't see the need to cite long lists of doctors' and scientific researchers' names, nor every name of every journal in which their studies were published. But the study results have appeared in the top medical journals, and the places we used for our research included such respectable sources as *The Oxford Companion to Wine, The New Frank Schoonmaker Encyclopedia of Wine, The Wine Spectator, The Wine Trader, 60 Minutes, The New York Times,* and so on.

All seem to agree that it's time to raise up your glass and holler, "Here's to my health!"

WINE AND HEART DISEASE

Everyone knows that the federal government isn't exactly on the cutting edge when it comes to officially approving and recognizing certain foods, vitamins, medicines, herbs, and medical techniques that citizens have known for years to be beneficial to their health. Yet the most recent U.S. Government Dietary Guidelines for Americans states that *moderate drinking is associated with a lower risk for coronary heart disease.* (This statement is brought to us by the folks who created the now well-known Food Pyramid, which suggests the food groups we should eat from daily, and in what proportion; as well as the ones who redesigned all the Nutritional Guidelines labels on our packaged foods and determined the RDA, or Recommended

Daily Allowances, for vitamins and minerals). If Uncle Sam approves, you'd better believe it's true.

Hundreds of people from all over the globe—Japanese men living in Hawaii; Chicago General Electric workers; the good folks of Framingham, Massachusetts; Aussies in Busselton, Western Australia; elderly villagers in rural Greece; Californians from Alameda County—these and others have been poked, prodded, and questioned in studies related to drinking and the heart. The results are consistently positive: moderate drinking is good for your heart in a number of ways.

Prevents arterial clotting. Wine, and especially red wine in this case, contains *phenolics* (found in tannin, in the pigment of dark-skinned grapes, and in certain flavor compounds called *flavonoids*), which have been found to possess antioxidant properties that may help prevent clotting of the arteries and other internal blood clots (such as those that cause strokes). Wine's ability to inhibit the clotting activity of platelets, a condition known as thrombosis, substantially reduces the risk of heart attack.

Improves cholesterol levels. Heart disease is the number one killer of Americans. And while there may be any number of contributing factors, including smoking or a genetic predisposition, everyone agrees on the main culprit: fatty foods. But study after study has shown that *drinking wine with your meal can counter the adverse effects of fat in your bloodstream by positively affecting your cholesterol levels.*

Together with the alcohol in wine, phenolics found in wine alter blood lipid (fat) levels by lowering your overall cholesterol and by raising the level of HDL, the so-called good cholesterol, in your blood. What's more, one study discovered that people who consumed wine with dinner, as opposed to those who drank mineral water, not only experienced improved cholesterol numbers, but the effects were still detectable until early the next morning.

Our conclusion? Have salad for breakfast, and for dinner have eggs, thick-cut slabs of bacon, butter-slathered biscuits, and hot-off-the-grill hash browns—but remember to wash it all down with a supple Merlot!

Lowers blood pressure. Experts agree that high blood pressure contributes to coronary heart disease and overall mortality. A recent Harvard study only adds to the evidence of wine's cardioprotective benefits, in its ability to positively affect systolic and diasystolic blood pressure. The lowest blood pressure levels were found in those who consumed one to three drinks per day (wine or other alcoholic spirits), even factoring in such things as smoking, a family history of hypertension, adjustments for pulse rate, medication use, and so on.

WINE AND STROKES

Just as moderate wine drinking benefits the heart by helping to prevent the formation of arterial plaque, which can clog arteries and blood vessels, it also aids in preventing cerebrovascular disease caused by internal blood clotting. Several renowned researchers have determined in a number of different studies that wine drinkers, whether it's white or red, enjoy a dramatically reduced risk of the most common type of stroke.

WINE AND AGING/MORTALITY

We've never understood mortality studies. Isn't mortality always 100 percent? Anyway, a lot of research has been done in the field of aging and mortality as it relates to wine consumption, and there's a lot of good news.

The 12-Year Copenhagen Study, perhaps the most famous research project involving wine's health benefits, found a *49 percent reduction in mortality* among the study's participants who drank three to five glasses of wine per day (not exactly "moderate," in our opinion!). It was those flavonoids again, with their antioxidant properties, that were found to have a significant preventive effect on diseases of the heart as well as some forms of cancer.

Another long-term health study in Alameda County, California, focused on factors important in predicting healthy aging, defined as living independently at a high level of physical and mental function, without requiring outside aid. Guess what? Except for being a nonsmoker, *the most important factor predicting healthy aging was being a moderate drinker.*

A Greek research team studied the elderly inhabitants of three rural Greek villages to see if they could find the secret to their "fountain of youth." It turned out that the old folks there practiced healthy Mediterranean-style eating of legumes, fruits, vegetables, grains, and monounsaturated fats (mostly olive oil), small amounts of meat and dairy, *and a moderate amount of wine*. Since wine was an integral part of the daily diet, the researchers concluded that it was also an essential element in helping them to live to such ripe old ages.

By the way, wine drinkers have significantly lower mortality rates than either beer or spirits drinkers.

WINE AND CANCER

When mainstream television ads talk about antioxidants, you can figure that everyone knows the term. But just in case you don't, here's the concept: there are compounds in our body called free radicals, which are highly reactive forms of molecules that can weaken cell walls, thus allowing those cells to oxidize. When cells are oxidized, they die or are subject to mutation, which can mean cancer. Phenolics, found mostly in red wine, block free radicals, thus preventing harmful oxidation. Antioxidants are good since they've been proven to decrease the incidence of many forms of cancer.

WINE AND BACTERIAL DISEASES

An exciting new study done at West Virginia University has found that wine can protect you from the kinds of bacterial diseases you get from tainted shellfish, bad water while traveling, and spoiled meat or poultry. The three culprits studied were E. coli, salmonella, and shigella. The results? *Wine kills bacteria.*

Wine was tested alongside pure alcohol, tequilla, and bismuth salicytate (the active ingredient in Pepto Bismol) to see what effect each had on 10 million colony-forming units of shigella, salmonella, and E. coli. Wine was most effective in destroying these critters, with good old Pepto coming in a distant second, and alcohol and tequilla coming in last. In other words, it's something specific to wine, and not its alcohol, that has this beneficial effect.

Because of this wonderful new revelation, it's even more important that you have some Mexican red wine *with your meal* when you're traveling, or some nice Virginia Riesling with those raw oysters.

WINE AND OTHER ILLNESSES

There's a laundry list of other maladies that wine has proven to be beneficial in preventing, but before we get into what the experts say, we'd like to add one of our own: joylessness. After a trying day at the office or with the kids, isn't it nice to sit down to a lovely home-cooked meal (or to be waited on at your favorite restaurant) and to sip a glass of wine with your dinner? Our wholly unscientific research and anecdotal experience tell us that the Europeans have the right idea by making wine part of their overall culture of relaxing at the dinner table. It leads to sanity, it prevents depression, and it soothes those tired brain cells. Now on to the experts.

Lowers the risk for bone and joint diseases. Studies continue to associate moderate wine consumption with a lower risk of developing such conditions as arthritis and those related to diminished bone density, such as osteoporosis.

Reduces the likelihood of diabetes. Two recent studies have confirmed earlier reports that moderate drinkers (in this case, wine *or* spirits) experience a *40 percent decrease* in the likelihood that they will develop adult onset diabetes.

Reduces the risk of gallstone disease. It's been shown that red- and white-wine drinkers benefit from a *one-third reduced risk of developing gallstones* and the subsequent complications of gallstone disease.

PART II

A Reference Guide to Winespeak

Chapter 8

WINE VARIETALS AND TYPES
What's Blank de Blank?

We were recently offered the choice of "red or white" at a particularly colorful dive one night while hunting for some late-night grub. Ah, if only the wine world were that simple. But it's not, so you've got to become oenophiliterate (we made that up) so you'll know where to start when faced with an especially daunting wine list or when roaming the aisles of a well-stocked wine shop.

We discovered, for example, that there are quite a few wine names made up by wine producers or by industry professionals to lend a certain exotic air to a class of wine that has suffered from a bad reputation in the past, hoping to rehabilitate its image. If you know that Fumé Blanc and Sauvignon Blanc are the same, life is simpler. If you like reds, but want one that has a friendly and uncomplicated personality, you need to know what your best options are. Most of the wine types and varietals found in Part III are included here.

Aleatico   This red grape is related to the Muscat variety, and produces rather esoteric, sweet red wines with strong aromas reminiscent of Muscat. It is most commonly grown in Italy, but can also be found in the warmer regions of California.

Alicante Bouchet   This hybrid was developed in the nineteenth century by Louis Bouchet and his son, who were looking to find a grape high in sugar and deeply colored—for making cheap bulk wine. Widely planted in California during Prohibition, its heavy skin made it easy to ship to home-wine makers across the country. Many amateur winemakers still grow it in their backyards. Although it has not been able to compete with today's more glamorous Cabernet Sauvignons and Pinot Noirs, a well-made Alicante Bouchet yields a rich, dark purple wine that has tremendous character and ageability. At its best the varietal is somewhat reminiscent of a Châteauneuf-du-Pape, with earthy, spicy flavors and loads of body. It is also known simply as Alicante.

Baco Noir A French-American hybrid developed at the turn of the century, Baco Noir gets its name from Maurice Baco, a French hybridizer who had some success creating grapes that could withstand North American climates. Also known as Baco 1, this grape produces a hearty red wine that's capable of aging, somewhat similar to Cabernet Sauvignon. It is grown in the cool regions of the eastern United States.

Barbera Until twenty-some years ago, Barbera was the fourth leading red variety grown in California. Unfortunately, Barbera's reputation as a hardworking gal who could blend in most anywhere did not serve her well in elite wine circles. And she's been relegated to the role of jug wine ever since. To find a high-quality Barbera in an upscale wine shop is rare. However, much of that is beginning to change, particularly in California and, interestingly, in Argentina.

This variety, of Italian origin, has strong vines, is adaptable to any soil, and produces high yields. What's more, Barbera has good aging features (high acidity, strong tannins, full body) and a historic ability to blend well with other grapes, most notably other Italian varieties such as Nebbiolo and Sangiovese, and Bordeaux varieties such as Cabernet Sauvignon. The rising popularity of these "Italian-style blends" may restore Barbera's sullied reputation.

In cooler regions, Barbera becomes rich and complex; in hot climates, it produces a light fruity wine. The more complex version goes well with beef, sausage, and game such as rabbit, while the lighter version is classically paired with pasta dishes, as the Italians have known for years.

Black Muscat SEE MUSCAT.

Blanc de Blancs In French this means, literally, "white from whites" and refers to both still and sparkling white wines that are made exclusively from white grapes. Many are blends of different white varieties, with Chardonnay commonly a key component.

Blanc de Noirs Literally "white from blacks" in French, these are light-colored wines that are made from black-skinned (red wine) grapes by fermenting the crushed grapes or grape juice (known as the must) without the skins. (It is the skin of the grape that gives wine its ruby hues.) The term Blanc de Noirs refers to both sparkling wines and, increasingly, to still wines that would have otherwise been called rosé. When one thinks of rosé, what comes to mind is your rotund Aunt Matilda lugging a jug of it to your annual Thanksgiving dinner. The French name gives those pink wines a highfallutin ring, thus helping to sell the wines by making them sound more attractive. Blanc de Noirs ranges from light red to straw-colored.

Bordeaux-Style Blends SEE MERITAGE.

Brut "Brut" and words like it tie us word nerds into knots and cause us to thrash in our beds at night, losing valuable sleep. The reason is because "Brut" is an adjective meaning "very dry" or "being the driest made by the producer," yet it's frequently used as a noun: "a Brut." Either way, it refers to sparkling wines. In Europe, the term refers to the driest champagnes and other sparkling wine. There, Common Market laws dictate that a sparkling wine labeled Brut must have no more than 1.5 percent residual sugar. In America and elsewhere, the term is merely a descriptive one that means "very dry." There is no good way to tell if a non-European Brut sparkling wine will be dry, very dry, or very, very dry without tasting it. The best you can do is to know that by labeling the sparkler "Brut," the winery wants you to *think* it's very dry and not sweet.

Cabernet Franc One of the primary blending grape varieties, Cabernet Franc can rarely stand by itself because it produces a red wine that generally lacks enough fruit to balance out the tannins. But it has been used for many decades in the Old World as a blending agent, along with Merlot, to add complexity to Cabernet Sauvignon. Significantly lighter in color and body than either of the two latter, Cabernet Franc nevertheless adds cedary, raspberry, and floral suggestions to the more assertive Cabernet Sauvignon.

In California and the American Northwest it was seldom grown until two decades ago, but now interest in Cabernet Franc is increasing as vintners have begun to successfully use it like the French to prettify and add dimension to Cabernet Sauvignon.

Cabernet Sauvignon Everyone says it and so will we: for most of the world, Cabernet Sauvignon is king of the reds. Imagine you're sitting in the deep leather chair of your oak-paneled library, using your Mont Blanc fountain pen to write a nearly forgotten ex-lover. It's snowing outside and you're in front of the fire. This is what a classic Cab can conjure up because it's, well, classic.

A small, tough-skinned grape, it produces wines with a higher level of tannin than most, deep color, and rich body and aroma. A great Cab is capable of—indeed requires—long aging in your cellar. But there are many examples of New World Cabs that are complex and age worthy yet ready for early drinking.

Because of its assertive personality, Cabernet Sauvignon is frequently blended with other varieties. (As long as it's 75 percent Cab, the wine can be called Cabernet Sauvignon in the United States.) Merlot, a grape whose subtle herbal and cherry character contrasts nicely with the former's tight, brooding one, is often used to make Cab more approachable in its youth. Blending it with Cabernet Franc adds an aromatic quality reminiscent of herbs, violets, and spring berries, but doesn't soften the tannins much.

Ideally suited for cool coastal climates, Cabernet Sauvignon has been grown in California for more than a hundred years, but it's only been in the last thirty that it has come to represent some 11 percent of all California wine grapes; the number of Cabs bottled in California has increased fiftyfold since 1970. So successful has it been in Washington State that some wineries are staking their success on that variety alone. The quality of America's best Cabernet Sauvignon, and that includes certain producers in Argentina and Chile, is giving the finest (and oldest) wineries in France the jitters.

While Cabs will vary from country to country and vineyard to vineyard, one can characterize them generally. They tend to be deeply colored, richly fruity, with complex structure, which means lots of acid and plenty of tannin. This is good news for wine lovers who want to cellar a special wine until their teenager gets her master's in anthropology. If deferring gratification isn't your thing, there are plenty of New World Cabernets that are intensely fruity, less complex, and ready for early drinking. This style will usually be less expensive. The Reservas from Chile represent great value and lots of personality, and Argentina has some wonderfully approachable Cabernets as well. Wine writers often describe the varietal with these words: black cherry, blackberry, plums, herbs, green olives, truffles, loamy earth, tobacco, leather, violet, mint, eucalyptus, tea, cedar, bell pepper, tar, and chocolate. These aren't subtle flavors and aromas!

Because of its strong character, Cabernet Sauvignon goes well with simple, hearty foods such as roast or grilled beef, venison, pork, veal, and duck. With medium to lighter versions, one can be more creative, pairing Cab with fruit-based sauces (on meat), garlicky tomato sauces with pasta, herbs such as rosemary, basil, dill, and savory condiments such as chutneys. Hard cheeses and goat cheeses make a good accompaniment, and some even suggest that you can quaff down your last glass with a rich chocolate dessert.

Cabernet Sauvignon is best served at room temperature, and can be cellared anywhere from not at all to a dozen or more years, depending on the bottle.

Carignane Carignane is the hardest working grape in France. A Rhône variety, it is the most widely planted grape there, and for many years the same could be said of its predominance in California. (From the early 1900s through Prohibition, some fifty thousand acres of Carignane were the source of most of America's red wine. That number has decreased about 80 percent.) The reason is because growers can net higher yields per acre from Carignane when it's grown in warm and fertile areas, and therein lies both its strength and its weakness. Alone, Carignane often produces what could be called an ordinary jug wine—light, low in acidity, tannin, and extract—and oceans of it. But as a blending agent in the so-called Rhône-style blends, or

"Rhône Rangers," both in France and now in America, it is useful and delicious.

This is not to say that Carignane is an unpleasant wine. When the vines are old, yields are kept low (thus increasing the amount of fruit extract in each grape), and the grapes are allowed to fully ripen before they are harvested, a good Carignane-based wine can be grand in the best Rhône tradition. These earthy wines, with surprising intensity, richness, and size, are full of black fruit and spicy flavors and go well with hearty beef dishes such as winter stews, hamburger, and steak, and can hold their own next to gamey meat such as venison. SEE RHÔNE-STYLE VARIETALS/BLENDS.

Carlos The Carlos grape is a Muscadine cultivar, which is a grape native to the southern United States. Carlos, unlike its European cousins, is able to thrive in hot, humid climates that would devastate the fussy European varieties with fungus, mold, and general rot. Wines from Carlos are generally finished sweet. However, with barrel fermentation or aging these wines are gaining attention as fine dry wines.

Cayuga This is a new white wine hybrid that was developed by the experiment station in Geneva, New York, by researchers trying to create a variety that could withstand Northeast and Great Lakes climates and produce premium-quality dry table wines with distinctive characters. Cayuga is just such a grape. It is a cross between Seyval and Schuyler, the latter being a cross between an American hybrid and Zinfandel. What is promising about Cayuga is that it's hardy and high yielding. It has been described as pleasant, nicely balanced, fruity, with delicate aromas. The variety it most closely resembles is Riesling.

Champagne We New World rebels insist on referring to our sparkling wines as champagne, much to the horror of the French, for whom champagne means *only* the sparkling wine produced in the Champagne area of France. (In France it is illegal to use the name incorrectly; all violators are guillotined. In the good old U.S.A., there is no such law, although most vintners call their bubbly "sparkling wine.") Must we eat gelled fruit dessert rather than good old Jell-O? Can't we wear a Band-Aid rather than wrestling with an adhesive bandage strip? We *like* to turn brand names into generic words, so there!

But let's get to the real issue. Champagne, sometimes synonymous (in the United States) with sparkling wines, is a sparkling wine whose carbonation is derived naturally during a second fermentation in a closed container. There are three ways to produce champagne: (1) by the *méthode champenoise,* (2) by the transfer method, or (3) by the bulk, or Charmat, method. (See glossary of wine terms, Chapter 9.) Champagne is usually made from a blend of Chardonnay, Pinot Noir, or Pinot Meunier. SEE ALSO SPARKLING WINES.

Charbono A little-known varietal that is grown almost nowhere besides in a handful of Napa and Mendocino, California, vineyards, Charbono produces a dark-colored, agreeable red wine with lots of body.

Chardonnay This white vinifera grape is the grape of France's white burgundy and champagne, and is a major force in American sparkling wine. It is also by far the most popular white wine produced in the New World. Wine producers love Chardonnay because it is easy to grow, adapting well to most cool coastal regions. Wine drinkers favor it because it is easy to like. Chardonnay ages well, and more than other whites, the interesting aromas and flavors derived from oak barrel fermentation and aging assume a key role in its personality, resulting in toasty, creamy, or spicy notes.

There are two predominant Chardonnay styles. The first is fresh, fruity, and lightly oaked; the second is toasty, spicy, buttery, and big. Either way, most Chardonnay is fairly fruity, with plenty of balancing acidity, and has a flavor and bouquet that may include apple, pineapple, peaches, tangerine, and lime, cinnamon and clove spices, and buttery, vanilla, smoky, nutty, or grassy hints.

Among the New World stars for producing Chardonnay are Australia, with its voluptuous, showy wines nearly bursting with flavor, and California, whose Chardonnays are considered some of the best on earth. Oregon's climate allows the grapes to reach full maturity on the vine, as they do in Burgundy, France, which brings out the natural acidity (most California producers, for instance, have to balance their Chardonnays by adding tartaric acid) and creates marvelously piquant wines that are giving the French a run for their money. New Zealand and Washington State are also having good luck with this varietal. Because Chile and Argentina have just begun to plant Chardonnay, the fresh and uncomplicated Chardonnays being produced there will no doubt improve as the vines age.

Like Cabernet Sauvignon, most Chardonnay has so much personality that it tends to compete with complex foods. The basic rule is to serve this wine with unassuming dishes such as raw vegetable dippers before a main meal; seafood and shellfish (without fancy sauces); pasta with cream sauce; and roasted turkey or chicken. Leaner Chardonnays can complement mild cheeses.

Like all white wines, serve Chardonnay chilled. Depending on the bottle, most Chardonnays can be consumed immediately, and some can be cellared for a handful of years.

Chenin Blanc Poor Chenin Blanc. While in France's Loire Valley this native French variety reaches its true height (in the Vouvray, Saumur, and Savennières regions) Chenin Blanc has largely been ignored in the New World. However, that trend is changing as consumers are beginning to look for simple, appealing white wines at reasonable prices. Often blended with other whites, Chenin Blanc is a crowd pleaser and is coming into its own in places like California, Washington State, and Chile.

Chenin Blanc comes in two basic styles. The drier of the two is Chardonnay-like, taking on oak-barrel flavors and aromas (spicy, roasted, or vanilla). The second is sweeter, marked by delicate hints of flowers, melons, pears, and honey. Because this grape produces buds earlier and ripens later than most, either style will usually have lots of natural clean, crisp acidity and plenty of fruit, which means it ages well.

When you think of Chenin Blanc, think summer: August picnics with antipasto, raw clams or oysters, crudité, fresh fruit, pasta salad, and chicken. This wine also goes well with spicy Thai and Mexican dishes. Serve it cold, and drink it up or cellar it for a handful of years.

Cinsault A tiny amount of Cinsault is grown in California, but it is also grown in southern France, Lebanon, and South Africa. It is a large-berry, black-fruited grape that is often used to balance out red wine blends, particularly those composed of Syrah, Grenache, or Mourvèdre, adding fragrance and finesse.

Concord If there's such a thing as an all-American grape, this is it. One of us used to sit in the backyard with a childhood girlfriend each year, pinching Illinois Concord grapes hot from the sun until the green pulp popped into our mouths. We always ate too many. Concord grapes, because they are native to the United States, thrive in places with low temperatures, such as the Midwest and the eastern United States. Although most often used for grape juice and jelly, Concord can produce a wide range of wines, usually on the sweetish side, with the pronounced musky flavor that's distinctive of native American varieties.

Cortese A white wine grape, grown mostly in the Piedmont region of France, that yields an appealing, light, fresh wine.

Cynthiana SEE NORTON.

Ehrenfelser The Germans wanted a Riesling-type grape that would ripen in a broader range of sites, so they crossed Riesling with Sylvaner and got Ehrenfelser. Unlike many such attempts, this marriage was a happy one. Ehrenfelser has a clean, pure quality with delicate aromas similar to Riesling, but without as much acidity. That means that it won't age well, and you'll have no choice but to drink it right up. Canada is having a lot of success with this grape, producing lovely New World whites that are easy to like.

Fumé Blanc Fumé Blanc is nothing more than a smoke-and-mirror marketing ploy to confuse people who either like Sauvignon Blanc or don't. These two are one and the same, except that the latter is an actual grape variety. It all started back in the Hippie decades when Robert Mondavi coined the name "Fumé Blanc" to distinguish his dry, oak-style Sauvignon Blanc from the sweet jug wines of the same name so prevalent at the time. The name caught on for a while, and still pops up now and then. One thing Mondavi is generally credited with, however, is the restoration of Sauvignon Blanc's good standing. Because of this, most wineries don't even bother with Fumé Blanc, but if they do, American government labeling police require that they print "Dry Sauvignon Blanc" under the name.

Gamay Although Gamay has been produced in the New World for decades, specifically California, it appears that the only things American Gamay grapes have in common with France's Beaujolais region variety (Gamay Noir à Jus Blanc) are their name and, often, the style of wine they render. In the New World, Gamay refers to a wine made from one of two grapes: Gamay Beaujolais, which is in fact a misnamed clone that belongs to the Pinot Noir family, or Napa Gamay, which is actually the Valdiguié grape, also from France. Both Gamay Beaujolais and Napa Gamay wines are sometimes simply called Gamay, confusing the issue even further.

The best producers of Napa Gamay and Gamay Beaujolais make three characteristic styles of wine. The first, known as Nouveau, is made using the carbonic style of maceration, and produces fruity, fresh wines that are easy to understand and to gulp down—usually within nine months to a year of their release. The second style, a product of conventional fermentation, is less sweet than Nouveau, and can be cellared several months longer. The third style is drier still and more closely resembles Pinot Noir, displaying oak-aged qualities and more age worthiness.

Like French Gamay, these charming New World wines benefit from slight chilling, are friendly in their youth, and go well with picnic foods such as cold cuts, fresh vegetables, chicken, and pasta salads. SEE ALSO GAMAY BEAUJOLAIS AND NAPA GAMAY.

Gamay Beaujolais Gamay Beaujolais is also sometimes called simply Gamay. In the 1970s scientists determined that the red vinifera grape identified as Gamay Beaujolais was a fraud—that is, it was in no way related to its French cousin of Beaujolais fame. These same experts identified Pinot Noir as the likely source of this lesser clone. Although American vineyards have been allowed to keep "Gamay" on their labels, the trend will no doubt fade away as vintners recognize that the name Pinot Noir demands a higher price in the marketplace ("Pinot Noir" is allowed by the U.S. government for wines made from Gamay Beaujolais) and as regulators feel the need to keep up with modern scientific knowledge in their labeling requirements.

This hardworking grape does well in cooler regions and produces charming, quaffable wines that are delicious when served slightly chilled with uncomplicated foods. SEE ALSO GAMAY.

Gewürztraminer We learned five different ways to say the name of this white grape variety while compiling our first edition, and every winemaker we spoke with was adamant about *his* pronunciation. Here it is, the definitive version, but we won't reveal our source: *guhverts tra MEENer.* (If you want to be hip, just call it "Gewürz.") Besides being difficult to pronounce, this wine is a problem to grow. If it ripens too early (warm climates), it gets bitter and loses acidity. But if the growing season is too cool, it never achieves full aromatic intensity. New Zealand seems to have had the best luck with it, with Australia and Oregon, and then Washington and California not far behind.

In German *gewürz* means spicy, and the words commonly used to describe this wine's flavors and bouquet are clove, nutmeg, lychee nut, carnations, and wildflowers. A great Gewürz will indeed be spicy, with a heady perfume and slight sweetness. Serve it with pork sausages, foie gras, Oriental cuisine (especially mouth-searing Thai), crab, or trout.

Grenache In the New World, particularly in California, this red wine varietal (there is also a White Grenache varietal wine) has been used primarily to make port and rosé. However, it is gaining popularity in California, Australia, and the Northwest as a key component in the medium-bodied red wines known as Rhône-style blends (a blend of two or more grapes traditionally grown in southern France's Rhône Valley). Grenache-based wines go well with ham and turkey. SEE RHÔNE-STYLE VARIETALS/BLENDS.

Grignolino There's very little of this Italian grape grown in the New World, mostly in California, where it yields a light-bodied, delicate red wine, rosé, or sparkling rosé with a very fruity aroma. Grignolinos are meant to be drunk in their youth, within a year of the vintage.

Icewine Known sometimes as Ice Wine or by its German name, Eiswein, this is a type of very sweet dessert wine made from an interesting process. The grapes are allowed to freeze right on the vine, producing a high concentration of sugar in the juice when pressed. A handful of North American—particularly Canadian—wineries make this treasured oddity, and some wineries are even experimenting with producing it from grapes artificially frozen in freezers. Try it as dessert, or with sweets such as cakes, fruit tarts or pies, and flan.

Italian Varietals/Blends New World wine drinkers, it seems, are tiring of the same old reds. In California, where there are a lot of Italians and where the pioneering spirit still runs deep, Italian varieties are gaining ground. These are usually Barbera, Sangiovese, and Nebbiolo, either made into varietal wines, or blended with each other and sometimes with Cabernet Sauvignon to produce heavenly reds loaded with fruit, personality, and ageability. Italian-style wines can stand up to hearty dishes such as beef and tomato-sauced pastas.

Johannisberg Riesling SEE RIESLING.

Lemberger In the New World, Washington State has the monopoly on Lemberger, a grape of German origin that produces fresh and fruity, light red wines that are made to be drunk young.

Malbec Malbec produces intense red wines that are nearly black in color, firm, ripe, and lush, with the ability to age well. In Argentina, Malbec is the most planted red wine grape, and in Chile it is number three. California wineries use Malbec in much the same way as it has been used in France: as a blending wine, often with Merlot, to create charismatic Bordeaux-style blends. SEE MERITAGE.

Malvasia Bianca Widely planted in Italy, Malvasia is a grape, or family of grapes actually, with ancient origins. Malvasia Bianca is a white wine made from Malvasia, which is rare in the New World. The variety is capable of producing deeply colored whites that are high in alcohol and often slightly sweet.

Mataro SEE MOURVÈDRE.

Melon Pronounced *muh-LAWN*, and short for Melon de Bourgogne, this French variety is also sometimes known as Pinot Blanc in California, where it produces fruity white table wines. SEE PINOT BLANC.

Meritage This is a trademarked name coined by American wineries to solve a marketing problem. The problem was this: in order to call a wine by its varietal name, say Cabernet Sauvignon, that wine is required by U.S. laws to be composed of 75 percent Cabernet Sauvignon at minimum. When that was not the case, high-class wineries were forced to call their red or white gems "table wine," or else to give the wine some proprietary name that gave consumers no clue as to what was inside the bottle. And so "Meritage" came to be.

Meritage wines, also known as Bordeaux-style blends, have to be made up of certain varieties to be thus called. For red Meritage these are Cabernet Sauvignon, Merlot, Cabernet Franc, Petit Verdot, and Malbec. For white Meritage the grapes are Sauvignon Blanc, Sémillon, and Muscadelle. Wineries who use Meritage on their label have to join an association and agree to follow its requirements, which deal with such issues as maximum case production and pricing, in order to set a high standard for Meritage. It seems to be working, because the ones we've tried, at least, have not been run-of-the-mill wines. In fact, they've been stupendous.

Merlot Is there anyone who doesn't like Merlot? Judging by the way plantings of this red grape variety are increasing exponentially throughout the New World, the answer would have to be no. And who couldn't like its soft, fruity, supple personality? Its charm lies in its array of wonderful flavors and aromas—among them black cherries, caramel, herbs, and sometimes a hint of orange peel—as well as its high alcohol and lush, chewy texture. California, Washington State, and even Long Island, New York, are among the New World regions where it is thriving in the nineties, as well as South America, New Zealand, and Australia.

Because it has what Cabernet Sauvignon lacks, it is often used to soften the latter in the style of the great Bordeaux Cabs. But increasingly it is used the other way around: as a base for its own varietal wine, with small amounts of Cabernet Sauvignon added to the Merlot to give it more structure and focus.

Because it is less tannic than Cabernet Sauvignon, Merlot shouldn't be cellared for years. Have it with chicken, duck, ham, or turkey, as well as Mediterranean dishes and even spicy Chinese foods. Or sip it before dinner alongside soft cheeses.

Mourvèdre Mourvèdre is enjoying a resurgence in the New World, mostly in California, where it is often called Mataro. The trend to create wines in America that mimic those of France, in this case France's Rhône Valley, have resulted in some wonderfully new and creative blends. Mourvèdre, often a key component in these Rhône-style wines, is a robust grape that adds color, body, and hints of green tea–like herbal aromas. SEE RHÔNE-STYLE VARIETALS/BLENDS.

Müller-Thurgau This cross between Riesling and Sylvaner was developed in the late nineteenth century in Germany. It ripens earlier than Riesling, is easy to grow, and is high yielding. New Zealand, Oregon, and Washington have had some success with this grape, producing white wines that bear a slight resemblance to Riesling, are flowery yet acidic, and fresh.

Muscadelle It sounds similar, but Muscadelle is no relation to Muscat. The Australians use this variety better than almost anyone, to make their fine Tokay, a dark amber fortified wine known the world over for being alcoholic, mysterious, sensual, and sumptuous. It is sometimes called Flame Tokay. Some California wineries also use it in white Bordeaux-style blends. SEE MERITAGE.

Muscat Here's a family of grapes that's been around for centuries and centuries. There are at least four varieties of Muscat, ranging in hues, thus producing wines that vary from pale golden to dark, dark brown. Some Muscats have nicknames that reflect their hue, hence Orange Muscat, Black Muscat, and so on. Muscat of Alexandria and Muscat Canelli are but two Muscat varieties; the names and nicknames of the various Muscats could take up their own chapter.

Muscat grapes are known for their incredibly perfumed berries. Made all over the world, in most places Muscat is finished slightly sweet, with the exception of some dry-style Australian ones. New World varieties include off-dry sipping wines and sweet late harvest styles that often have a distinctive spicy aroma. In California some sweet fortified dessert wines made from Muscat varieties produce remarkably fragrant wines loaded with tropical fruit. Washington can render delicious, crisp, aromatic wines incredibly refreshing on hot summer days. When used in sparkling wine, Muscat grapes yield a sparkler that resembles Italian spumante.

Depending on the wine, of course, Muscat is generally ideal as an aperitif. Try it with hard cheese, foie gras, or with prosciutto and melon. For dessert it complements fruit pies or puddings.

Muscat of Alexandria SEE MUSCAT.

Muscat Canelli SEE MUSCAT.

Napa Gamay The Napa Gamay grape is no relation to the true Gamay grape, but is in fact the Valdiguié, a workhorse (and sometimes uninspiring) grape of the sizzling hot Midi region of France. At its best this misnamed grape can produce round, fruity reds that have popular appeal. Napa Gamay has been overshadowed by its other misnamed noncousin, Gamay Beaujolais (related not to Gamay, but to Pinot Noir), and therefore is not a major shelf stocker. SEE ALSO GAMAY.

Native American Varieties The wine grape is from the genus *Vitis*. The *species* of grape depends on where that grape originally grew, before the intervention of man. Native American grapes are different species from *Vitis vinifera,* the chief European species that includes most of the wine grapes grown in the world. There are more than a dozen native American species of wine grape.

Nebbiolo Nebbiolo is one of Italy's two finest grapes, Sangiovese being the other. It is responsible for some of that country's best wines, among them world-famous Barbaresco and Barolo. In the New World, especially California, but South America to a lesser degree, Nebbiolo is making its presence known.

California wineries are using it in Italian-style blends, or to make delicious varietal wines that can be long-lived, tannic, acidic, alcoholic, richly textured, big, big reds. Nebbiolos almost always require aging to evolve into distinctive and high-class wines.

Niagara Niagara is a French-American hybrid, the American parent being Concord, developed at the end of the 1800s. It thrives in the Midwest and East, and produces distinctive white wines that are usually on the sweet side, aromatic, with that grapy, musky, pungent quality that's a trademark of native American wine grapes.

Noble   The Noble is a hybrid of native American Muscadine grapes that originated and continue to thrive in the southern United States and Gulf Coast, where they can withstand the extreme heat and humidity that would kill off most varieties. It produces red wines that are usually finished slightly sweet.

Norton   Also known as Cynthiana, Norton is an American hybrid that thrives in the warmer regions of the United States. It produces light reds that display flavors and aromas hinting of spice and coffee.

Orange Muscat   SEE MUSCAT.

Palomino   This is a white grape variety that's most commonly associated with the making of sherry. Outside of Spain, Palomino is found in South Africa, with smaller amounts planted in California, Australia, and New Zealand.

Petite Sirah   This grape is no relation to Syrah, although it was once thought to be. It grows in North and South America, where it can produce red, almost black, wines that are extremely tannic but well balanced, with distinctive flavors and aromas that include black pepper. California wineries produce varietal wines of Petite Sirah, but more often it is used as a blending grape, to add backbone and color to Pinot Noir or Cabernet Sauvignon. Serve it with hard cheeses, lamb, and beef dishes.

Petit Verdot   This classic red wine Bordeaux grape is fairly new to California, the majority of whose vines are just now coming of the age to yield fruit. Some wineries make a varietal wine out of Petit Verdot, and it has many of the same strengths as Cabernet Sauvignon: rich color, hefty tannins, and excellent flavor concentration. The problem with Petit Verdot is that it ripens so late, and sometimes not at all, which has limited its practicality in the New World. But where it thrives, some wineries use it in their red Meritage blends to add color and tannic backbone to these Bordeaux-style wines. SEE MERITAGE.

Pinot Blanc   This grape is a mutation of Pinot Gris, and bears some resemblance to Chardonnay. In fact, in California some wineries use the same winemaking techniques on Pinot Blanc as they use for Chardonnay, and end up with a wine that is similar in some respects, although without as much fruit concentration. Other Pinot Blancs are subtly fruity and light, with crisp acidity. Pinot Blanc is also used to make California sparkling wines.

It turns out that older vines of Pinot Blanc may actually be Melon, and sometimes the two names are used interchangeably. SEE MELON.

Pinot Gris The grapes of this Pinot Noir variant are a beautiful pink-grey. Pinot Gris is not found widely in the New World, although the varietals made from it in Oregon have made the world sit up and take notice. New Zealand has also had some success with Pinot Gris. It is capable of producing full-bodied yet soft white wines that are gently perfumed.

Pinot Noir More than almost any wine we can think of, Pinot Noir is often described in poetic, sensual terms. A great Pinot Noir has subtlety, elegance, complexity, and finesse. On the palate it can be lush and broad and seductive, with essences of raspberries, loganberries, cherries, herbs, earth, and bouquets of fresh wildflowers. Because it loses its tannins quickly, Pinot Noir should be consumed within a couple years of the vintage, no more than seven or eight years max.

But more than these wonderful qualities, which winemakers the world over try to achieve with their Pinot Noirs, the grape's most dominant feature is how exasperating it is to grow. Winemakers spend their entire careers wrestling with the grape. It is thin-skinned, and therefore susceptible to various maladies to which fragile grapes fall prey. It also buds early, making it vulnerable to frost.

Nevertheless, you'll find Pinot Noir in almost every country where ambitious winemakers ply their trade. It is the sole grape of which red burgundy is made, and France is the country that has been able to take Pinot Noir to its most celestial heights. However, California, Washington, and especially Oregon, with a climate very similar to Burgundy's, are beginning to do wonders with this fickle grape. Canada, Australia, South Africa, and New Zealand are also attempting Pinot Noir, with Australia the real wild card, since its vines are just now of the age that they will bear fruit. Stay tuned.

Pinot Noir is also one of the grapes used to make excellent sparkling wines, especially the *méthode champenoise* sparklers made in California.

Have Pinot Noir with swordfish, fresh tuna steak, roast chicken or turkey, and game such as pheasant.

Port Port refers to a type of fortified wine that can be made from any grape variety. Portugal is where the world's most famous ports hail from, but South Africa, California, and Australia are the New World leaders in producing sometimes outstanding ones.

Here's the process: red wine grapes are crushed and begin to ferment in the usual way. After two to four days, the partially fermented grape juice has about 6 percent alcohol and about 10 percent residual sugar, which is quite sweet. At this point, the grape juice is run off into containers holding whopping 154-proof neutral wine spirits. The spirits act to immediately stop the fermenting process, and what's left is very flavorful, very sweet wine with around 20 percent alcohol.

There are two main types of port: wood aged and vintage ports. Wood-aged ports are ready to drink when bottled, and are made from many different vintages, added during the aging process to achieve a continuity of style. Ruby port is one type of wood-aged port that is dark red, young, fruity, and flavorful, and aged for three to four years on average before it is bottled. Tawny port is the other wood-aged port, and it is aged for eight to ten years. As a result, it is lighter in color, more mellow and subdued.

Vintage ports, on the other hand, are made from a single vintage, and they are bottled after about two years, but it takes from ten to twenty years or more of bottle age before they reach maturity. Therefore, vintage ports may be produced only two or three times in a decade.

Since ports pack a whollop in terms of alcohol and sweetness, they are best enjoyed after dinner. We like to have our port for dessert, without any other sweets to interfere with the heavenly experience.

Rhône-Style Varietals/Blends California winemakers, in particular, have for some time been on a quest to recreate—and top—the great red wines of France, and increasingly the whites as well. Thus, the famous grapes of the Rhône Valley are much in demand and are being made into varietal wines in addition to delicious Rhône-style blends, known as the "Rhône Rangers." These adventuresome winemakers are producing wonderful wines from Syrah, Carignane, Grenache, Mourvèdre, Alicante Bouchet, and Viognier grapes.

Riesling In Oregon it's White Riesling. In Australia it's Rhine Riesling. In America and other places it's Johannisberg Riesling, or sometimes just Riesling. These are all one and the same.

Riesling is a grape variety of German origin that makes wines in two basic styles: dry to off-dry, and lusciously sweet. The reason for the latter is that it is often harvested late (see "late harvest," in Chapter 9) and allowed to be infected with the "noble rot," also known as *Botrytis cinerea,* which produces juice that is highly concentrated and sweet, with lots of fragrance, and apricot and peach overtones. The drier versions are fresh, flowery, and delicate, with hints of apples and pears. What they both have in common is their surprisingly inexpensive price.

What you eat with your Riesling depends on the style of the wine. The medium-dry versions go well with cold meats, oysters, pasta salads, chicken, Thai cuisine, and even sushi. The sweeter ones can accompany hard cheeses, prosciutto, and fresh fruit.

Rosé Also called blush or Blanc de Noirs, *rosé* means "pink" in French. To make rosé, dark-skinned grapes are crushed as in red-wine making, but after just enough time to extract the desired amount of pigment from the skins, the juice is separated from the skins and then fermented like white wine. These wines can be anywhere from the palest pink to pale red, and are made from any number of red-wine grapes. Rosés are made in virtually every winemaking region, and at their best are light but flavorful, sometimes sweet, and meant to be consumed young. The best foods to accompany a delicate rosé are ones that won't overpower them, simple dishes such as pizza, pasta salads, and cold meats. Always serve rosé chilled.

Ruby Cabernet Developed in 1949 in California, Ruby Cabernet is a cross between Cabernet Sauvignon and Carignane. It is not widely planted anymore, but produces a pleasant red wine with some resemblance to Cabernet Sauvignon, although not as intense.

Ruby Port SEE PORT.

Sangiovese Along with Nebbiolo, Sangiovese is one of Italy's two great grape varieties. Because it ripens slowly and late, it can yield rich, alcoholic, long-lived red wines with cherry and plummy flavors. Sangiovese can also be made into light, fresh and fruity, early drinking reds.

In South America it is being grown in Argentina. In North America California leads the way and receives international recognition for its Sangioveses. As a result, plantings are increasing in California, so in the next decade we will no doubt see more of this wine in America.

Like other Italian-style reds, Sangiovese wonderfully complements Mediterranean dishes.

Sauvignon Blanc This variety is responsible for some of the most distinctive and popular white wines of the world. It is grown virtually everywhere, with New Zealand, Australia, California, and South Africa the New World leaders, Washington State, Texas, and South America following.

What is most distinctive about wines made from Sauvignon Blanc is their uniquely sharp aromas. Terms commonly used to describe the wine are grassy, musky, herbaceous, green fruits, nettles, and gooseberries. The wine has lively acidity, making it a great match with Sémillon, with which it is frequently blended and called white Meritage. Dry versions of Sauvignon Blanc are sometimes called Fumé Blanc.

Serve it chilled, of course, with all sorts of seafood and shellfish dishes.

Sauvignon Vert There's very little of this Muscadelle clone planted in the New World. It is grown in limited amounts in California, and produces light, agreeable white wines.

Semchard A white wine blend of Sémillon and Chardonnay.

Sémillon This is an excellent, high-yielding grape that produces classy and distinctive white wines that are low in acidity. Because of its weight and plentifulness, Sémillon is frequently used as a blending wine, to add background to Chardonnay, or to add weight and fruit to Sauvignon Blanc. Susceptible to botrytis, Sémillon is often made into rich, sweet dessert wine.

California, Washington, and Australia are making wonderful Sémillon, as are Chile and Argentina.

Seyval Blanc This French-American hybrid thrives in cool climates, and does well in Canada and the eastern United States, most notably New York. Unlike many French-American grapes, Seyval has no hint of that "foxy" or musky flavor that American grapes tend to have. It is increasingly being made into a varietal wine in America, where it yields a crisp white wine that can also be aged in oak to produce a richer, longer-lived white.

Sherry Australia, South Africa, and California are the New World regions producing sherry, a fortified wine made from white grapes, that gets its distinctive flavors from a yeast that forms on the top of the wine as it's fermenting. California "sherry" often refers to fortified wines, usually sweet ones, that have been baked, aged, or artificially infused with yeast to create a product similar in flavor to Spanish sherry.

Shiraz SEE SYRAH.

Sparkling Wines Any wine that has noticeable bubbles—not just the mild spritz sometimes found in still table wines—and goes *krushhh-unk!* when you open it is a sparkling wine. We'll test you on that one later since it's a pretty hard concept to grasp. At any rate, there are lots of sparkling wines produced outside of France's Champagne district, and they may be made from Chardonnay, Pinot Noir, Pinot Blanc, Riesling, Muscat, Symphony, or other varieties. Most commonly it's the first two. The more complicated the method of integrating the carbon dioxide into the wine, the more expensive the wine. The primary two used are the *méthode champenoise* and the bulk, or Charmat, method (see wine terms in Chapter 9).

New York State led the way for sparkling wines in the United States, but California has since taken over as the top producer, in no small part because the cooler coastal regions have attracted well-known French champagne makers who've transplanted their operations to the United States. Sparkling wines, however, are made virtually everywhere in the New World.

A great sparkling wine will be crisp and clean, with varying degrees of yeast and citrus. Some say the perfect sparkling wine is like "apple pie in a glass." This makes sense if you consider that the various fruit flavors (apple, lemon, pineapple, strawberry, cherry) come from the grapes, and the fresh-baked bread flavors come from the yeasts, which of course are the little buggers that convert grape sugar into alcohol and carbon dioxide—better known as bubbles. Sparkling wines vary in sweetness ("brut" means driest, "sec" and "demi-sec" are progressively sweeter).

If you want to impress your friends, know that the perfect sparkling wine should have tiny bubbles (this shows that the CO_2 is well integrated into the wine) that last a long time and form a thin layer on top of the glass. When tasters describe a sparkling wine as being "creamy," they're talking about the sensation of the multitudinous minuscule bubbles rolling gently across the tongue and down your throat.

One well-known California bubbly bottler says that sparkling wines should ideally be served at 42 degrees—which is very cold. To achieve this, they suggest placing it on the top shelf of your refrigerator for 30 minutes, then for 15 minutes in an ice bucket filled with ice, water, and salt (the salt makes the ice melt faster, thus making it colder). If you don't have an ice bucket, place the bottle in your freezer for 15 minutes just before serving.

Sparkling wine is more versatile than serving as the traditional toast at weddings and anniversaries. Try it with nuts and piquant olives, spicy Oriental foods, sushi and sashimi, shellfish, pâté, duck, beef, and goat cheeses. By the way, it's not easy to find a quality sparkling wine for under ten dollars.

Sylvaner   This good-quality German white wine variety barely has a foothold in the New World anymore. There is a small amount of Sylvaner in California, where it yields light, soft, short-lived whites that are fresh, fruity, and pleasant. Be aware that in California Sylvaner can be marketed under the names Monterey Riesling and Sonoma Riesling. These are not Rieslings! Sylvaner is less distinguished than Riesling, and is being replaced by more charismatic whites as its popularity declines.

Tawny Port   SEE PORT.

Vignoles   The French hybridizer J. F. Ravat was successful when he created this French-American cross. Vignoles is also known as Ravat 51, and does well in the cooler climates of North America, particularly New York State. High in acidity, it produces white wines with restrained fruitiness and good balance that can range from off-dry to very sweet and honeyed. The grape is susceptible to botrytis, or "noble rot," and can thus be turned into delicious dessert wines. Vignoles is also used to make icewine.

Vintage Port   SEE PORT.

Viognier   This rare but well-loved Rhône Valley grape has captured the imagination of California winemakers, who love its unusual spicy flavors and its aromas of violets, peaches, and apricots. It makes an excellent Riesling-like white wine, but it can also be made like Chardonnay, depending on the vinification methods used. With American consumers tiring of the Chardonnay monopoly, Viognier's fortunes will steadily rise. SEE RHÔNE-STYLE VARIETALS/BLENDS.

White Zinfandel Although a "white" wine made from the Zinfandel grape, White Zinfandel is actually pink. It has become wildly popular in the last few years, and California is the biggest New World producer. The wines are fresh and fruity, on the sweet side, but with enough acidity to balance out the sugar. Some White Zins have a bit of spritziness. Others have some Riesling or Muscat blended in to add more character and spunk.

This is a light and lively wine that is made to be drunk young, and can accompany light foods such as picnic fare.

Zinfandel This exotic European red-wine grape has taken the New World by storm. California is where most Zinfandel is cultivated these days, with Australia and South Africa new entrants in the field. One reason it's so appealing is that it lends itself to any number of styles. Zinfandel can be fruity, light, Beaujolais-like, or medium-bodied with definite character, or extremely rich, intensely flavored, tannic, and long-lived, like a great Cabernet Sauvignon. Some winemakers also make it into a sweet dessert wine.

Zinfandel has an easily recognizable varietal character: aromas and flavors of black pepper and brambles, with cherries, blackberries, and raspberries, and a lush, supple texture.

Chapter 9

WINE LANGUAGE
Who Writes This Stuff?

Because the wines in this book were all excellent enough to receive one or more gold medals in blind tastings, and because the tasting notes in Part III were written either by the winemakers themselves or by raving reviewers (and occasionally by us—one of the perks of writing a wine book!), you won't see common unflattering wine terms like "flabby," "cloying," or "dumb" defined here.

You'll find that once you learn the lingo, it's fun to understand what the heck they're talking about and to be privy to the mysteries of winespeak. You'll discover that innocent terms like "fresh" and "hint of vanilla" are actually code words that refer to specific components of the wine or the process by which it was made, in this case "acidity" and "oak-barrel aging," respectively.

We now no longer ask, "Who writes this stuff?" We are now part of the problem rather than the solution, using these silly terms freely and without shame, and spicing up our own wine appraisals with some of our favorite words such as "pugnacious," "mischievous," and "brazen."

By the way, words in SMALL CAPITALS are cross references to other definitions in this chapter that illuminate the term being defined.

acid/acidity Acid is to wine what a good zing of lime juice is to food: it adds zest and liveliness. In the language of wine, terms such as "crisp," "tart," "lively," and "refreshing" are used to describe wines that have a good balance of acid. Acidity is what keeps sweet and semisweet wines from being too cloying, and it's what helps to deliver the flavor in sparkling wines, since the mousse (the foamy bubbles) can sometimes disperse the fruity flavor elements. It's also what makes white wines such a good dinner guest, since acid stimulates the appetite, cleanses the palate, and cuts through rich foods.

Because white wines lack the tannin of reds, acidity is especially important because it contributes to a wine's ability to age well in your cellar. Acidity is used on wine labels to express the total acid content by volume. Ideal levels of acid on dry wines fall between 0.6 and 0.75 percent of the wine's volume. For sweet wines it should not be less than 0.70 percent of the volume. Didn't you always want to know that? SEE ALSO MALOLACTIC FERMENTATION.

age worthy Age worthy simply means that a wine is capable, or worthy, of being cellared or aged. This is one of those terms with a double meaning. It could either mean that the wine you just purchased really isn't ready to drink yet (perhaps those mouth-puckering tannins in the red wine haven't had a chance to break down inside the bottle), or that the wine will be good now, but perhaps even better later if cellared properly. Usually it's a complimentary term that refers to wines with greater character and complexity than your Saturday barbecue variety. SEE AGING.

aging Many would be surprised to learn that 90 percent of the wines produced worldwide are drunk "young" (soon after they're bottled and released), and they're meant to be. For one thing, a newly purchased bottle of wine has already been aged to some extent—otherwise you'd be drinking grape juice. SEE BARREL AGING.

But more to the point, a bottle of wine is a living thing. That is, wine is composed of natural elements such as water, acids, alcohols, and tannins that interact with one another until the wine finally decays. It doesn't sound very romantic, but that's the way it is. In the case of fine reds, such as the more expensive Cabernet Sauvignons or Italian varietals (SEE TANNIN), and some of the sweet white wines or vintage ports, this aging process can bring the various elements into greater BALANCE, so that the wine's flavors and aromas, color, body, and finish improve. But for rosés, most white wines, and many lighter red wines, aging is merely an exercise in the misconceived notion that all wine improves with age.

Even if you've purchased a keeper, the way you store the bottle and even the size of the bottle (the smaller the bottle, the more rapidly it will "mature") will determine the length of time it should be cellared. Some people like to keep wine, and if you're one of them, be aware that wine does not like temperature extremes or bright light. (SEE CELLARING.) The easiest way to determine if you've purchased a wine that will be better later than it is now is to read the tasting notes. The winemaker will say something like "will improve even further in the bottle" or "drink it until 2010," or "needs time to develop more focus," or "this wine is still young." If a wine is "balanced" or "mature," it's "ready to drink now."

aperitif Although the wine and spirits police state that an aperitif must not contain less that 15 percent alcohol by volume in order to be labeled as such, the term has come into popular usage to mean *any* alcoholic beverage that is consumed before a meal. The point is to stimulate the appetite. Generally speaking, the French prefer a sweet aperitif such as Tawny Port. But many Americans like wines that are neither too alcoholic and nor too sweet. Good choices include sparkling wine, dry sherry, and white wine. (The ACID found in white wine and dry sparklers actually makes you hungrier.)

appellation In France there are rigid laws that determine which appellation (or wine-growing region) a wine can lay claim to. A burgundy cannot be produced in any appellation other than Burgundy. However, the Americans have adopted the term and made it synonymous with "region." So in California, for example, the appellations would include those of Sonoma, Napa, the Sierra Foothills, and so on.

aroma How a wine smells after you pour it into a glass will tell 90 percent of the story, at least in terms of what kinds of flavors you can expect. (For more on tasting and smelling wine, see Chapter 4.) A wine's aroma, in winespeak, is often referred to as its nose or its bouquet, and may include everything from flowers to tropical fruits to herbs to saddle leather to flint. It takes a bit of imagination to dream up these smells, but they're there. Many varietals have aromas that distinguish them from all others, and you'll sometimes see these described as "typical varietal bouquet," a lazyman's way of telling you that your Zinfandel smells the way it's supposed to, rather than his describing its aromatic components. SEE VARIETAL CHARACTER.

astringent/astringency Did you ever bite into an unripe persimmon or green banana? If so, you know what astringent means. Your mouth turns inside out, and no amount of water will bring the pink-and-slidy feeling you long for back to your tongue, inner cheeks, and gums. Astringency in wines is associated with high levels of tannin. Very tannic wines need some extra time in the bottle to mellow out, since tannins normally decrease with age. (SEE AGE WORTHY.) As long as there's plenty of fruit to outlive excessive tannins, astringency won't be a problem once the wine matures. A little bit of astringency is to be expected in robust, rich, full-bodied red powerhouse wines. What you don't want is a mouth-puckering experience that ruins your pleasure. SEE TANNIN.

backbone Like many terms in wine language, "backbone" can be taken rather literally. It generally refers to either tannin or acid levels that "hold up" or "support" the wine. Wines with firm tannic or acidic backbones are full bodied; those without backbones would be soft or light bodied. SEE ACID AND TANNIN.

balance This a term of praise that describes that magic moment in a wine's life when its components—chiefly acid, sugar, fruit, and alcohol—are working together in harmony. Acid is what balances sweetness; the fruit concentration is what balances tannin and oakiness; and the overall flavor and acidity of the wine are what keep the alcohol from making you spin around on your saloon stool gasping "whoo-hahh!" It's reasonable to assume that all balanced wines won't have the same intensity. For example, a balanced light wine should be delicate, while a balanced full-bodied wine should have the appropriate concentration and punch. SEE BODY.

barrel aging Most wines spend only a brief period of time in large vats or tanks to rid them of impurities and to prepare them for bottling. But the fuller-flavored reds and some whites (such as drier-style Chardonnays, Sauvignon Blancs, Chenin Blancs, and Pinot Blancs) are aged in large or small oak barrels or larger casks, which matures them, adds structure, and improves their taste, if done correctly. Barrel aging requires time, money, knowledge, and considerable effort, so winemakers like to brag about it.

But there's another reason they mention it, especially in the case of white wines, which has to do with identifying a certain style of wine, as barrel-aged wines have specific flavor characteristics that nonbarrel-aged wines lack. Some terms that will clue you in to the fact that the taster is describing qualities that come from oak barrel aging are oak, vanilla, clove, nutmeg, cinnamon, and sometimes chocolate.

There's a whole oenological science devoted to oak barrels, one that we won't get into here. But suffice it to say that the size of the barrel and its percentage of new oak, not to mention the character of the particular tree from which it came and the nationality of that tree, as well as the time the wine spends in barrel—all come into play. Oak barrel aging imparts all-important tannin (necessary for longer shelf life) to whites but, oddly, *mellows* the sharp tannin levels in robust red wines. SEE STRUCTURE.

barrique A French word for "barrel," *barrique* refers to oak barrels or casks of 225 liters (or about 59 U.S. gallons) in which wines are often stored. A *barrique* yields 25 cases, or 300 bottles, of finished wine.

berrylike Often used to describe Zinfandel, this term refers to sweet and ripe blackberries, raspberries, cherries, and cranberries. When aromas conjure up other berries, winemakers will usually name them, such as currants, black currants, strawberries, etc.

big SEE BODY.

blend/blending Blending is not too different in winemaking than it is when you're cooking up the perfect curry—a dash of this, a pinch of that, all to accomplish the perfect balance of flavors, bite, and piquancy. A wine might be a blend of the same varietal grown in different vineyards (SEE MICROCLIMATE), a blend of the same wine that is aged in different casks

(SEE BARREL AGING), a blend of wines from different vintages, or a blend of two or more wine varieties.

The purpose of blending is, naturally, to achieve a winemaker's goal. In some cases, it is to produce a wine that will be consistent year after year, something consumers can depend on, regardless of weather conditions and other factors that affect a particular vintage. In other cases, it may be that a certain varietal, say Cabernet Sauvignon, becomes "friendlier" when mellowed out by Cabernet Franc or Merlot. Blending is a perfectly legitimate practice, and every wine-producing region and country has laws that dictate how a blended wine can be labeled. (For more on wine varietals and characteristics, see Chapter 8, especially ITALIAN VARIETALS/BLENDS, MERITAGE, AND RHÔNE-STYLE VARIETALS/BLENDS.)

body This is a term that's difficult to describe, but a sensation that's fairly simple to identify if you pay attention. Body describes how a wine feels in your mouth—its weight and fullness—and refers to a combination of the wine's alcohol, sugar, and glycerin content (glycerin, a by-product of fermentation, is a colorless, sweet, slippery liquid that adds "smoothness" to wine). Body is substance: think of body as being the opposite of thin and watered-down. A light- or medium-bodied wine might be described as "simple," "soft," "attractive," or "delicate." A full-bodied one might be called "brawny," "mouth filling," "big," or "weighty." Most wines are not full bodied, and there is nothing anywhere that says a medium-bodied wine is inferior to a full-bodied one. They are different, will feel different in your mouth, and will be compatible with different foods. Remember that the key to a wine's greatness is its balance—not the measure of its body.

botrytis Its formal name is *Botrytis cinerea,* and it's also known as "noble rot." When wine grapes grow in just the right conditions—dry, sunny days alternating with damp, foggy mornings—they may become botrytized, or infected with the beneficial mold that transforms normal grape juice into a honeyed, aromatic, *magical* liquid. Since this condition is apt to happen after harvest season, as late as December in some places, the resultant wines are called LATE HARVEST wines, and they're prized the world over.

It works like this: the beneficial mold covers the grapes, sending little filaments into the skin that perforate the grapes and cause them to shrivel up. The mold doesn't rot the grape, but 90 percent of the water evaporates, and the sugar and acids remain in the grape pulp. When this is pressed and fermented, you get very sweet wine (since all of the sugar is not fermented into alcohol) that has extremely concentrated flavors and aromas. Think, for example, of how intense a dried tomato or dried pear tastes, and you get the idea.

Over time the botrytized wine turns pale yellow to dark gold, the flavors maturing and concentrating. The most common grapes used to make late harvest wines are Sémillon, Sauvignon Blanc, Riesling, Gewürztraminer, and

Chenin Blanc, although there are others that are susceptible to the noble rot. These wines age extremely well in the bottle, and are best served alone after a meal, although sweet-toothed diners might like to try them with fruit tarts, berries, or bland custards.

bouquet SEE AROMA.

brawny SEE POWERFUL.

breathing/airing Here's a simple concept that makes wine connoisseurs' noses redden even further as the debate rages on. To breathe or not to breathe seems to be the question, and the answer, at least as far as we're concerned, doesn't seem all that unclear. Breathing refers to the act of pouring wine into another container, such as a decanter, in order to allow the wine to aerate and mix with oxygen. The point of this is that the aroma components of the wine are allowed to oxidize, which makes them more intense. (Breathing does *not* refer to simply uncorking a wine. The narrow neck of the bottle prohibits an adequate supply of oxygen from making any discernible difference in the wine's bouquet.)

But the material we've read, written by noted world wine experts, seems to lean on the side of the pour-the-wine-into-your-glass-and-just-drink-it side of the argument. Their reasoning is that only the surface is getting oxidized anyway, and some of the fruitiness and flavor is at risk if a wine is exposed to oxygen too long. (This makes sense; otherwise, why would we bother to recork a half-consumed bottle?)

If you are serving a young, tannic red wine, breathing may lessen some of the tannins. If you are serving a very old wine, careful decanting should be done to separate the wine from the sediments that have settled in the bottom of the bottle. But in general, those who say a wine needs to breathe probably want you to look at their vacation pictures before you get too involved in enjoying yourself.

If you want to please both sides, serve your wine in a large, wide wine glass (for maximum surface contact with the air) and swirl it around a bit before sipping it. (For more on tasting and smelling wine, see Chapter 4.)

brut This is a term that refers to the driest champagnes and other sparkling wine. In Europe, Common Market laws dictate that a sparkling wine labeled brut must have no more than 1.5 percent sugar. In America and elsewhere, the term is merely a descriptive one that means "very dry." There is no good way to tell if a non-European brut sparkling wine will be dry, very dry, or very, very dry without tasting it.

bulk/Charmat process To transform wine into sparkling wine, a second fermentation process has to occur. In the case of French champagne or New World sparkling wines made by the *MÉTHODE CHAMPENOISE,* that second fermentation takes place inside individual bottles. But with the bulk or Charmat process, it takes place in large tanks. After the second fermentation, the wine is filtered, the appropriate dosage is added (a mixture of wine and sugar added to sparkling wines before they are bottled that will determine how dry they will be), and then it is bottled.

The tanks may be very large or rather small, and the process can take less than a month. Some wines are left *sur lie* in these tanks (that is, the wine is left in contact with the LEES, a deposit consisting mainly of dead yeast cells that is a by-product of fermentation, and adds a distinctive flavor and complexity to sparkling wines) for several months in the tanks before being bottled. The Charmat process is widely used in the United States, and sparkling wines made this way must be labeled Charmat Process or Bulk Process.

buttery SEE CREAMY.

carbonic maceration Known also as whole berry fermentation, this is a process by which whole bunches of grapes (usually red) are placed in a tank that also contains carbon dioxide. The weight breaks the skin of the grapes at the bottom, thus beginning fermentation at an intracellular level. (Normally grapes are crushed and the yeast ferments the juice in the presence of air.) The resulting wines have less acidity and are light and fruity—so you should drink them young. Beaujolais and wines labeled Nouveau are usually made this way.

cellaring/storing Let's not get crazy here. The truth is, if you have 244 bottles of wine in your temperature- and humidity-controlled, computer-organized, state-of-the-art wine cellar, you probably already know how to take care of that liquid gold. But for the rest of us, here are a few tips.

The first, most important tip is: don't cellar your wine for too long unless you know for a fact that it will improve with bottle aging. (SEE AGING.) Most wines won't. We can't think of anything worse than holding on to that special bottle for your fortieth birthday, only to discover on the night you're looking for a spirit lifter that you're in possession of some flat, rotten red stuff that's not even fit for your salad.

After you've obeyed tip number one, the rest is easy. Just find a place in your house or apartment that is relatively cool, dark, vibration-free, and not prone to extreme temperature changes. Then call it your "cellar." Although the ideal cellar temperature is between 55 and 60 degrees F, with 45 to 70 degrees acceptable extremes, the main issue here is consistency. In other words, it's better to have a good medium temperature that will stay that way than to have a cooler place that will sometimes be warm.

Always store your wine bottles on their sides so that they are in contact with the cork. This keeps the cork from drying out and shrinking.

The final tip is to keep a well-organized cellar book (or, if you must, put the data in your computer) so that you know which wines go best with what foods, and when they will be at or past their prime. (For more on wine cellars, see Chapter 5.)

cepage You don't have to be a wine snob to sound like one. It's fun: just tell Walker W. Wilcox III who lives next door that the Pinot Gris *cepage* is making fantastic strides in Oregon. *Cepage* just means a variety of grapevine.

chewy You'll know a chewy wine when you drink one, but explaining it is another thing. Imagine that the wine you're drinking requires a knife, fork, and some healthy molars. You've got yourself one chewy wine. The term is used to describe red wines that have high levels of tannin and are rich, heavy, and full of fruit extract. SEE ALSO BODY AND MOUTH FEEL.

cigarbox A term used to describe the aroma of cedar and/or tobacco in a wine. It's not an uncomplimentary adjective. In fact, one of us had a grandfather who smoked cigars, and those old wooden boxes made wonderful treasure keepers for paper-doll clothes, exotic dead bugs, and the like with their little brass clasps that locked shut. The treasures all smelled like the cigarbox, a wonderfully pleasant aroma.

citrus Although citrus fruits include oranges, lemons, and limes, among others, the winespeak term "citrus" most often refers to grapefruit. Chardonnays grown in cool climates will often display a grapefruitlike character.

clone Don't think of sci-fi monsters; think of a white-jacketed, bespectacled scientist strolling through Napa Valley vineyards in August, clipboard in hand. Clones are plants reproduced asexually by means of cuttings or grafts so that they retain the genetic characteristics of the parent plant. Cloning is used extensively throughout the world to find and reproduce grapes of a certain variety that ripen later, for example, or yield more, or are resistant to disease. There are many different clones of a single variety.

closed Even though it sounds like an insult, to say that a wine is closed is to say that it has great potential. In other words, the wine has a lot of concentration and good character, but needs more time in the bottle to mature to its full intensity.

complex This is what you want in your favorite boyfriend, and what makes a great wine unbelievable. A complex wine is one in which layers and layers of different flavors and aromas reveal themselves, all combined with a lovely MOUTH FEEL, a smashing FINISH, in perfect BALANCE. Complexity is elusive, but the best wines have it.

concentrated Annie Greensprings could figure this one out. Concentrated wines are ones that are not watery and thin, where the flavor components jump out at you and make a distinct impression on your palate. Concentrated wines will have effects that linger on and on. SEE ALSO FINISH.

cooperage A term that refers to any container for storing or aging wine, from stainless steel to oak, from small to very large.

creamy Some wines are described as having a creamy or buttery texture, or creamy, buttery flavors. In sparkling wines, this is a result of LEES contact. In certain Chardonnays, this may be a result of MALOLACTIC FERMEN-TATION. Creamy is the opposite of CRISP, which refers to the level of ACIDITY.

crisp Like so many wine terms, crisp is a code word that indicates a wine's acid content, in this case a pleasing level of acidity. It is synonymous with "refreshing," "fresh," and "tart." SEE ACID/ACIDITY.

cuvée This word comes from the French *cuve*, meaning vat or tank, particularly a large one used for blending or fermenting wines. In places other than Europe, the term has come to mean a specific lot or batch of a particular wine or blend.

delicate SEE BODY.

demi-sec Is the glass half full or half empty? "Demi" is from the French meaning half, and "sec" means dry. But demi-sec wines are closer to being half sweet than they are to being half dry. This term is usually applied to sparkling wines that are sweet to medium sweet.

depth Some of these wine terms get tricky, and you have to use your imagination a bit. Where weight refers to a wine's body, or how a wine "feels" in your mouth, depth has more to do with how *much* of your mouth experiences the wine. It's a subtle distinction, but a wine that has good depth is one full of layers of flavors that seem to fill your mouth from front to back.

disgorging Sparkling wines made by the *MÉTHODE CHAMPENOISE* undergo a final step, disgorging, whereby the sediment, or LEES, is removed from each bottle before the wine receives its dosage (a mixture of wine and sugar that determines how sweet the champagne or sparkling wine will be), and before the bottle gets corked.

dry Quick: What's the opposite of dry? If you said wet, you haven't read enough of this book. The opposite of dry, in wine terms, is sweet. A wine, still or sparkling, in which an ordinary wine taster can perceive no sweetness is dry, and that would fall somewhere between 0.5 and 0.7 percent RESIDUAL SUGAR, which is the amount of sugar left after a wine has finished fermenting. Dry does not necessarily mean better; there are many wines that are *supposed* to be sweet. SEE SWEET.

earthy Will there be a lot of brown stuff floating around in a wine that has "earthiness"? No. This term can mean any number of things, but when used in a complimentary sense, as found in *this* book, it is being used to describe that elusive flavor quality that comes from the soil. Eat a radish just picked and still hot from the sun-drenched black dirt and you'll know what the winemaker is talking about. You can almost taste the minerals in the soil. This one requires a bit more imagination than some other wine terms.

en tirage SEE LEES.

estate bottled In the United States, "estate bottled" on a label means that the wine comes from the winery's own vineyards, or from vineyards leased on a long-term basis, only if the vineyards and winery are both located within the APPELLATION shown on the label. In other words, the grape juice wasn't purchased from a winery a thousand miles away, and then made into wine. Or conversely, the wine wasn't grown in the vineyards, and then made into wine a thousand miles away. Estate bottled wines are supposed to connote superior quality.

extract Elements that add flavor, aroma, and character to a wine are known as extract. A "highly extracted" wine, or one with "loads of extract," implies that the grapes used to make this wine had very concentrated juice, and this could be for any number of reasons, among them a great vintage; careful avoidance of overcropping; OLD VINES; LATE HARVEST; or possibly because they were just plain great grapes.

fat Fat is good when you're talking about dessert wines. It refers to the naturally occurring glycerin in sweet dessert wines, the oily richness that coats your mouth. Fat is slightly less complimentary when referring to nondessert wines that are medium to full bodied, slightly low in acid, and leave a fat or full impression on your palate.

filtered There's a lot of stuff floating around in wine after it's been fermented. After all, fermentation is caused by little living critters, and they don't just disappear, nor do their by-products. Therefore, the vast majority of winemakers fine and filter their wine at least a little. The reason is because most people expect a nice clear glass of wine in their wine glass.

Explaining the types of filters and extent to which wines should be filtered could fill the rest of this book. Know, however, that even as you read this, someone, somewhere is getting hot under the collar debating how much wines should be filtered. Why? Because wine lovers complain that overfining and overfiltering wine removes from it the very thing we love: its character.

Therefore, many winemakers are moving back to the traditional (European) practice of not overdoing it, figuring that New World wine lovers would rather put up with a little sediment rather than drink something that has no personality and might as well be swigged from a gallon jug. Some of the wines in this book have "Unfined, Unfiltered" on their labels to alert consumers to a purist approach, a more handcrafted winemaking method that, theoretically at least, leads to a higher quality, more sensuous wine-drinking experience. SEE FINED.

fined Fining is similar to filtering, resultwise at least. As opposed to filtering, where the wine is poured through something that screens out the sediments and other junk, in fining something is *added* to the wine that captures the unwanted solid particles. It's the same process cooks use to clarify broth or to make jelly clear (by adding egg whites). In fact, winemakers also use egg whites sometimes, but more commonly gelatin or bentonite (a type of clay). Like filtering, it's a controversial practice if done to excess, because it's a bit like giving the wine a lobotomy: a lot of personality gets lost in the process. SEE FILTERED.

fine-grained tannins When a winemaker refers to TANNINS as being fine-grained, he or she is saying that tannins are present, but they're smooth and not overpowering. In other words, the tannins are refined and well behaved.

finish We hope that winespeakers come up with some new ways to describe a great finish other than "long and lingering." Like so many wine terms, finish is just a highfallutin way of saying aftertaste. Actually, it's a bit more involved. After you swallow the wine, its finish is characterized both by how long the flavors linger in your mouth, and by what kind of qualities are still perceptible. So, a finish in a quality wine might be medium or long, but it could also be soft, creamy, slightly tannic, or just "good." A wine's "LENGTH" or "persistence" is a component of its finish.

firm Used to describe a wine that hits your palate with an acidic or tannic bang, this is a complimentary term that implies that a wine may be rather young, but will make a great accompaniment to strong-flavored foods.

fleshy/meaty These terms refer to body and texture, and often suggest a wine of great smoothness and richness, where suppleness and flavor are in harmony. SEE CHEWY.

fortified wine Sherry and port are the best-known examples of fortified wines in the New World. These are wines in which the alcoholic content has been increased to the tune of 17 to 21 percent in the finished product by the addition of brandy or neutral spirits. Because of their high alcohol, fortified wines are less likely to spoil after opening than table wines, and they also have long, long cellaring potential. In the United States, sweet fortified wines have to be labeled "Dessert Wine" because the federal authorities want to prevent the temptation of alcoholics to buy up and glug down all the expensive twenty-year-old rare port they can get their hands on.

fruity This is a term that often applies to young wines. A fruity wine is full of intense fruit flavors such as berries or apples, and possesses freshness.

glycerin A by-product of fermentation, glycerin is found in all wines, but is most obvious in higher-alcohol and late harvest wines. At high levels it feels slippery and smooth on the tongue, and adds fullness to the wine's body.

grassy You will often see this term when Sauvignon Blanc is being described because it is part of that wine's VARIETAL CHARACTER. Grassiness is a nice quality if you think of the light, fresh, green smell of a summer lawn being mowed. Sometimes "gooseberry" is used to describe a similar flavor/aroma. Too much grassiness is a negative, but you won't find the term used as such in this book.

grip Here's a term that's easy to understand. When a wine, like a handshake, is forceful, it has grip. Grip is used to describe a red wine distinguished by rich texture and an assertive personality.

herbs/herbaceous Certain wines (for instance, Cabernet Sauvignon, Sauvignon Blanc, and Merlot) are sometimes described as having herbal aromas and/or flavors. *Which* herbs depends on the wine's VARIETAL CHARACTER.

hybrid When two or more grape varieties are genetically crossed by human intervention, you get a hybrid. The idea is to create a grape that's superior to the parents, or one that's better able to cope with such conditions as climatic extremes or proneness to disease. In the northern United States, French-American hybrids have resulted in wines that are much better than those of native varieties in many cases. It may take thousands of crosses to come up with a commercially successful wine, and it takes about fifteen years to determine if that hybrid will produce consistently sound wine.

late harvest If harvest time is autumn, then grapes picked later than that would be late harvest, right? Well, yes, but late harvest on a label really refers to how *ripe* the grapes were at harvest time. If grapes are picked at a stage where they're riper than normal (i.e., they have a higher-than-normal sugar content), then they will be made into a late harvest wine. Often, but not always, these later-picked grapes have been infected with noble rot, or BOTRYTIS. Either way, late harvest on a label means that the wine will be sweeter than normal—possibly very, very sweet—or with higher-than-normal alcohol levels. Most late harvest wines are after-dinner wines, sipped in place of dessert.

layers A really complex wine may be described as having *layers* of fruit. We always think of Charlie's Chocolate Factory, and that magical chewing gum that reveals an entire six-course meal when chewed long enough. Actually, "layers" is another wine term that is fairly obvious. When, for example, the winemaker has created a blend from four different grapes, and has done it masterfully, a discerning taster will be able to distinguish different nose and flavor components from each of the grape varieties used, and will see how these all come into balance. Once you get the hang of what to expect from each type of grape, you too will notice layers of flavors from some of the wines in Part III. By the way, it's not just blends that possess layers. Some of the more classic varietals can conjure up three and four different flavor sensations.

lees You'll often read that a wine "sat on the lees" or that it was "left in contact with the lees" for several months. Lees means sediment, or more precisely, dead yeast cells that are a by-product of fermentation. When wine ferments, this sediment sinks to the bottom of the barrel or tank and is promptly removed so as not to contribute unwanted odors or flavors. But some wines, particularly some Chardonnays and Sauvignon Blancs, are left in contact with the lees (called *sur lie)* after fermentation. This adds complexity and an attractive toasty, roasted grain character. Sparkling wines get much of their character from aging on the lees (called *en tirage),* except the aging is done during a second fermentation inside the bottle—sediment and all—before DISGORGING takes place. This is why the best sparkling wines taste akin to freshly toasted homemade bread. The lees contact also contributes richness and creaminess to these sparkling wines.

length The amount of time the aftertaste lingers in your mouth after swallowing your wine is a wine's length. Ten seconds is good, fifteen is great, and twenty seconds is spectacular. SEE FINISH.

maceration Broadly, this term means to steep or to soak something (in this case, grapes) in order to separate the liquid from the solids. In winemaking, this important process involves dissolving the tannins, pigments, and flavor compounds from the grape skins, seeds, and stem fragments into the new wine. Produced during fermentation, alcohol, being a solvent, achieves this.

One could write a book about the various ways maceration takes place, including cold maceration and CARBONIC MACERATION, but be satisfied to know that the process will produce different results depending on such variables as temperature, duration, size of the vat, and degree of agitation.

malolactic fermentation   This technical term refers to the secondary fermentation that most red wines, and a few whites, undergo that converts malic acid (the acid of most fruits, especially apples) into lactic acid (the acid of milk). It sounds strange, but specially propagated lactic acid bacteria are introduced into the wine to induce malolactic fermentation, and the resulting wines are more complex, softer and more supple, less harsh and less tart. Think of it as adding cream to your coffee, except it's done on a microscopic level. Few whites undergo malolactic fermentation because crisp, lively ACIDITY is precisely what we *want* in white wines. However, some cool-climate whites, such as certain Chardonnays, may be too acidic, and malolactic fermentation is used to add a creamy, buttery texture.

méthode champenoise   All champagnes from France are produced by the *méthode champenoise*. For producers of sparkling wine in the New World (some of whom insist on calling their sparklers "champagne," which is punishable by law in France if not produced in that eponymous region!), this wine term has definite snooty connotations. In fact, wines made by this method take a lot more expertise, time, and money, so the resultant sparklers are generally higher quality.

Basically, after the wine has fermented it is bottled, and a measured amount of sugar and yeast is added. When the bottle is corked, fermentation occurs, but the carbon dioxide that is produced gets trapped inside, thus creating those wonderful bubbles. The sediment that is a by-product then must be expelled (SEE DISGORGING). These *champagnes* (go ahead: arrest us) are marketed in the bottle in which the second fermentation took place. (For more on sparkling wines, see Chapter 8.)

microclimate   It's been known for thousands of years, but not fully understood. Why does one vineyard produce extraordinary grapes, while the one right next to it doesn't? Microclimate may be the answer. In winespeak it refers not just to climate, but to a combination of soil type, soil drainage, the angle of slope, altitude, and orientation toward the sun. Many wineries produce several bottles of the same varietal in a given vintage, but on one label might appear the name of a vineyard from which the grapes were grown to distinguish that particular wine. Microclimates, similar to the French word *terroir,* are part of the reason why certain individual vineyards seem to produce wines that have unique and identifiable qualities year after year.

mousse   Mousse is to champagne/sparkling wine as "head" is to beer.

mouth feel/mouth filling If we could remove a single term from wine language, this would be it. Who made it up? What does it mean? And why do so many winemakers and wine tasters use it to describe wine? We can only answer the middle question, or try to. Mouth filling seems to refer to wines with intense, round flavors, often in combination with glycerin or slightly low acidity. The idea here is that the wine's various characteristics seem to expand in the mouth, thus "filling" it up (as opposed, say, to an acidic wine that would have a distinct cutting or biting edge). Mouth feel is often used in conjuction with the modifiers "chewy" or "fleshy." SEE ALSO BODY.

must This is the juice of grapes produced by pressing or crushing, before it is fermented.

natural In *MÉTHODE CHAMPENOISE* sparkling wines, after DISGORGING, a small amount of wine is lost. So winemakers commonly add a mixture of wine and sugar (known as the dosage*)* to fill up the bottle and to add some degree of sweetness, depending on how dry they want the final sparkler to be. Natural (sometimes spelled naturel) sparkling wines have no sweetener added. Thus, a natural champagne or sparkling wine is driest of all. Winemakers sometimes refer to these as "no dosage" wines.

noble rot SEE BOTRYTIS.

no dosage SEE NATURAL.

nose SEE AROMA.

NV These initials, commonly seen on labels, stand for nonvintage. The word means that the wine you're drinking is a blend of several different vintages, usually based mainly on the most recent one, with the products of some past vintages, sometimes called "reserve wines," blended in. Just because a wine has no vintage does not mean it is of lower quality. Indeed, some winemakers attempt to produce wines year after year that will be consistent and always excellent. NV is often seen on sparkling wine or champagnes.

oak/oaky Aging in oak barrels imparts certain flavors and aromas to wines, including, obviously, oakiness. Vanillin, which comes from the oak itself, and toasty or roasted qualities, derived from the charring that comes from the open flames used to heat the barrel staves during barrel making, are common ways to describe oaky wines. "Woody" is another word for oaky.

old vines Like classic, well-cared-for cars, old grapevines are considered valuable. The reason, oddly enough, is that the older a vineyard becomes, the lower its yield. But since each vine has to devote all of its energy into producing fewer grapes, those fewer grapes will have a higher level of EXTRACT. In the New World, Australia seems to have the most old vines, since many of the vineyards there were planted in the last century. Since conventional wisdom would state unabashedly that old vines make better wines, you'll often see "Old Vines" or "80 Year Old" or some such right on the label to announce to potential buyers that this wine will be jam-packed with flavor.

pencil lead   There comes a time when we have to admit we've been beat. Having checked through several up-to-date, ten-pound tomes on wine by the world's leading wine authorities, we failed to come up with an explanation for this one. We don't know what pencil lead tastes or smells like. But we do know that it's not a derogatory thing to say about a wine's bouquet. (Robert Parker, considered by some the god of American wine writers, uses this term frequently.) So there you are. If you can recognize and detect pencil lead in the bouquet, be happy about it.

phylloxera   If you're seeking revenge on a mean and nasty winemaker who has dis'd you, whisper "phylloxera" in his ear and walk away. He'll turn several shades of white, for this vine disease, brought about by tiny aphids or lice that attack the roots of most grapevines, was responsible for wiping out virtually all vineyards in France and America in the last century. Grape growers are deadly afraid of it, and for good reason. The little critters live on in the soil, and will attack *Vitis vinifera* vines (which includes all of the European varieties from which the finest wines in the world are made) like there's no tomorrow.

In the late nineteenth century, it was discovered that most native American varieties were immune to phylloxera, so grafting the European varieties onto American rootstock was done, both in America and throughout Europe. Unfortunately, that didn't solve the problem completely, since the little devils have found a way to show up again on the American rootstock that was widely used in the 1980s. (By the year 2000, for instance, 30 to 50 percent of all U.S. coastal vineyards will have to be systematically replanted because of phylloxera.) Some varieties are more resistant than others, and some regions—Chile, for example—have never had the problem at all.

powerful   Powerful red wines are ones that are high in alcohol and tannin, also sometimes called "brawny" reds. A powerful white wine would be a dry wine with lots of body.

private reserve   SEE RESERVE.

proprietary wine   This is a name or brand dreamed up by a producer that is exclusive to that producer, and is used instead of the varietal name. So for example, if a producer wants his 1993 Cabernet Sauvignon to stand out from the pack, he might name it Midnight Red, and the next year's wine would be the 1994 Midnight Red. It's a bit like trademarking your wine. The problem for consumers, of course, is that it's impossible to determine from the proprietary name what kind of wine they're buying. On the other hand, this growing trend has added some sparkle, fun, and mystique to the formerly stuffy wine world, especially in America.

proprietor's reserve SEE RESERVE.

reserve Although there is no official regulation governing how this term is used, a reserve wine usually represents a wine of higher quality than the regular bottling of that same variety. You'll see the term alone, or sometimes as Private Reserve, Proprietor's Reserve, Special Reserve, Vintner's Reserve, and the like. A quality producer with a conscience won't abuse the term; it should be merited.

Reserve wines get their name because the wine has been separated out, or reserved, from the rest of the batch. It might be the same as the regular wine, but aged longer or differently. It might be from selected vineyards, or from selected lots of wine. Or sometimes reserve wines are merely chosen and bottled from the top 5 to 10 percent of the existing batches.

Regardless, expect to pay more for reserve wines. If both the reserve and the regular bottling have won gold medals, try both and see if the difference in quality warrants the difference in price.

residual sugar After a wine is done fermenting, there is usually at least a small amount of unfermented grape sugar, known as residual sugar. Winemakers put this statistic in their notes, and occasionally on their labels, especially for dessert wines, to let consumers know how sweet the wine is and how and with what foods to enjoy it. It is expressed as a percentage by volume or weight. SEE SWEET.

roasted SEE OAKY.

round A wine described as being round has enough residual sugar to balance out any rough edges such as tannin and acid, and may be rich and ripe, leaving a full sensation in your mouth. The key word here is balance, since round wines have a quality of fullness or completeness, without any one taste or tactile sensation dominating.

sec Applied to sparkling wines, sec, which in French means "dry," actually means sweet or very sweet. You figure it.

soft SEE BODY.

spicy   Certain varietals are often, and appropriately, described as being spicy. Gewürztraminer's VARIETAL CHARACTER evokes such a description, as does Zinfandel often, and sometimes Chardonnay. Spicy generally refers to pungent, attractive aromas and flavors including black pepper, clove, cinnamon, anise, cardamom, and caraway, depending on the wine.

structure   How body, acid, alcohol, glycerin, and tannin interact in a wine make up its structure. A good wine will have "firm" or "good" structure.

supple   This is a complimentary term that's generally used to describe full-bodied reds that have achieved a kind of softness, in spite of high levels of tannin and acidity, and a fairly firm STRUCTURE.

sur lie   SEE LEES.

sweet   As we've mentioned, sweetness is not a fault. Sweet wines are *supposed* to be sweet. The key is to have enough ACID present for BALANCE. According to the *Connoisseur's Guide to California Wine,* the following is a key to RESIDUAL SUGAR levels (expressed in percentage by volume or weight) that you can use to determine the level of sweetness in a wine from its label statistics:
   Less than 0.5% residual sugar = dry
   0.6% to 1.4% residual sugar = slightly sweet
   1.5% to 2.9% residual sugar = medium sweet
   3.0% to 5.9% residual sugar = sweet
   More than 5.9% residual sugar = very sweet

tannin   Tannin, or tannic acid, comes from the stems, seeds, and skins of grapes, as well as the wooden barrels in which the wines are stored and aged. Red wines have about five times more tannin than whites.
   Tannins are detected not by taste but by *feel.* That puckery feeling in your mouth, also known as ASTRINGENCY, is from tannin. Brawny young reds will often have overpowering tannin, which means you should cellar them until the tannins soften and make room for the fruit. If the tasting notes say the wine is fairly tannic, that's winespeak for "don't touch this bottle for a year or two at least." Since tannin is a natural preservative, it is a necessary component of wines that are meant to have a very long life. However, in order to age gracefully, a tannic wine must have adequate acid, sugar, and alcohol to stay in BALANCE.

tart   SEE ACID/ACIDITY.

terroir   SEE MICROCLIMATE.

toasty   "Caramel" and "toffee" are toasty aromas. SEE ALSO OAKY AND YEASTY.

transfer method Like the *MÉTHODE CHAMPENOISE*, the transfer method is a process for making sparkling wines that are fermented *in the bottle,* as opposed to those made by the BULK PROCESS. Where the transfer method and *méthode champenoise* diverge is after the second—or bubble-forming—fermentation. With the former method, the wine is poured out of the bottle after the second fermentation into pressurized tanks, where it is filtered. Once the sediment has been removed, the wine is rebottled. (In the latter method, the wine never leaves the bottle, but the sediment is removed using a complicated process called DISGORGING.) In France, wines made by the transfer method cannot be called champagne. New World winemakers aren't compelled to follow such rules. One advantage to the transfer method, from a winemaker's point of view, is that it is modern, cheaper, and less labor intensive than the *méthode champenoise.*

vanilla/vanillin When you see vanilla or vanillin in tasting notes, think oak. The reason is because aromas of vanilla come from the vanillin that is contributed by oak barrel staves. Just as in food, a whiff of vanilla, however subtle, gives an impression of sweetness.

varietal Varietal is a wine that takes its name from the grape variety of which it's primarily (at least 75 percent) composed.

varietal character Each variety of grape has a distinct set of taste and nose characteristics when picked at the optimum moment of ripeness. Occasionally a winemaker will say that a wine "displays typical varietal *characteristics*," (or *bouquet* or *flavors*), which means, in effect, that you'll need to see Chapter 8 to get an idea of what to look forward to. But once you know, for example, that California Zinfandels are berrylike, the phrase is convenient shorthand that replaces describing all the berry flavors you'll already expect.

vinifera Short for *Vitis vinifera,* this is the species of grape used for the world's finest and most acclaimed wines. Except for the native American species, all the wines in this book are made from vinifera grapes.

vintage Vintage basically means year, so a vintage 1993 bottle would contain wine that was grown and harvested in 1993. The rule is that at least 95 percent of that wine has to have come from 1993-grown grapes.

vintner's reserve SEE RESERVE.

weight SEE BODY.

whole berry fermentation SEE CARBONIC MACERATION.

yeast/yeasty   Commonly used to describe sparkling wines, yeastiness comes from—you guessed it—the yeast that is part of the fermentation process. "Toastiness" and "fresh baked bread" express the same aromas.

young   To say that a wine is "still young" means that it could still use some time in the bottle to reach its full potential. A young wine might be good, but will be better still if given time to mature.

PART III

The Gold Medal Winners

Chapter 10

RED WINES

Cabernet Franc
Cabernet Sauvignon
Italian Varietals
Merlot
Native American Reds
Other Reds
Petite Sirah
Pinot Noir
Red Blends
Syrah/Shiraz
Zinfandel

Cosentino   *1992 Cabernet Franc*
Region: USA—California   Suggested Retail: $16.00
Availability: Limited   Golds: NW

We applaud Cosentino for making a great Cabernet Franc, a variety often used for blending with Cabernet Sauvignon. This wine has blueberries, cranberries, and cracked pepper in the nose. In the mouth it is rich and full bodied with blueberries and cranberries, followed through with notes of black cherries and a long, peppery finish. It is well balanced with excellent structure and supportive tannins.
Special Award: *Best Overall Red Wine (NW)*

Gold Hill Vineyard   *1990 Estate Cabernet Franc*
Region: USA—California   Suggested Retail: $14.00
Availability: Limited   Golds: SD

This one has intense cherry, berry fruit flavors and aromas, and a velvety finish.
Special Award: *Best of Class (SD)*

Guenoc Estate   *1991 Lake County Cabernet Franc*
Region: USA—California   Suggested Retail: $13.50
Availability: Limited   Golds: PR, TG, IE, TN

Deep garnet tones, a silky texture, nuances of nutmeg, clove, and allspice characterize this wine. A long, full finish and elegant structure promise excellent aging potential. Try it with sage and basil pasta; venison; or baked chèvre in olive leaves.

Gundlach-Bundschu   *1992 Rhinefarm Vineyards Cabernet Franc*
Region: USA—California   Suggested Retail: $14.00
Availability: Limited   Golds: DA

Founded in 1858, this winery says the secret of their delicious Cabernet Franc (which, by the way, is normally used as a blending grape) is that all of its fruit is massed up front and the tannins are softer than those of Merlot. This wine can be cellared, but it drinks beautifully right now.

Kendall-Jackson   *1992 Grand Reserve Cabernet Franc*
Region: USA—California   Suggested Retail: $20.00
Availability: NP   Golds: OC

This wine has pure raspberry and peppermint aromas, with rich, sweet fruit and a backdrop of tannin. Incidentally, Cabernet Franc is a wine that not too many California wineries will dare to produce, so extra recognition should go to those who try it—and succeed so well.

Did You Know . . . ?

At one Presidential State Dinner, Cosentino's Cabernet Franc was the most consumed red wine. Unfortunately, we weren't told which president quaffed it down with such enthusiasm. More trivia: Mitch Cosentino also informed us that his wine reportedly goes well with bear. Would he be talking about the Russian Bear at that State Dinner?

Latcham Vineyards *1993 Sierra Foothills Cabernet Franc*
Region: USA—California   Suggested Retail: $15.00
Availability: Limited   Golds: CA, EL, ML
This wine has excellent, deep color with classic spicy blueberry aromas and tremendous blueberry and black cherry fruit flavors, as well as good oak. A very full bodied, deeply flavorful wine with a rich, spicy nose and a powerful finish.
Special Awards: Best Cabernet Franc of California (CA); Best Cabernet Franc of Appellation (CA)

Madrona Vineyards *1992 Estate Bottled Cabernet Franc*
Region: USA—California   Suggested Retail: $11.00
Availability: Limited   Golds: OC, SD
Of deep, dark color with tinges of violet around the edges, this wine displays intense cherry and raspberry fruit along with floral notes and the slightest hint of toasty oak. It has soft tannins and a crisp, fruity finish.

Mount Konocti *1993 Lake County Cabernet Franc*
Region: USA—California   Suggested Retail: $10.00
Availability: Good   Golds: CA, CL
Fresh, ripe berries and a touch of black pepper spice with toasty vanilla complexities make up this wine's aroma and flavors. You'll be rewarded if you cellar this one, as it will age elegantly through 1999 and beyond.
Special Award: Best Cabernet Franc of Appellation (CA)

Nevada City Winery *1993 Cabernet Franc*
Region: USA—California   Suggested Retail: $20.00
Availability: Limited   Golds: OC
You'll find a rich, purple color; aromas of plums and cherries, floral scents of lilacs and violets, with a hint of spice; French oak; and depth, complexity, and charm. It's fruity, soft, and "absolutely delicious." Engaging now, this wine will benefit from 1 to 2 years cellaring. The original case production of this wine was low, but the winery released a small number of cases in the spring of 1996 with artist labels. The new labels feature an iris by nationally recognized watercolorist Nancy Kaestner.

Did You Know . . . ?

Long overshadowed by Cabernet Sauvignon, Cabernet Franc is gaining ground in the New World as an exciting alternative to its better-known cousin. In 1992, one-third of California's plantings of Cabernet Franc were still too young to bear fruit. The same was true of Australia's Cabernet Franc vines. The end of this decade should be promising for red-wine lovers looking for a delicious change of pace.

Bandiera Winery   *1993 Napa Valley Cabernet Sauvignon*

Region: USA—California   **Suggested Retail: $8.00**
Availability: Very Good   **Golds: OC, NW**

Even as a youthful wine, this Cabernet displays very concentrated cassis, cherries, and plum notes in the nose. The tannins are well integrated with the fruit, and in the background is an accent of vanilla from the French oak. Some Cabernet Franc lends complex aromatic qualities. By the way, only 4 golds were awarded at Orange County in this category out of 95 entries.

Barefoot Cellars   *NV "Barefoot Cab" Cabernet Sauvignon*

Region: USA—California   **Suggested Retail: $4.99**
Availability: Very Good   **Golds: OC**

Barefoot Cab has a blackberry and cherry bouquet enhanced by the complexity of oak. Its smooth, spicy finish appeals to new and experienced wine lovers alike. It is perfect with red sauce pasta, hearty soups, and sharp cheeses, stands up to spicy foods, and is an ideal complement to all red meat. Only 4 golds were awarded out of a field of 95 at Orange County. By the way, we love this wine and buy it all the time for large gatherings; it's as friendly in a crowd as it is to our pocketbooks.

Bel Arbors   *1992 California Cabernet Sauvignon*

Region: USA—California   **Suggested Retail: $6.99**
Availability: NP   **Golds: NW**

This is a medium-bodied Cabernet with a soft, pleasing mouth feel. Its stylish cherry fruit character is complemented by toasty oak-spice from barrel aging. Classic Cab cassis and black cherry fruit fill the flavors, which linger in a full finish with complexities of coffee and vanilla.

Canyon Road   *1993 Cabernet Sauvignon*

Region: USA—California   **Suggested Retail: $6.00**
Availability: Very Good   **Golds: OC**

Out of 95 entries in its field, only 4 Cabernets were awarded golds at Orange County. This one is a blend of Cabernet Sauvignon (80%) and Ruby Cabernet (20%). It was matured in a combination of small French and American barriques and redwood tanks. You'd be hard-pressed to find a better price!

Corbett Canyon Vineyards   *1992 Reserve Cabernet Sauvignon*

Region: USA—California   **Suggested Retail: $9.00**
Availability: Good   **Golds: SD, NW, AT, TG, MO**

A complex wine that conjures up scents and aromas of cedar, vanilla, leather, white pepper, and fresh boysenberries.

Did You Know . . . ?

Winemaker Davis Bynum of Barefoot Cellars nicknamed his wine the "Château La Feet" of California. The nickname stuck, but Château Lafite Rothschild of France was so upset that Bynum had to change it!

Errazuriz Panquehue　*1993 Don Maximiano Cab. Sauvignon Reserve*
Region: Chile　　　　　　　　Suggested Retail: $8.40
Availability: NP　　　　　　　Golds: CI
Luscious and delicious, oozing with fruit flavors, and nicely accented by nutmeg and vanilla notes, this Cab has a well-polished texture that nicely blends the oak, black cherry, and currant flavors, and a distinctive mintiness that carries through to the finish. Best of all, it is available in the United States.

Fetzer　*1992 Valley Oaks Cabernet Sauvignon*
Region: USA—California　　　Suggested Retail: $7.99
Availability: NP　　　　　　　Golds: CA
An engaging wine with forward cherry and oak-spice aromas. Mellow tannins provide a mouth feel with classic Cabernet fruit and a long finish with lingering flavors of vanilla and coffee.
Special Award: *Best Cabernet Sauvignon of Appellation (CA)*

Forestville Vineyards　*1992 California Cabernet Sauvignon*
Region: USA—California　　　Suggested Retail: $6.00
Availability: NP　　　　　　　Golds: FF
Look for superb balance and tasty flavors of black cherry fruit, with smooth tannins, all nicely framed by oak.

McGuigan Brothers　*1993 Bin 4000 Cabernet Batch 2*
Region: Australia　　　　　　Suggested Retail: $8.99
Availability: Good　　　　　　Golds: IW
This and many other McGuigan Brothers wines can be found in the United States, and they represent wonderful values as well as high quality. The wine is deep red with purple hues, and has a bouquet that emits lifted fruit and light oak aromas. On the palate the wine demonstrates medium to heavy weight, with good integration and flavor. The finish is quite astringent but is balanced with soft fruit and fresh acid.

Napa Ridge Winery　*1992 Central Coast Cabernet Sauvignon*
Region: USA—California　　　Suggested Retail: $8.00
Availability: Very Good　　　Golds: FF, MO
The winemaker selected grapes from vineyards in California's coastal regions. With their sandy, rocky soils, these regions provide excellent drainage and encourage extensive root development by forcing the vines to work hard for nourishment. This Cab has full flavor extract and gorgeous color.

Did You Know . . . ?

The Spanish Conquistadors were responsible for introducing *Vitis vinifera* vines (those that produce the world's finest wines) to Chile in the mid-sixteenth century. By the eighteenth century, Chile was well known for its copious quantities of inexpensive wines, much to the dismay of the Spanish wine producers.

Ste. Genevieve *NV Texas Cabernet Sauvignon*
Region: USA—Texas   Suggested Retail: $4.99
Availability: NP   Golds: SD, TG
This wine is softened with a hint of Merlot and Cabernet Franc for a rich, smooth quality with an essence of fresh peppers, cherries, and raspberries. It will bring out the best in fresh venison or juicy beef.

Stone Creek *1990 Chairman's Reserve Cabernet Sauvignon*
Region: USA—California   Suggested Retail: $9.85
Availability: Limited   Golds: DA
This wine is a claret style with spicy aromas, complexity, Napa Valley components, and a rich, lingering finish.

Vina Domaine Oriental *1993 Cabernet Sauvignon*
Region: Chile   Suggested Retail: $5.99
Availability: NP   Golds: IV
Look for a deep, beautiful, and young red-violet color with intense aromas of raspberry, cherry, and fine leather, with touches of vanilla, butter, and toasted almond. The wine has an intense palate, with good structure and balance. If you have trouble finding this one, call Brennan's of Wisconsin at (414) 785-6606. Right now they're the only wine shop that carries this prizewinner, but some East Coast stores may have it by the time this book is in print. It's a steal for the price.

Weinstock Cellars *1993 Alexander Valley Cabernet Sauvignon*
Region: USA—California   Suggested Retail: $8.99
Availability: Good   Golds: RE
The complex mixture of berry and pepper notes is balanced with full-bodied fruit and oak notes that round out the flavor. This distinctive wine will age very well for 4 to 6 years and should gain added interest and complexity as it ages.

Wente Bros. *1992 Livermore Valley Cabernet Sauvignon*
Region: USA—California   Suggested Retail: $8.00
Availability: Limited   Golds: DA
This wine has solid berry and herb flavors and picks up interesting notes of spice on the finish.

Did You Know . . . ?

The growth of the Texan wine industry has been amazing, from 50,000 gallons bottled in 1982 to more than a million gallons in 1991. Texas wineries have a total economic impact of $106.9 million and provide jobs for nearly 3,000 Texans each year.

Beringer Vineyards *1992 Knights Valley Cabernet Sauvignon*
Region: USA—California   Suggested Retail: $16.00
Availability: NP   Golds: CA
Here's a terrific bargain. This wine, with its deep ruby/purple color, offers delicious ripe cassis fruit along with aromas of jammy cherries, herbs, and spices. It is concentrated yet supple, and can be drunk over the next 7 to 10 years.

Brutocao Cellars *1990 Estate Cabernet Sauvignon*
Region: USA—California   Suggested Retail: $13.50
Availability: Limited   Golds: LA, CL
Rich cherry, berry, black pepper, and vanilla flavors abound. This winery, in beautiful Mendocino County, prides itself on its hands-on winemaking processes and has something else that's offbeat—a female winemaker. If you have difficulty finding this or other Brutocao wines, call (800) 433-3689 and the winery says "we'll do our best to get our wines to your neighborhood."

Buena Vista Carneros *1991 Estate Bottled Cabernet Sauvignon*
Region: USA—California   Suggested Retail: $12.00
Availability: Good   Golds: IW, PR
Here's a luscious Cab of deep, intense red color, with aromas of black cherries, cassis, and light oak. Flavors of ripe berries, jam, and black pepper will greet your palate, and nicely balanced oak rounds things out. It has a full-bodied structure with a round, mouth-filling finish.

Chapel Hill Winery *1993 Cabernet Sauvignon*
Region: Australia   Suggested Retail: $14.25
Availability: Very Good   Golds: IV
The winery did not provide a lot of information about this wine, and we only wish we had the time to seek out every gold medal wine to personally taste. But know that Chapel Hill, which exports to the United States, has been consistently winning golds for their Cabs, so we suggest you try it.

Chapel Hill Winery *1992 Cabernet Sauvignon*
Region: Australia   Suggested Retail: $14.00
Availability: Good   Golds: IW
This wine also won five trophies and seven golds in 1994. Like the 1993, it's available in the United States. Look for elegant varietal fruit with soft tannin and deep crimson color. The lifted, complex nose shows herbaceous green bean, cassis, and violets, with an overlay of oak. The palate is elegant and medium bodied, with French oak enhancing the flavor intensity and imparting subtle astringency, American oak adding vanilla spiciness—both balanced to allow fruit expression.

Did You Know ... ?
By the year 2000, Brutocao Cellars will be producing all of their wines organically.

Château Souverain *1991 Winemaker's Reserve Cabernet Sauvignon*
Region: USA—California   **Suggested Retail: $16.00**
Availability: NP   **Golds: RE, LA**

This is a rich, extracted Cabernet Sauvignon with a classic nose of chocolate, boysenberry, and cedar. The deep purple color hints of the complex flavor concentration, which echoes the wine's classic aromas. Intensely fruited, this wine finishes with ripe tannins and a soft, balanced acidity. Although enjoyable now, it will improve even more with 5 to 10 years of cellaring.
Special Award: *Finalist for Sweepstakes Award, Red Wine (RE)*

Château Souverain *1992 Alexander Valley Cabernet Sauvignon*
Region: USA—California   **Suggested Retail: $12.00**
Availability: NP   **Golds: CA, IV, NW**

Rich, dark ruby color precedes a classic nose of black currant fruit, cloves, vanilla, and a hint of smoky oak. The concentrated Cab flavors have good continuity with the aromas, and are carried in a mouth-filling, extracted frame that will keep gaining complexity with proper cellaring.
Special Awards: *Trophy for Best New World Cabernet Sauvignon (NW); Best of Price Class (NW)*

Creston Vineyard *1991 Paso Robles Cabernet Sauvignon*
Region: USA—California   **Suggested Retail: $10.00**
Availability: Good   **Golds: RE, CA, LJ, TG**

Paso Robles, known for its wild temperature swings (daytime temperatures can reach 100 degrees F, while at night it can plunge to 50 degrees F), is ideal Cabernet country, according to some. This Cabernet struck the right notes for the judges in 1995. Creston's Cabernets have won 100 medals in 10 vintages. The 1991 exhibits the color, depth of flavors, tannin, and structure that will benefit from further bottle aging. And look at that price!

De Loach *1993 Sonoma Cuvée Cabernet Sauvignon*
Region: USA—California   **Suggested Retail: $10.00**
Availability: Good   **Golds: LA**

De Loach's Cabs seem to pick up the gold wherever they're entered, and this one has an unbeatable price. It is a medium-bodied, well-balanced wine full of black cherry and rich cassis flavors.

Did You Know . . . ?
Prohibition wrecked the American wine industry for many years. In 1919 the production of wine was 55 million gallons. By 1925 it had dwindled to just 3.4 million gallons (wineries were still permitted to produce wine if used for religious, medicinal, or flavoring purposes). Most wineries went out of business, and in spite of their protests, none were compensated.

De Loach   *1992 Estate Bottled Cabernet Sauvignon*
Region: USA—California   Suggested Retail: $14.99
Availability: Good   Golds: CA, SF
Here's a well-balanced wine that has a smooth texture, medium body, and a deep, rich garnet color. It has an intensely varietal nose with pleasant cedar tones. Flavors of black cherry and rich cassis mingle through the lingering finish. The winemaker recommends trying this wine with rich cheeses or a dark chocolate dessert for a delicious finale to a fine meal.
Special Award: *Double Gold (SF)*

Douglas Hill Winery   *1992 Cabernet Sauvignon*
Region: USA—California   Suggested Retail: $15.00
Availability: NP   Golds: OC
Richly flavored with complex tiers of currant, cherry, and spice that turn supple and generous, this wine has excellent fruit/tannin balance. In its category at Orange County, incidentally, only 7 golds were awarded out of 121 in the field.

Filsinger Vineyards   *1991 Temecula Cabernet Sauvignon*
Region: USA—California   Suggested Retail: $11.99
Availability: Limited   Golds: PR
You can buy this wine directly from the winery by calling (909) 676-4594. It has medium body, with blackberry, cassis, and spicy overtones, light acids, and good balance.

Geyser Peak Winery   *1993 Alexander Valley Cabernet Sauvignon*
Region: USA—California   Suggested Retail: $12.00
Availability: NP   Golds: LA
The nose displays typical berry Cabernet fruit characters enhanced by sweet vanillin oak. The wine has a soft, round palate with good depth and lingering flavor.
Special Award: *Best of Class (LA)*

Grant Burge   *1993 Cabernet Sauvignon*
Region: Australia   Suggested Retail: $15.95
Availability: Good   Golds: BR, PE, SW
An excellent purple color, this wine has a bouquet typical of the varietal. On the palate the wine is full of flavor and is beautifully complexed with new French oak, good structure, but soft tannins. It is available in the United States and Europe.

Did You Know . . . ?

Australian and New Zealand restaurants have a liberal view of wine drinking. BYO, or Bring Your Own, restaurants are common in those two countries, where the owners have a special license permitting diners to tote their own favorite bottle to dinner. Even many that have regular wine-serving licenses often allow their patrons to bring favorite wines and have them uncorked for a modest fee.

Gundlach-Bundschu *1992 Rhinefarm Vineyard Cabernet Sauvignon*

Region: USA—California   **Suggested Retail: $15.00**
Availability: Good   **Golds: NW**

There are close to 50 Cabernet Sauvignons that come out of Sonoma Valley. What makes this one so special? According to the winemaker, it's because the fruit comes from the oldest continually harvested vineyards in the state (1995 marked their 137th consecutive harvest). The wine is rich and smooth, with balanced fruit and a lingering finish. It drinks marvelously now, but will age well in your cellar.

Hanna Winery *1992 Alexander Valley Cabernet Sauvignon*

Region: USA—California   **Suggested Retail: $16.00**
Availability: NP   **Golds: RE**

Curranty, with cassislike fruit and a round, almost velvety palate, this Cab is long and consistent, and will improve with age. If you want to order this and other Hanna wines directly (discounted from the retail price), call (800) 854-3987.

Herzog Wine Cellars *1993 Special Reserve Cabernet Sauvignon*

Region: USA—California   **Suggested Retail: $11.00**
Availability: Limited   **Golds: CA, LJ**

This wine has the complex characters of berry and cherry aligned with light notes of green pepper. It is full bodied and rich in the mouth, but very soft and pleasant to drink. It should age gracefully for 5 to 7 years.
Special Awards: *Tie for Best Cabernet Sauvignon of California (CA); Tie for Best Cabernet Sauvignon of Appellation (CA)*

Hop Kiln Winery *1991 Russian River Valley Cabernet Sauvignon*

Region: USA—California   **Suggested Retail: $14.00**
Availability: Limited   **Golds: RE**

Firm and intense, with racy black cherry and cider flavors, this Cab has aromas of dense fruit, dried flowers, and spice with a subtle added dimension of olives. Cellar it until 1997 for the smoothest quaffing.

Indian Springs Vineyards *1993 Cabernet Sauvignon*

Region: USA—California   **Suggested Retail: $10.00**
Availability: Limited   **Golds: RE, CA, LA**

This is a large, structured wine with intense, forward fruit flavors. Hints of chocolate and black cherries are complemented by extended barrel aging. Rich and complex, yet soft enough to enjoy now, this wine will reward cellaring into the next century. Look at that price!
Special Award: *Tie for Best Cabernet Sauvignon of Appellation (CA)*

Did You Know . . . ?

Thomas Jefferson wrote: "No nation is drunken where wine is cheap and none sober where the dearness of wine substitutes ardent spirits as the common beverage."

Joullian Vineyards *1990 Carmel Valley Cabernet Sauvignon*
Region: USA—California   **Suggested Retail: $14.00**
Availability: Limited   **Golds: RE**

This wine has a dark, garnet color with a spicy, blackberry, chocolate aroma. It finishes with a touch of vanilla mint.

Kendall-Jackson *1992 Vintner's Reserve Cabernet Sauvignon*
Region: USA—California   **Suggested Retail: $14.99**
Availability: NP   **Golds: PR**

Here's a Cab that is broad, rich, and full bodied with flavors of blackberry and cassis backed with notes of cedar, tobacco, and toast. This wine drinks well now, but will continue to gain complexity with time in the cellar. A great deal for the price.

Lambert Bridge *1993 Sonoma County Cabernet Sauvignon*
Region: USA—California   **Suggested Retail: $15.00**
Availability: Good   **Golds: OC**

The nose is filled with loads of cassis, berry, and spice, which combine with subtle nuances of toasty, smoky oak, roasted coffee, and cedar. These bright berry flavors carry forward in the mouth and are joined with hints of sweet vanilla oak. This is a rich wine, where each layer reveals more depth and complexity. It's luscious now, but will cellar well. Cabernet Franc (8%) and Merlot (2%) were added to the blend to provide additional structure and backbone and to enhance the fruit flavors.

Lava Cap *1991 Estate Bottled El Dorado Cabernet Sauvignon*
Region: USA—California   **Suggested Retail: $15.00**
Availability: Limited   **Golds: SD**

Berry flavors with full, round, soft tannins characterize this wine.

Leasingham Wines *1993 Classic Clare Cabernet Sauvignon*
Region: Australia   **Suggested Retail: $14.99**
Availability: Good   **Golds: RM, AD, GR, BR**

Brick red colored, here's a wine with an aroma that exhibits herbaceous characters with rich berry and black currant fruit and toasty oak components. On the palate it is rich and full, showing soft, complex berry fruit and cassis, with persistent lingering tannins. You'll be able to find it in the United States.

Did You Know ... ?

In ancient Greece, wine was stored and transported in amphorae, large ceramic vessels with two handles, a narrow mouth that could be stoppered with a cork or narrow piece of clay and then mortared shut, and a bottom that tapered to a point. (Very few Greek amphorae were constructed with flat bottoms.) With the development and use of aqualungs after World War II, the exciting discovery of many ancient cargo ships containing amphorae shed much light on ancient wine trading.

~~singham Wines~~ *1994 Classic Clare Cabernet Sauvignon*
~~on:~~ **Australia**   **Suggested Retail: $14.99**
~~lability:~~ **Good**   **Golds: RU**

~~~s~~ Cab, like the prizewinning 1993, is available in the United States. It is deep ~~~ick~~-red with purple hues and has rich aromas of blackberry and black currant ~~~ruit~~, with hints of charry oak. The palate shows rich, intense flavors of black currant and cassis. It has sweet fruit concentration and generosity on the palate.

J. Lohr *1992 Seven Oaks Cabernet Sauvignon*
Region: USA—California   **Suggested Retail: $12.00**
Availability: Very Good   **Golds: SF, PR**

This wine has a deep garnet color with bright, crisp hues. The aromas are of plum and blueberry with a hint of raspberry. The bouquet is full of chocolate and toasted oak. On the palate you'll find flavors of plums and chocolate. A rich and full-flavored wine, it has a soft, round texture and a long, lingering finish.

Madrona Vineyards *1991 Estate Bottled Cabernet Sauvignon*
Region: USA—California   **Suggested Retail: $11.00**
Availability: Limited   **Golds: CA**

Berry fruit, subtle herbaceous notes, and hints of cedar and earthiness come forth in the aroma. Supple yet solid tannins allow early drinkability (but with cellaring potential of 10-plus years). This wine has a smooth and lingering finish and an aftertaste reminiscent of cherries.
Special Award: *Best Cabernet Sauvignon of Appellation (CA)*

Magnotta Winery *1991 Cabernet Sauvignon Limited Edition*
Region: Canada   **Suggested Retail: $10.75**
Availability: NP   **Golds: IW, TG**

This wine is dense purple in color with black currant and berry aromas along with mouth-filling flavors of oak, spice, plum, berries, and a hint of chocolate. Although full bodied and balanced, it maintains richness and softness on the palate.

Magnotta Winery *1990 Cabernet Sauvignon Limited Edition*
Region: Canada   **Suggested Retail: $10.75**
Availability: Limited   **Golds: IV**

Like the 1991, this purple-colored wine features black currants and berries on the nose, and oaky, spicy, plummy, berry flavors, with just a hint of chocolate. It is soft and rich on the palate, but full bodied and mouth filling.
Special Award: *Black Diamond Award (IV)*

Did You Know . . . ?
In 1916, Prohibition began in Canada, but with the help of some wheeling and dealing on the part of the savvy grape growers, wine was exempted from the general interdiction against alcohol.

Mario Perelli-Minetti Winery *1991 Cabernet Sauvignon*
Region: USA—California   Suggested Retail: $14.50
Availability: Limited   Golds: LA
This winery, with a history of winemaking in both Italy and America, has been making wine in California for about 100 years. The wine is produced in a full robust style with an accent on fruity flavor. Using judicious grape selection and cellaring techniques, it is made smooth enough to be drunk now, but will improve with age.

Matua Valley Wines *1993 Waimauku Cabernet Sauvignon*
Region: New Zealand   Suggested Retail: $13.00 CAN
Availability: Outside USA   Golds: NZ
1993 was a superb year for the Auckland region. This wine has a deep, impenetrable color with youthful purple-red tints. The aroma is ripe Cabernet overlayed with oak to give a cigarboxlike character; the palate is full bodied with clean fine tannins and good fruit weight and length. Cellar this one up to the year 2000. Matua's wines are available in Canada, Japan, Europe, the UK, and Australia.

Meeker Vineyard *1991 Gold Leaf Cuvée Cabernet Sauvignon*
Region: USA—California   Suggested Retail: $14.00
Availability: Limited   Golds: OC
The intense fruit concentration of this wine comes from a very low yielding vineyard. The wine was aged in American oak and has moderate tannins, deep fruit, a big plummy and leather component, and wonderful aromatic scents.

Messina Hof Wine Cellars *1992 Private Reserve Cabernet Sauvignon*
Region: USA—Texas   Suggested Retail: $14.99
Availability: Limited   Golds: LA, TX
A wonderful, rich, full-bodied wine with great wood and berry flavors. It has a deep, dark color and a long, lingering finish.

Napa Ridge Winery *1991 Reserve Cabernet Sauvignon*
Region: USA—California   Suggested Retail: $13.00
Availability: Limited   Golds: SD, AT
This wine has excellent structure, depth, richness, and intense fruit concentration.

Navarro *1990 Mendocino Cabernet Sauvignon*
Region: USA—California   Suggested Retail: $17.00
Availability: Limited   Golds: PR, OC
Even with 18 months of aging in French oak barrels, this wine was still loaded with cherry and thick with flavors of smoke, tar, briar, and olive.

Did You Know . . . ?

Messina Hof wines are showing up in unusual places. Theirs is the only Texas wine served in the skyboxes of Texas Stadium, home of the Dallas Cowboys. And look for them in the "home" of Shirley MacLaine on the set of the sequel to the movie *Terms of Endearment*.

Perry Creek Vineyards   *1992 El Dorado Cabernet Sauvignon*
Region: USA—California   **Suggested Retail: $10.00**
Availability: Limited   **Golds: PR**

Ripe, almost jammy, raspberry and plum fruit with a touch of dark chocolate. Very generous and soft in texture, this vintage is enjoyable now but has enough backbone to take it through the next 3 to 4 years.

A. Rafanelli Winery   *1992 Cabernet Sauvignon Unfiltered*
Region: USA—California   **Suggested Retail: $16.00**
Availability: NP   **Golds: RE, PR, NW, OC**

This wine was only one of three gold medalists in its field of 92 entries at Orange County. We didn't get information on this wine from the winery, but the four golds should say everything. Also, the Rafanelli wines we've tried have been outstanding, so we don't think you'll go wrong with this one. For a wine of this magnitude, says Robert Parker, the price is a bargain.
Special Award: *Best of Class (PR)*

Renaissance Vineyard and Winery   *1991 Cabernet Sauvignon*
Region: USA—California   **Suggested Retail: $13.00**
Availability: Good   **Golds: CI**

This wine shows a medium to deep garnet color. Its classy nose with ripe blackberry and cherry fruit has subtle hints of almonds, flowers, and gentle oak. On the palate it is medium bodied and silky, with an unusually elegant structure and ripe, vibrant, berrylike fruit. Delicious now in its youthful fruitiness, the wine shows outstanding promise for a long evolution in the bottle. The critics raved on and on about this Cab, and all were astounded at its price.

Richard L. Graeser Winery   *1991 Estate Bottled Cabernet Sauvignon*
Region: USA—California   **Suggested Retail: $13.50**
Availability: Limited   **Golds: SD**

Look for full body with a hint of oak, cherry, and blackberry aromas and a long finish.

Sebastiani Vineyards   *1992 Sonoma County Cabernet Sauvignon*
Region: USA—California   **Suggested Retail: $11.00**
Availability: Very Good   **Golds: SD**

Dark garnet in color, this wine has dusty currant and vanilla/oak aromas complexed by herbal earthiness. Full bodied, it has dense flavors of olive-toned fruit and a smooth oak finish with considerable soft tannins. The wine will soften and develop with another 2 to 5 years aging, and will hold for another 3 to 5 years. Hearty meat and mushroom dishes will sing alongside this Cab.
Special Award: *Best of Class (SD)*

Did You Know . . . ?

At 2,300 feet elevation, with clear views of the snow-covered Sierra Nevada Mountains, Renaissance is the largest mountain vineyard estate in North America, and also one of the most beautiful.

Sierra Vista Winery *1992 Estate Bottled Cabernet Sauvignon*
Region: USA—California   **Suggested Retail: $14.00**
Availability: Limited   **Golds: LA, EL**

The winemaker says one reason this Cab is so exceptional is that it is grown on its own roots (as opposed to wines that are grown on grafted rootstock). This is an elegant, supple wine with great depth. Its black cherry fruit character is the result of leaf pulling and hedging to open the vines. A cedary character is evidence of a Cabernet Sauvignon grown on it own roots. And 18 months in small oak barrels adds complexity to the Cab fruit. Try it with chicken in morel sauce or sauces flavored with blue or soft-ripening cheeses.

St. Supery Vineyards *1991 Dollarhide Ranch Cabernet Sauvignon*
Region: USA—California   **Suggested Retail: $14.00**
Availability: Good   **Golds: CA, NW**

Tantalizingly rich aromas of fresh, ripe black cherries, delicate oak, and vanilla introduce the plum and cherry flavors. Soft, firm tannins add an alluring complexity, and balance the deliciously forward fruit. Ready now, this wine will continue to develop in the bottle for many years.

Stonier's Winery *1993 Cabernet Sauvignon*
Region: Australia   **Suggested Retail: $11.00**
Availability: Good   **Golds: SY, BL, ST**

Here are some of the comments from the judges at Sydney, who loved this wine enough to name it one of the top 100: "Interesting, sweet, rather sagelike"; "very fine, elegant soft fruit nose with hints of eucalyptus"; "well balanced, with a long finish and good aftertaste." With a bit of age, commented one, "this wine will end up being perfectly delicious." This wine is available in the United States, and you can call Australian Great Estates at (301) 587-8344 if you have trouble finding it.

Trapiche *1993 Medalla Tinto*
Region: Argentina   **Suggested Retail: $17.99**
Availability: Very Good   **Golds: AR**

Intense and robust, with red-purple hues, this Cab has a slightly smoky aroma of toasted honey and blackberries, and a persistent wide taste with ample body. Touches of black pepper at the finish promise great longevity. By the way, Argentinean wines represent some of the best value-for-quality New World wines. You'll find this and other Trapiche wines in the United States, Canada, and Europe.

Did You Know . . . ?

Argentina is number five in world wine production. So why aren't there more Argentinean wines on North American tables? First, *Argentineans have been drinking most of their wine!* And second, until recently, foreign investors were scared off by the unsettled political situation there. However, the former statistic is going down, and the latter is soaring upwards with a new infusion of foreign interest.

W.B. Bridgman   *1992 Cabernet Sauvignon*
Region: USA—Washington   **Suggested Retail: $10.99**
Availability: Limited   **Golds: TC, GH**

This wine has an inviting nose of cedar, cassis, blackberry, and damson plum with a pretty garnet color. On the palate it delivers mouth-filling flavors, moving smoothly through fruit, oak, and tannin. Try it with rosemary and garlic lamb, as well as tomato-sauced dishes.

Wente Bros.   *1991 Charles Wetmore Estate Reserve Cab. Sauvignon*
Region: USA—California   **Suggested Retail: $17.95**
Availability: Limited   **Golds: PR**

In the 1880s Charles Wetmore first imported this clone of Cabernet Sauvignon from the commune of Margaux. This wine has a silky texture and wonderful aromas with layers of currant, black cherry, tobacco, and spice flavors. Subtle vanilla and toasty oak flavors add to the structure and deliver a soft, rich taste experience that balances a lively finish with medium tannin. The winery will be releasing a limited number of cases of this wine in November 1996 as a "Library Wine Release," at which time the price will also go up.

Wild Horse Winery   *1992 San Luis Obispo Cabernet Sauvignon*
Region: USA—California   **Suggested Retail: $13.00**
Availability: Limited   **Golds: DA**

This wine has bright flavors and aromas of blueberry, currant, mocha, and mint. Enjoy it with rich cuts of beef and lamb, blue-veined cheeses, herbed pastas, and braised vegetables.

Windsor Vineyards   *1992 Cabernet Sauvignon*
Region: USA—California   **Suggested Retail: $10.17**
Availability: Good   **Golds: OC, TG**

Look for a toasty oak aroma and straightforward cherry-berry flavor.

Yalumba   *1992 "The Menzies"*
Region: Australia   **Suggested Retail: $14.00**
Availability: Good   **Golds: RM**

Named after "the consummate politician and red wine aesthete," Sir Robert Gordon Menzies, this wine is a youthful red plum color. The very scented nose comprises plums, red berries, and mocha oak. Medium bodied on the palate, it has great sweetness coming from ripe fruit and also 23 months oak maturation. Cellar this one for 5 to 8 years. This wine is available in the United States.

Did You Know . . . ?

If you've kept up on all the great health news about phenolics and flavonoids found mostly in the skin of red-wine grapes (see Chapter 7 to read more about these amazing substances), then you should be drinking Cabernet Sauvignon, since it has a high skin-to-pulp ratio.

Altamura Winery   *1990 Napa Valley Cabernet Sauvignon*
Region: USA—California   **Suggested Retail: $25.00**
Availability: NP   **Golds: SF**
Well rounded, beautifully balanced, with medium acid and medium tannins, this wine has lush fruit and sweet oak on the finish. It's drinkable now, but will improve over the next 10 to 12 years.

Apex   *1992 Yakima Valley Cabernet Sauvignon*
Region: USA—Washington   **Suggested Retail: $22.00**
Availability: Limited   **Golds: TC, BT**
This wine has a beautiful ruby hue. The aroma is seductive with complex nuances of cassis, tobacco, cedar, eucalyptus, and spice. Expansive fruit flavors unfold on the palate with velvety tannins before a lengthy finish. Rack of lamb, stuffed flank steak, and barbecued meats make three outstanding combinations with this Cab.

Beaulieu   *1990 Georges de Latour Private Reserve Cab. Sauvignon*
Region: USA—California   **Suggested Retail: $40.00**
Availability: NP   **Golds: IV**
A beautiful dark ruby color, this Cab has aromas of black currants, cherries, and toasty oak, especially complex and intense in this vintage. With similar flavors and tremendous depth and richness, this wine will age beautifully for decades and will be one of the great vintages of Georges de Latour.

Beringer Vineyards   *1991 Cabernet Sauvignon Private Reserve*
Region: USA—California   **Suggested Retail: $45.00**
Availability: NP   **Golds: SF, PR**
According to Robert Parker, Beringer's Cabernet Sauvignons and Merlots have gone from strength to strength. This is a big wine for that very special occasion.

BRL Hardy Wine Company   *1991 Thomas Hardy Cabernet Sauvignon*
Region: Australia   **Suggested Retail: $24.00**
Availability: Limited   **Golds: SF, RM, GR**
Here are excerpts from several Sydney International judges (who gave the wine a gold last year): "intense, sweetly ripe"; "strong cedar and cassis"; "vanillalike oak on the palate"; "elegant with some power"; " really blackberry"; "quietly classy." Best of all, it is available in the United States.
***Special Award:** Double Gold (SF)*

Did You Know . . . ?
Vineyards that have been consistently nurtured and protected from stresses, pests, and diseases, and from a lack or an excess of water and mineral nutrients, can live and thrive for a very long time. Perhaps the most famous vine is at Hampton Court Palace near London. Planted in 1769, it's *still* yielding a lot of grapes every year, although it has to be kept under glass.

BRL Hardy Wine Company   *1992 Thomas Hardy Cabernet Sauvignon*
Region: Australia   **Suggested Retail: $25.00**
Availability: Limited   **Golds: IV, RU, PE**

Deep brick red in color, this stunning wine exhibits black currant aromas, with hints of tobacco and vanilla. The palate is well balanced and displays plum, black currant, and capsicum with soft vanilla oak overtones. You can find this one in the United States.

Buena Vista Carneros   *1990 Grand Reserve Cabernet Sauvignon*
Region: USA—California   **Suggested Retail: $24.00**
Availability: Limited   **Golds: SM, FF**

This wine is round, smooth, and exceptionally well balanced. Forward aromas of ripe berries, currants, and delicate herbs are complemented by hints of black pepper and chocolate. The wine's classic Cabernet flavors are of berry and cassis, leading to a rich, supple, mouth-filling finish.

C. A. Henschke   *1993 Cabernet Sauvignon*
Region: Australia   **Suggested Retail: $40.00**
Availability: Good   **Golds: RM, SY, AU, HO, PE, QU**

It would be difficult to heap enough praise onto this Cab, and you can see by the number of golds it has won in 1995 and 1996 that the judges agree. This is a serious wine to cellar and to save for a very special occasion 5 or more years down the road. P.S. It is available in the United States.

Canepa Winery   *1993 Canepa Magnificum Cabernet Sauvignon*
Region: Chile   **Suggested Retail: $25.00**
Availability: Limited   **Golds: CI**

The totally unirrigated vines from which this Curico Valley wine was produced result in very low yields, thus producing juice with high fruit extract and concentrated flavors. This rich and interesting wine is characterized by its complex yet discreet nose, with scents of ripe fruit, black currants, and prunes, and hints of vanilla, chocolate, and spices. The initial taste is superb. The wine offers a strong personality of considerable complexity, with all the power from the still-young tannins, a marked presence of the wood, and mellowness that gives it length on the palate and a pleasant lingering aftertaste. Released in June 1996 in the United States, you'll be able to find this beauty in some U.S. states. It was the only Chilean wine to receive the Grand Prize at Challenge International du Vin.
Special Award: *Grand Prix d'Honneur (CI)*

Did You Know . . . ?

Australia's C.A. Henschke is under the control of the *fifth* generation of the family, which has been producing top-quality wines since the mid-1860s. In Australia, it's more common to find wineries that have been operating for over a century than it is in the United States.

Carmen Vineyards   *1993 Gold Reserve Cabernet Sauvignon*
Region: Chile   **Suggested Retail: $25.00**
Availability: Good   **Golds: LJ**
Chile is now producing some of the finest Cabernet Sauvignons in the world. The 1990 vintage also won a gold in 1995 (at Selections Mondiales), so this winery is obviously doing something very right. This wine has a deep ruby color with intense, complex aromas of red fruit (strawberries, berries, cassis), and some tobacco and coffee nuances. On the palate it is full bodied with ripe tannins, has beautiful structure, complex flavors, a huge mouth feel, and a long finish. It is available in the United States.

Château Julien   *1991 Cabernet Sauvignon Private Reserve*
Region: USA—California   **Suggested Retail: $20.00**
Availability: Limited   **Golds: OC, IV, CA, TG, MO**
Lingering sweet oak and ripened berry finesse the way to a remarkably smooth finish. More than 2 years in small French oak barrels produced a rich, hearty wine with great color. The aging potential is 10 to 15 years from the vintage date.

Château St. Jean   *1989 Reserve Cabernet Sauvignon*
Region: USA—California   **Suggested Retail: $38.00**
Availability: NP   **Golds: RE, CA, LA**
Intensely purple in color, this Cabernet has a very complex, well-integrated nose with rich aromas of ripe, black cherries, black currants, plums, and cedar, as well as hints of chocolate and toasty French oak. On the palate a silky entry gives way to bright fruit flavors of blackberry and cranberry, and the wine finishes long with pleasant tannins and spicy oak nuances.
Special Award: *Best of Class (LA)*

Château St. Jean   *1991 Cinq Cepages Cabernet Sauvignon*
Region: USA—California   **Suggested Retail: $18.00**
Availability: NP   **Golds: NW, FF**
Intense aromas of ripe berries, plums, cassis, and spice fill the nose of this wine, which offers hints of chocolate and French oak in the background. The fruit aromas carry over onto the palate, with layers of black cherry and berry, balanced tannins, and oak toast persisting throughout an elegant finish.

Did You Know . . . ?
Perhaps the most dramatic revolution happening in the wine world is occurring in Chile. For decades the wineries there struggled with outdated equipment and technology, as well as a lack of funds. But in the late 1980s the government, together with the wine industry, mobilized to transform Chile into a top-class, world-competitive wine-producing country. With the additional help of foreign investment, new equipment and wine expertise flooded the country. Get ready!

Coldstream Hills   *1993 Reserve Cabernet Sauvignon*
Region: Australia   **Suggested Retail: $16.65 CAN**
Availability: Outside USA   **Golds: HO**
The wine is a strong purple-red color, with a clean, smooth bouquet of cassis and black currant aromas backed by a hint of sweet oak. The palate is softly rich and mouth filling, with dark berry fruit, a hint of dark chocolate, and lingering fine tannins. Cellaring potential: 4 to 10-plus years. Try it with mature cheeses and lamb. This wine is not available in the United States, but you can buy it in Canada, the UK, the Far East, Europe, and New Zealand.

De Loach   *1991 Estate Bottled O.F.S. Cabernet Sauvignon*
Region: USA—California   **Suggested Retail: $25.00**
Availability: Limited   **Golds: SD, FF**
"Our Finest Selection" is what the initials stand for, and this is a deep, rich garnet color with a smooth texture and deep body. A well-balanced wine, it has an elegant, deeply varietal nose with cedar and pepper notes and a touch of anise. Black cherry and rich cassis flavors with just a hint of chocolate mingle with generous oak components through the wine's lingering finish. The winemaker recommends having this one with game—or a rich chocolate dessert!
Special Award: *Chairman's Award (FF)*

Dry Creek Vineyard   *1991 Reserve Cabernet Sauvignon*
Region: USA—California   **Suggested Retail: $20.00**
Availability: Limited   **Golds: SD, NW, HH, TG**
Intense berry aromas blossom in this plush, textured wine. Subtle layers of chocolate amplify the brightly focused cherry and plum flavors. Undertones of cedar and mint unfold gently on the palate. Rich oak and sweet vanilla concentrate all the elements into an opulent, harmonious wine. This graceful, impeccably balanced Cabernet is approachable now, but will continue to improve with further cellaring.
Special Award: *Double Gold (TG)*

E. & J. Gallo Winery   *1991 Estate Bottled Cabernet Sauvignon*
Region: USA—California   **Suggested Retail: $50.00**
Availability: Good   **Golds: SF, DA**
The single-spaced, two-column oenological notes for this wine read like a doctoral thesis on winemaking! Take our word for it: this is liquid gold, and the care taken in making it from only the "best of the best" barrels means that this is a wine to take seriously. Save it for a special occasion and sip it with great joy.

Did You Know . . . ?
Quercus alba, also known as American white oak and used for barrel making, is found primarily in the Eastern United States extending east from Minnesota, Iowa, Missouri, and Arkansas, north of Mexico, and south of Canada and Maine. American oak is widely used in the wine industries of Spain, North and South America, and Australia.

Freemark Abbey   *1987 Sycamore Vineyards Cabernet Sauvignon*
Region: USA—California   Suggested Retail: $22.00
Availability: Limited   Golds: IV
Look for intense color and depth, with blackberry and allspice in the nose. The wine possesses rich Cabernet aromas. Ripe currants and blackberry add to the richness and complexity.

Freemark Abbey   *1990 Bosche Vineyard Cabernet Sauvignon*
Region: USA—California   Suggested Retail: $28.00
Availability: Good   Golds: IV
This wine is deep garnet with a slight ruby edge and has bright cherry aromas with cassis and currants. Lots of depth, dark chocolate, rich flavors, a long crisp finish, and moderate tannins complete the profile.

Geyser Peak Winery   *1993 Reserve Cabernet Sauvignon*
Region: USA—California   Suggested Retail: $22.00
Availability: NP   Golds: LA, LJ
The folks at Geyser Peak are producing several different Cabernet Sauvignons each year, and they all seem to be winning gold after gold after gold. This one, like its 1992 sibling, is not fined or filtered, so expect some sediment along with a lot of rich and sophisticated flavors and aromas.

Geyser Peak Winery   *1992 Reserve Cabernet Sauvignon*
Region: USA—California   Suggested Retail: $22.00
Availability: NP   Golds: CA, LA, PR, CL, MO
The nose displays herbaceous berry fruit characters enhanced by lifted vanillin oak. Some smokiness is also evident from the barrel fermentation. The palate is well structured with evident but soft tannins.
Special Awards: *Tie for Best Cabernet Sauvignon of Appellation (CA); Double Gold (CA); Red Sweepstakes (CL)*

Greenwood Ridge   *1992 Estate Bottled Cabernet Sauvignon*
Region: USA—California   Suggested Retail: $18.00
Availability: Limited   Golds: RE, SF, LA, NW
The spicy cedar bouquet combines with cherry and berry aromas, accented by vanillin and herbaceous undertones; deep briary flavors linger on the palate. This intensely flavored Cabernet Sauvignon will enhance hearty meals such as red meat and dishes in tomato sauce.
Special Awards: *Double Gold (SF); Best of Class (LA); Division Sweepstakes (LA); Governor's Award (LA)*

Did You Know . . . ?
Anywhere from 30 percent to 50 percent of all coastal vineyards in the United States will have to be systematically replanted by the year 2000 due to phylloxera.

Grgich Hills *1990 Napa Valley Cabernet Sauvignon*
Region: USA—California   **Suggested Retail:** $24.00
Availability: Very Good   **Golds:** FF

Balance and harmony are two outstanding attributes of this wine. The dark, brooding, purple-red color leads to a spicy aroma with mouth-filling flavors of ripe berry fruit and a counterpoint of sweet oak. This wine won first place in the April/May 1995 edition of California Grapevine.

Guenoc Estate *1992 Bella Vista Reserve Cabernet Sauvignon*
Region: USA—California   **Suggested Retail:** $25.50
Availability: Limited   **Golds:** LA, IV, FF, FW, BT, LJ, IN

Look for brilliant color, cherry fruit on the nose, with deep flavors of black currant, chocolate, and roasted coffee. It goes well with roasted meats; baked full-flavored salmon or mahi-mahi; lasagna with oregano and tarragon; and rich cheeses.
Special Award: *Chairman's Award (FF)*

Guenoc Estate *1992 Beckstoffer Reserve Cabernet Sauvignon*
Region: USA—California   **Suggested Retail:** $40.50
Availability: Good   **Golds:** SD

This one is tight and intense, with a trim band of spice, currant, black cherry, and tobacco, turning tannic on the finish. A young and complex wine that needs cellaring to soften and evolve. It will be best after 1999.

Hardy Wine Company *1993 Thomas Hardy Cabernet Sauvignon*
Region: Australia   **Suggested Retail:** $25.00
Availability: Good   **Golds:** HO

Three vintages of this Cab won golds in 1995 alone, so Hardy obviously has mastered the art of making gold medal full-bodied reds. This one is available in the United States, and has a nose dominated by ripe black and red currant aromas, with a leafy oaky influence. The palate is rich and generous, displaying the perfect balance of black currant, vanilla, and herbal overtones.

Heitz Cellar *1990 Trailside Vineyard Cabernet Sauvignon*
Region: USA—California   **Suggested Retail:** $45.00
Availability: Limited   **Golds:** OC, RE, BT

Here's a dark, enticing wine with wonderful hints of black cherry and new oak nuances in the aroma. The layers of fruit and complexity offer delicious flavors on the palate, thus showing extraordinary harmony and abundance of flavor and balanced elegance.

Did You Know . . . ?
Robert Parker, the famed American wine critic credited with developing a numerical system for evaluating wine, tastes *over 100 wines a day!*

Hess Collection Winery   *1991 Napa Valley Cabernet Sauvignon*

Region: USA—California ** Suggested Retail: $18.50**
Availability: Good **Golds: OC, SD, NW**

Here's a dark, cherry red wine with aromas of blackberries, currants, cassis, and black cherry, with a second layer of roasted nuts, coffee, and French oak, as well as hints of chocolate and fig. It has flavors of cherries, spices, mint, and nutmeg; then roasted coffee, vanilla, and cassis. The body is very full, layered, and rich. The tannin profile is smooth and rich with an element of softness. Fruit, oak, and youthful tannins close the wine. This wine is slightly softer than previous vintages and needs more bottle aging—up to the year 2005—to fully marry the many flavors.
Special Award: *Best of Price Class (NW)*

Justin Vineyards   *1992 Unfined Unfiltered Cabernet Sauvignon*

Region: USA—California **Suggested Retail: $20.00**
Availability: Limited **Golds: CA, NW, IE**

This liquid gold was made in an extremely limited quantity from this family-owned and -operated winery. But we include it because Wine Spectator *gave it an 88 rating, and* The Wine Advocate *called it "the star of Paso Robles." Because of the winery's careful hands-on production practices, it seems a safe bet that any Justin Cabernet Sauvignon will be a winner. If you can't find it, try calling the winery at (800) 726-0049. Incidentally, Justin labels are designed by a different artist every year, and have become the envy of label collectors.*
Special Awards: *Tie for Best Wine of Region (CA); Best Cabernet Sauvignon of Appellation (CA)*

Kendall-Jackson   *1991 Grand Reserve Cabernet Sauvignon*

Region: USA—California **Suggested Retail: $30.00**
Availability: Limited **Golds: DA, NW**

A big, intense wine with deep ruby color and a bouquet of blackberry, cherry, cedar, toasty vanilla, and cassis. This one has loads of jammy fruit flavors in the mouth that linger through the finish.

Louis M. Martini   *1990 Monte Rosso Vineyard Cabernet Sauvignon*

Region: USA—California **Suggested Retail: $22.00**
Availability: Limited **Golds: RE**

Fragrant aromas of cassis, mint, and herbaceous black pepper with a beautiful complement of oak distinguish this wine. A rich, complex wine with a balance and tannin structure that will enable it to age for decades.

Did You Know ... ?

Prehistoric potters of ancient Greece used to stand their pots on grape leaves to dry in the sun before firing. As a result, some of the recovered pots have beautiful and perfect impressions of grape leaves baked right onto their bases.

Markham Vineyards *1991 Napa Valley Cabernet Sauvignon*
Region: USA—California   **Suggested Retail: $20.00**
Availability: Very Good   **Golds: SD**

Deep ruby garnet in color, this intensely extracted, fruit-focused wine shows cassis and black cherry notes with hints of cedar and tobacco on the nose. The rich, ripe berry flavors meld with hints of vanilla oak toastiness and are harmoniously balanced with delicate, yet youthful, chewy tannins. The long, juicy finish lingers on.

Mazzocco Vineyards *1991 Sonoma County Cabernet Sauvignon*
Region: USA—California   **Suggested Retail: $18.00**
Availability: Limited   **Golds: LA**

This is a fragrant wine with vibrant berry notes and a hint of spice. Rich black cherry fruit flavors burst in the mouth, underscored by vanilla and anise. Full bodied with sufficient tannins, the wine finishes with textured layers of focused fruit and soft oak.
Special Award: *Best of Class (LA)*

Merryvale Vineyards *1991 Napa Valley Cabernet Sauvignon*
Region: USA—California   **Suggested Retail: $25.00**
Availability: Good   **Golds: SD**

Check out that brilliant dark ruby color. The wine has a concentrated yet elegant nose with aromas of cassis, vanilla, and clove. Expect very bright fruit character displayed on the palate, with good concentration. Cassis seems to be the dominant fruit character here, allowing for a refined and balanced wine with good depth and a promising future.

Michel-Schlumberger *1990 California Reserve Cabernet Sauvignon*
Region: USA—California   **Suggested Retail: $35.00**
Availability: Limited   **Golds: NW**

This wine has outstanding color and is rich in layers of berry and spice. According to the winemaker, it is the "hallmark of the vintage."

Mitchelton Wines *1995 Cabernet Sauvignon*
Region: Australia   **Suggested Retail: $19.99**
Availability: Very Good   **Golds: RM**

The press material from the winemaker on this one is not yet completed, because this wine was tasted, judged, and awarded a gold while the wine was still in barrel—before it was bottled or released. That's good news for Aussie-wine lovers, because this one should be plentiful and new on U.S. shelves at press time. Snag a bottle quickly from this well-known, consistent gold-medal-winning winery.

Did You Know . . . ?
Cork is central to Portugal's economy. Portugal's cork forests make up about 30 percent of the world's cork trees, and that country produces more than half of the world's total output of cork.

Mont St. John *1991 Napa Valley Cabernet Sauvignon*
Region: USA—California   **Suggested Retail: $25.00**
Availability: Limited   **Golds: SD**
This Cabernet Sauvignon has an exceptionally fruity nose and an aroma of luscious raspberries, plums, perfumed oak, and unmistakable "Rutherford Dust" characteristic of the area in which the grapes were grown. In the mouth the full, lush texture is perfectly balanced with the flavors of raspberries, currant, and a hint of spice. The lingering finish is clean and mouth-watering.

Newlan Vineyards *1991 Cabernet Sauvignon Estate Bottled*
Region: USA—California   **Suggested Retail: $18.00**
Availability: Limited   **Golds: SF**
A rich and complex wine boasting subtle aromas of licorice, black cherry, and black currant. It has firm, well-integrated tannins and a long finish.

Peju Province *1991 HB Vineyard Cabernet Sauvignon*
Region: USA—California   **Suggested Retail: $65.00**
Availability: NP   **Golds: SF, AT**
Aromas of oak, blackberries, allspice, and walnuts combine in a lovely spiciness. Blackberry and chocolate flavors are balanced by a strong tannic backbone and crisp acidity. Proportioned for a long, graceful saturation, this Cab will develop over the next few years; its intensity will soften with age. By the way, this wine has received a gold every year since the 1985 vintage, including three Double Golds.
***Special Award:** Double Gold (SF)*

Penley Estate *1993 Coonawarra Cabernet Sauvignon*
Region: Australia   **Suggested Retail: $40.00**
Availability: Very Good   **Golds: SY**
This wine also won a gold at Royal Melbourne in 1994, and was just released in July 1996, so you should have no problem finding this gem in the United States. The wine is deep crimson colored with some amber tints. Its aroma has striking berry and smoky oak tones, which highlight the intense character and concentration. A powerful wine, medium to full bodied, this one will age gracefully, and will achieve its full potential in 5 to 10 years.

Preston Vineyards *1992 Washington State Reserve Cab. Sauvignon*
Region: USA—Washington   **Suggested Retail: $28.00**
Availability: NP   **Golds: WW**
The Reserve Cabs produced by Preston consistently score in the 90s in the Wine Spectator. *This beauty was bottled unfiltered to bring out the full varietal character.*

Did You Know . . . ?
Around 600 A.D., a Bedouin poet wrote, "If I die bury me by the vine, so that its roots may satiate the thirst of my bones."

Robert Mondavi *1990 Napa Valley Cabernet Sauvignon Unfiltered*
Region: USA—California   Suggested Retail: $20.00
Availability: Good   Golds: IV
A naturally balanced wine possessing the varietal's classic aromas and flavors of cassis, berry, and spice, with the added components of vanilla and wood imparted by oak aging. Look for lots of forward fruit flavors.

Rodney Strong *1991 Reserve Cabernet Sauvignon*
Region: USA—California   Suggested Retail: $30.00
Availability: NP   Golds: LA, SD
This wine already shows rich black currant flavors with cedar, tobacco, and ripe green olive complemented by firm yet soft tannins and a velvety finish.

Sequoia Grove Vineyards *1992 Napa Valley Cabernet Sauvignon*
Region: USA—California   Suggested Retail: $18.00
Availability: Good   Golds: PR
This wine is full bodied and rich, with a good balance of fruit. The finish is long, rich, and satisfying. Cellar it for a couple of years, as it will improve with age.

Seven Hills Winery *1991 Klipsun Vineyard Cabernet Sauvignon*
Region: USA—Washington   Suggested Retail: $20.00
Availability: Limited   Golds: DA
Here's a full-bodied wine with wonderful depth and breadth on the palate, and a long finish. It's a beautiful example of Washington State Cabernet.

Shafer Vineyards *1991 Hillside Select Cabernet Sauvignon*
Region: USA—California   Suggested Retail: $45.00
Availability: Limited   Golds: NW, BT
A Cab with very dark color, this one has intense blackberry jam flavors and a sweet core of fruit that lingers on the midpalate. It possesses deep concentration, and has approachable tannins and great depth of flavor.
Special Award: *Best of Price Class (NW)*

Did You Know . . . ?

Small animals have always been a problem for vineyard managers, since they feed on young vines as well as grapes. Napa Valley's Shafer Vineyards has found a way to deal with those pesky gophers, rabbits, voles, field mice, meadow mice, and ground squirrels without resorting to traps and toxic poisons. Doug Shafer built nesting boxes and perches, and brought in owls and hawks. It's an ingenious system, since the owls work at night hunting down the large rodents, while the hawks take over the shift at daylight, catching smaller animals. A pair of barn owls and their young can eat up to *1,000 rodents* in one nesting season!

Shafer Vineyards *1992 Stag's Leap District Cabernet Sauvignon*
Region: USA—California   **Suggested Retail: $22.00**
Availability: Good   **Golds: SD, TG**
Silky and easy drinking, this wine has hints of oak and aromas of currant and blackberry. Rich fruit, excellent balance, and soft tannins complete the picture.

Silverado Vineyards *1992 Napa Valley Cabernet Sauvignon*
Region: USA—California   **Suggested Retail: $19.00**
Availability: Very Good   **Golds: SD**
This one is brilliant, medium deep, slightly purple-ruby in appearance. It has pungent aromas with sweet vanilla, cedar, herbs, clove, and ripe fruit, with slightly tart undertones. Medium acidity, medium-full body, sweet fruit, chocolate, and vanilla flavors, and slightly chalky tannin are in evidence. A firm backbone, fleshy mouth feel, and long finish tell the rest of the story.

Stonestreet Winery *1992 Estate Bottled Cabernet Sauvignon*
Region: USA—California   **Suggested Retail: $24.00**
Availability: NP   **Golds: CA**
This wine is rich, dark, and supple. Following fermentation using native yeast, the wine underwent an extended maceration to maximize the extraction of color, flavor, and round, mouth-filling tannins. Sculpting these tannins by careful racking and aerating during barrel aging helped develop the complex aromas and flavors of dark fruits, cedar, spice, and earth.

Tefft Cellars *1992 Yakima Valley Cabernet Sauvignon*
Region: USA—Washington   **Suggested Retail: $27.00**
Availability: Limited   **Golds: WW**
Here's a robust and spicy Cab with toasty oak. It is bursting with sweet plum, currant, and black cherry, and has a long finish and smooth tannins.

V. Sattui Winery *1991 Mario's Reserve Cabernet Sauvignon*
Region: USA—California   **Suggested Retail: $60.00**
Availability: Limited   **Golds: RE, IW, PR, SD**
"Undoubtedly the finest wine ever produced by V. Sattui," according to this top-class winery, from which you can order this wine directly at (707) 963-7774 or by fax at (707) 963-4324. The judges in various prestigious competitions obviously agree. It's pricy because it's now scarce, so splurge before it's too late.
Special Award: *Best of Class (SD)*

Did You Know . . . ?
In the 1930s Washington State's wine industry centered around the Concord grape, a native American variety better known as the source of grape juice and jelly. In 1969 there were only two wineries in Washington, around the time when California's wine industry was soaring. By 1990 there were eighty fine wineries in Washington.

V. Sattui Winery *1992 Preston Vineyard Cabernet Sauvignon*
Region: USA—California   **Suggested Retail: $35.00**
Availability: Limited   **Golds: CA**
Wow! The judges at California State Fair loved this Cab. The price of this wine has gone up because bottles are getting scarcer and scarcer. Luckily, you can get a bottle (limited to 3 per customer) directly from the winery, which is the only way V. Sattui sells their wines. They describe this one as having an intense, spicy, black currant nose, full body, and highly structured flavors. It can be cellared for 7 to 10 years. Phone: (707) 963-7774. Fax: (707) 963-4324.
Special Awards: *Tie for Best Cabernet Sauvignon of California (CA); Best Cabernet Sauvignon of Appellation (CA)*

V. Sattui Winery *1991 Preston Vineyard Cabernet Sauvignon*
Region: USA—California   **Suggested Retail: $40.00**
Availability: Limited   **Golds: NW**
V. Sattui wines are only available from the winery, and this one is limited to 2 bottles per person, which might account for the price, since it's becoming scarce. Sweet herbal spices in the nose and on the mouth, with rich palate sensations, great balance, and firm structure are what characterize this Cab. This wine also won a gold at the 1994 Los Angeles County Fair. Phone the winery at: (707) 963-7774, or fax them at: (707) 963-4324.

Willamette Valley Vineyards *1992 Our Very Best Cabernet Sauvignon*
Region: USA—Oregon   **Suggested Retail: $25.00**
Availability: Limited   **Golds: OR**
This is a deep purple-red wine with aromas of cedar, tobacco, and cassis. It has rich, intense flavors of black cherry and chocolate and a full body.

ZD Wines *1992 Napa Valley Cabernet Sauvignon*
Region: USA—California   **Suggested Retail: $25.00**
Availability: Limited   **Golds: LA, NW, CN, TG, BT**
Look for a medium-dark ruby color, aromas of rich cherry and plum fruit, vanilla/toasty oak, and medium tannins. A spicy finish that lingers tops it off. Here's a wine that can be cellared for 4 to 5 years.
Special Award: *Double Gold (TG)*

Did You Know . . . ?
At ZD Wines, they believe in recycling everything. After the grapes are fermented and pressed, workers load up the pomace and truck it across the trail to feed the very excited cows. According to the winery, the cows actually start running when they see the truck heading their way. The cows also annually enjoy bovine appetizers of grape stems and seeds.

Brindiamo *1993 South Coast Nebbiolo*
Region: USA—California   **Suggested Retail: $14.00**
Availability: Limited   **Golds: IV, NW, AT**
We root for underdogs, and Nebbiolo is off the beaten path, so we like it. The vineyard is at the base of the Santa Rosa Mountains, where warm days and cool nights help develop the grape's character. This one is similar to an Italian Barbaresco with its rich fruit flavors dominating the nose, lovely plum and spicy notes on the palate, and an alcohol level between 12.5 and 13%. A good tannic structure assures that this wine will age beautifully through 1999.

Emilio Guglielmo Winery *1993 Private Reserve Grignolino*
Region: USA—California   **Suggested Retail: $8.00**
Availability: NP   **Golds: CA, LA**
Deep aromas of fresh cracked pepper and juniper greet your nose. Soft, rich, inviting flavors of plums, berries, and subtle herbs, with a smooth lingering finish tell the rest. We say be adventurous and try a different red wine for a change.
Special Award: *Best Other Red Varietal of Appellation (CA)*

Montevina Winery *1992 Amador County Barbera*
Region: USA—California   **Suggested Retail: $9.00**
Availability: Limited   **Golds: SD, NW, AM**
This 1992 vintage boasts a beautiful aroma of black cherries, with a hint of the toasty, nutty character typical of the Barbera variety. Full, rich, and soft on the palate, the wine offers fresh, vibrant, cherry fruit flavors with a dash of spice and toasted herbs, and a lingering, long finish.
Special Awards: *Best of Price Class (NW); Best New World Barbera (NW)*

Preston Vineyards *1993 Dry Creek Valley Estate Bottled Barbera*
Region: USA—California   **Suggested Retail: $13.00**
Availability: NP   **Golds: FF**
Look for a deep crimson color and fresh ripe raspberries dominating the nose, which also shows notes of spicy leather and oak. This is a very crisp and lively wine with lots of sweet berry fruit. Aging potential: 6 years.

Did You Know . . . ?
When shopping for hard-to-find wines, let your fingers do the walking. No, we don't mean in the Yellow Pages. Take a virtual visit to the wine shops on the Internet. Hundreds of wineries from all over the New World have home pages offering their wines by the case, discounted from the retail price you'd pay in the wine shop. Many of these wineries also have mailing lists you can get on so that you can receive newsletters with information about special events at the winery, advance offers on upcoming vintages, and other fun stuff of particular interest to wine enthusiasts.

Vino Noceto   *1993 Shenandoah Valley Noceto Sangiovese*
Region: USA—California   **Suggested Retail: $10.00**
Availability: Good   **Golds: CA**
Here's a full- to medium-bodied wine with deep color and a cherry/berry aroma with intense cherry fruit. The Sierra Foothills terroir lends a not-so-subtle spiciness as well. Part of the lot of grapes contributed bright, fruit flavors and wonderful violet aromas. The other lot added a rich, Sangiovese jamlike undercurrent to the final blend. Careful control of oak helped to capture the floral aromas without overpowering oakiness. The wine can be enjoyed now or set aside for later. Try it with Mediterranean or Italian dishes, or even spicy Southwestern cuisine.
Special Awards: *Double Gold (CA); Best Sangiovese of Appellation (CA)*

Did You Know . . . ?
The price of a French oak barrel is around $600, while an American oak barrel goes for about $250.

Atlas Peak Vineyards *1992 Napa Valley Sangiovese Reserve*
Region: USA—California   Suggested Retail: $24.00
Availability: Limited   Golds: OC, IV, PR
A full, rich, elegant wine with fruit aromas of wild berries, plums, and lots of spice. The hints of oak are well integrated with the ample fruit.

Eberle Winery *1993 Norman Vineyard Barbera*
Region: USA—California   Suggested Retail: $18.00
Availability: Limited   Golds: RE, CA, SF, PR, IE
This wine has ripe berry flavors with a velvety mouth feel. It is well balanced with firm acid and soft tannins. Its ripe fruit has a backbone of tartness and "begs for a plate of pasta."
Special Awards: *Best Barbera of Appellation (CA); Double Gold (CA); Best of Class (PR)*

Mosby Winery *1993 Vigna Della Casa Vecchia Sangiovese*
Region: USA—California   Suggested Retail: $16.00
Availability: Limited   Golds: OC
Medium ruby in color, with an essence of lilacs, violets, and black cherry that follows in the taste. It is moderately tannic, with well-balanced fruit and oak. The Vecchia Della Casa vineyard, where the wine is bottled, is the site of the oldest house in California, according to the proprietor. It is an adobe house built in 1853.

Mount Palomar Winery *1992 Castelletto Estate Bottled Sangiovese*
Region: USA—California   Suggested Retail: $18.00
Availability: NP   Golds: CA
Low crop yields created rich, intense flavors without heaviness on the palate. In the glass the wine has attractive bright red hues and is highly aromatic. Look for flavors reminiscent of raspberry and dried cherries, with smoky, roasted undertones.
Special Awards: *Best of Region (CA); Best Sangiovese of Appellation (CA)*

Renwood Winery *1993 Reserve Select Barbera*
Region: USA—California   Suggested Retail: $20.00
Availability: Limited   Golds: SF, LA
This is a large-scale wine with a firm mouth feel, dense body, and great extraction. Since Barbera is used as a blending grape more often than it is made into its own wine, we salute Renwood for taking a chance with this varietal, which is sorely underrated and every bit as complex and delicious as its more popular cousin, Cabernet Sauvignon.

Did You Know . . . ?
Don't dust off your grandmother's beautiful lead crystal decanter for your next party. These are not good vessels for wine, since the acid in the wine leaches the lead from the glass, thus adding the neural toxin to your wine. Most modern decanters are no longer made of lead.

Renwood Winery *1993 Clockspring Vineyard Sangiovese*
Region: USA—California   **Suggested Retail: $16.95**
Availability: Good   **Golds: CA**
The Noble red grape of all of central Italy is the Sangiovese, though its varietal name is far less known than the Chianti and Brunello that are made from it. Here's a red wine of medium body, dry and firm, with a tannic spine and a floral bouquet. It is amply endowed with all of the virtues we seek in a fine and elegant red wine.

Robert Pepi Winery *1991 Colline di Sassi Sangiovese*
Region: USA—California   **Suggested Retail: $20.00**
Availability: NP   **Golds: LA, PR**
The 1993 vintage of this wine won golds as well. Obviously, Robert Pepi knows how to make Italian varietal reds that are delicious—especially with hearty pasta dishes and grilled red meats.

Robert Pepi Winery *1993 Colline di Sassi Sangiovese*
Region: USA—California   **Suggested Retail: $25.00**
Availability: NP   **Golds: CA**
Classic varietal aromas of cherry, strawberry, and rose petal characterize this wine, with notes of roasted oak and spice. A wine of great texture and richness, with firm tannins, and a velvety finish. By the way, both the 1991 and 1993 bottlings of this wine won golds in 1995.
Special Awards: *Best Wine of Region (CA); Best Sangiovese of Appellation (CA)*

Robert Pepi Winery *1991 L'Anima Sangiovese*
Region: USA—California   **Suggested Retail: $20.00**
Availability: Good   **Golds: RE, OC**
This Italian varietal is bright, spicy, and exotic with firm tannins and a velvety finish. The judges loved it, and so will you. Robert Pepi won golds for three of their Sangioveses in 1995, proof that this is a winery that has mastered this variety. Get out of your Cabernet Sauvignon rut and go "Italian" for a change of pace.

Did You Know . . . ?

The Sangiovese grape has ancient origins. It's probably indigenous to Tuscany, and some even postulate that it was known to the Etruscans (eighth century B.C.). The literal translation is "blood of Jove," which further indicates the age of this variety. It is Italy's most planted variety, but in California it's gaining ground as well. California wineries producing "Supertuscans" are beginning to get international recognition. Robert Pepi and Atlas Peak, both in Napa, are considered the important pioneers in introducing America to California-style Italian varietals.

Sebastiani Vineyards *1992 Barbera*

Region: USA—California　　　**Suggested Retail: $15.00**
Availability: Good　　　**Golds: RE**

Sebastiani has been producing Barbera since their founding in 1904. This one has Zinfandel (12%), Mourvèdre (7%), and Carignane (1%) blended in to create a marvelous synergy of flavors, complexity, and spice. Notable oak aromas and flavors, along with clove, spice, and bright fruit hints, lead to a smooth finish. A lively, medium-bodied wine, it will go nicely with grilled meats or poultry, and especially any dish with tomato sauce.

Swanson Vineyards *1993 Estate Bottled Sangiovese*

Region: USA—California　　　**Suggested Retail: $18.00**
Availability: Good　　　**Golds: RE, OC**

The wine critics' scores for this wine are in the 90s. Look for medium red color with fruity scents of raspberry, cherry, blackberry, violet, and spice. The aromas are echoed on the palate, adding dried cherries and vanilla from the "light kiss" of oak barrels. Balanced and almost silky in texture, it also has the structure to develop additional complexity with further bottle aging.

Did You Know . . . ?

Residues of harmful agrochemicals and pesticides are less worrisome in wine than in other foods and beverages, for the reason that these chemicals are likelier to be eliminated through the processes of clarification, fermentation, and filtration than, say, those found on just-picked strawberries.

Carmen Vineyards *1993 Reserve Merlot*
Region: Chile   **Suggested Retail: $9.99**
Availability: Good   **Golds: LJ**

This winery's other Merlot also won a gold in 1995. Value is the name of the game with Carmen's gold medal winners. This one is a deep ruby color with intense aromas of red fruit (strawberries, berries, prunes) and spicy nuances on the nose. It has nice complexity with vanilla aromas from barrel aging, a palate that is medium to full bodied, and a lot of firmness. The wine is rich in flavors, voluminous in the mouth, and has a long finish. Best of all, you can buy it in the United States.

Carmen Vineyards *1993 Merlot*
Region: Chile   **Suggested Retail: $6.99**
Availability: Very Good   **Golds: LJ**

You should have no problem finding this Chilean Merlot in the United States; Carmen made a whopping 40,000 cases. It has a deep ruby color with intense aromas of red fruit, with spicy nuances, a light to medium body, and concentrated varietal flavors.

Grand Cru Vineyards *1993 Premium Selection Merlot*
Region: USA—California   **Suggested Retail: $8.00**
Availability: NP   **Golds: OC**

Look for complexity and elegance with ripe herb, currant, and oak flavors. The texture of this Merlot is smooth and supple, and the wine has a long finish.

Louis M. Martini *1992 North Coast Merlot*
Region: USA—California   **Suggested Retail: $9.50**
Availability: Good   **Golds: OC, NW**

Cherry aromas leap out of the nose with hints of white pepper woven through from the French oak. Minor herbal, mint, and cedar also emerge in the bouquet. The wine is medium bodied with full flavors of tingling tannins and has a long, lively finish.

Messina Hof Wine Cellars *1993 Barrel Reserve Merlot*
Region: USA—Texas   **Suggested Retail: $9.99**
Availability: Good   **Golds: LA, LS**

Blackberry and wood flavors combine to produce a classic Bordeaux blend with a long, lingering finish.

Did You Know . . . ?
Louis P. Martini (son of founder Louis M. Martini, founder of the eponymous California winery) made the first varietal Merlot in the United States with his 1968/70 vintage.

Paul Thomas Winery   *1993 Columbia Valley Merlot*

Region: USA—Washington   **Suggested Retail: $9.50**
Availability: Good   **Golds: WW**

We buy this wine frequently in Woodstock, New York, at our favorite wine shop. It goes well with any number of foods, and the best thing we can say about it is that it's agreeable in every sense of the word—fruity, easy to understand, and lovely to drink all by itself. (In other words, we don't want to spoil this wine with food!) The winemaker says it has a bright, spicy, peppery nose with black cherries, currants, licorice, and earthy flavors.

Round Hill Vineyards   *1993 California Merlot*

Region: USA—California   **Suggested Retail: $8.00**
Availability: Very Good   **Golds: CA**

Having aromas of ripe cranberry and cherry with hints of plum, anise, and subtle vanilla oak, this wine delivers round, rich flavors of cranberry and red cherry that display nice length in the finish.
Special Awards: *Tie for Best Merlot of California (CA); Best Merlot of Appellation (CA)*

Washington Hills Cellars   *1993 Columbia Valley Merlot*

Region: USA—Washington   **Suggested Retail: $9.99**
Availability: Good   **Golds: NW**

Traditional black sweet cherry combined with cedar and spice contribute to a complex bouquet. Firm tannins, sweet vanilla oak, and fruit combine nicely for a long, appealing finish. Try this Merlot with duck, veal, pastas, and even chocolates.

Did You Know . . . ?

Wineries in Washington's sunny inland Columbia Valley are producing consistently fine and delicious, fruity, well-structured Merlots. Merlot is that state's most popular red-wine grape. In 1991 the acreage planted in Merlot had doubled in just three years, and continues to increase.

Belvedere Winery *1992 Sonoma County Merlot*
Region: USA—California   **Suggested Retail: $12.00**
Availability: Good   **Golds: NW**
Fragrant aromas of cherries, raspberries, and toasty oak are followed by hints of spice and herbs. The aromas carry through to the flavors, resulting in a Merlot that is fruity but has great depth and complexity. This is a beautifully balanced wine with a rich, long, lingering finish. Very enjoyable now or with up to 6 years bottle age. An outstanding dinner wine that will go very well with a variety of pasta dishes, meats, and poultry.
Special Award: *Best of Price Class (NW)*

Buena Vista Carneros *1992 Merlot*
Region: USA—California   **Suggested Retail: $13.00**
Availability: Good   **Golds: IV**
Cranberry, black cherry, and cassis are the predominant aromas of this wine, with subtle scents of vanilla. With flavors of berry and spice, this Merlot has rich texture and a supple finish. The winemaker suggests serving it with polenta topped with walnuts, feta cheese, and sun-dried tomatoes. Yum!

Caterina Winery *1992 Columbia Valley Merlot*
Region: USA—Washington   **Suggested Retail: $13.95**
Availability: Limited   **Golds: DA**
The wine shows clean, focused cherry, berry flavors with a toasty, vanilla finish. It has a bright and appealing nose, but is made to age and should improve through 1998.

Château St. Jean *1992 Sonoma County Merlot*
Region: USA—California   **Suggested Retail: $12.00**
Availability: NP   **Golds: PR, SO**
This Merlot offers aromas of violets, juicy plums, black cherries, and oak spice. On the palate the wine shows soft textures and ample flavors of ripe plums, blackberries, cinnamon, and vanilla, which persist through the soft, rich, and enduring finish.

Château Ste. Michelle *1993 Columbia Valley Merlot*
Region: USA—Washington   **Suggested Retail: $16.00**
Availability: Limited   **Golds: WW, NE**
This Merlot is characterized by a deep ruby color and aromas of black cherry, vanilla, and ripe raspberries. The flavors are very concentrated yet soft on the palate, enhanced by the contributions of French and American oak.

Did You Know . . . ?
The Romans invented the first glass-blown bottles, and some believe they were the first to store wine in glass.

Columbia Crest *1992 Columbia Valley Merlot*
Region: USA—Washington   Suggested Retail: **$10.00**
Availability: Limited   Golds: IV
Ripe, summertime berries and toasty oak aromas complement rich, chocolate-berry flavors. Hints of coffee and cocoa linger on the palate. Enjoy this one with rosemary-roasted lamb or poultry with sage, says winemaker Doug Gore.

Covey Run Vintners *1993 Yakima Valley Merlot*
Region: USA—Washington   Suggested Retail: **$10.99**
Availability: NP   Golds: IV
This wine has a supple texture, with low tannins and an appealing velvety mouth feel. The elegant aromas resemble sweet black cherry and berry, with subtle hints of pepper and spice, which follow through on the palate. Expect good aging potential in this Merlot.

Creston Vineyard *1993 Paso Robles Merlot*
Region: USA—California   Suggested Retail: **$13.00**
Availability: Good   Golds: SD, TG, BT
This blend of 81% Merlot, 10% Cabernet Sauvignon, and 9% Cabernet Franc is as good as gold, or at least that's how the judges felt. The last four vintages of Creston Merlots have tallied up 63 medals, including Best of Class and Best of Region. This one can be consumed now, but will benefit from further cellaring.

De Loach *1993 Estate Bottled Merlot*
Region: USA—California   Suggested Retail: **$15.00**
Availability: Good   Golds: CA, LA
This rich, well-balanced, full-bodied Merlot has aromas of currants and black cherries. The wine exhibits subtle flavors of oak with hints of mint and plum. Undercurrents of spice and cedar round it out. Try it with rack of lamb or beef tenderloin.
Special Award: *Best Merlot of Appellation (CA)*

Fetzer *1993 Barrel Select North Coast Merlot*
Region: USA—California   Suggested Retail: **$11.99**
Availability: NP   Golds: CA
Here's a warm, round-flavored Merlot with ripe cherry fruit and hints of blueberry, mint, and toasty vanilla. With varietal fruit and fine oak well married in aroma and flavor, this elegant red offers style, depth, and complexity.
Special Awards: *Tie for Best Merlot of California (CA); Best Merlot of Appellation (CA)*

Did You Know . . . ?
Creston wines were poured at the inaugurations of three presidents: Reagan, Bush, and Clinton. We knew all three had *something* in common besides their office.

Firestone   *1993 Santa Ynez Valley Merlot*

Region: USA—California   Suggested Retail: $12.00
Availability: Very Good   Golds: CA, IE

This wine is ripe, rich, and soft, with layers of chocolate and cherry flavors, balanced by notes of herbs and vanilla.
Special Award: *Best Merlot of Appellation (CA)*

Forest Glen Winery   *1993 Barrel Select Merlot*

Region: USA—California   Suggested Retail: $10.00
Availability: NP   Golds: LA

Look for a bright cherry color and aromas of ripe berries and green olives. The wine has mouth-filling flavors of ripe plums, cherry, and oak. Its soft finish makes it easy to drink now.
Special Award: *Best of Class (LA)*

Freemark Abbey   *1992 Napa Merlot*

Region: USA—California   Suggested Retail: $16.00
Availability: Good   Golds: PR

Dark ruby cherries and plums dominate the aroma with a hint of lavender. This Merlot has medium soft tannins and plummy flavors.

Grant Burge   *1989 Hillcot Merlot*

Region: Australia   Suggested Retail: $13.60
Availability: Limited   Golds: PE

The wine shows excellent purple color and its bouquet has a depth of raspberrylike fruit with wood overtones. The palate has good structure and flavor, yet is still soft. You'll find this one in the United States, as well as in Europe.

Hogue Cellars   *1992 Columbia Valley Merlot*

Region: USA—Washington   Suggested Retail: $14.99
Availability: Very Good   Golds: IV

The aromas of this Merlot are an appealing mélange of gardenia, bramble, raspberry, cherry, blueberry, and blackberry, with accents of leather, chocolate, and oak spice. Moderate tannins, good structure, and a long vanilla and cherry finish enhance this wine.

Indian Springs Vineyards   *1993 Merlot*

Region: USA—California   Suggested Retail: $12.00
Availability: Good   Golds: PR

This wine displays concentrated berry flavors with pleasing toast nuances from oak aging. Smooth and well balanced enough to drink now, it will reward cellaring into the next century. Previous vintages of the Merlot have been consistent gold medal winners.

Did You Know ... ?

The first grapevines introduced to Australia were brought by the Anglo-Saxons way back in 1788, on the First Fleet.

Kenwood Vineyards *1992 Sonoma County Merlot*
Region: USA—California　　　　**Suggested Retail: $16.00**
Availability: Good　　　　**Golds: NW**
A ripe, aromatic wine with hints of plum, nutmeg, and cloves continuing into the smooth finish. Perfect with paella.

Konocti Winery *1993 Lake County Merlot*
Region: USA—California　　　　**Suggested Retail: $10.00**
Availability: NP　　　　**Golds: PR**
A luscious, berry-fruit Merlot that is fragrant and flavorful. While not complicated, this one will be a delight, and is ready to consume right now.

Lambert Bridge *1993 Merlot*
Region: USA—California　　　　**Suggested Retail: $14.99**
Availability: Good　　　　**Golds: CA**
This Merlot is deep purple, soft, supple, smoothly textured, and full flavored. The nose is filled with loads of bright berry and plummy fruit that combine with subtle smoky nuances and spice. These flavors carry forth in the mouth and are joined with hints of blackberry and sweet toasty oak. Ideal for current consumption, this wine still possesses the structure that will mature nicely with age. Cabernet Sauvignon (15%) was added to the blend to provide additional structure, backbone, and complexity.

Leeward Winery *1993 Napa Valley Merlot*
Region: USA—California　　　　**Suggested Retail: $15.00**
Availability: Limited　　　　**Golds: SD**
Aromas of black cherries, violets, cocoa, and spice greet the nose. This balanced wine exhibits plum and black cherry flavors with a lingering, rich, full finish.

Magnotta Winery *1991 Merlot Limited Edition*
Region: Canada　　　　**Suggested Retail: $10.75**
Availability: NP　　　　**Golds: IV**
This Merlot has a velvety texture and striking aromas of chocolate, coffee, and ripe black plum that give way to concentrated flavors of plum, toast, and licorice. It is ripe, balanced, and lingers on the finish. Try it with wild game and aged cheeses.
Special Award: *Black Diamond Award (IV)*

Did You Know ... ?
The cork industry has fallen on hard times more than once. It began in Catalonia, then was disrupted by the Spanish Civil War. In Algeria, another once-major cork producer, the political situation of the 1960s put a stopper on the economic viability of that industry. Finally, in the late twentieth century, Portugal has taken the lead.

Meerlust   *1989 Merlot*
Region: South Africa   **Suggested Retail: $16.00**
Availability: Very Good   **Golds: IV, WC**

Meerlust Merlot is a mellow, velvety wine, deep garnet in color, with a hint of sweetness. It is full bodied, and because of its intense concentration has the potential to improve in complexity in the bottle. This wine is available in the United States, and has won many other honors, including being chosen one of the top 40 red wines in 1995 by Wine Enthusiast.

Mill Creek Vineyards   *1992 Dry Creek Estate Merlot*
Region: USA—California   **Suggested Retail: $14.00**
Availability: Limited   **Golds: RE**

Intense flavors of cherry and cassis with hints of cedar make the structure of this wine one of the best ever from Mill Creek Vineyards. Its texture is soft and silky and it has a rich, black cherry bouquet.

Napa Ridge Winery   *1992 North Coast Merlot*
Region: USA—California   **Suggested Retail: $10.00**
Availability: Good   **Golds: IV**

A rich, creamy, and velvety wine with hints of oak, spice, and vanilla from oak aging. Tinges of berry and currant flavors will greet your tongue, and the wine has soft tannins and a delicate finish.

Pedroncelli Winery   *1992 Dry Creek Valley Merlot*
Region: USA—California   **Suggested Retail: $10.00**
Availability: Good   **Golds: NW**

The wine is ruby red in color and rich in style. Its aroma is accented by cedar, black pepper, and blueberry. These components are combined with spicy oak, black cherry, and berry flavors on the palate. With depth and broad, mouth-filling flavors, the wine weaves together the best of the varietal. A lengthy finish is emphasized by medium tannins. The winemaker suggests serving it with osso bucco, roast leg of lamb, grilled Italian sausage and polenta, or Cornish game hens stuffed with fennel and wild rice.

Rabbit Ridge Vineyards   *1992 Sangiocomo Vineyards Merlot*
Region: USA—California   **Suggested Retail: $16.00**
Availability: Limited   **Golds: FF**

You'll find a rich, full-bodied Merlot with a velvety mouth feel, and notes of currants, berries, chocolate, and vanilla. This wine has an exceptionally long finish.
Special Award: *Chairman's Award (FF)*

Did You Know . . . ?
Until recently, South African winegrowers were restricted from importing high-quality vines to plant because of rigid quarantine laws. The next decade will be one to watch as the classic varieties mature.

Rodney Strong *1992 Sonoma County Merlot*
Region: USA—California   **Suggested Retail: $15.00**
Availability: NP   **Golds: PR**
The outstanding growing season of 1992 yielded Merlot grapes with intense varietal character and firm, well-balanced tannins. Handcrafted lots of Cabernet Sauvignon (15%) and Cabernet Franc (5%) enhance the wine's complexity and longevity. It has a velvety quality and is ideally suited to rich savory cheeses and flavorful meat dishes. "All in all, quite a seductive wine," according to the winemaker.

Stevenot Winery *1993 Sierra Foothills Reserve Merlot*
Region: USA—California   **Suggested Retail: $12.00**
Availability: Good   **Golds: IV, SD**
The winery was a bit skimpy with the description they provided, but there's nothing skimpy about the two gold medals awarded to this fabulous Merlot. Look for black cherry flavors with hints of vanilla, and soft tannins.

Storrs Winery *1993 San Ysidro Merlot*
Region: USA—California   **Suggested Retail: $17.00**
Availability: Limited   **Golds: CA**
Deep garnet with a purple edge, this Merlot has aromas of black cherries, ripe plum, black currant, and sweet oak, with an accent of granite. It is bold and full bodied, yet soft on the palate. It offers up generous fruit—black cherries, raspberry, and black currant—and soft vanilla, and is complex with a lush texture and firm tannins that permit aging.
Special Award: *Best Merlot of Appellation (CA)*

W.B. Bridgman *1993 Yakima Valley Merlot*
Region: USA—Washington   **Suggested Retail: $11.99**
Availability: Limited   **Golds: TC**
The fragrance of ripe black cherries and pomegranates is balanced with complex oak aromas. On the palate are well-developed fruit, oak, and supple tannins that subside gracefully through a long finish. Hearty meats and flavorful sauces are well matched to this full-flavored wine. Try it with rib roast and gravy.

Wellington Vineyards *1992 Merlot*
Region: USA—California   **Suggested Retail: $15.00**
Availability: Limited   **Golds: OC**
This wine has intense black cherry fruit, deep color, and is rich and full bodied with long aging potential.

Did You Know . . . ?
Does this tidbit fall under "medicine" or "marketing"? In the 1970s one French doctor began recommending wines (French, of course), from specific producers and vintages, to his patients for maladies ranging from cystitis to flatulence. La Tâche for la rash?

Whitehall Lane Winery *1992 Knights Valley Merlot*
Region: USA—California   **Suggested Retail: $16.00**
Availability: NP   **Golds: RE, OC**

Deep purple/black colors and gushing floral and fresh fruit flavors with excellent acid balance characterize this wine. It has full body and dense aromas and flavors.
Special Award: *Finalist for Sweepstakes Award, Red Wine (RE)*

Wild Horse Winery *1992 Central Coast Merlot*
Region: USA—California   **Suggested Retail: $14.00**
Availability: Good   **Golds: NW**

A medium-bodied wine with aromas of plum, tobacco, olive, pimento, and spice. On the palate this wine is round with modest tannin and flavors of plum and blueberry. Enjoyable now, this Merlot's fruit and richness will continue to develop with bottle aging. It nicely complements spicy Southwestern foods, as well as grilled chicken and vegetables.

Did You Know ... ?
Haven't wine and poetry *always* gone together? In the seventh century B.C., Archilochos wrote:

> Along the rowers' benches bring your cup
> And lift the lids of the big wine jars up
> And drain the good red wine: we can't, tis clear
> Be sober all the time we're watching here.

Andrew Will Winery   *1993 Washington Merlot*
Region: USA—Washington   **Suggested Retail: $20.00**
Availability: NP   **Golds: NE**
This wine has a relatively plush feel and a good structure. (The winery may have been a bit brief with their description, but know that some of the finest Merlots are now coming out of Washington State.) Since the expert judges loved it, you will too.

Beringer Vineyards   *1991 Bancroft Ranch Merlot*
Region: USA—California   **Suggested Retail: $28.00**
Availability: NP   **Golds: IV, NW**
This wine offers up ample aromas of black cherry fruit and cocoa, with herbs and oak adding complexity. A full-bodied, big-personality Merlot, it has layers of flavor, lots of ripeness, and a knock-out chocolate finish.
***Special Awards:** Best of Price Class (NW); Trophy for Best New World Merlot (NW)*

Château Ste. Michelle   *1992 Indian Wells Vineyard Merlot*
Region: USA—Washington   **Suggested Retail: $30.00**
Availability: NP   **Golds: NW**
Ripe, supple fruit characteristics are apparent in this vintage. A spectrum of lively oak notes is also present: vanilla, smoke, and spice. Here's a graceful wine with soft tannins and a supple mouth feel. The winery has a culinary director who recommends foods and dishes that this wine will complement. Among the herbs are basil, oregano, rosemary, and thyme—sounds like a Mediterranean chicken and pasta meal to us!

Dry Creek Vineyard   *1991 Estate Merlot*
Region: USA—California   **Suggested Retail: $20.00**
Availability: Limited   **Golds: CI**
Produced from a 12-acre estate vineyard adjacent to the winery, this 100% Merlot is rich with black cherry fruit and chocolate flavors. Its intense bouquet of spice and plum intermingles with hints of cinnamon and pear. A bold spiciness combines with rousing tannins and smoky oak to create a luxuriously textured wine. The balanced finish is elegant and velvety smooth. The judges said: "The deep color of the wine goes with an extremely appealing nose, with complex fruity, animal, and milky aromas. On the palate, it is still young, but very powerful. The good balance, length, and softness of the mellowed tannins provide for extremely pleasant drinking."
***Special Award:** Grand Prix d'Honneur (CI)*

Did You Know ... ?
The most common remains found of ancient grapes are the seeds, which were often charred at the time they fell to the ground. As charcoal these can be studied, since they remain recognizable for many thousands of years. Paleoethnobotanists scrutinize these seeds for hints about whether they were from wild or cultivated grapes, thus shedding light on ancient winemaking practices.

Gary Farrell Wines   *1992 Ladi's Vineyard Merlot*

Region: USA—California	**Suggested Retail: $20.00**
Availability: Limited	**Golds: OC, PR, SD, SO**

This wine is full bodied and rich with layers of black cherry, raspberry, and currant flavors throughout. While highly extracted and solid through its integrated, tannic backbone, the wine remains in balance and focused on its intense and unyielding fruit concentration. Although approachable and enjoyable in its youth, this Merlot will cellar beautifully for many years. In addition to multitudinous golds and extra honors, trophies, and awards, this one was named "Best Merlot of the Year" in Wine & Spirits *magazine.*

Special Awards: *Best of Class (PR); Grand Champion Wine (PR); Best Pacific Rim Red Wine (PR)*

Kendall-Jackson   *1992 California Grand Reserve Merlot*

Region: USA—California	**Suggested Retail: $30.00**
Availability: Limited	**Golds: FF**

Out of a field of 104, only 4 Merlots were awarded golds at Farmer's Fair, this being one of them. Pick up a bottle now! This one has intense flavors of blackberry, cassis, and "sweet" black cherry fruit, with notes of roasted nuts, coffee, brown sugar, and vanilla oak.

Special Award: *Chairman's Award (FF)*

Matanzas Creek Winery   *1992 Sonoma Valley Merlot*

Region: USA—California	**Suggested Retail: $30.00**
Availability: Good	**Golds: IW**

This young wine was remarkable from the start. Its toasty, rich oak blends nicely with loads of dense, spicy berry fruit.

Merryvale Vineyards   *1992 Napa Valley Merlot*

Region: USA—California	**Suggested Retail: $25.00**
Availability: Limited	**Golds: DA**

A very dense and concentrated wine, showing powerful elegance. Concentrated ripe fruit aromas emerge from the glass, with complex plummy, dried cherry, and cassis qualities, balanced with sweet vanilla undertones. Look for a very full palate sensation with rich and supple tannins, allowing for both a pleasant and long finish now and a promising future for those choosing to lay it down for many years.

Did You Know . . . ?

Literally rooted in the soil, wine is a way of life that involves capital, labor, and a complex distribution system. Because of its material and symbolic importance to culture, vineyards have always been particularly vulnerable during times of war. Ancient Greeks used to cut down and burn the vines of their enemies, and barbarian invaders of Roman Europe announced their victory in the same way.

Pine Ridge　*1993 Selected Cuvée Estate Bottled Merlot*
Region: USA—California　　　Suggested Retail: $18.00
Availability: NP　　　Golds: OC
You'll find raspberry and cherry aromas and flavors in this medium-bodied wine. It has excellent depth and a silky smooth texture. Drink it over the next 5 to 7 years.

Seven Hills Winery　*1993 Walla Walla Valley Merlot*
Region: USA—Washington　　　Suggested Retail: $20.00
Availability: Limited　　　Golds: OR
A very nicely balanced Merlot in an elegant style. This one has red cherry and raspberry notes that harmonize with delicate vanilla and spice from French and American oak.

Shafer Vineyards　*1993 Napa Valley Merlot*
Region: USA—California　　　Suggested Retail: $23.50
Availability: Good　　　Golds: RE, CA, FF, BT
Drawing complexity from diverse vineyard sources, this Merlot is aromatic with herbs and spice and jam-packed with ripe plum fruit on the palate. Cabernet Sauvignon (10%) contributes backbone, while a touch of Cabernet Franc (5%) enhances the wine's perfumy aromatics.
Special Awards: Double Gold (CA); Best Merlot of Appellation (CA)

Smith & Hook Winery　*1992 Santa Lucia Highlands Merlot*
Region: USA—California　　　Suggested Retail: $18.00
Availability: NP　　　Golds: NW
Fresh aromas of blackberries, cherries, cinnamon, and toasty oak are presented in the nose, as well as a touch of vanilla, and the flavors follow the aromas, complemented with a hint of currants and ripe plums. With soft, moderate tannins, this wine is approachable in its youth, yet will age well for 4 to 6 years.
Special Award: Best of Price Class (NW)

St. Francis Vineyards　*1992 Sonoma County Estate Bottled Merlot*
Region: USA—California　　　Suggested Retail: $18.00
Availability: Good　　　Golds: CA
This Merlot has typical richness and varietal character. Unblended and aged in French and American oak, and bottled unfined and unfiltered, it will develop further in the bottle, but can be enjoyed now.

Did You Know . . . ?

Trends in winemaking have been largely fueled by what's "in fashion" at the time. For example, the late twentieth century saw a worldwide, frenzied demand for international (as opposed to native) varietals. This led to the phenomenal prevalence of Cabernet Sauvignon and Chardonnay in virtually every winemaking region of the world.

Sterling Vineyards *1991 Three Palms Merlot*
Region: USA—California   **Suggested Retail: $22.00**
Availability: NP   **Golds: PR**
The aroma is reminiscent of raspberry and plum, and the palate is fleshy, with a fine, supple finish.

Stonestreet Winery *1992 Alexander Valley Merlot*
Region: USA—California   **Suggested Retail: $24.00**
Availability: NP   **Golds: IV**
The 1992 Merlot is rich, dark, and concentrated with complex aromas of plum, black cherry, berries, and spice, with soft tannins and deep color. But it is also a supple wine that is very approachable.

Swanson Vineyards *1993 Napa Valley Estate Merlot*
Region: USA—California   **Suggested Retail: $18.00**
Availability: Good   **Golds: OC**
This Merlot is intense and luscious, with aromas of black olive, dark cherry, vanilla, smoke, chocolate, and spice. The palate is rich, round, and soft, with complex flavors that persist through a long, supple finish. Though crafted for early appeal, the wine will reward several years' cellaring with additional depth and complexity.

Truchard Vineyards *1992 Carneros Merlot*
Region: USA—California   **Suggested Retail: $18.00**
Availability: Limited   **Golds: OC**
Look for floral aromas with violets, plum overlaid on spice, chocolate, and coffee. The wine offers up concentrated fruit in the mouth with plum and chocolate flavors dominating. It has good acidity followed by firm tannins that provide focus and length. This wine will continue to develop and hold for at least 10 years in the bottle.

Whitehall Lane Winery *1993 Napa Valley Merlot*
Region: USA—California   **Suggested Retail: $18.00**
Availability: NP   **Golds: SF**
This is a well-balanced wine with wonderful fruit and silky tannins. It is full bodied and dense with fruit aromas and flavors. It will age well into the next century.

Whitehall Lane Winery *1993 Leonardini Vineyard Merlot Reserve*
Region: USA—California   **Suggested Retail: $28.00**
Availability: Limited   **Golds: SF**
After 11 years of making Merlot from the Napa and Knights valleys, Whitehall Lane "has created possibly the finest Merlot to come out of the Napa Valley since 1985," according to the winemaker.

Did You Know . . . ?
Most of the devastating diseases and pests of *Vitis vinifera*, the species used for most fine wines, have been spread from the United States.

Augusta Winery *1992 Missouri Cynthiana*
Region: USA—Missouri   Suggested Retail: $14.99
Availability: Limited   Golds: FF
A dry red wine with full-bodied, intense flavors that's mouth filling and oak aged.

Chautauqua Vineyards *Semi-Sweet Noble*
Region: USA—Florida   Suggested Retail: $5.50
Availability: Limited   Golds: LA
This Floridian wine has medium depth and excellent clarity. It exhibits the powerful aroma and earthy complexity of the variety. The wine is medium bodied, with nice acid balance, berry and currant notes, and a long finish. On the beach after a beautiful meal, have it for dessert, and enjoy the hot sand between your toes.

Meier's Wine Cellars *NV American Concord*
Region: USA—Ohio   Suggested Retail: $3.95
Availability: Limited   Golds: DA
The essence of Concord is captured in this rich, flavorful, semisweet wine.

St. James Winery *1993 Missouri Norton*
Region: USA—Missouri   Suggested Retail: $10.99
Availability: Limited   Golds: PR, SD, NW, LB
The 1993 has opulent fruit on the nose with blackberries, black cherries, and a note of spice and coconut. Fermented to dryness in stainless-steel tanks and aged in 100 percent American oak, this full-bodied Missouri wine sings with red meat and pasta.

Stone Hill Wine Co. *1992 Estate Bottled Norton*
Region: USA—Missouri   Suggested Retail: $16.99
Availability: Limited   Golds: SF, PR
A robust deeply colored dry red wine with distinctive varietal flavor and aroma of the Norton grape variety. Ripe jammy fruit is framed by a touch of oak and subtle earthy notes. The mouth feel is full, yet soft tannins are reminiscent of some Merlots.
***Special Award:** Double Gold (SF); Best of Class (PR)*

Swedish Hill Vineyard *NV Svenska Red*
Region: USA—New York   Suggested Retail: $5.49
Availability: Good   Golds: SF, FL
The fresh, grapy aromas and flavors and semisweet finish make this fruity wine perfect for those who like the "puckery" taste of traditional, dry, oaky red wines. It is a blend of mostly native American grapes.

Did You Know . . . ?
"Scuppernongs," as Floridians call the fruity Muscadine grapes, a wild native variety that thrives in that state's humid, hot environment, are. the same grapes that produced America's first wine when French Huguenots controlled the area some 430 years ago.

Beringer Vineyards   *1993 North Coast Gamay Beaujolais*
Region: USA—California   Suggested Retail: $6.50
Availability: NP   Golds: NW
If you like your wines fruity, floral, light, and fun, you won't go wrong with this delicate beauty from Beringer. It is made to be consumed right away.
Special Award: *Best of Price Class (NW)*

Covey Run Vintners   *1993 Yakima Valley Lemberger*
Region: USA—Washington   Suggested Retail: $5.99
Availability: NP   Golds: WW
A medium-bodied red wine with fruity aromas and a cherry-berry character. Fresh and lively berry flavors dominate the palate. Look for smoothness and low tannins.

Fetzer   *1994 California Gamay Beaujolais*
Region: USA—California   Suggested Retail: $6.99
Availability: NP   Golds: CA
Fresh aromas of strawberry jam and sweet spice are followed by lightly sweet cherry and berry fruit flavors. This is especially refreshing served chilled.
Special Award: *Best Gamay of Appellation (CA)*

Geyser Peak Winery   *1994 Sonoma County Gamay Beaujolais*
Region: USA—California   Suggested Retail: $8.00
Availability: NP   Golds: PR, CL
Like all of the best Gamay Beaujolais wines (usually blends, in this case Pinot Noir, Syrah, and Petite Sirah), this one is fresh, fruity, and light in style. In other words, you don't have to be a Rhodes scholar to appreciate it, which we have to admit we like. Serve it slightly chilled.
Special Award: *Best of Class (CL)*

Glen Ellen Winery   *1994 Proprietor's Reserve Gamay Beaujolais*
Region: USA—California   Suggested Retail: $5.00
Availability: Very Good   Golds: LA, IE
This is a light, flavorful wine with hints of boysenberry and roasted coffee. Aromas of boysenberry mingled with undertones of mint characterize the nose of this fruity wine. The flavors reflect a nice balance of fresh cherry and boysenberry, and the mouth feel is full, with a light, flavorful finish. The winery sent us availability data by the gallon rather than by the case. At this wonderful price, it sounds like a wine to drink gallons of.

Did You Know ... ?

Ampelographers, whose precise science it is to identify different grape varieties, have turned the wine industry on its head several times. Their discovery that Gamay Beaujolais and Napa Gamay are different varieties, and unrelated to the French Gamay, set wineries scratching their heads on how to market their New World "Gamay."

Lakeview Cellars *1993 Baco Noir VQA*
Region: Canada   **Suggested Retail: $9.95**
Availability: NP   **Golds: IV**
The 1993 shows the deepest purple color, with full body, and good tannins and acid. The bouquet expresses a complexity of berries, smokiness, leather, and chocolate. It will cellar well and makes a nice accompaniment to lamb, game, and spicy foods.

Parducci Winery *1991 Mendocino Charbono*
Region: USA—California   **Suggested Retail: $7.00**
Availability: Limited   **Golds: CA**
The color of this wine is a superb, inky purple-red. It has spicy berry aromas, is pleasantly tart with fruity flavors, and has a very long aftertaste.
***Special Award:** Best Other Red Varietals of Appellation (CA)*

Pedroncelli Winery *1992 Sonoma County Gamay Beaujolais*
Region: USA—California   **Suggested Retail: $7.00**
Availability: Good   **Golds: NW**
Look for a ruby red color and aromas of black pepper and berries. Blackberry fruit and pepper flavors highlight the taste, and the fruitiness characteristic of this varietal is carried through to a rounded finish. Light tannins give the wine some backbone.

Preston Vineyards *1994 Estate Bottled Gamay Beaujolais*
Region: USA—California   **Suggested Retail: $8.25**
Availability: NP   **Golds: DA**
With brilliant crimson color, this wine has fresh, lively cranberry aromas that are highlighted by floral and strawberry notes. It is soft and round on the palate with a crisp finish. Drink it over the next 2 years.

Rabbit Ridge Vineyards *1992 "Allure"*
Region: USA—California   **Suggested Retail: $7.00**
Availability: NP   **Golds: OC**
This wine has smoky, cherry flavors with hints of cinnamon and anise. It is medium bodied with a nice fruit finish.

Did You Know . . . ?
University of California at Davis's Department of Viticulture and Enology developed the "Aroma Wheel," a visual tool to help novices identify and understand the various smells found in wine. The center ring has broad categories such as Fruity and Earthy. The next ring out gets more narrow, for example "Fruity" is further divided into "Tropical Fruit" and "Citrus." Around the outside of the wheel are the most specific terms of all. "Tropical Fruit" is described by "Apple, Pineapple, Melon." Every great wine book (besides this one) has a reprint of Ann Noble's Aroma Wheel. Pick up a copy and check it out.

Audubon Collection   *1993 Harris Vineyard Carignane*
Region: USA—California **Suggested Retail: $10.00**
Availability: Limited **Golds: CA**
Ripe plum and cherry flavors intermingle with hints of black pepper and fresh herbs. This Carignane is bright and fruity with soft tannins for current drinkability.

Château Julien   *1993 California Mourvèdre*
Region: USA—California **Suggested Retail: $14.00**
Availability: NP **Golds: LA**
Rich, mouth filling, yet soft, this Mourvèdre has cherry, berry, plum, and licorice flavors and aromas. Dark purple edges and deep fruit slightly hint of Petite Sirah. According to the winemaker, this is "a statement wine," strikingly different from other reds and ready for drinking now.
Special Award: *Best of Class (LA)*

Cline Cellars   *1990 Contra Costa Mourvèdre*
Region: USA—California **Suggested Retail: $14.00**
Availability: Limited **Golds: NW**
This wine is full and rich with flavors of dark cherries and chocolate, herbs, violets, and anise, and has a long, lingering vanilla finish.
Special Award: *Best of Price Class (NW)*

Hart Winery   *1992 California Mourvèdre*
Region: USA—California **Suggested Retail: $12.00**
Availability: Limited **Golds: PR**
Expect a soft style with a hint of smoke and cranberries. This Rhône grape has a typical light brownish-red color. Vines that are 110 years old (!) make a more concentrated flavor.

La Motte   *1991 La Motte Millenium*
Region: South Africa **Suggested Retail: $11.85**
Availability: NP **Golds: CI**
South Africa is an up-and-coming winemaking region to keep your eyes open to since the political strife of the past few decades has come to a resolution, at least for now. This wine has a forward and robust style with assertive black currant and plummy fruit, and nice undertones of oak. It is available in the United States.

Did You Know...?
The Smithsonian Institution in Washington has placed bottles of the winning wines from the legendary Paris Tasting of twenty years ago in its permanent collection. The aftershocks from the Paris Tasting, where two California wines took first place in the red and white categories against Burgundy's and Bordeaux's most revered wines, were so great that the wine media still talks about it. It put California on the fine-wine map permanently.

Rabbit Ridge Vineyards *1992 Heoin Vineyard Carignane*
Region: USA—California　　　**Suggested Retail: $11.00**
Availability: Limited　　　　**Golds: PR, FF**
Look for big, bold fruit up front with a very dry finish and chocolate, tobacco, pepper, and spice aromas.

Ridge Vineyards and Winery *1992 Evangelo Vineyard Mataro*
Region: USA—California　　　**Suggested Retail: $15.50**
Availability: Good　　　　　**Golds: OC**
Mataro is another name for Mourvèdre. Here's a purple-tinged ruby wine with a nose of blackberry and roasted marshmallow and a substrata of plum, saddle leather, hay, pepper, and yeast. It is smooth in the mouth with clove, spice, and balanced blackberry/plum fruit. There is a slight gaminess in its layered, lingering finish. It's very drinkable now, although it will develop for the next 3 to 5 years.

Rosenblum Cellars *1993 TLK Ranch Carignane*
Region: USA—California　　　**Suggested Retail: $10.00**
Availability: Limited　　　　**Golds: RE, OC, FF**
Here's a medium-bodied, fruity wine that shows a bouquet of ripe plum and rose petal with hints of violets and cream. The flavors are cherry, plum, and cream with nuances of spice. The judges loved this one!
Special Awards: Finalist for Sweepstakes Award, Red Wine (RE); Chairman's Award (FF)

Sebastiani Vineyards *1992 Mourvèdre*
Region: USA—California　　　**Suggested Retail: $15.00**
Availability: Limited　　　　**Golds: CA**
The source of this Mourvèdre is from 50- to 70-year-old vines. It has a nose of currants, jam, young port, and woody, barklike notes. In the mouth the black cherry flavors come alive. The wine finishes with smooth tannins, flavors of roasted walnuts, and just a hint of chocolate. Try it with Italian and Provençal dishes, as well as Mexican and Middle Eastern cuisine.
Special Award: Best Mourvèdre of Appellation (CA)

Weinstock Cellars *1994 Paso Robles Napa Gamay*
Region: USA—California　　　**Suggested Retail: $15.99**
Availability: Good　　　　　**Golds: LA, TG**
Look for a deep purple-red color with intense cranberry, cotton candy, and blackberry aromas. This wine can be enjoyed at either room temperature or out of the refrigerator, as one would serve a white wine. Drink it while it's young.

Did You Know ... ?
Hydrogen fluoride, found in air pollution, has reduced vineyard yields in many countries. Mourvèdre is particularly sensitive to this kind of pollution.

Geyser Peak Winery   *1993 Alexander Valley Petit Verdot*
Region: USA—California   **Suggested Retail: $20.00**
Availability: NP   **Golds: LA, NW**
This beauty is available only if you visit the tasting rooms of Geyser Peak. We're not sure why this is so, but if you should happen to be in Sonoma County, give them a call at (800) 945-4447 and have a few sips of this out-of-the-ordinary wine made from a variety that's often used in Bordeaux, France, to add color and depth to the wines produced there.

Geyser Peak Winery   *1993 Winemaker's Selection Malbec*
Region: USA—California   **Suggested Retail: $20.00**
Availability: NP   **Golds: CA, LA, NW, SO, MO**
Very few vintners are producing Malbec these days, so kudos should go to Geyser Peak for doing something off the beaten track—and obviously doing it well.
Special Awards: *Best Other Red Varietals of Appellation (CA); Double Gold (SO); Double Gold (MO)*

Jekel Vineyards   *1992 Arroyo Seco Sanctuary Estate Malbec*
Region: USA—California   **Suggested Retail: $35.00**
Availability: NP   **Golds: NW**
Here's a massive wine packed with blackberry, olalliberry, and grape jam flavors along with vanilla, nutmeg, violets, and toasty oak. This wine needs several years to soften and will continue to mature for at least a decade. It will complement your most intensely flavored red meat dishes.

Jekel Vineyards   *1992 Sanctuary Estate Petit Verdot*
Region: USA—California   **Suggested Retail: $35.00**
Availability: NP   **Golds: NW**
Jekel's winemaker, Rick Boyce, believes that his role is to "preserve and enhance natural and distinctive attributes and character specific to each grape variety." This is a soft wine with deep red color and lovely ripe cherry and raspberry aromas with hints of earth. French oak provides a complement of sweet toasty vanilla and helps develop the wine's smooth, velvety texture. Try it with roasted game foul or delicate cuts of beef.
Special Award: *Best of Price Class (NW)*

Prince Michel Vineyard   *1989 Lot 89 Le Ducq Red*
Region: USA—Virginia   **Suggested Retail: $55.00**
Availability: Limited   **Golds: IV**
This wine displays complex red fruit aromas reminiscent of black cherry, cassis, and mulberry. The bouquet is firm and deep with strong toasty, vanillin barrel notes. On the palate the fruit is pleasantly integrated with the vanilla bean influence from the oak. This wine should last 10 years or more. A Virginia gold? We can't wait to try it.

Did You Know . . . ?
Geyser Peak's Trione family loves polo so much that the Peak is the official sponsor of the U.S. Polo Association.

Bogle Vineyard   *1993 California Petite Sirah*
Region: USA—California   **Suggested Retail: $7.00**
Availability: Good   **Golds: FF**
This is a deep ruby wine with aromas of cherries, violets, and cedar. Jammy blackberry and plum flavors are accented with subtle black pepper and spice. A full-bodied, concentrated wine, this one has soft, lush tannins. By the way, Wine Spectator *has named this wine a Best Buy two years in a row.*
Special Award: *Chairman's Award (FF)*

Colorado Cellars   *1993 Petite Sirah*
Region: USA—Colorado   **Suggested Retail: $8.00**
Availability: Limited   **Golds: TG, IE**
An extremely rich, robust, dry red wine with an intense dark—almost black—color. It is full bodied, with a raspberry nose and black pepper highlighting the nose and flavor components. Try a gold medal winner from Colorado for a change.

Concannon   *1992 Reserve Petite Sirah*
Region: USA—California   **Suggested Retail: $9.95**
Availability: Limited   **Golds: PR, HH, GH**
This full-bodied wine has blackberry, black cherry, blueberry, and currant aromas and flavors with pepper, earth, vanilla, oak, light tea, and tobacco undertones—all ending in a lengthy finish. One reviewer called it "outstanding." A Wine Enthusiast *Cellar Selection, rated 91.*

Parducci Winery   *1992 Petite Sirah*
Region: USA—California   **Suggested Retail: $7.00**
Availability: Good   **Golds: OC**
Parducci's philosophy is to produce reds that reflect the best in the varietal. One of the winemaker's favorites, this one is minimally filtered so that wine lovers can taste the quality and complexity of the vintage and the winemaker's art. It is full bodied and has fruit that is earthy and concentrated. The 1993 vintage also won a gold.

Parducci Winery   *1993 California Petite Sirah*
Region: USA—California   **Suggested Retail: $8.00**
Availability: Very Good   **Golds: LA**
Parducci was one of the first wineries to bottle Petite Sirah as a varietal. Here's a full-bodied wine with complex aromas, possessing rich, earthy fruit. The varietal flavors are well balanced by moderate tannins. This exceptional wine is delicious with turkey or pork.
Special Award: *Best of Class (LA)*

Did You Know . . . ?
Colorado's Grand Valley, nestled in the Rockies, has about a dozen wineries that are producing delicious wines some say are reminiscent of Washington State's.

Deer Park Winery *1990 Howell Mountain Petite Sirah*
Region: USA—California   Suggested Retail: $16.00
Availability: Limited   Golds: PR
A rich, full-bodied wine with intense varietal character, including a peppery spiciness. This one is an excellent candidate for extended cellaring.

Fetzer *1991 Petite Sirah Reserve*
Region: USA—California   Suggested Retail: $12.99
Availability: NP   Golds: OC, SD
Deep and dark in color with dense wild berry and currant aromas and flavors, this wine has undertones of jam, black pepper, and oaky spice that add seductive complexity.
Special Award: Best of Class (SD)

Foppiano Vineyards *1991 Reserve Napa Valley Petite Sirah*
Region: USA—California   Suggested Retail: $20.00
Availability: Limited   Golds: RE
A wonderful, heavy-bodied, tannic wine. Spicy fruit aromas combine with rich flavors in a full, smooth body from old vines. If stored properly, the wine should last 15 to 20 years.

Guenoc Estate *1991 North Coast Petite Sirah*
Region: USA—California   Suggested Retail: $13.50
Availability: Good   Golds: OC, LA, NW, FL, CL, CN, HH, TN
We barely have space to fit in all the golds this wine won. Full and packed with fruit, the opulent, seductive scent of delicate tropical flowers on a bed of chocolate and black cherries lends an exotic touch to this Petite Sirah. Deep earth flavors seem to linger in a finish burnished with crushed fresh pepper and vanilla. Its touch of soft wildness makes it an ideal companion to lamb, venison, or pheasant, as well as chili or blackened foods. Or try it with bittersweet chocolate.
Special Awards: Best of Class (LA); Trophy for Best New World Red Wine (NW); Best of Price Class (NW)

Guenoc Estate *1992 North Coast Petite Sirah*
Region: USA—California   Suggested Retail: $13.50
Availability: Good   Golds: CA, SF, FF, AT
Bright purple hues with aromas of blackberry and cherry backed with a smoky, coffee bouquet characterize this wine. Easy and round in the mouth, this full-bodied, rich, and complex wine is a perfect match for braised and grilled beef or roasted poultry. The judges at California State Fair were gaga over it.
Special Awards: Best Wine of Region (CA); Best Petite Sirah of Appellation (CA); Runner Up for Best of Show (CA)

Did You Know . . . ?
The percentage of Americans who abstain from drinking alcoholic beverages is 30 percent.

Latcham Vineyards *1992 El Dorado Petite Sirah*

Region: USA—California   Suggested Retail: $13.50
Availability: Limited   Golds: NW

This is a rich, dark purple wine with classic black pepper aromas. Wonderfully mellow with an excellent balance of intense black cherry and berry fruit, black pepper, and oak, this one is rich and full bodied with a brilliant nose and finish.

Lolonis Wine Cellars *1991 Orpheus Petite Sirah*

Region: USA—California   Suggested Retail: $16.00
Availability: NP   Golds: NW

The power and inky tannin of this Redwood Valley Petite Sirah are balanced by the inclusion of very fruity, floral elements of Napa Gamay (20%). The Napa Gamay was produced by whole berry fermentation (carbonic maceration), which adds a particular perfume to the wine. The vines are organically grown since 1956.

Mirassou Vineyards *1992 140th Anniversary Petite Sirah*

Region: USA—California   Suggested Retail: $13.50
Availability: Limited   Golds: OC

The nose opens with rich, forward blueberry fruit components within a background of black pepper and French oak. On the palate the blueberry characters are balanced against the firm, but not aggressive, tannin structure, adding grace to the underlying strength of the wine.

Storrs Winery *1993 Santa Cruz Mountains Petite Sirah*

Region: USA—California   Suggested Retail: $16.00
Availability: Limited   Golds: RE, CA

The color is deep purple-black. The nose is jam-packed with ripe black raspberry and cherry fruit, with accents of pepper, spice, and moderate oak. It is full bodied on the palate with a lush texture and generous flavors of black cherry, olallieberry, and notes of vanilla. Supple tannins under the fruit promise a long life ahead.
Special Awards: *Best Wine of Region (CA); Best Petite Sirah of Appellation (CA)*

Windsor Vineyards *1992 North Coast Petite Sirah*

Region: USA—California   Suggested Retail: $10.17
Availability: Good   Golds: RE, TG

This wine is soft and round and has a deep garnet color with lush blackberry-pepper flavors and smoky aromas.

Did You Know . . . ?

The *Oxford Companion to Wine* makes a compelling argument against those who claim that Petite Sirah is actually the little-known French grape, Durif. Since Petite Sirah showed up in California wine literature in the early 1880s, and since Durif had hardly been propagated in France at that time, it's nearly impossible that they're one and the same variety.

Cartlidge & Browne *1993 Pinot Noir*
Region: USA—California   **Suggested Retail: $7.50**
Availability: Limited   **Golds: OC**

A lighter style of Pinot Noir with developed aromas of black cherry and hints of anise and clove, this wine has charred, bacony oak, and exotic mocha spices to boot. Made from a lush blend of Ruby Cabernet, Carignane, and Grenache, it is extremely versatile as a companion to food, ideal for lunches, picnics, and barbecues—a refreshing alternative to light whites or heavier reds. The winemaker suggests serving it slightly chilled. Its texture is dense and firm, yet its tannins are soft enough to make for very enjoyable drinking now. If your local wine merchant doesn't carry this one, order it directly from the winery at (800) 946-3635.

Napa Ridge Winery *1993 North Coast Pinot Noir*
Region: USA—California   **Suggested Retail: $7.50**
Availability: Very Good   **Golds: IV, DA, NW, TN**

Look for delicate cherry and berry flavors in this Pinot Noir. Here's a wine with vibrant fruit but soft tannins, at a price that absolutely no one can complain of.

Villa Mt. Eden *1993 Cellar Select Pinot Noir*
Region: USA—California   **Suggested Retail: $8.00**
Availability: Limited   **Golds: OC**

Fruit and spice aromas treat the nose to a velvety ride that suggests cranapple, leather, and smoke. These elegant aromas carry through to the palate where ripe cherries, dairy cream, cocoa, and a hint of mint taper to a lingering, strawberry cream finish. Try it with smoked fowl, richly sauced pasta dishes, or salmon.

Willamette Valley Vineyards *1993 Oregon Pinot Noir*
Region: USA—Oregon   **Suggested Retail: $9.00**
Availability: NP   **Golds: NW**

The wine is dark ruby/purple and has flavors and aromas of berries and earth, with spicy undertones and a medium body and firm tannins. The 1994 Whole Berry Fermented Pinot Noir was also a gold medal winner, so it's doubtful that any Pinot from this winery will disappoint.

York Mountain Winery *1991 San Luis Obispo County Pinot Noir*
Region: USA—California   **Suggested Retail: $6.00**
Availability: Limited   **Golds: LA, NW**

Cherries and violets are the main aroma components with a nice toasty oak background. This medium-bodied Pinot accompanies lamb, beef, and even salmon very well—and what a price! The winery was established in 1882, which is quite old for an American winery.
Special Award: *Best of Price Class (NW)*

Did You Know ... ?
Increasingly, great American chefs are steering away from automatically recommending those same old whites to accompany their seafood creations. Pinot Noir, apparently, is the darling of the new American seafood chefs.

Acacia Winery   *1993 Carneros Pinot Noir*
Region: USA—California   **Suggested Retail: $15.00**
Availability: Very Good   **Golds: LA**

This wine is deep in color and ripe in character. It is complex yet delicate, with black cherry, plum, and cranberry notes hinting of cinnamon and toast. The optimum time to drink it is now through 1999. You might call matching food with Pinot Noir a no-brainer—at least according to the winemaker, who says that "it supports the delicate and tames the strong."

Beaulieu   *1993 Carneros Pinot Noir*
Region: USA—California   **Suggested Retail: $11.99**
Availability: NP   **Golds: SD**

The beautiful ruby red color of this wine matches well with the red raspberry and cherry fruit aromas. The wine also displays a distinct minty and spicy character unique to Carneros, as well as a vanilla and toasty oak character from the barrels. With a soft mouth feel and long finish, this Pinot Noir is very inviting today, but it will age well for another 3 to 8 years easily.

Brindiamo   *1993 Edna Valley Pinot Noir*
Region: USA—California   **Suggested Retail: $12.00**
Availability: Good   **Golds: NW**

Depending on climate, growing conditions, clonal selections, and viticultural practices combined with winemaking techniques, the nuances of Burgundy, California, or Oregon Pinot Noir become vastly different. This one reflects many of the best attributes of Pinot Noir. Beautiful color extract and intense berry and rose petal aromas, a nice balance of tannins and fruit character, and a subtle kiss of oak make this an elegant and complex wine.

Byron Vineyard   *1993 Santa Barbara County Pinot Noir*
Region: USA—California   **Suggested Retail: $16.00**
Availability: Good   **Golds: LA**

Complex and seductive, this wine possesses a profound richness and opulence. Lush, sweet fruit tones with a hint of red cherry are harmoniously intermingled with the right touch of French oak. While ready to drink now, the pronounced fruit expression and intricate nature of this wine suggest excellent aging potential.

Did You Know . . . ?

While Cabernet Sauvignons all over the world share some recognizable characteristics, it's harder to pin down varietal character for Pinot Noirs, other than a certain sweet fruitiness, in general, and lower levels of tannins and pigments than the other "great" French red varieties. Part of this wide variation lies in Pinot's genetic makeup. It is a particularly old vine variety, in all probability a selection from wild vines made by man at least two thousand years ago. In other words, it's had a lot of time to mutate. There's strong evidence that Pinot existed in Burgundy in the fourth century A.D.

Camelot Winery *1993 Central Coast Pinot Noir*
Region: USA—California **Suggested Retail: $12.00**
Availability: NP **Golds: OC, LA, DA**
The aroma combines black cherry and plum fruit with hints of cedar and nutmeg. Harmonious and mouth filling, the graceful black cherry fruit is nicely supported by the toasty oak complexity derived from aging in small oak barrels, with both elements contributing to the lingering finish.

Château Souverain *1993 Winemaker's Reserve Pinot Noir*
Region: USA—California **Suggested Retail: $16.00**
Availability: NP **Golds: IV**
Medium red garnet in color, the 1993 Pinot Noir has bright strawberry jam, cherry, and cola aromas backed by smoky, toasty oak notes. The tannins are already soft and silky, and are balanced by moderate adicity. The flavor and finish are rich and varietal with a concentrated character that is typical of cool-climate Carneros Pinot Noir, and enhanced by the carbonic storage technique.

Château St. Jean *1992 Sonoma County Pinot Noir*
Region: USA—California **Suggested Retail: $14.00**
Availability: NP **Golds: SD, NW**
The nose of this Pinot Noir is opulent and complex, full of ripe cherries with hints of plum, spice, and violet. The wine is rich and mouth filling with intense flavors of cherries, plums, and tea roses, and finishes with a warm complement of French oak toast. Look at all the extra kudos it received from the judges!
Special Awards: *Best of Class (SD); Best of Price Class (NW); Trophy for Best New World Pinot Noir (NW)*

Coldstream Hills *1993 Reserve Pinot Noir*
Region: Australia **Suggested Retail: $9.99 CAN**
Availability: Outside USA **Golds: RM**
This is a medium red wine with plum and cinnamon aromas and flavors predominating. On the palate it is harmonious and balanced, and deceptively light. The finish is long; the aftertaste lingers. This wine can be cellared for 1 to 4 years, and the winemaker recommends serving it with, among other things, Asian dishes. Coldstream Hills exports to you lucky Canadians, as well as to Europe, Hong Kong, Singapore, Japan, Thailand, Indonesia, Taiwan, and New Zealand—but alas, not to the United States.

Did You Know . . . ?
Heard enough bad news about ozone in the atmosphere? Here's more. Ozone from air pollution causes a condition known as oxidant stipple, which forms lesions on the upper surfaces of the grape leaf. This happens next to heavily industrialized areas, and has been detected and studied in California and New York vineyards. The economic effects of this pollution have yet to be determined.

Coldstream Hills　*1991 Pinot Noir*
Region: Australia　　　　　　　**Suggested Retail: $16.99 CAN**
Availability: Outside USA　　　**Golds: AU**

This purple-red Pinot Noir has a full, complex bouquet with strong plummy fruit and a touch of gaminess. On the palate it has strong, spicy fruit with depth and complexity. It is fruit- rather than oak-driven, although there is a touch of spicy oak. Cellar it for 1 to 5 years. You can buy this one if you live in Canada, Europe, New Zealand, the Far East, or the UK.

Creston Vineyard　*1993 Paso Robles Pinot Noir*
Region: USA—California　　　　**Suggested Retail: $12.00**
Availability: Limited　　　　　**Golds: RE**

This elegant red wine was produced primarily by the carbonic maceration method. After hand harvesting, the grapes were gently placed into open-top fermenters to initiate the 10-day whole-berry fermentation. The wine spent 9 months in older French oak barrels, and has intense, spicy Pinot Noir aromas. It is ready to drink now but will develop gracefully with further bottle aging.
Special Award: *Sweepstakes Award, Red Wine (RE)*

David Bruce Winery　*1993 Vintner's Select Pinot Noir*
Region: USA—California　　　　**Suggested Retail: $12.00**
Availability: NP　　　　　　　**Golds: IV, SD, TG**

David Bruce is written about and praised by every wine writer, in every wine magazine you can think of. His 1993 Vintner's Select is yet another gold medal Pinot Noir, and has toasty oak, smoky bacony notes, herb suggestions, and a touch of roasted grain. The combination of aromas is unique, and gives way to medium-deep fruit, spice, and herbs in the mouth. It is supple now, but could benefit from 3 to 4 years in the cellar—if you can wait that long!
Special Award: *Best of Class (SD)*

Edna Valley Vineyard　*1993 Estate Bottled Pinot Noir*
Region: USA—California　　　　**Suggested Retail: $15.00**
Availability: Good　　　　　　**Golds: OC**

This wine has an abundant, perfumed, raspberrylike fruitiness with hazelnut and vanilla flavors. It is ready to drink now and will continue to improve for the next 5 to 8 years.

Did You Know . . . ?
It seems there are a surprising number of winemakers who are currently or formerly of the medical profession. David Bruce, of the eponymous winery, is one of them. He's a Santa Cruz dermatologist. Our theory is that these were kids who loved to blow up chemicals in their basement beakers while Mom was cooking dinner upstairs. Now they can satisfy their lust for alchemy while making a dual contribution to our quality of life.

Fess Parker Winery   *1993 Santa Barbara County Pinot Noir*
Region: USA—California   **Suggested Retail: $15.00**
Availability: NP   **Golds: CA, PR**
Here's a high-class winery that's producing golds year after year. We didn't get tasting notes for this wine, but considering the competitions it won golds in, as well as the special awards conferred upon it, we don't think you'll miss with this Pinot Noir.
Special Awards: *Best Pinot Noir of Appellation (CA); Best of Class (PR)*

Fetzer   *1992 Barrel Select North Coast Pinot Noir*
Region: USA—California   **Suggested Retail: $12.99**
Availability: NP   **Golds: CA**
Flavors of oak-spice and dried cherries combine with minty vanilla to create a superb wine that is infinitely versatile on the table.
Special Award: *Double Gold (CA); Best Pinot Noir of Appellation (CA)*

Fetzer   *1992 Olivet Lane Vineyard Reserve Pinot Noir*
Region: USA—California   **Suggested Retail: $16.99**
Availability: NP   **Golds: SD, FF**
Here's a stylish Russian River Pinot Noir, a rich wine with classic varietal flavor intensity: cherry fruit and tomato-herbal qualities enhanced by vanilla spice and fresh strawberry complexities.

Greenwood Ridge   *1993 Pinot Noir Anderson Valley*
Region: USA—California   **Suggested Retail: $15.00**
Availability: Limited   **Golds: RE**
The smoky bouquet of toasted oak enhances sweet strawberry and cherry aromas and soft, ripe, fruity flavors. This Pinot Noir can be enjoyed as an aperitif or with lightly sauced meat, grilled chicken, or pork.

Magnotta Winery   *1991 Pinot Noir Limited Edition*
Region: Canada   **Suggested Retail: $10.75**
Availability: NP   **Golds: IW, BT**
This full-bodied Burgundy-style wine has peppery, vanilla overtones. It is slightly smoky with wood flavors from the oak aging. Plentiful fruit is surrounded by earthy, mushroomlike flavors. Try it with duck pâté, old cheeses, and liver, lamb, or pork.

Did You Know . . . ?
The size of the berry is considered essential to the quality of the wine. The best-quality wine varieties have small grapes, and thus a higher skin-to-volume ratio. After all, it is the skins of the grapes, not the flesh, that contribute most of the flavor and aroma compounds, as well as the color.

Navarro   *1991 Anderson Valley Méthode Ancienne Pinot Noir*
Region: USA—California   Suggested Retail: $15.00
Availability: Limited   Golds: FF, SY, TG, IE
This lighter-bodied Pinot competed and won a gold in Sydney, Australia, among other places. It has ripe cherry and plum aromas with flavors of cherry-raspberry supported by sweet oak.

Robert Mondavi   *1993 Unfiltered Napa Valley Pinot Noir*
Region: USA—California   Suggested Retail: $15.00
Availability: Very Good   Golds: CA
This Pinot Noir has bright cherry and raspberry flavors layered with hints of sweet spices and oak. It has a rich, velvety texture with a long silky finish.

Rodney Strong   *1993 River East Vineyard Pinot Noir*
Region: USA—California   Suggested Retail: $16.00
Availability: NP   Golds: CA
Ripe with scents and flavors of red cherry, the wine is elegant and has a silky finish with a hint of creamy vanilla and smoky toasty oak in the bouquet.
Special Awards: *Best Pinot Noir of California (CA); Tie for Best Pinot Noir of Appellation (CA)*

Schug Carneros Estate   *1993 Carneros Pinot Noir*
Region: USA—California   Suggested Retail: $16.00
Availability: Limited   Golds: SD
Look for a bouquet of cherries, berries, and spicy, smoky oak with a hint of mint on the finish. Flavors of cherries and spice, a silky texture, and a long finish are framed by delicate oak nuances. It will improve with additional cellaring for 5 to 7 years.

Villa Mt. Eden   *1993 Grand Reserve Carneros Pinot Noir*
Region: USA—California   Suggested Retail: $16.00
Availability: Limited   Golds: PR, NW, OC, SF
Supple and lush, velvety bright fruit permeates the wine. Pinot Noir's elusive characters charm, tease, and entertain. This rendition of cherry-plum, spiced fruit makes the search for Pinot Noir, the winemaker's "Holy Grail," an enviable one. Try it with firm cheeses, blackened fish, rich sauces, pheasant, and smoked duck.
Special Award: *Double Gold (SF)*

Willamette Valley Vineyards   *1994 Whole Berry Ferm. Pinot Noir*
Region: USA—Oregon   Suggested Retail: $11.50
Availability: NP   Golds: OR
Robert Parker says the Whole Berry Fermented Pinots from this vineyard "may be the world's most delicious and accessible Pinot Noir." It has deep color, powerful raspberry-cherry fruit aromas, soft and subtle flavors, and a smooth, silky finish.

Did You Know . . . ?
The Greek physician Hippocrates recommended drinking wine as part of a healthy diet. He also used it as a disinfectant on wounds.

Ata Rangi Vineyard *1993 Pinot Noir*
Region: New Zealand   **Suggested Retail: $25.00 NZ**
Availability: Outside USA   **Golds: IW**
The nose yields a sweet, succulent, plummy fragrance laced with clovy oak and a suggestion of gamey notes, which are still to develop. On the palate are fine soft tannins and an explosion of layers of flavor. Because of Ata Rangi's increasing fame, Americans should be able to find this one very soon.
Special Award: *Trophy for Best Pinot Noir (IW)*

Ata Rangi Vineyard *1994 Pinot Noir*
Region: New Zealand   **Suggested Retail: $25.00 NZ**
Availability: Outside USA   **Golds: NZ**
Talk about consistency! Ata Rangi's Pinot Noirs have won golds since the 1991 vintage. Although it was not available in the United States at press time, export inquiries are running hot, according to the owners, so Americans take note, and keep checking the New Zealand section of your wine shop. The winemaker describes this one as having a nose that is lifted and aromatic—a spicy potpourri of cherry-chocolate, sweet tobacco, and roses. The wine has very good structure, with a full, supple palate and a fruity sweetness. There are hints of the savory complexities that will further develop over the next 3 to 4 years.
Special Award: *Trophy for Best Pinot Noir (NZ)*

Coldstream Hills *1994 Reserve Pinot Noir*
Region: Australia   **Suggested Retail: $31.00 CAN**
Availability: Outside USA   **Golds: SY, AD**
Here are some excerpts from some of the Sydney judges: "deep in color with a pungently smoky, almost charry oak nose"; "savory, with cherry flavors"; "complex bouquet with almost Oriental spiciness"; "lively acid, good balance." Lucky Canadians can buy this wine, which is also available in the UK, Europe, the Far East, and New Zealand.
Special Award: *Best Pinot Noir (SY and AD)*

Cosentino *1993 Unfined Unfiltered Punch Cap Fermented Pinot Noir*
Region: USA—California   **Suggested Retail: $18.00**
Availability: Limited   **Golds: LA, NW**
Cosentino, according to their winemaker, might be the best-kept secret in Pinot Noir. "Very few know that we make this varietal. Those who do follow our Pinot Noir releases selfishly and do not want to share, as production is small and the wines are sold on an extremely limited basis." You heard it from the source. Now don't you want to find this wine? The judges obviously thought it was tops.
Special Award: *Best of Class (LA); Best of Price Class (NW)*

Did You Know . . . ?
Are you *determined* to try a great Pinot Noir from New Zealand? Then mail order it! Ata Rangi's fax is 06 306 9523. See also Appendix 3 for mail-order vendors who can handle the odd exotic request.

David Bruce Winery   *1992 Estate Reserve Pinot Noir*

Region: USA—California   **Suggested Retail: $33.00**
Availability: NP   **Golds: OC, SF, TG, BT, GH, IE**

The awards, recommendations, Best Buys, and general kudos for this wine are too numerous to list here. Just know that this is a winner, and run out a buy a bottle! Sweet oak mingling with dark, intense red fruits combine to create a complex, concentrated wine that has layers of flavor, rich, mouth-filling textures, and a finish that goes on and on.

Davis Bynum Winery   *1992 Le Pinot*

Region: USA—California   **Suggested Retail: $32.00**
Availability: Limited   **Golds: CA**

This wine is not available in retail stores outside California, but can be ordered directly from the winery, at (800) 826-1073. Gary Farrell, whose own label wins golds galore, is the winemaker at Davis Bynum, and after tasting the fruit from the spectacular 1992 vintage, decided to produce a special bottling of 100% Pinot Noir from two special vineyards. Farrell has been called the "master of the Russian River Valley."

Special Awards: *Double Gold (CA); Tie for Best Pinot Noir of Appellation (CA)*

Davis Bynum Winery   *1992 Limited Edition Pinot Noir*

Region: USA—California   **Suggested Retail: $22.00**
Availability: Limited   **Golds: NW**

Reminiscent of a fine French red burgundy, this Pinot Noir has complex black cherry, wild strawberry, clove aromas, and no hard tannins. As its name suggests, production was limited. But we've found that great wines like these can often be found on restaurant and hotel wine lists even when they're long gone in the wine shop, so keep your eyes open for it. Incidentally, the 1993 is also getting great press so far.

De Loach   *1992 O.F.S. Estate Bottled Pinot Noir*

Region: USA—California   **Suggested Retail: $25.00**
Availability: Limited   **Golds: LA, PR, NW**

The 1992 Pinot Noir O.F.S. (Our Finest Selection) is a deep ruby color, with abundant fruit in the nose and rich, smoky, earthy flavors complexed by toasty oak. It is layered and full in the mouth, with medium body and an elegant, lingering finish.

Did You Know . . . ?

Archaeologists have found clay tablets dating back to the eighth century B.C., from what was once the Assyrian capital Kalhu. They're part of a once-vast archive that detailed the rationing of wine to the 6,000-people palace household, from the queen and king down to the lowliest shepherd boy. It's estimated that one wine magazine uncovered at the ruin stored at least 4,000 gallons.

Elkhorn Peak *1993 Fagan Creek Vineyards Pinot Noir*

Region: USA—California **Suggested Retail: $24.00**
Availability: Limited **Golds: OC**

Here's a medium ruby wine with attractive, intense, slightly stemmy, tight cherry fruit aromas with notes of spiced apples and tobacco. It has medium to medium-full body, slightly rich, supple, herbal, cherry fruit flavors, medium to medium-full tannin, and a soft finish with a lingering aftertaste.

Gary Farrell Wines *1993 Bien Nacido Vineyard Pinot Noir*

Region: USA—California **Suggested Retail: $28.00**
Availability: Limited **Golds: OC, EL**

This handsomely crafted, youthful wine offers generous blackberry and black cherry aromas with underlying spice and vanilla scents. Layers and layers of similar flavors abound in a lengthy finish that is underlaid by properly proportioned tannins and joyful acidity. Wonderful to drink now, but don't be fooled—it will be best in a few years.

J. Rochioli Vineyards *1993 Estate Bottled Pinot Noir*

Region: USA—California **Suggested Retail: $18.00**
Availability: Good **Golds: CA**

Here you'll find concentrated aromas of black cherry fruit with hints of spice and rose petals combined with supple flavors of ripe cherries and vanilla, all balanced by a firm structure.
Special Award: *Tie for Best Pinot Noir of Appellation (CA)*

La Crema *1993 Grand Cuvée Pinot Noir*

Region: USA—California **Suggested Retail: $22.50**
Availability: NP **Golds: CA**

Here's a classic Pinot Noir with distinctive aromas of raspberry jam and black cherry. It is rich and round with notes of spice and toasty oak, matched with a velvet mouth feel and a long, lingering finish. It will gain further complexity with bottle age, although it's luscious now.
Special Awards: *Best of Show (CA); Best Wine of Region (CA); Best Pinot Noir of Appellation (CA)*

Did You Know . . . ?

In California's Napa Valley, and elsewhere where valley floors are prone to frost, some high-tech producers use wind machines to stir up the cold, dense air that has settled on the ground with the warmer air from above. On windless spring nights one might see one of these contraptions in action, looking a bit like a windmill fitted with a jet propeller. Helicopters are often used to the same effect.

Sanford Winery   *1993 Santa Barbara County Pinot Noir*
Region: USA—California   **Suggested Retail: $18.00**
Availability: Very Good   **Golds: CA**
Although this wine is lightly bodied and more restrained than the 1992 offering, it still has a forward, assertive style with lots of varietal characteristics. Showing black cherry, raspberry, and strawberry aromas, followed by spicy berry, oak, and herbs, the finish is lingering and the fruit intensity prevails.

Sterling Vineyards   *1993 Winery Lake Pinot Noir*
Region: USA—California   **Suggested Retail: $18.00**
Availability: NP   **Golds: CA**
Look for a bright garnet hue with spicy fruit and touches of mocha, cola, and black cherry. Full and concentrated, the wine finishes with firm and supple tannin.
Special Award: *Best Pinot Noir of Appellation (CA)*

Stonestreet Winery   *1992 Sonoma County Pinot Noir*
Region: USA—California   **Suggested Retail: $21.00**
Availability: NP   **Golds: NW**
This wine expresses a broad range of flavors: cherry, berry, plum, vanilla—all backed by notes of toast and spice. It's a rewarding wine that will gain complexity with further bottle age.

Trout Gulch Vineyard   *1991 Santa Cruz Mountains Pinot Noir*
Region: USA—California   **Suggested Retail: $18.00**
Availability: Limited   **Golds: NW**
This is a full-flavored and well-balanced wine with a long aftertaste of berry fruits, cherries, roses, and just a hint of spice. Not all great Pinots come from France! This wine will age well with proper cellaring. By the way, this wine has won a gold two years in a row at New World International.

Tualatin   *1993 Private Reserve Barrel Select Pinot Noir*
Region: USA—Oregon   **Suggested Retail: $20.00**
Availability: Limited   **Golds: OR**
This is a wine of great concentration. It has deep color, an intense aroma, and rich, complex flavors. It is just now opening up and should enjoy a long life. Quantities of this and other Oregonian wines are often limited, so we advise you to snag a bottle right away when you see one.
Special Award: *Best of Show, Red Wine (OR)*

Did You Know . . . ?
The world's most expensive bottle of wine, auctioned off at Christie's for *105,000 pounds,* was displayed standing upright under warm lights. Unfortunately, the cork dried up, fell into the bottle, and the wine was oxidized and rendered undrinkable!

Cline Cellars *1993 Côtes D'Oakley*

Region: USA—California   **Suggested Retail: $8.50**

Availability: Very Good   **Golds: OC**

A blend of 47% Carignane, 38% Mourvèdre, 8% Syrah, 5% Zinfandel, and 2% Alicante Bouchet, this wine gets its various characteristics from the contributing grapes: dark cherry fruit from the Carignane; tobacco, violet, plum flavors and aromas from the Mourvèdre; spices and plumminess from the Syrah; dusty berry flavors from the Zin; and color and structure from the Alicante Bouchet. Drink it now or cellar it for 3 to 5 years. By the way, we drank this with one of our mothers visiting from Illinois after a long moving day. She is used to French wine, but thought this one was snappy and different. We felt it possessed a beautiful punch. It was oh so dry but very fruity and complex. The color was a brilliant deep purple, and it went down well with stir-fried chicken and vegetables.

Leasingham Wines *1994 Cabernet Malbec*

Region: Australia   **Suggested Retail: $9.99**

Availability: Very Good   **Golds: RM, RU**

Deep, intense brick red in color, this wine shows subtle cassis and mulberry fruit on the nose, intertwined with herb and pepper notes. The palate is rich and generous with attractive sweet fruit, and displays a fine balance of tannins. The Malbec (15%) adds herbal complexity and weight. This wine is available in the United States.

Madrona Vineyards *1993 Shiraz/Cabernet*

Region: USA—California   **Suggested Retail: $9.00**

Availability: Limited   **Golds: CA**

This wine has deep, dark color and is bursting with ripe berry and cherry fruit. It displays subtle floral notes with a distinctive smokiness, moderate tannins, and offers crisp palate-cleansing acidity. Robert Parker calls this one a "noteworthy value." The blend is 70% Syrah and 30% Cabernet Franc.

Special Award: *Best Other Specialty Red Varietal Blends of Appellation (CA)*

Pedroncelli Winery *1992 Primo Misto*

Region: USA—California   **Suggested Retail: $6.50**

Availability: Good   **Golds: NW**

Here's a classic red wine blend that's 45% Zinfandel, 41% Cabernet Sauvignon, and 14% Napa Gamay. Ruby red in color with berry and spice aromas and flavors of raspberry, currant, and black pepper, this wine is dry, rich, and full bodied, and it finishes with a hint of spicy oak.

Special Award: *Best of Price Class (NW)*

Did You Know . . . ?

World War II was devastating for European wine producers, and is one of the factors that launched the rise of the American wine industry.

Rosemount Estate   *1995 Shiraz Cabernet*
Region: Australia   **Suggested Retail: $7.90**
Availability: Very Good   **Golds: RS**

This 65% Cabernet/35% Shiraz is delicious, fresh, and soft, and ready for early drinking. It can easily be served chilled and drunk as an everyday wine. The color is bright red, the aromas are of plums and cherries, and it is unoaked to bring out the lively fresh fruit. On the palate it is ripe and soft with abundant fresh fruit flavors, good length, and texture. It's widely available in the United States, and a great price to boot.
Special Award: *Best of Class (RS)*

Yalumba   *1993 Oxford Landing Cabernet Sauvignon/Shiraz*
Region: Australia   **Suggested Retail: $5.50**
Availability: Very Good   **Golds: NW**

Full, deep cherry red in color, this wine has a ripe and aromatic nose with scents of plums, stewed fruits, and a cedar oak lift. The palate has great weight and intensity with excellent balance and length. Full flavored and rich, this wine is the most complex of this label. It is available in the United States as well as Canada, the UK, and New Zealand.

Did You Know . . . ?
Rosemount Estates is the official wine of the Australian Olympic team. Leave it to those Aussies to endorse their athletes' after-events activities!

Beringer Vineyards *1992 Knights Valley Red Meritage*
Region: USA—California   Suggested Retail: $14.00
Availability: NP   Golds: RE, OC
This blend of Cabernet Sauvignon with Petit Verdot and Merlot added for good measure is not only delicious, but a great bargain as well. Impressive color; large, jammy, spicy, black and red fruit flavors and aromas; rich texture with a supple mouth feel; medium to full body; and a long finish characterize this winner.
Special Award: *Finalist for Sweepstakes Award, Red Wine (RE)*

Beringer Vineyards *1991 Knights Valley Meritage Red*
Region: USA—California   Suggested Retail: $13.00
Availability: NP   Golds: PR, FF
We couldn't get much information on this wine, but know that the 1992 version was also a gold medal winner. Therefore, you can't go wrong in your wine shop with either vintage of this wine. At this price, with Beringer's outstanding reputation, it's bound to be a bargain.

Brindiamo *1993 Rosso Vecchio*
Region: USA—California   Suggested Retail: $10.00
Availability: Limited   Golds: OC, LA
This one has beautiful red-plum color with damsonlike qualities in the nose. The four varietals used in this blend (44% Mourvèdre, 30% Grenache, 21% Petite Sirah, 5% Negrette) have melded to yield a wine with rich complexity: berries, rose petals, plums, a touch of tobacco, and cedar. This multidimensional wine has a subtle touch of oak and soft, mouth-filling tannins that yield to the rich fruit flavors and long lingering finish.
Special Award: *Best of Class (LA)*

Castoro Cellars *1992 Undici Anni*
Region: USA—California   Suggested Retail: $15.99
Availability: Limited   Golds: PR
After ten years of winning wines, the winemaker decided to name this the Undici Anni ("eleven years" in Italian). When you fill your glass, note the deep color from maximum character extraction during fermentation. The aromas are filled with rich plum, spices, herbs, and aged oak coupled with flavors of red currants, black pepper, and smoky characters. The blend is 37% Cabernet Sauvignon, 37% Zinfandel, and 26% Cabernet Franc. Yum!

Did You Know . . . ?
If you're looking for Brindiamo wines of more recent vintages, look for Thornton instead. They've changed their name, but not their standard of quality. (Incidentally, *brindiamo* means "let's toast" in Italian.) In 1995, their wines won 75 medals in major competitions, many of them golds and double golds.

Château Reynella   *1994 Cabernet Merlot*
Region: Australia   **Suggested Retail: $10.99**
Availability: Very Good   **Golds: HO, RU, MC**

Widely available in the United States, this deep cherry red wine has fruit aromas of plums and red currants, with herbal overtones. The palate is powerful, displaying the plum and cherry spice of Merlot (35%) and the red currant and wintry flavors of Cabernet Sauvignon (65%).

Château Reynella   *1995 Cabernet Merlot*
Region: Australia   **Suggested Retail: $10.99**
Availability: Very Good   **Golds: RU**

The 1994 vintage of this wine won several golds as well, and we suspect that this one will win more, since it was just released. You'll have no problem finding either one in the United States. This one is medium deep red, with a nose that exhibits sweet fruit aromas of red currant and blackberry, with a hint of herbs. The palate is intense with complex berry fruit and spices. The softness of this wine can be attributed to the use of traditional basket presses.

Cline Cellars   *1990 Oakley Cuvée*
Region: USA—California   **Suggested Retail: $13.50**
Availability: Good   **Golds: OC**

Here's a blend of 48% Mourvèdre, 27% Carignane, 20% Zinfandel, and 5% Alicante Bouchet. Yum! The winemaker describes it as being similar to a Châteauneuf-du-Pape or Gigondas, although it is "unmistakably Californian." The wine has rich flavors and aromas that are a blend of dark cherries and herbs, fresh-picked raspberries and blackberries, chocolate and earthy zest, and spices and radiant gemlike color. Enjoy it now or cellar it for 5 to 7 years.

Concannon   *1992 Central Coast Reserve Assemblage*
Region: USA—California   **Suggested Retail: $17.95**
Availability: Limited   **Golds: DA, IE**

Here's a wine that is 73% Cabernet Sauvignon, 22% Cabernet Franc, and 5% Merlot, and what a blend. It has a deep color, with leather and coffee flavors and aromas to go with the jammy cherry, and a big, chalky tannin structure to allow for age worthiness. One reviewer calls this a gem. Call the winery directly if you have trouble finding it or other Concannon wines: (510) 447-3760.

Did You Know . . . ?

Corkscrews, apparently, have national identities, or so say those who spend their valuable time studying corkscrew history. The British win hands down when it comes to design, function, and quality of workmanship. The British used bronzed finishes, while the French favored nickel plating. Antique American corkscrews were often wooden-handled affairs with—guess what?—*advertisements* printed on them.

Golden Creek Vineyard   *1992 Sonoma County Reserve "Caberlot"*
Region: USA—California   **Suggested Retail: $15.00**
Availability: Limited   **Golds: NW, SD**
This 50% Cabernet Sauvignon, 50% Merlot has a beautiful, deep ruby color, with flavors and aromas of blueberries and oak with a nice, lingering aftertaste.
Special Award: *Best of Price Class (NW)*

Hillstowe   *1993 McLaren Vale Buxton Cabernet Merlot*
Region: Australia   **Suggested Retail: $16.00**
Availability: Very Good   **Golds: RM**
This 85% Cabernet Sauvignon, 15% Merlot is a concentrated wine with lifted violet and berry aromas. Subtle oak handling adds structure to rich fruit flavors, producing a complex wine with great depth of character. Best of all, it's a decent price and will be available in the United States about the same time this book hits the shelves.

Joseph Phelps Vineyards   *1992 Le Mistral*
Region: USA—California   **Suggested Retail: $15.00**
Availability: Good   **Golds: NW**
This mouth-filling wine is full of spice, plum, and berry flavors, has excellent richness and purity, and a long heady finish. The blend is 75% Grenache and Mourvèdre, 25% Syrah and Carignane. It is compatible with a variety of meats and stews, as well as Mediterranean cuisine.
Special Award: *Best of Price Class (NW); Best New World Rhône Style Red (NW)*

Les Côteaux Kefraya   *1988 Château Kefraya*
Region: Lebanon   **Suggested Retail: $12.30**
Availability: Limited   **Golds: IW**
Aromas of ripe fruit, eucalyptus, cloves, coffee, and cocoa emerge from the glass. Toasty at first, the bouquet develops smoky roasty overtones, licorice, resin, spices, and white pepper. The 1988 also has a pleasing aspect that coats the mouth, yet remains silky and feminine, with a nice backbone of tannin. This is a very powerful wine, aromatic, very intense. Kefraya has a compelling story of survival— winemaking in a war zone, where 2,000 Moslem residents of Kefraya village look the other way as grapes are made into wine, which their religion prohibits. 40% of Kefraya's wines are exported to France and elsewhere in Europe, but they can be obtained ex winery if you live in the United States and want to buy or distribute these wines. For more information, call 96-11-494171 or fax 96-11-494820.

Did You Know . . . ?
Monsieur de Bustros, owner of Lebanon's Les Côteaux de Kefraya, bulldozed the desert, planted 2 million plants, built a châteaux, hired French consultants and a French oenologist to establish a state-of-the-art winery, and is now producing world-renowned gold-medal wines—all while his country was ravaged by war and anarchy, and while his home in Beirut was burning to the ground.

Matua Valley Wines   *1993 Ararimu Cabernet Sauvignon/Merlot*
Region: New Zealand   **Suggested Retail: $23.00 CAN**
Availability: Outside USA   **Golds: NZ**
This wine has a rich color and a fragrant, mature bouquet. Oak maturation has developed a soft round finish and pleasing complexity on the palate. Soft grainy tannins complete a well-structured wine style. Cellar this one up to 1999. By the way, the blend is 70% Cabernet Sauvignon and 30% Merlot. Matua's wines are available in Canada, as well as in Australia, the UK, Europe, and Japan.

Quivira Vineyards   *1993 Dry Creek Cuvée*
Region: USA—California   **Suggested Retail: $12.00**
Availability: Limited   **Golds: OC, NW**
The aromas of strawberries and cherry-berry "jump out of the glass," according to the winemaker. This California Rhône-style wine is a blend of 56% Grenache, 24% Mourvèdre, 13% Syrah, and 7% Zinfandel. Spicy berry and black cherry fruit flavors are supported by base notes from the Mourvèdre and Syrah, as well as the French oak. The winemaker describes this blend as "wonderfully aromatic and fruit focused," and says it is loaded with charm and ready for immediate consumption. Try it with grilled meats and vegetables. Incidentally, keep your eyes out for more "Rhône Rangers," as California producers are increasing acreage of these exciting alternatives to Cabernet Sauvignon.

River Run Vintners   *1992 Côte d'Aroma*
Region: USA—California   **Suggested Retail: $15.00**
Availability: Limited   **Golds: OC, NW**
This Rhône-style blend is a combination of Syrah (47%), Mourvèdre (26%), Carignane (24%), and Grenache (5%). Layers upon layers of complementary flavors blend together in this liquid gold.

Santino Wines   *1991 Satyricon*
Region: USA—California   **Suggested Retail: $12.95**
Availability: Limited   **Golds: CA**
This Rhône-style wine was produced utilizing a partial whole-berry fermentation and aging in small French oak cooperage for 16 months. The blend is 41% Grenache, 34% Syrah, 18% Mourvèdre, and 7% Cinsault. It hints of jam and raspberry fruit, enhanced by a touch of cigarbox cedar and earth.
Special Award: *Best Rhône Varietal Blend of Appellation (CA)*

Did You Know ... ?
New Zealand has some unique animal problems—and solutions. Kangaroos have to be fenced out, but sheep are sometimes fenced *in* and used to munch on and thin down excessive grape leaves.

Trentadue Winery *1993 Old Patch Red*

Region: USA—California   **Suggested Retail: $11.00**

Availability: Good   **Golds: CA**

This is a blend of Petite Sirah, Zinfandel, Carignane, and Alicante Bouchet. It displays an opaque purple color to go with a nose that has ripe, jammy, red and black fruit characters with notes of coffee and toasted oak. This is a rich, lush wine with soft tannins and tons of plum and black cherry flavors.

Special Award: *Best Red Generic of Region (CA)*

Zaca Mesa Winery *1993 Z Cuvée Red*

Region: USA—California   **Suggested Retail: $14.00**

Availability: Good   **Golds: OC, FF**

This is a truly Mediterranean-style wine with fresh, juicy red fruit impressions from the Grenache (49%), spicy aromas from the Mourvèdre (43%), and color, structure, and ripe blackberry fruit flavors from the Syrah (8%). It longs to have 6 to 8 months in the bottle to develop complexity and bouquet, and longer aging, from 4 to 5 years, is possible. Try it with Cajun and Creole dishes.

Did You Know ... ?

Around 1860, vines brought over to Europe for experimental purposes accidentally carried the insects that cause phylloxera, and within two decades virtually all of the vineyards of France were destroyed. The disease spread as far as Russia, South Africa, Australia, and New Zealand.

Bonny Doon Vineyard *1993 Le Cigare Volant*
Region: USA—California   Suggested Retail: $18.00
Availability: Good   Golds: SF
Bonny Doon (who also owns the Ca' del Solo label) wins our kudos for the most entertaining and creative press material. We think the winemaker is actually a poet in disguise. This incredibly delicious wine, which we've tried, is described as follows, in part: "Crushed junipers, mulberries, fraises de bois, wild plums, dried cherries, anise root, and raw meat make this a wine for the urban hunter/gatherer. But what is it really like? It is like living to be 200 years old. It is a bouquet of ultra-violets. It is the sun pouring through one's sievelike body. It is all of the virtues and more vices than are dreamt of in Miami." Well, we'd love to quote more, but for now we recommend that you try it and find out why the judges went mad over this one. By the way, it's made from 37% Mourvèdre, 25% Syrah, 23% Grenache, and 14% Cinsault.
Special Awards: *Double Gold (SF); Best of Show, Red Wine (SF)*

C. A. Henschke *1992 Shiraz/Cabernet Sauvignon/Malbec*
Region: Australia   Suggested Retail: $22.00
Availability: NP   Golds: IV, AD, QU
This wine won 2 gold medals in 1994, and another in 1993. Obviously it's a winner. Not only that, but the 1993 vintage was also a tremendous hit at prestigious wine competitions. Henschke wines demonstrate a lot of consistency from vintage to vintage, so check it out because you'll find it in U.S. wine shops.

C. A. Henschke *1993 Keyneton Estate Shiraz/Cabernet/Malbec*
Region: Australia   Suggested Retail: $25.00
Availability: Good   Golds: RM, PE
This wine is available in the United States, and it sounds like a beauty. Made from 80% Shiraz, 15% Cabernet Sauvignon, and 5% Malbec grapes, it is bright deep crimson in color, and has aromas of lifted sweet plums, chocolate, and blackberry fruits, with hints of vanilla, scented balsam oak nuances, and subtle raspberries and sappiness. The palate shows sweet rich berry fruits, is full, soft, and complex, and is rounded off with ripe soft tannins and excellent length. It will be at its best in the year 2003! Great with beef, game, lamb, veal, pork, quail, and chicken.

Did You Know . . . ?

Spitting, as opposed to *swallowing* wine is commonly practiced in professional wine tastings. Since the throat has no taste receptors, a taster can swirl the wine around in the mouth, getting the full flavor impressions of the wine without having to contend with the deleterious effects of alcohol on one's judgment. (For more on tasting wine, see Chapter 4.) However, tasting thirty wines, even while spitting, *is equivalent to drinking one glass of wine,* since some ethanol is vaporized and absorbed on the palate, and some of the wine, however minute, slips down your waiting gullet.

Carmenet Vineyard   *1991 Vin de Garde*
Region: USA—California   **Suggested Retail: $35.00**
Availability: Limited   **Golds: OC**
This blend of Cabernet Sauvignon (71%), Cabernet Franc (19%), and Merlot (you guessed it: 10%) is a winner. In French, a wine made to cellar before drinking is called a vin de garde. *An age-worthy Bordeaux-style wine, also known as Red Meritage, must in its youth have relatively high amounts of tannin, but also a lot of color and fruit to bind with the tannin and make it taste rich and sweet rather than overly astringent. Carmenet accomplished this with their 1991 Red Meritage, which should improve for decades if cellared properly. This one has a full mouth feel, complex layers of flavor reminiscent of black currants, cedar, wild mountain sage, and the sweet floral spice of native bay laurel bruised by spring rains—the scent wafting through the breeze.*

Cosentino   *1992 M Coz Unfiltered*
Region: USA—California   **Suggested Retail: $45.00**
Availability: Limited   **Golds: SF**
Cosentino consistently wins golds for their Red Meritage blends. This one is 55% Cabernet Sauvignon, 21% Cabernet Franc, 19% Merlot, and 5% Petit Verdot, and is made the old-fashioned way—without filtering, which leaves a lot of flavor and character complexity in the bottle. We think you'll love it.

Cosentino   *1991 The Poet*
Region: USA—California   **Suggested Retail: $25.00**
Availability: Limited   **Golds: SF**
We like Meritage, because it is a nice change of pace from the more commonly found reds. This winner is a blend of Cabernet Sauvignon (44%), Merlot (35%), and Cabernet Franc (21%). It is young and intense, with a classic spicy and aromatic nose, full body, broad flavors, complexity, and a long, harmonious finish. Incidentally, the previous eight vintages of The Poet have all been gold medal winners! We think you can't go wrong with this one, or even the next vintage, if this one is too hard to find.

Firestone   *1991 Vintage Reserve Red Meritage*
Region: USA—California   **Suggested Retail: $20.00**
Availability: Limited   **Golds: FF, GH**
This wine reveals a nose of black cherries, herbs, and spices, and is rich, deep, and full bodied with superb color saturation and purity. It's delicious now, but the fine tannins could use until 1998 or 1999 to soften. The blend is 57% Cabernet Franc, 27% Merlot, and 16% Cabernet Sauvignon.

Did You Know ... ?
Carmenet's vineyards, accessible only by four-wheel drive, are patrolled by diamond-backed rattlers.

Flora Springs Wine Company *1991 Napa Valley Trilogy*
Region: USA—California   **Suggested Retail: $28.00**
Availability: Limited   **Golds: DA**
The superior 1991 vintage made the winery's reputation with its lingering flavors of blueberries, cherries, currants, and chocolate. Ample but not intrusive tannins are apparent. Wait for three acts of complexity—a wild beginning, a reflective middle, and an ending that makes you want to applaud. The blend is 41% Cabernet Sauvignon, 38% Merlot, and 21% Cabernet Franc.

Geyser Peak Winery *1993 Reserve Alexandre Red Meritage*
Region: USA—California   **Suggested Retail: $27.00**
Availability: NP   **Golds: OC, LJ, IN**
Elegant, full bodied, and extremely complex, this is another gold medal Red Meritage from Geyser Peak, a magic blend of 48% Cabernet Sauvignon, 29% Merlot, 12% Malbec, 7% Petit Verdot, and 4% Cabernet Franc. Since the Red Meritage keeps winning golds every year, it's reasonable to assume that any vintage of this one will be extraordinary.

Geyser Peak Winery *1992 Reserve Alexandre Red Meritage*
Region: USA—California   **Suggested Retail: $27.00**
Availability: NP   **Golds: FF, SO, TG, AT**
When you add up all the component grapes used in this blend, it won't equal 100. (40% Merlot, 28% Cabernet Sauvignon, 28% Petit Verdot, 5% Cabernet Franc, 5% Malbec.) But is that so important? We don't think so. What matters here is that Geyser Peak seems to be making great Red Meritage (their 1993 is also a several-times-over gold medal winner). Ripe cherry and berry aromas enhanced by vanillin oak lead to lush flavors of raspberry fruit, spice, and cigarbox herbaceousness. This wine has medium tannins, a long, spicy finish, and can be further improved by cellaring for several years.
Special Awards: *Chairman's Award (FF); Double Gold (TG)*

Hedges Cellars *1991 Red Mountain Reserve*
Region: USA—Washington   **Suggested Retail: $25.00**
Availability: Limited   **Golds: SF, NE, TA**
The nose offers up aromas of cedar, spice, red and black fruits, and a whiff of chocolate. A blend of 67% Cabernet Sauvignon/33% Merlot, it's medium to full bodied and rich, with fine length and concentration, and an overall sense of balance. It can be consumed now or over the next 5 to 7 years. This wine got major praise in the wine press, so grab it at your nearest wine shop, or look for their 1992 release, which could be just as fine. Their mail-order number is (206) 391-6056.

Did You Know ... ?
The cork tree, *Quercus suber,* is a species of oak that grows only in the western Mediterranean, notably Spain and Portugal.

Hillebrand Estates Winery *1991 Truis Red*
Region: Canada   **Suggested Retail: $24.95**
Availability: Limited   **Golds: IW**

This intense, dark, and brilliant ruby red wine has well-matured aromas and a rich nose of red fruits, cassis, blueberry, and spices. On the palate some tannins and spiciness are enhanced by flavors of vanilla. With a long aftertaste and nice oak balance, it is enjoyable now, but will age well. It has enough structure to stand up to old cheese. Incidentally, the blend is 66% Cabernet Sauvignon, 31% Cabernet Franc, and 3% Merlot.
Special Award: *Trophy for Best Blended Red Wine (IW)*

Joseph Phelps Vineyards *1991 Napa Valley Insignia*
Region: USA—California   **Suggested Retail: $55.00**
Availability: Good   **Golds: SF, IV, NW, LJ**

This is a blend of 80% Cabernet Sauvignon, 10% Merlot, and 10% Cabernet Franc. Suffused with intense flavors of black cherry, chocolate, cassis, and herbs, this seductive wine is supported by a firm structure of tannin. It has great depth of color and sweet, toasted aromas, as well as elegant and concentrated fruit with a heady finish of vanilla and deep red fruit that lingers. All the reviewers raved, and one said, "It could last 30 years and never have a bad day." Can we wait that long?
Special Awards: *Best New World Meritage Red (NW); Best of Price Class (NW)*

Justin Vineyards *1992 Isosceles Reserve*
Region: USA—California   **Suggested Retail: $24.50**
Availability: Limited   **Golds: IV**

Rich fruit aromas of cassis and blackberries overlaid by fragrances of pencil lead and cigarbox characterize this one. The mouth feel and flavors are rich and powerful, but the interplay of fruit, acid, and tannin allows the wine to retain its wonderful sense of elegance. This wine will improve for a decade or more. The Wine Spectator *highly recommends it, rating it 92.*

Langtry *1991 Meritage Red California*
Region: USA—California   **Suggested Retail: $36.00**
Availability: Limited   **Golds: IV, CL, LJ, TG**

With deep garnet nuances, this wine has a mouthful of flavors that evoke raspberries, blueberries, and chocolate in a garden of spices. A wonderfully full body, concentration of extracts, and noble balance culminate in a rich, lingering finish blessed with soft aftertones. It is made with 58% Cabernet Sauvignon, 32% Cabernet Franc, 9% Petit Verdot, and 1% Merlot. Serve this multigold winner with blue-veined cheeses, sautéed mushrooms, and roasted meats with fresh cracked pepper.
Special Award: *Double Gold (TG)*

Did You Know . . . ?
The number of yeast cells in one drop of fermenting grape juice is 5 million.
Do You Care . . . ?

Mount Veeder Winery   *1991 Reserve Napa Valley Red Meritage*

Region: USA—California   **Suggested Retail: $40.00**
Availability: Good   **Golds: RE, SD**

A dark ruby wine with aromas of plum and black currant with hints of toasty oak, spice, and vanilla. Effusive berry, cedar, and spice fill the palate. The broad mouth develops into cocoa and sweet toasty oak supported by supple tannins. Powerful and mouth filling, this is a blend of Cabernet Sauvignon (52%), Merlot (33%), Cabernet Franc (12%), Petit Verdot (2%), and Malbec (1%).

Penley Estate   *1992 Penley Estate Shiraz Cabernet Sauvignon*

Region: Australia   **Suggested Retail: $22.00**
Availability: NP   **Golds: SY, AI**

In 7 years and only 7 vintages, Penley's wines have won 10 trophies and 53 golds. This one is bright crimson, with some amber tints indicating oak maturation and some bottle age. The nose is distinctive and commanding with a berrylike aroma. The length of flavor shows strong and rich berry Cab character. Complexity is the main feature here. Look for the promising 1993 vintage in U.S. wine shops as well.

Richard Hamilton Winery   *1993 Coonawarra Cabernet/Merlot*

Region: Australia   **Suggested Retail: $20.00**
Availability: Limited   **Golds: IV, SY**

The wine was matured in new French oak casks for 12 months and is redolent of dark cherries, ripe plums, firm tannins, and toasty oak. On the palate it is light to medium bodied with rich, complex fruit and a firm lingering finish complemented by fine-grained tannins. Allowing the wine to breathe before serving is recommended, and further cellaring (2 to 4 years) will only enhance its inherent character. It's available in the U.S., UK, Denmark, New Zealand, Canada, and Hong Kong.

Stonestreet Winery   *1992 Legacy*

Region: USA—California   **Suggested Retail: $35.00**
Availability: NP   **Golds: CA, NW**

We love red wine blends. This one is 53% Cabernet Sauvignon, 44% Merlot, and about 2% Petit Verdot. It is made with the best barrels of the richest, most supple lots, with the greatest depth of flavor and complexity, chosen to go into this blend of Stonestreet's signature wine. The wine has many layers of plummy, dark berry fruit flavors, a note of tobacco and cedar, and a mouth-filling texture.

Stonestreet Winery   *1991 Legacy*

Region: USA—California   **Suggested Retail: $35.00**
Availability: NP   **Golds: NW**

A mouth-filling wine with layers of plum and dark berry fruit and notes of tobacco, cedar, and toast. It has very fine silky tannins and a long, vanilla-laced finish. The blend is 41% Cabernet Sauvignon, 34% Cabernet Franc, and 25% Merlot.

Did You Know...?

The average number of taxes levied on a bottle of wine in Chicago is five.

Leasingham Wines *1993 Domaine Shiraz*
Region: Australia   **Suggested Retail: $9.99**
Availability: Good   **Golds: AU, CE**
Vibrant brick red in color, this Shiraz has aromas that conjure up spice and herbs, cassis and berry fruit, and integrated vanillin oak. The palate is rich and generous with lively fruit characteristics, with the added complexity of toasty oak. It is available in the United States, as is the 1994 gold medal version of this wine.

Leasingham Wines *1994 Domaine Shiraz*
Region: Australia   **Suggested Retail: $9.99**
Availability: Very Good   **Golds: WR**
This wine is deep brick red in color. The aroma is complex, showing lifted plum, with chocolate and spice characters and charry oak suggestions. The palate exhibits overall finesse, but also sweetness and rich berry flavors. You'll not have a problem finding this one in the United States.

McGuigan Brothers *1992 Hunter Valley Black Shiraz*
Region: Australia   **Suggested Retail: $6.99**
Availability: Good   **Golds: IV**
The Black Label is made in a unique way to accentuate the soft "velvety" flavors. It has ruby color, cherry/plum aromas, and is soft and velvety on the palate. An easy-drinking, all-seasons wine. This wine is available in the United States as well as the UK, and what a price!

McGuigan Brothers *1991 Black Shiraz*
Region: Australia   **Suggested Retail: $6.99**
Availability: Good   **Golds: IW**
The technical sheet sent by the winery for this wine describes a complicated process using a rotary fermenter, or "Vinimatic," which uses mechanical agitation to extract color and flavor from the grapes and skins. There's more, but the end result is a colorful, soft wine with cherry flavors and medium body. It's a tremendous value, and can be found in the United States and the UK.

Rothbury Vineyards *1993 South Eastern Australia Shiraz*
Region: Australia   ·   **Suggested Retail: $8.99**
Availability: Very Good   **Golds: WC**
It has long been regarded that multiregional blends add both completeness to wines and afford better consistency of style. This is a Shiraz with a depth of complexity that is the hallmark of regional blends, with all the characteristics of the famous Rothbury style. It is available in the United States, as well as Europe and Japan, and you can't beat the price.

Did You Know . . . ?
The average number of grapes in a cluster is 85. The approximate number of grapes in a bottle of wine is 600. (You never know when this information may come in handy.)

Yalumba *1993 Family Reserve Shiraz*

Region: Australia   **Suggested Retail: $8.65**
Availability: Good   **Golds: RM, BR, BL, HO**

The vines used for this wine are very old—planted in 1913. The core is plums and prunes with good weight and alcohol sweetness, with a hint of rhubarb and spicy lift on the nose. A beautifully balanced and intense wine with creamy oak sweetness that will mature gracefully for 5 to 8 years. This wine is available in the United States, Canada, the UK, and New Zealand. Incidentally, the 1994 vintage of this one is also a gold medal winner.

Yalumba *1994 Family Reserve Shiraz*

Region: Australia   **Suggested Retail: $8.65**
Availability: Very Good   **Golds: HO**

The nose imparts a noticeable lifted rhubarb tone that mingles sweetly with the American oak. The palate is rich and full with sweet, ripe plum and prune flavors. A classic Barossa Valley Shiraz that will continue to improve for 10 years. This wine is available in the United States, Canada, New Zealand, and the UK.
Special Award: *Best Shiraz in Show (HO)*

Did You Know . . . ?

Popular Australian and New Zealand wineries commonly package "bag-in-box" wines. These are collapsible laminated bags inside a strong carton with a handle and a tap, known as casks or, prosaically, bladder packs. As one Australian friend told us, "We just open up the 'fridge and pour out a tall glass of cool wine to have at lunch like you Americans have your soda pop."

Arrowfield Wines *1992 Show Reserve Shiraz*
Region: Australia   **Suggested Retail: $15.50**
Availability: Good   **Golds: IV**
The complex nose displays hints of pepper and spice, lifted berry aromas, and well-integrated oak. This complexity is carried through onto the palate where rich fruit flavors are more evident. Look for a good acid balance, soft tannins, and a long flavorsome finish. This one is available in the United States, as well as New Zealand, Europe, and Japan.

Ashwood Grove *1991 Kingston Reserve Shiraz*
Region: Australia   **Suggested Retail: $14.00**
Availability: NP   **Golds: IV**
A wine of deep brick-red hues having pungent ripe fruit aromas on the nose, this Shiraz also has overtones of pepper, licorice, and blackberry. A complexity of flavors with integrated oak characters and fine, soft tannins, and a long finish with great persistence top it off. This wine is available in the United States.

BRL Hardy Wine Company *1991 Eileen Hardy Shiraz*
Region: Australia   **Suggested Retail: $14.85**
Availability: NP   **Golds: SM**
Long and concentrated, with a chewy mouth feel, this wine conjures up rich and spicy sensations. It has a fruity and fragrant palate. This wine is available in the United States.

C. A. Henschke *1992 Mount Edelstone*
Region: Australia   **Suggested Retail: $34.00**
Availability: Limited   **Golds: IW, IV, SY, AU, AD, BA**
Made from 86-year-old Shiraz vines, this wine will make you glad to be alive. It is available in the United States.
***Special Awards:** Trophy for Best Shiraz/Syrah (IW); four other "Best" trophies from among the competitions above*

Cambria Winery *1992 Tepusquet Vineyard Estate Bottled Syrah*
Region: USA—California   **Suggested Retail: $30.00**
Availability: Limited   **Golds: RE, OC, LA**
Spicy, peppery, black cherry, and black currant aromas will greet your nose, followed by rich and full-bodied flavors in your mouth. Look for plenty of concentrated fruit and medium tannin levels. Layers of fruit complexity suggest that this one will last for the next 10 to 12 years.
***Special Awards:** Finalist for Sweepstakes Award for Red Wine (RE); Best Red Wine (OC); Double Gold (OC); Best of Class (LA)*

Did You Know ... ?
When cork is sliced, million of cells are opened and function as tiny suction cups. They provide an exceptional power of adhesion to wet, smooth surfaces (such as the inside of a bottle neck), and compensate for any microscopic flaws in the glass that could let air through.

Chapel Hill Winery   *1994 McLaren Vale Shiraz*
Region: Australia   **Suggested Retail: $11.00**
Availability: Good   **Golds: MC**

You should have no problem finding Chapel Hill wines in the United States, as well as in the UK, Hong Kong, and New Zealand. McLaren Vale's Mediterranean climate ripened grapes of high sugar and acidity, medium tannin levels, and deep crimson color in 1994. The nose of this Shiraz shows blackberry, black currants, and vanillin-enhanced oak. With integrated fruit and oak, and medium body, the wine is drinkable now, but further bottle aging will smoothen the palate and bring out more complex flavors.

Château Reynella   *1993 Shiraz*
Region: Australia   **Suggested Retail: $10.99**
Availability: Good   **Golds: AU**

Deep red with purple hues, this is a wine with concentrated aromas of blackberry and mulberry fruit. Typical rich, sweet berry fruit, chocolate, and spice characters combine to form a wine of great richness and length. The 1994 also won golds, and both are available in the United States.

Château Reynella   *1994 Shiraz*
Region: Australia   **Suggested Retail: $10.99**
Availability: Very Good   **Golds: AU, HO, WR**

An inky-purple-colored, peppery/leafy- and berry-scented red. Mulberry and cherry fruit flavors dominate with delicious pepper and spice overtones. It's a soft wine with fine tannin structure. This one is available in the United States.

Columbia Winery   *1992 Red Willow Vineyard Syrah*
Region: USA—Washington   **Suggested Retail: $21.00**
Availability: Limited   **Golds: WW**

A very dark, deep red wine, this Syrah has a charming berry aroma with hints of vanilla and smoked meat. It is full and round in the mouth, has sweet fruit, and a velvety texture. The finish is long and sumptuous.

Eberle Winery   *1993 Fralich Vineyard Syrah*
Region: USA—California   **Suggested Retail: $16.00**
Availability: Limited   **Golds: RE, CA, SF, PR, FL, IE**

Bursting with blueberry and bright fruit aromas, this Syrah opens up to reveal a smoky, bacon aroma reminiscent of a true French Hermitage. The judges went bonkers over this wine!
Special Awards: *Tie for Best Wine of Region (CA); Best Syrah/Shiraz of Appellation (CA); Best of Class (PR)*

Did You Know . . . ?
Syrah, better known as Shiraz in Australia, is the most widely planted red-grape variety in that country.

Geyser Peak Winery   *1993 Shiraz*

Region: USA—California   **Suggested Retail: $12.50**
Availability: NP   **Golds: PR, OC, TG**

The 1993 Reserve Shiraz from Geyser Peak is also a gold medal winner, but is $20 more per bottle! There must be a reason for that, but if you like a wine with blackberries, anise, and black pepper in the nose, with subtle vanillin hints, and a palate that's soft and silky, then buy two bottles of this one and get a great deal.

Geyser Peak Winery   *1993 Reserve Alexander Valley Shiraz*

Region: USA—California   **Suggested Retail: $32.00**
Availability: NP   **Golds: OC, SF, SO, AT**

The folks at Geyser Peak have decided to call their Syrah (a perfectly lovely name for a grape, in our opinion) by its Australian nickname, Shiraz. (Their winemaker is Australian.) Shiraz sounds to us more like a mishmosh between "cheers" and "hurrahs," both of which are appropriate for this award winner. This one has concentrated color, with a nose that displays rich licorice and blackberry characters typical of ripe Shiraz fruit. Strength, structure, and soft tannins round it out.

Hardy Wine Company   *1993 Eileen Hardy Shiraz*

Region: Australia   **Suggested Retail: $14.85**
Availability: NP   **Golds: RM**

The best thing to say about this wine is "go for it." We didn't get a lot of information on this particular wine, but it seems like a sure bet to us, since the 1992 and 1994 were also gold medal winners. It can be found in the United States.

Hardy Wine Company   *1992 Eileen Hardy Shiraz*

Region: Australia   **Suggested Retail: $14.85**
Availability: Limited   **Golds: IW, WR, RU, PE**

This must be great stuff, since the 1991, 1993, and 1994 vintages of this wine all won numerous national and international gold medals. Pick up a bottle of this deep red wine that has pungent, ripe blackberry fruit with hints of black pepper and spicy complexity. The palate exhibits big, rich, chocolatey flavor and length with a fine dusty tannin finish. Available in the United States.

Hardy Wine Company   *1994 Eileen Hardy Shiraz*

Region: Australia   **Suggested Retail: $18.00**
Availability: Very Good   **Golds: AD, WR**

Deep purple red, this wine has a nose exhibiting rich varietal fruit with mint and spice. The palate is intense with solid plum and blackberry flavors, balanced by rich chocolate and fine-grained tannins. It is available in the United States, as are its siblings, the gold medal 1991, 1992, and 1993. Now that's consistency.

Did You Know . . . ?

Here's the classic formula for serving one or more wines with a meal: dry before sweet, young before old, ordinary before fine. It sounds to us like the way you could arrange your dinner guests as well.

Kingston Estate *1991 Riverland Reserve Shiraz*
Region: Australia   **Suggested Retail: $14.95**
Availability: NP   **Golds: NW, IV**
Deep red brick in color, this wine exhibits pungent ripe fruit aromas with overtones of pepper, licorice, and blackberry on the nose. The flavors are intense, with ripe berry fruit backed up by spice and licorice. Complex, integrated oak characters, fine soft tannin, and a persistent finish complete the package. This Shiraz has the flavor intensity and structure to continue to improve in the bottle for 10 more years, and it's available in the United States.
Special Awards: *Trophy for Best New World Shiraz (NW); Best of Price Class (NW)*

Leasingham Wines *1993 Classic Clare Shiraz*
Region: Australia   **Suggested Retail: $14.99**
Availability: Good   **Golds: SF, HO, RU, BR**
Look at those golds! Best of all, this wine is available in the United States. It is brick-red colored with purple hues. Plum and berry fruit characters dominate the aroma, with hints of mint and charry oak. The palate is big, rich, and generous, displaying chocolate and plums coupled with smoky vanilla oak, providing great length and depth.

Leasingham Wines *1994 Classic Clare Shiraz*
Region: Australia   **Suggested Retail: $14.99**
Availability: Good   **Golds: RM, AU**
This brilliant and complex, deep brick red wine displays lifted plum, chocolate, spice, and herbs on the nose. The palate shows considerable concentration of Shiraz flavors, with sweet, rich berry and smoky, vanilla oak. It is available in the United States.
Special Award: *Top Gold (AU)*

Merrivale Wines *1993 Tapestry Shiraz*
Region: Australia   **Suggested Retail: $14.25**
Availability: Limited   **Golds: SY**
Medium to full red purple in color, this Shiraz has a rich, ripe, juicy berry and spice nose with some vanilla oak. The palate is soft and sweet, with good oak and tannin balance. It is full bodied with a firm dry finish and fine length. One judge at Sydney called this a "giant wine"; another said "it's a very seductive, sensual, pleasing Shiraz"; a third called it "a very, very smart Shiraz indeed." Although this one may be hard to find in the United States, the 1994 vintage will be in stores soon, so look for it.

Did You Know . . . ?
Ever pop the cork on a wine bottle to let the wine "breathe"? Experts say it's pointless. Breathing entails exposing as much of the surface of the wine to air as possible. But the neck of a wine bottle is so small that very little of the wine actually comes in contact with oxygen.

Miranda Wines *1992 Show Reserve Old Vines Shiraz*
Region: Australia   **Suggested Retail: $13.50**
Availability: NP   **Golds: IW**
The vines that yielded the concentrated fruit for this wine are 80 years old. The color is deep, rich, almost black with a very slight brick-red hue along the edges. It has pleasant lifted blackberry/spice fruitiness and toasty vanilla oak aromas. The flavors are a mixture of intense ripe blackberry and spicy black cherry fruit, with a slight pepperiness and luscious soft vanilla overtones. Full bodied, elegant on the palate, and well balanced, this wine may be available in the United States by press time. Look for it.

Normans Wines *1994 Chais Clarendon Shiraz*
Region: Australia   **Suggested Retail: $19.75**
Availability: Good   **Golds: RM, AU**
This and other Normans wines are available in the United States. Look for rich, spicy/plummy fruit complemented by American oak vanillin notes. It is medium to full bodied with rich flavor and a firm tannic finish.

Rosemount Estate *1992 Balmoral Syrah*
Region: Australia   **Suggested Retail: $31.60**
Availability: Good   **Golds: SY, ZU**
Balmoral is an uncompromising "old vines" Syrah drawn from 100-year-old vines. It is deep ruby, staining the glass with the power of its fruit, and intensely perfumed with a ripe berry and spice aroma that shows lovely floral lift as a young wine, and evolves into a complex savory character. The palate is full bodied, loaded with ripe fruit, spice, and soft tannins that are at once round and ripe as well as long and mouth filling. The finish is multilayered and complex with American oak, long flavors, and excellent balance of oak and acidity. One of the judges at Sydney called it "right in the top league." You'll find this wine in the United States.
Special Award: *Perfect 20 out of 20 Score (ZU)*

Swanson Vineyards *1992 Napa Valley Estate Syrah*
Region: USA—California   **Suggested Retail: $25.00**
Availability: Limited   **Golds: FF**
The enormous extract of this wine allowed the winemaker to use techniques designed to maximize its depth and concentration. Huge, brooding aromas of cherry, plum, smoke, vanilla, cassis, and wild game fill the glass. The palate feel is equally complex and plush, pumping out mouth-watering, unctuous fruit and round, velvety tannins.
Special Award: *Chairman's Award (FF)*

Did You Know ... ?
Australia has the highest annual per capita wine consumption in the English-speaking world.

Truchard Vineyards   *1993 Carneros Estate Bottled Syrah*
Region: USA—California   **Suggested Retail: $18.00**
Availability: Limited   **Golds: CA**
Blackberry and white pepper aromas with hints of leather and spice emerge from the glass, with similar flavors in the mouth. The wine is big and intense in the mouth while retaining a silky texture. Spice, pepper, and berries follow through in the finish. The wine is drinkable now, but should last if properly cellared.
Special Award: *Best Syrah/Shiraz of Appellation (CA)*

Yalumba   *1992 "The Octavius" III*
Region: Australia   **Suggested Retail: $31.50**
Availability: Limited   **Golds: PE**
The vines that bore the fruit for this wine date back to the 1900s, which means low yields and high concentration of fruit. This wine is a thick red plum color, and displays very youthful hues. The nose is a mix of briary red cherry aromas with spice and sweet vanillin mocha oak. The old vines have the ability to provide great strength in the middle palate through the concentration of the berries. Potential cellaring time is 20 to 30 years! You'll find this beauty in the United States, Canada, the UK, and New Zealand.

Zaca Mesa Winery   *1993 Zaca Vineyards Syrah*
Region: USA—California   **Suggested Retail: $12.00**
Availability: NP   **Golds: OC**
Lush and full bodied, with layers of fruit and well-integrated oak, this wine has gobs of currant, bright cherry, and raspberry characteristics that pick up a spicy note on the finish. It will improve for at least a year or two.

Did You Know ... ?
When, after a state dinner, President Clinton was so impressed with Zaca Mesa's 1993 Syrah that he ordered three cases, winery owner John Cushman ransacked his own personal cellar to fill the order. Such patriotism!

Castoro Cellars *1992 Zinfandel*
Region: USA—California   **Suggested Retail: $9.50**
Availability: Good   **Golds: OC, LA**
A big Zin full of fruit, ripe plums, raspberries, and cinnamon spice. Once it's in your mouth, taste the oak, rich fruit, and balancing tannins followed by a long, lingering finish. This wine is great now, but hiding some in your cellar will only be a treat down the road. Drink it with a hearty Italian entree. Incidentally, there were only 5 golds awarded at Orange County in this field of 72 entries.

Estrella River Winery *1992 Proprietor's Reserve Zinfandel*
Region: USA—California   **Suggested Retail: $5.25**
Availability: NP   **Golds: NW**
Look for a light garnet color and intense blackberry characteristics with hints of oak in the nose. Soft tannins and moderate acidity combined with lush, ripe berry flavors all add up to a real bargain.

Fetzer *1992 Mendocino County Barrel Select Zinfandel*
Region: USA—California   **Suggested Retail: $8.99**
Availability: NP   **Golds: NW**
Here's a classic Fetzer Zinfandel: ripe, full flavored, and well structured. Its blackberry flavors have complexities of toasted coconut, black pepper, and vanilla. Delightful now, it will repay 3 to 5 years of bottle aging.
Special Award: *Best of Price Class (NW)*

Granite Springs Winery *1992 Estate Bottled Zinfandel*
Region: USA—California   **Suggested Retail: $8.00**
Availability: Limited   **Golds: CA**
A typical "foothills Zinfandel," according to the winemaker, this wine has lots of fruit and spice, medium body, nice fruit aroma, and typical varietal fruit mixed with interesting spice.

Montevina Winery *1993 Brioso Zinfandel*
Region: USA—California   **Suggested Retail: $7.00**
Availability: Good   **Golds: CA, EL**
This 1993 Brioso smells like a bowlful of freshly picked strawberries and boasts a smooth, delicious berry fruit flavor enhanced by a hint of varietal spice. Brighter and paler in color, lower in tannin and acid, and displaying fruity aromas and soft, red juicy flavors, it is a classic Beaujolais-style wine.
Special Award: *Double Gold (EL)*

Did You Know ... ?
Known as the "Wine State," California produces 90 percent of all wine made in the United States.

Rosenblum Cellars *NV California Vintners Cuvée X Zinfandel*
Region: USA—California   Suggested Retail: $8.00
Availability: NP   Golds: FF
This wine is a great bargain from one of California's leading Zinfandel producers. Look for superripe berry fruit, a soft texture, and a long and mouth-filling finish.

Sausal Winery *1993 Zinfandel*
Region: USA—California   Suggested Retail: $9.00
Availability: Limited   Golds: OC
This Zin possesses medium body, abundant fruit, and a smooth finish.

Villa Mt. Eden *1993 Cellar Select Zinfandel*
Region: USA—California   Suggested Retail: $8.00
Availability: Limited   Golds: LA
Aromas of briar and vanilla introduce the jammy blackberry oak characters that are prevalent on the palate. This Zinfandel has ripe fruit characters and an assertive nature. Get out the barbecue and savor this wine's bold spiciness with grilled sausages or a good pepper steak, or have it with pizza prepared with generous amounts of garlic and onion.

Villa Mt. Eden *1992 Cellar Select Zinfandel*
Region: USA—California   Suggested Retail: $8.00
Availability: Limited   Golds: NW
This appealing Zin is fruity, round, and soft, with clean berry fruit and spicy, toasty oak notes. Drink it while it's young.
Special Awards: *Best of Price Class (NW); Trophy for Best New World Zinfandel (NW)*

Did You Know . . . ?
Zinfandel had a firm hold on the California wine business in the 1880s. It was the most popular wine of the miners who worked the California Gold Rush.

Adelaida Cellars *1992 San Luis Obispo County Zinfandel*
Region: USA—California   **Suggested Retail: $14.00**
Availability: Limited   **Golds: LA**
Produced from 80-year-old vines grown on rough and tumble terrain, this rustic wine has full body, medium acid, lots of wild berry fruit, and earthy, chocolate, peppery, dried fruit notes. It's almost a dessert style. The Wine Enthusiast *named this a Best Buy and gave it a gold medal.*

Alderbrook *1993 Dry Creek Valley Zinfandel*
Region: USA—California   **Suggested Retail: $14.00**
Availability: Good   **Golds: CA**
Vines more than 85 years old were used to make this full-bodied Zin. Aromas of ripe raspberry and blackberries are complemented with undertones of fresh ground pepper and sweet/toasty vanilla oak. Ripe flavors of berries, sweet oak, and supple tannins finish dry and smooth. This is a very age worthy wine.
Special Award: *Tie for Best Zinfandel of Appellation (CA)*

Baron Herzog *1993 Sonoma County Zinfandel*
Region: USA—California   **Suggested Retail: $11.99**
Availability: Good   **Golds: SD, TG**
This is a robust, full wine eliciting all of the positive characteristics of the Zin varietal. It has a distinctive stemmy aroma and pleasing oak nuances as part of the aftertaste. Although quite high in alcohol (15%), it is quite soft yet full in the mouth.

Belvedere Winery *1991 Dry Creek Valley Zinfandel*
Region: USA—California   **Suggested Retail: $11.00**
Availability: Good   **Golds: LA, SD**
Some of the vines used to make this great Zin date back to 1900, which is pretty darn old for American grapevines. This wine benefits from French and American oak barrel aging, offering classic Zinfandel character. Full bing cherry flavors are accented with black pepper. Other spice aromas mix with the oak's softening finish, creating a well-balanced, thoroughly delightful wine.
Special Award: *Best of Class (LA)*

Cline Cellars *1993 Contra Costa County Zinfandel*
Region: USA—California   **Suggested Retail: $12.00**
Availability: Good   **Golds: DA, TN**
This rich wine has flavors of ripe raspberry and blackberry, mocha, and white pepper. It has a great spicy oak character and a long, lingering finish. Concentrated flavors and a beautiful balance make this wine drinkable now, or after 5 to 7 years of cellaring.

Did You Know . . . ?
In ancient Persia, during the Archaemenid Dynasty, women laborers who bore sons were rewarded with ten quarts of wine. Those who bore daughters received five quarts.

Davis Bynum Winery *1992 Russian River Valley Zinfandel*
Region: USA—California   Suggested Retail: $12.00
Availability: Good   Golds: RE
Produced from vines with an average age of 80-plus years, this Zin is full bodied and concentrated.

Dry Creek Vineyard *1992 Zinfandel*
Region: USA—California   Suggested Retail: $14.99
Availability: Good   Golds: SD, HH
Opulent brambleberry and blackberry scents impart an intriguing bouquet of ripe fruits and spice. Sweet vanilla and oak intermingle with earthy notes and jammy, berry flavors. The soft, voluptuous texture leaves an impression of elegance, yet the nicely balanced finish is long and moderately powerful.
Special Award: *Best of Class (SD)*

E. & J. Gallo Winery *1992 Frei Ranch Vineyard Zinfandel*
Region: USA—California   Suggested Retail: $15.00
Availability: NP   Golds: NW
Here's a concentrated, full-bodied wine with deep black cherry and ripe raspberry fruit components, enhanced by spicy black pepper and rich vanilla oak aromas and flavors.

Eberle Winery *1993 Sauret Vineyard Zinfandel*
Region: USA—California   Suggested Retail: $13.00
Availability: Limited   Golds: SF, IE
This is a medium-dark ruby wine with purplish tinges. It hds a rich, intense, slightly jammy, cedary, spicy, briary, ripe berry fruit aroma with hints of vanilla. This extroverted wine has a finish that lasts nearly a minute, providing a huge mouthful of wine, and will be best if cellared for a few years. Incidentally, it won first place in Belgium's Vino Veritas tasting against 49 other California Zins.

Edmeades Estate *1993 Zeni Vineyard Zinfandel*
Region: USA—California   Suggested Retail: $20.00
Availability: NP   Golds: NW
Here's a classic Zinfandel, ripe and intense, with bold aromas of blackberry, raspberry, black pepper, and spice. It is full bodied with a rich, round mouth feel.

Did You Know . . . ?
DNA fingerprinting is used to track down elusive grape varieties that try to get by on an alias. Many a fraud has been found this way. One of the first discoveries took place fairly recently with this state-of-the-art technique, when in the early 1990s Zinfandel was found to be identical to Italy's Primativo grape.

Edmeades Estate *1992 North Coast Zinfandel*
Region: USA—California   **Suggested Retail: $12.00**
Availability: NP   **Golds: FF**
This is a rich, intense wine with forward flavors of raspberry, black cherry, spice, and black pepper. It is a full-bodied Zin with soft tannins and a round and sensuous mouth feel. Although the wine is 96.15% Zinfandel, the winemaker chose to make the other 3.85% a blend of Grenache, Alicante Bouchet, and Sangiovese. That's a perfectionist!

Gary Farrell Wines *1993 Collins Vineyard Zinfandel*
Region: USA—California   **Suggested Retail: $15.00**
Availability: Limited   **Golds: NW, FF, BT, SO**
Medium dark ruby, with attractive, intense, herbal, earthy, slightly spicy, ripe berry fruit aromas and hints of cedar and pepper, this wine is well balanced, with medium tannins. Drink it while it's young.
Special Award: *Best of Category (FF)*

Greenwood Ridge *1993 Scherrer Vineyards Zinfandel*
Region: USA—California   **Suggested Retail: $13.50**
Availability: Limited   **Golds: RE, OC, CA, LA, NW, FF**
These Zin grapes come from 70-year-old vines. The wine was fermented in small, open vats and aged for 6 months in French oak barrels. It has a soft, round texture with jammy berry flavors and will enhance a variety of dishes, from pizza and hamburger to pasta and roast duck.

Haywood Estate *1992 Rocky Terrace Estate Zinfandel*
Region: USA—California   **Suggested Retail: $18.00**
Availability: Limited   **Golds: NW, FF**
This Zin draws fruit from the fractured rock terraces of Los Chamizal Vineyard in Sonoma Valley. The grapes from this tiny plot are noted for their concentrated spice and blackberry flavors. The resulting wine, aged in new oak barrels, is intensely flavored and elegantly structured. Only a few hundred cases are made each year, so if you should see a bottle on a wine list or in a wine shop, by all means grab it.

Hop Kiln Winery *1993 Primitivo Zinfandel*
Region: USA—California   **Suggested Retail: $18.00**
Availability: Limited   **Golds: CA**
This ruby red wine has sweet and buttery aromas of raspberry, vanilla, chocolate, and cinnamon spice. On the palate it has firm tannins and structure with ripe grape, juicy blackberry, and raspberry flavors. In the finish are hints of black pepper. This is a dense, solid, elegant, and complex wine.

Did You Know . . . ?
Missionaries played a large role in the establishment of viticulture in New Zealand, California, and South America, mainly for the production of sacramental wines.

J. Fritz Winery *1993 80 Year Old Vines Zinfandel*
Region: USA—California   **Suggested Retail: $12.00**
Availability: Good   **Golds: OC, LA, SD, SO, AT**
Made from 80-year-old vines, this wine has cherry, berry, and spice aromas that waft from the glass. It has mouth-filling fruit flavors, which are deep, rich, and full bodied. The raspberry finish concludes with a good balance of tannins and plenty of warm vanilla, spice, and toasty oak. If you like Zinfandel, or are ready for a change of pace, check this one out. You aren't going to find a Zin with many more golds than this one—and look at that price!
Special Award: *Sweepstakes Winner, Red Wine (SO)*

Jankris Vineyards *1993 Zinfandel*
Region: USA—California   **Suggested Retail: $20.00**
Availability: NP   **Golds: PR**
This wine has raspberry and smoky flavors with a little oak finish. It was made with 25% whole berry fermentation and was seasoned in French oak. The Wine Spectator *rated this one an 89.*
Special Award: *Best of Class (PR)*

Kendall-Jackson *1992 Grand Reserve Zinfandel*
Region: USA—California   **Suggested Retail: $20.00**
Availability: NP   **Golds: RE, NW**
Spicy aromas and cherry fruit greet the nose and mouth, along with medium tannin and body. Rich color and fine depth complete the picture. Drink this wine over the next 4 to 5 years.

Lava Cap *1993 El Dorado Estate Bottled Zinfandel*
Region: USA—California   **Suggested Retail: $20.00**
Availability: Limited   **Golds: CA, EL, AM**
With intense fruit and spicy flavors, this Zin is full bodied and has soft tannins. If the judges went so crazy over this wine, you will too.
Special Awards: *Double Gold Medal (CA); Best Zinfandel of California (CA); Tie for Best Zinfandel of Appellation (CA); Best of Show (EL); Double Gold (EL)*

McIlroy Family Wines *1993 Porter-Bass Vineyard Zinfandel*
Region: USA—California   **Suggested Retail: $15.00**
Availability: Limited   **Golds: RE, OC, LA, PR, FF**
This wine has spice and berry flavors and is a beautiful deep red color with a medium body and fruity, berry jam aromas. It is rich in the mouth with ripe fruit and wonderful tangy notes with a soft, elegant finish. Look at all those golds!
Special Awards: *Best of Class (LA); Chairman's Award (FF)*

Did You Know . . . ?
Leftover wine, even if it's no longer great to drink, makes perfectly acceptable cooking wine. Coq au vin, anyone?

<u>Meeker Vineyard</u> *1993 Gold Leaf Cuvée Zinfandel*
Region: USA—California　　**Suggested Retail: $13.00**
Availability: Limited　　**Golds: LA**
This is the quintessential Dry Creek Zinfandel with lots of berry components and pepper spice. It has an intense concentration of new French oak and a little bit of American oak. The 35- to 100-year-old vines were low yielding and head pruned.

<u>Mission View Vineyards</u> *1993 Estate Bottled Zinfandel*
Region: USA—California　　**Suggested Retail: $11.50**
Availability: Limited　　**Golds: CA**
Rich, wild blackberries, ripe blueberries, and a medley of spice boldly dictate the aromas and flavors of this wine. This is a "monster Zin" at 15.8% alcohol, allowing one to enjoy warm, round, full, and yet supple flavors.
Special Award: *Best Zinfandel of Appellation (CA)*

<u>Nichelini</u> *1991 Joseph A. Nichelini Vineyard Zinfandel*
Region: USA—California　　**Suggested Retail: $12.00**
Availability: Limited　　**Golds: CA**
The grapes used for this wine were from 67-year-old vines. The wine has ripe berry aromas, heady perfume, garnet hues, and is full bodied, luscious, smooth, and elegant.
Special Awards: *Double Gold (CA); Best Zinfandel of Appellation (CA)*

<u>Peachy Canyon Winery</u> *1993 Dusi Ranch Zinfandel*
Region: USA—California　　**Suggested Retail: $20.00**
Availability: Limited　　**Golds: OC**
This is a dry-farmed, head-pruned, pre-Prohibition vineyard. Planted in the 1920s, the Benito Dusi Ranch has become, according to the winemaker, "our favorite source of 'sine qua non' Zinfandel . . . the best grown anywhere, in our humble opinion." This is a full-bodied wine with concentrated, jammy raspberries on the nose, spicy currants, and a little prune. Total elegance!

<u>Preston Vineyards</u> *1993 Dry Creek Valley Zinfandel*
Region: USA—California　　**Suggested Retail: $12.00**
Availability: NP　　**Golds: SF**
Anticipate hues of ruby with purple highlights; flavors and aromas of cherries, raspberries, cinnamon, and pepper; ripe tannins; and crisp acidity. The wine has a long and savory finish, with 3 to 10 years aging potential.

Did You Know . . . ?
California and Oregon are the only states, to our knowledge, that have a specific "wine doggie bag" statute allowing you to cork your unfinished bottle of (usually overpriced) wine in the restaurant where you've just dined, and take it home with you.

Rabbit Ridge Vineyards *1993 Dry Creek Valley Zinfandel*
Region: USA—California   Suggested Retail: $11.00
Availability: Good   Golds: RE, PR, NW

Look for rich, dark color in this full-bodied wine with a long finish. You'll love its very jammy style with blackberry, currant, and cherry flavors along with hints of spice.

A. Rafanelli Winery *1993 Dry Creek Valley Zinfandel*
Region: USA—California   Suggested Retail: $13.00
Availability: Limited   Golds: CA

Recently in Portland, Oregon, we had an unforgettable dinner at a restaurant called Wildwood. On the super wine list we found this Zin, and ordered a bottle to have with our meal. Between the mouth-watering cuisine and the unbelievable wine, we were in heaven. The winery, according to Wildwood's coowner, is family owned and operated, and their wines are not made in vast quantities. However, he made sure and got a case or two of this beauty for his spectacular wine list. We're so glad he did. If you see it anywhere, whether shopping or dining, don't hesitate to buy a bottle. You'll love its array of spicy fruit flavors that go on and on. It's a great accompaniment to buffalo steak.
Special Award: Tie for Best Zinfandel of Appellation (CA)

A. Rafanelli Winery *1992 Dry Creek Valley Unfiltered Zinfandel*
Region: USA—California   Suggested Retail: $14.00
Availability: NP   Golds: NW

Here's a dark ruby/purple-colored Zin with a knock-out nose of ripe black raspberries, pepper, and spice. Look for medium to full body, flavors that never stop, and a velvety texture. This wine has loads of concentrated fruit, with light tannin and a heady finish. If cellared properly it can be drunk over the next 7 to 10 years.

River Run Vintners *1992 California Zinfandel*
Region: USA—California   Suggested Retail: $15.00
Availability: Limited   Golds: RE, PR
This Zin has a rich, raspberry nose, modest tannins, and a full finish.

Did You Know . . . ?
Most of the greatest vineyards of Europe were created or owned by cathedrals and churches during the Middle Ages. The Church came to be identified with wine, not only as Christ's blood, but as a symbol of the luxury and comfort in this world. The twelfth-century Benedictines became so notorious for their way of life that one writer referred to them as "rising from the table with their veins swollen with wine and their heads on fire."

Rodney Strong *1992 Old Vines River West Vineyard Zinfandel*
Region: USA—California **Suggested Retail: $14.00**
Availability: NP **Golds: NW**

The gnarled 90-year-old vines produced a small amount of fruit with intense blackberry, raspberry/briar patch flavors, spiced with a peppery character. The fruit is enhanced with moderate oak tones and is rich and full in the mouth with fine acid-tannin balance. It promises excellent aging potential.
***Special Award:** Best of Price Class (NW)*

Rombauer Vineyards *1993 Napa Valley Zinfandel*
Region: USA—California **Suggested Retail: $18.00**
Availability: NP **Golds: PR**

This wine greets you with a splash of vanilla. Look for highlights of tropical fruits and ripe peaches with aromas that are complemented with layers of honey and hints of fresh, creamy butter. The finish is long and rich.

Rosenblum Cellars *1993 Brandlin Ranch Zinfandel*
Region: USA—California **Suggested Retail: $19.00**
Availability: Limited **Golds: OC**

This high-extract Zinfandel exhibits a ripe, opulent, brambly, blackberry bouquet with hints of chocolate and spicy cream. The flavors are explosively ripe currant and blackberry with a vanilla and black cherry aftertaste. It has the potential to age for 8 to 15 years.

Rosenblum Cellars *1993 Paso Robles Zinfandel*
Region: USA—California **Suggested Retail: $12.00**
Availability: NP **Golds: RE, TG**

According to Robert Parker, Rosenblum Cellars continues to rank among California's "leading Zinfandel producers." We didn't get a lot of information on this one, but you can be sure that it is delicious. Rosenblum won several golds in 1995 for several of their Zins. We say, if you can do one thing extremely well, do a lot of it!

Rosenblum Cellars *1993 Old Vines Zinfandel*
Region: USA—California **Suggested Retail: $12.50**
Availability: NP · **Golds: OC, CA**

The vines that bore the fruit for this winner are 80 years old and from four different vineyards. This is a medium-bodied claret-style Zin. The bouquet shows ripe raspberries, cherries, and blackberries with nuances of cracked pepper and vanilla bean. The flavors are rich blackberry and cherry with chocolate and spices. A full, lingering aftertaste shows nicely. Recommended cellaring: 5 to 9 years.

Did You Know . . . ?
Most of the world's wine grapes are not vinified by the grape grower, but are sold as fresh fruit to be made into wine elsewhere.

Sierra Vista Winery *1993 Estate Bottled El Dorado Zinfandel*
Region: USA—California   **Suggested Retail: $10.00**
Availability: Limited   **Golds: LA**
Here's an elegant wine without the nitty-gritty mouth feel of many Zinfandels. It has a distinct, red raspberry character with a blackberry and peppery spice. Good acid balance, plenty of intense fruit, toasty oak, and soft tannins will allow this wine to improve for 5 to 10 years. As it ages, the range of flavors will continue to expand. Try it with Cajun, South American, or Mediterranean food.

Silver Horse Vineyards *1992 Paso Robles Zinfandel*
Region: USA—California   **Suggested Retail: $12.00**
Availability: Limited   **Golds: RE, SD**
Look for deep garnet color in this wine with a wonderful nose of cedar and chocolate. The intense, juicy Zinfandel characteristics fill your mouth with soft and generous fruit. Silver Horse wines can be found in California, Ohio, Washington, Canada, and Texas, and soon will be available in Colorado, Oklahoma, Arizona, and New Mexico as well.
Special Award: *Finalist for Sweepstakes Award, Red Wine (RE)*

St. Francis Vineyards *1993 Sonoma Valley Zinfandel*
Region: USA—California   **Suggested Retail: $16.00**
Availability: Limited   **Golds: RE**
This Zinfandel was produced from old vineyards of between 70- and 100-year-old vines. The small crop yielded intense fruit, and a field blend of Petite Syrah and Alicante Bouchet provided the wine with a deep, rich color. Unfined and unfiltered, this wine will complement many hearty dishes.

Storrs Winery *1993 Santa Cruz Mountains Zinfandel*
Region: USA—California   **Suggested Retail: $16.00**
Availability: Limited   **Golds: SF**
The color of this Zin is deep ruby with a purple edge. The nose offers up ripe brambleberries—ollaliberry, raspberry, and loganberry—with accents of black pepper and vanilla. In the mouth it is bold and full bodied, yet with a very supple palate. Rich brambleberry notes reemerge, complemented by soft vanilla and a long, lingering finish.

Did You Know ... ?
Decanter labels, made to hang from a chain on a decanter to identify the type of wine inside, have been around for more than two centuries. Some are quite exquisite and fetch thousands of dollars from obsessed collectors. They can be made of everything from lowly lead, fabric, leather, or tin to ivory, silver, mother-of-pearl, or gold.

Storybook Mountain Vineyards *1991 Estate Reserve Napa Valley*
Region: USA—California   **Suggested Retail: $25.00**
Availability: Limited   **Golds: SD**
Look for intense, sweet red raspberry fruit with spicy hints of cloves and cardamom, accented by a touch of oak and a suggestion of orange peel. On the palate there is immense focus and length. This Zin has a sensuous balance of depth of fruit and judiciously soft tannins. A lingering finish leaves the mouth refreshed and suffused with bright raspberry flavor. Robert Parker rated this one a 90+.

Topolos at Russian River *1993 Sonoma County Zinfandel*
Region: USA—California   **Suggested Retail: $20.00**
Availability: Limited   **Golds: IV**
A restrained, complex, pedigreed wine that offers a range of flavors one might associate with a fine Bordeaux, such as berry, spice, oak, and earth. This one seems to have it all.

V. Sattui Winery *1991 Howell Mountain Zinfandel*
Region: USA—California   **Suggested Retail: $30.00**
Availability: Limited   **Golds: IW, IV, NW, AT, SE**
Limited to 6 bottles per person, this wine, described by the winery as "a great wine from a great vintage," can be purchased only from V. Sattui. It has a fine balance between concentrated, spicy fruit and tannin. Look at all of those golds! Call them before it disappears, at (707) 963-7774, or fax them at (707) 963-4324.
Special Awards: *Trophy for Best Zinfandel (IW); Cellar Selection (SE)*

Whaler Vineyard *1992 Zinfandel Estate*
Region: USA—California   **Suggested Retail: $10.00**
Availability: Limited   **Golds: OC**
Primarily coopered (barreled) in American oak, this Zin has elegance, a silky mouth feel, and flavors and aromas of berries. It is medium bodied and soft, and is ideal for drinking over the next 4 to 5 years. However, supplies are limited, so if you're determined to find this one, you might want to call the winery directly at (707) 462-6355, because it's been selling like hotcakes.

Did You Know . . . ?
The California Gold Rush in the mid-nineteenth century played a major role in the establishment of a thriving California wine industry. First, those thirsty miners created a big demand for wine, so production soared. Second, all the new wineries springing up needed laborers, so a new sector of mostly immigrant workers was born. And third, when gold became less attractive, frustrated miners seeking more security moved into the grape-growing and winemaking biz.

Windsor Vineyards *1991 Shelton Signature Series Zinfandel*
Region: USA—California   **Suggested Retail: $14.17**
Availability: Limited   **Golds: DA**

The color of this wine, according to the excitable winemaker, is "dark cranrazzberry" red. Decadent aromas of intense raspberry jam and rich, sweet, chocolatey oak toast, along with loads of peppery spice, leap out of the glass. The flavors are of raspberry truffles—dark chocolate through and through, vibrant with ripe berry fruit and spicy black pepper and anise, a hint of cloves, rounded out sweetly with smoky-sweet oak toast. Wow! A silky texture with lively acid and slightly chewy tannin backbone for graceful aging—energetically firm, yet developing soft voluptuous curves. The finish is long, with berry-chocolate flavors, and is soft and chewy. The winemaker suggests having "razzberry chocolate decadence cake" as a main course, along with this wine, of course. Or try it alongside chicken with not-too-spicy mole sauce.

Did You Know ... ?
With DNA typing or "fingerprinting," in which grape varieties can be distinguished from one another, the chances of two vine varieties having the same DNA pattern are one in 6 million.

Chapter 11

WHITE WINES

Chardonnay
Chenin Blanc
Gewürztraminer
Other Whites
Riesling
Sauvignon Blanc
Sémillon
White Blends
White Zinfandel

Andres Wines *1993 Niagara Peninsula Peller Estates Chardonnay*
Region: Canada   Suggested Retail: $8.95
Availability: Very Good   Golds: VI, CI
A soft, buttery, pleasant Chardonnay with nuances of American oak, this wine underwent malolactic fermentation, and has a lovely straw color. Flavors and aromas reminiscent of apple butter emerge from the glass and linger throughout the long finish.
Special Award: Grand Gold Medal (VI)

Arbor Crest *1993 Columbia Valley Cameo Reserve Chardonnay*
Region: USA—Washington   Suggested Retail: $9.50
Availability: Limited   Golds: NW
Butterscotch, vanilla, and toasty accents are prominent in this medium-bodied Chardonnay that is brightly fruity and lively. Fine ripeness, balance, and character make this wine a great bargain for the price. Cellar it up to 1998.

Beaulieu *1993 Beautour Chardonnay*
Region: USA—California   Suggested Retail: $9.99
Availability: NP   Golds: PR
This wine matches the forward fruity character of peaches, pears, and apricots with a subtle toasty oak character from the barrels. This Chardonnay is quite soft and drinkable now. You can savor it on its own or serve it alongside a variety of lighter foods.

Belvedere Winery *1993 Sonoma County Chardonnay*
Region: USA—California   Suggested Retail: $9.00
Availability: Very Good   Golds: NW
This is an abundantly fruity wine, with aromas and flavors of apples, pears, and pineapples and a hint of spice. Flavors of light, toasty oak and a touch of butterscotch make this a smooth, rich, and complex wine. A great value from one of Sonoma County's top Chardonnay wineries.

Canyon Road *1993 California Chardonnay*
Region: USA—California   Suggested Retail: $6.00
Availability: Very Good   Golds: FF
Out of a field of 214 Chardonnays in its class, only 8 golds were awarded, and this was one. This is a relatively full-bodied Chardonnay style, made of 79% Chardonnay and 21% Chenin Blanc. The price is definitely right.

Did You Know . . . ?
Ontario's Niagara Peninsula produces 90 percent of Canada's wines. Balmy breezes blowing off the Great Lakes create ideal vineyard conditions here. Surprised?

Carmen Vineyards *1994 Chardonnay*
Region: Chile   **Suggested Retail: $6.99**
Availability: Very Good   **Golds: LJ**
One of our favorite wines is Chilean, and we can't wait to try this one, which you should have no problem finding in the United States. This Chardonnay is a light brilliant color with fruity aromas and a touch of vanilla. It is a light-bodied wine with nice flavors, and is crisp, with a lingering finish.

Carmen Vineyards *1994 Reserve Chardonnay*
Region: Chile   **Suggested Retail: $9.99**
Availability: Very Good   **Golds: LJ**
Both the reserve and the "regular" Chardonnay from Carmen's 1994 vintage won golds, so we have confidence that this Chilean winery has its eyes on the top. Light and brilliant in color, it has intense aromas of tropical fruit, with the added complexity of oak. A good structure on the palate with a medium body end in a beautiful lingering finish. You can buy this in the United States.

Cartlidge & Browne *1993 Chardonnay*
Region: USA—California   **Suggested Retail: $7.50**
Availability: Good   **Golds: OC**
This was the only wine awarded a gold in its field of 50. It displays varietal character with especially aromatic qualities, combining the freshness and delicacy of apples and pears with suggestions of vanilla and cognac spiciness. Drink this one on hot summer evenings, since it is a lighter, fruit-focused Chardonnay. By the way, you can order it directly from the winery at (800) 946-3635.

Columbia Crest *1993 Columbia Valley Chardonnay*
Region: USA—Washington   **Suggested Retail: $8.00**
Availability: Limited   **Golds: PR**
It may be hard to find this wine, but keep trying. The winemaker says that picking up a glass of this wine is like holding a bowl of ripe fruit. Fragrant, tropical fruit aromas accompany well-rounded pear, apple, and butterscotch flavors. It also has a rich toasty finish and a nice balance between fruit and acid.

Concannon *1993 Central Coast Selected Vineyard Chardonnay*
Region: USA—California   **Suggested Retail: $9.75**
Availability: Very Good   **Golds: FF**
Out of 214 Chardonnays in its class, only 8 golds were awarded at Farmer's Fair. According to one reviewer, it is a well-crafted wine nicely balanced between its apple and ripe pear notes and its subtle oak flavors. "Easy to drink," said another, and very flavorful for the price. By the way, if you have difficulty finding this or other Concannon wines, contact the winery directly at (510) 447-3760.

Did You Know ... ?
Chardonnay has the distinction of being the variety of which the most cuttings have been smuggled—in places like South Africa, New Zealand, and Australia, where stringent quarantine laws are enforced.

Errazuriz Panquehue *1994 Maule Valley Chardonnay Reserve*
Region: Chile   **Suggested Retail: $8.00**
Availability: NP   **Golds: IV**

Here's a wine that shows fragrant, mature peach with some sweet oak tones. It possesses a ripe, soft, fat, chunky style with nice oak and good balance. This wine is available in the United States.

Estrella River Winery *1993 Proprietor's Reserve Chardonnay*
Region: USA—California   **Suggested Retail: $6.00**
Availability: NP   **Golds: LA**

Ripe apple flavors complement a lively, stylish aroma. Full-bodied, this wine shows excellent balance and harmony. The finish is long and flavorful.

Fetzer *1993 Bonterra Organically Grown Chardonnay*
Region: USA—California   **Suggested Retail: $8.99**
Availability: NP   **Golds: DA, NW**

Apple and citrus flavors with ripe overtones of tropical fruit are complemented by complexities of sweet vanilla-spice, butterscotch, and coconut. This wine is rich, creamy smooth, and elegant in the mouth.

Goundrey Wines *1995 Unwooded Chardonnay*
Region: Australia   **Suggested Retail: $9.50**
Availability: Very Good   **Golds: AU**

Fresh apricot and peach aromas, with some herbal hints, make up the bouquet. Pale straw in color, this wine has a round and persistent palate, displaying intense tropical fruit, with fig and peachy characters. This is the second vintage of Goundrey's unwooded-style Chardonnay, and it is proving to be immensely popular in Australia. It is also available in the United States.

Hope Farms Winery *1993 Chardonnay*
Region: USA—California   **Suggested Retail: $9.95**
Availability: Limited   **Golds: OC**

A buttery, full-bodied wine with light oak, and hints of vanilla and nutmeg. This was 1 of only 6 gold medalists in a field of 110.

Did You Know . . . ?

Sustainable viticulturalists practice techniques that attempt to avoid environmental degradation. Fetzer was one of the earliest wineries to try this approach and to achieve recognition for their efforts. Cover crops are used instead of fertilizers to enrich the soil, and undervine ploughing takes the place of using herbicides. Ploughing and driving heavy implements on wet soil are discouraged. Rather than fungicides, copper and sulphur sprays are used. In place of insecticides, soap sprays and natural oils control insects, along with "good" predator insects.

Indian Creek *1992 Anderson Valley Chardonnay*
Region: USA—California   Suggested Retail: $9.50
Availability: Limited   Golds: NW, CL
Here's a full-bodied wine loaded with spicy, toasty oak and ripe apple-pear and citrus fruit.

J. Furst Winery *1992 California Chardonnay*
Region: USA—New York   Suggested Retail: $9.99
Availability: Good   Golds: OC
At Orange County, out of 110 entries in its class, only 6 golds were awarded. This bargain-priced wine is fresh and complex with mouth-filling flavor. Expect flavors of vanilla, crisp citrus, spices, apple, and a hint of oak. Try it with friends over good conversation with cheese and nuts, or with roast duck.

Miranda Wines *1995 High Country Chardonnay*
Region: Australia   Suggested Retail: $9.45
Availability: Outside USA   Golds: RM, PE
Although this wine was not available in the United States at press time, the winery assures us that Miranda wines soon will be, so keep a look out for them. This one has fruit aromas of peach and apple. The palate is creamy in texture with rich fruit flavors. The natural crisp acidity of the Chardonnay fruit and its rich flavors are perfectly balanced with the wonderful toasty oak characters, creating a smooth lingering finish.

Parducci Winery *1994 Mendocino County Chardonnay*
Region: USA—California   Suggested Retail: $8.00
Availability: Very Good   Golds: CA
Expect aromas of apple and ripe fruit, crisp and fresh, with a rich varietal nose and a hint of oak in the background. It is brilliant green-gold in color, light medium in body, with just the right touch of oak.

Pillitteri Estates *1993 Oak Fermented Chardonnay VQA*
Region: Canada   Suggested Retail: $9.90 CAN
Availability: Outside USA   Golds: IV
Subdued oak aromas blend with hints of toast and apple. These are more pronounced on the palate where the mouth feel is round and the acidity is crisp. The clean finish slowly fades on a toasty note. The wine is available in Canada. For more information, call the winery at (905) 468-3147.

Did You Know . . . ?
As odd as it sounds, one common way of controlling frost damage to fragile grapevines is by aspersion, or sprinkling water over the vines. As the water freezes, it releases latent heat, thus protecting the vine tissue from injury.

R.H. Phillips Vineyard *1994 Barrel Cuvée Chardonnay*
Region: USA—California   **Suggested Retail: $7.99**
Availability: Very Good   **Golds: LA**
This wine has a citrus and apple fruitiness with yeasty, toasty oak, vanilla flavors. In the mouth it displays rich body. The oak aromas are apparent but complement the wine's natural fruitiness.

Robert Alison Winery *1994 California Chardonnay*
Region: USA—California   **Suggested Retail: $6.99**
Availability: Very Good   **Golds: LA**
Clean, well-defined varietal fruit teams up with crisp, partially barrel-fermented Chardonnay flavors to produce a delicious medium-bodied table wine. Although the wine is ready for consumption, it will easily hold in the cellar for another year.

Robert Mondavi *1993 Central Coast Chardonnay*
Region: USA—California   **Suggested Retail: $9.95**
Availability: NP   **Golds: IV**
Robert Parker says that Robert Mondavi's Chardonnays continue to go "from strength to strength." You can't argue with the price tag on this one, so if you see a bottle, pick it up.

Silver Lake Winery *1993 Columbia Valley Chardonnay*
Region: USA—Washington   **Suggested Retail: $5.99**
Availability: Good   **Golds: WW**
This Washington State wine is a pale golden color. The nose yields tropical fruit, especially bananas, followed by lemons and grapefruit. Expect a crisp and clean Northwest-style Chardonnay, moving toward maturity. A judicious touch of French oak adds to the full palate and medium finish.

Trapiche *1994 Chardonnay Oak Cask*
Region: Argentina   **Suggested Retail: $7.99**
Availability: Good   **Golds: IT**
The upper part of the Tupundato Valley in Argentina has a special fresh mesoclimate that is ideal for Chardonnay vines. A slow maturity process produced a complex and soft wine that combines with the natural flavors of the grape and the delicacy of the oak. You'll find this and other Trapiche wines in the United States, Canada, and Europe.

Did You Know . . . ?
One bottle in twelve of the world's wine is made in South America, and Argentina is number five in the world's production table.

Valley View Winery   *1992 Rogue Valley Chardonnay*

Region: USA—Oregon   Suggested Retail: $7.50
Availability: Limited   Golds: RE

Valley View has won more gold medals (11) in the past year than any other Oregon winery. This is a medium-bodied, straight-ahead style of Chardonnay with lovely tropical fruit, nice ripeness, and crisp, fresh acidity that gives the wine a zingy, refreshing finish. By the way, their Jazz Series label is a lot of fun.

Vichon Winery   *1993 California Chardonnay*

Region: USA—California   Suggested Retail: $9.99
Availability: NP   Golds: NW

Bright tropical fruit aromas dance with spice and toasted oak on the nose. This wine has rich texture, layers of fruit, and softness on the palate, which means you should run right out and drink it immediately. Try it with chicken tarragon or grilled shrimp.

Villa Mt. Eden   *1993 Cellar Select Chardonnay*

Region: USA—California   Suggested Retail: $8.00
Availability: Limited   Golds: NW

Honeyed fruits and toasted figs are pleasantly evident in this nicely rounded Chardonnay. Creamy butterscotch flavors progress into a generous basket of fruit with a rich finish of great length and focus.

Zellerbach Winery   *1994 California Chardonnay*

Region: USA—California   Suggested Retail: $8.99
Availability: Very Good   Golds: SD

A smooth, supple, and spicy wine with tiers of nutmeg, pear, and honey. The winemaker calls this a "no-nonsense" wine.

Did You Know . . . ?

Purchased by the Robert Mondavi family in 1985, Vichon Winery is a female-run operation, with a female general manager, and two females making the wine: Karen Culler, winemaker, and Pam Stevens, assistant winemaker. We're always happy to see women making remarkable wines in this male-dominated field.

Atlas Peak Vineyards *1993 Napa Valley Chardonnay*
Region: USA—California　　　　**Suggested Retail: $16.00**
Availability: Good　　　　　　**Golds: OC**

Here's a clean, crisp-style Chardonnay with tropical and citrus notes, and well-balanced oak overtones. Out of 103 entries in its class at Orange County, only 8 golds were awarded—this being one.

Baileyana *1993 Paragon Vineyard Chardonnay*
Region: USA—California　　　　**Suggested Retail: $13.50**
Availability: Very Good　　　　**Golds: OC**

Lemony, buttery fruit with rich pear and pineapple flavors are interlaced with small amounts of smoky oak. This one was 100 percent barrel fermented and underwent 100 percent malolactic fermentation. By the way, this Chardonnay received 1 of only 6 golds awarded out of a field of 110 entries.

Baron Herzog *1993 Chardonnay*
Region: USA—California　　　　**Suggested Retail: $10.99**
Availability: Very Good　　　　**Golds: IV**

Look for a traditional-style Chardonnay, dry and full bodied, with soft, buttery pear notes and a subtle oak aftertaste.

Beaulieu *1993 Los Carneros Chardonnay*
Region: USA—California　　　　**Suggested Retail: $11.99**
Availability: NP　　　　　　　**Golds: NW**

This wine has ripe peach and fruit aromas that blend well with the buttery, toasty character from barrel fermentation and malolactic fermentation. The mouth feel is rich and soft, making this a wine that is versatile with many foods.

Belvedere Winery *1993 Alexander Valley Chardonnay*
Region: USA—California　　　　**Suggested Retail: $11.00**
Availability: Good　　　　　　**Golds: RE, SD, TG**

A departure in style from previous vintages of this wine, the 1993 has more rich, creamy, and toasty oak components to complement the abundant varietal fruit. Aromas and flavors of pears and apples will greet your nose and palate. Wine Spectator *named this a Best Buy.*

Beringer Vineyards *1993 Napa Valley Chardonnay*
Region: USA—California　　　　**Suggested Retail: $10.00**
Availability: NP　　　　　　　**Golds: NW**

Look for plenty of fleshy, creamy apple and honeyed fruit. This wine is round and pure, has nice acidity, and can be consumed over the next several years. It's also an excellent value from this well-known winery.

Did You Know . . . ?
Think you can name half of all the world's grape varieties? Think again. It is estimated that there are 5,000 distinct grape varieties.

BRL Hardy Wine Company   *1994 Eileen Hardy Chardonnay*
Region: Australia   **Suggested Retail: $10.99**
Availability: Good   **Golds: RM, AD**

Medium to deep straw in color, this wine has citrus fruit characteristics and cashew nut, malt, and butterscotch evident on the nose. The palate is full and rich with creamy malt and vanilla complexities over sweet citrus. This Chardonnay has a soft, clean finish. By the way, this wine seems to win golds each and every vintage, and it is available in the United States.

Byron Vineyard   *1993 Santa Barbara County Chardonnay*
Region: USA—California   **Suggested Retail: $16.00**
Availability: Good   **Golds: CA, BT**

This vintage continues Byron's tradition of fragrant, harmonious Chardonnays. It has aromas of green apple and pear complemented by hints of vanilla and sweet oak. An exceptionally well balanced wine, this one displays a seamless structure and a rich, silky finish.

Callaway Vineyard   *1993 Calla-Lees Chardonnay*
Region: USA—California   **Suggested Retail: $10.00**
Availability: Very Good   **Golds: IW**

This wine is made in the classic sur lie *style, a process of aging the wine on the yeast lees to provide richness and complexity. Partial malolactic fermentation adds depth and texture. This one is full bodied and rich, and is an excellent complement to many dishes, including seafood, pasta in light cream sauce, and grilled chicken.*

Camelot Winery   *1993 Santa Barbara County Chardonnay*
Region: USA—California   **Suggested Retail: $16.00**
Availability: NP   **Golds: LA, OC, NW**

Characteristic of the finest Chardonnays from Santa Barbara County, this wine combines intensity and elegance. Papaya, peach, and mango flavors are balanced by soft vanilla and toast shadings from barrel aging. It has a smooth, silky texture that lingers through the drawn-out finish.
Special Award: *Best of Class (LA)*

Camelot Winery   *1993 Central Coast Chardonnay*
Region: USA—California   **Suggested Retail: $12.00**
Availability: NP   **Golds: IV**

The 1993 showcases opulent fruit in a smooth, polished style. The flavors of apple, citrus, and tropical fruit are enhanced by delicate spice and vanilla nuances developed during bottle aging. Intense flavors are nicely balanced by a creamy texture, continuing through a lingering finish.

Did You Know . . . ?
Didn't you ever wonder how long it takes that compressed cork to regain its full size after you've yanked it from the bottle? Wonder no more; catch up on lost sleep. The answer is: twenty-four hours.

Chapel Hill Winery   *1994 Reserve Chardonnay*
Region: Australia   **Suggested Retail: $14.25**
Availability: Good   **Golds: IV, HO**

This Chardonnay will last 7 to 10 years if cellared properly. It has an elegant, rich palate and medium lemon straw hues. The lifted nose exhibits the fresh citrus and melon characteristics of the Chardonnay spectrum overlain with the subtlety of malolactic and oak maturation. Like its French counterpart, this wine will peak after a period of bottle aging (1 to 5 years), rewarding the patient diner with its citrus, melon, and cashew nose, buttered toast and creamy palate. By the way, the wine-maker at Chapel Hill is a woman, and this and other wines she makes are available in the United States.
Special Award: *Trophy for Best Dry White (HO)*

Château Souverain   *1993 Rochioli Vineyard Reserve Chardonnay*
Region: USA—California   **Suggested Retail: $16.00**
Availability: NP   **Golds: LA**

This wine has a lively, green-gold color with complex aromas of tropical fruits, kiwi, and toasty/caramel nuances. The flavors follow naturally from the aromas and elicit impressions of sweet cream, peaches, clove, and oak toast. The ripe fruit from this cool-climate vineyard has been enriched by 100% malolactic fermentation and sur lie aging.

Château Souverain   *1993 Sonoma County Chardonnay*
Region: USA—California   **Suggested Retail: $12.00**
Availability: NP   **Golds: NW**

This wine is light straw in color and has an open, fragrant, floral-citrus quality in the nose, with undertones of caramel and cream. The aromas are followed by a soft, supple mouth feel, full of rich tropical, citrus, and yeasty/toasty flavors that combine to form an impression of richness that lasts into a long, clean finish.

Château St. Jean   *1993 Bell Terre Vineyards Chardonnay*
Region: USA—California   **Suggested Retail: $17.50**
Availability: NP   **Golds: PR**

Ripe pear and apple fruit, sweet oak and creamy, buttery nuances fill the nose of this complex Chardonnay. Richly textured, the wine offers layers of flavors of apple, hazelnut, vanilla, yeast, and French oak toast. The long, viscous finish is fresh and nicely balanced.

Did You Know...?

With the newly developed technology known as DNA typing or "fingerprinting," grape leaves or shoot tips provide the vine tissue to be analyzed. The DNA is isolated and then subjected to a series of biochemical manipulations, producing a sort of bar code pattern that can be read and stored in a computer, and used to determine a vine's genetic lineage.

Clos du Bois   *1993 Flintwood Vineyard Chardonnay*
Region: USA—California   **Suggested Retail: $17.00**
Availability: Good   **Golds: RE, LA**
Ripe pears and apples characterize the fruit flavors of this classic Chardonnay, which is light on the oak. Firm acidity and crispness round out the finish. Wine & Spirits *magazine named this one of the top 10 Chardonnays of 1995.*

Columbia Winery   *1993 Wyckoff Vineyard Chardonnay*
Region: USA—Washington   **Suggested Retail: $15.00**
Availability: Good   **Golds: LA**
This straw/lemon-colored wine has intense aromas of hazelnuts and vanilla mingling with tropical fruit, pineapple, and melon. It is full flavored and substantial, balanced with lively acidity, and has a fine, long finish.

Concannon   *1993 Livermore Valley Reserve Chardonnay*
Region: USA—California   **Suggested Retail: $14.95**
Availability: Limited   **Golds: NW**
Here's a surprising style of Chardonnay. It's pale yellow, austere, and lean but meaty, as opposed to milder, buttery, yeasty, sweeter ones that many have become accustomed to. Concannon was also named Winery of the Year by Wine & Spirits *magazine—for making consistently excellent wines. Try it and see what all the applause is about. The winery's number is (510) 447-3760; this wine was made in a small quantity, so they might be able to help you find it.*

Edmeades Estate   *1993 Mendocino County Chardonnay*
Region: USA—California   **Suggested Retail: $12.00**
Availability: NP   **Golds: DA, FF**
This wine is rich, complex, and concentrated with forward aromas of apple and citrus fruit and notes of butter and vanillin oak. A classic Mendocino Chardonnay. By the way, out of a field of 214 at Farmers Fair, there were only 8 golds awarded, this being one.

Edna Valley Vineyard   *1993 Estate Chardonnay*
Region: USA—California   **Suggested Retail: $15.00**
Availability: Very Good   **Golds: LA**
This wine presents concentrated aromas reminiscent of exotic fruits blended with elegant vanilla flavors slowly extracted from tight-grained French oak. It has a smooth mouth feel and creamy, yeasty flavors. The wine should be drinkable now, or can be cellared for 4 years. The winemaker says to try it with sashimi or lowfat popcorn!

Did You Know . . . ?
Before he became president, Thomas Jefferson served as the unofficial wine advisor to president George Washington.

Eola Hills Wine Cellars *1993 Oregon Chardonnay*

Region: USA—Oregon   **Suggested Retail: $10.00**

Availability: Limited   **Golds: OR**

Lemony, with a nice balance of acid, this Chardonnay has spicy oak and lots of fruit, but retains a fairly round body.

Fetzer *1993 Barrel Select Chardonnay*

Region: USA—California   **Suggested Retail: $10.99**

Availability: NP   **Golds: LA, NW**

Barrel fermented and barrel aged, this flavorful Chardonnay has finely layered aromas and flavors of creamy vanilla, enticing tropical lemon fruit, butterscotch, and lightly toasted oak. One reviewer suggests having a bottle with sautéed scallops, coconut prawns, and veal with mustard glaze. Yum!

Special Award: *Best of Price Class (NW)*

Franciscan Oakville Estate *1993 Napa Valley Chardonnay*

Region: USA—California   **Suggested Retail: $12.00**

Availability: NP   **Golds: RE**

This Chardonnay has complex aromas that include spice, tropical and citrus fruits, and toasty oak. The flavors are rich and slightly sweet, with a hint of oak—all ending on a long finish.

Geyser Peak Winery *1993 Sonoma County Chardonnay*

Region: USA—California   **Suggested Retail: $10.00**

Availability: NP   **Golds: RE, OC, PR, FF**

Out of a field of 214, only 8 wines were awarded golds at Orange. Of course, that shouldn't make a difference (a gold is a gold, after all, even if there's only 1 entry in a category), but we thought we'd mention it anyway. Please note that Geyser Peak is making many different Chardonnays, and they're all winning golds, so we would start with the least expensive one and work our way up.

Special Award: *Chairman's Award (FF)*

Did You Know . . . ?

Geyser Peak's new food and wine program, Great Chefs, Great Chardonnay, pairs America's premiere chefs with Peak Chardonnays, inviting them to create (and share) original recipes that make ideal accompaniments to the wines. Recipe No. 1 is by Chef Geral Hirigoyen of Fringale in San Francisco, and it's called Sea Scallops Napolean with Avocado and Melon. We have the recipe, but we're not sure we can share it!

Geyser Peak Winery *1994 Sonoma County Chardonnay*
Region: USA—California   **Suggested Retail: $10.00**
Availability: NP   **Golds: CA**

Here's the technical stuff from the winemaker: A medium-bodied Chardonnay displaying typical melon/apple fruit characters, complemented by buttery malolactic overtures and the complexity of yeastiness from the sur lie *process. The wine is balanced with sweet vanillin oak flavors that enhance the overall characters. An integrated, complex wine with a soft rounded palate and distinct flavor. Here's our advice: don't be scared off by winespeak—just try the wine and you'll see why Geyser Peak has won so many golds. You certainly won't be scared off by this price.*

Gloria Ferrer *1993 Carneros Chardonnay*
Region: USA—California   **Suggested Retail: $16.00**
Availability: Very Good   **Golds: DA, TG**

Look for a delicate balance of creamy pear, honey, vanilla spice, and nutmeg. On the palate the wine is smooth and creamy with toasted oak accents. It has a crisp, long, full finish and an understated style.

Goundrey Wines *1994 Reserve Chardonnay*
Region: Australia   **Suggested Retail: $14.25**
Availability: Limited   **Golds: AU, AD, MB**

Of medium gold-straw color and medium depth, this Chardonnay is clear and bright. The complex nose is redolent with scents of peach, cashew, and fig jam, with lovely integrated oak. On the palate the wine is round and full, with high-intensity fruit and peachy butterscotch flavors. The flavor goes on and on and ends with a clean, crisp finish. Winning many accolades from wine writers, this is a shining example of Chardonnay in a very competitive market, and is available in the United States.
Special Award: *Trophy for Best Chardonnay (MB)*

Guenoc Estate *1994 Estate Bottled Chardonnay*
Region: USA—California   **Suggested Retail: $14.50**
Availability: Very Good   **Golds: IV, FF, TG, IN**

With medium body and acid, subtle fruit, and moderate oak, this wine displays earth, lemons, and caramel. It is a crisp, straightforward Chardonnay with good balance and lingering oak and acids.

Did You Know . . . ?
Who exported the largest number of wines to the United States in 1994, behind first- and second-ranking countries France and Italy? The answer is Australia.

Hanna Winery   *1993 Sonoma County Chardonnay*

Region: USA—California   **Suggested Retail: $14.00**
Availability: NP   **Golds: OC, FF**

Out of 103 entries in its class at Orange County, only 8 golds were awarded, and this was one of them. Full and soft, this is a finely flavored, complex wine with apple, vanilla, hazelnut, and oak flavors and aromas. It has a moderate richness and a long, mildly oak finish. It's also a great value. For an even better deal, order it directly from the winery at (800) 854-3987.

Henry of Pelham Estates   *1993 Barrel Fermented Chardonnay*

Region: Canada   **Suggested Retail: $23.00 CAN**
Availability: Outside USA   **Golds: CI**

On the nose are pear, apple, and hints of nutmeg. Vanilla aromas emerge from French oak aging. This Chardonnay has a rich full-bodied texture with a long finish supported by citruslike acidity. The weight and complexity of this wine pair best with dishes that are neither too delicate nor overly cooked. A winemaker's favorite is grilled pork tenderloin, lightly marinated in tarragon, thyme, and a mixture of balsamic vinegar and Chardonnay. This wine is available in Canada, but not in the United States.

Hillebrand Estates Winery   *1992 Collector's Choice Chardonnay*

Region: Canada   **Suggested Retail: $13.95**
Availability: Limited   **Golds: IV**

This is a straw yellow wine with a pineapple, dry apricot, and vanilla nose. It has good fruit-oak balance, an oily mouth, and a full, round structure, with a touch of butterscotch and a bready aftertaste. Goes well with white meat or fish with a complex sauce, and is also great with soft cheese. It will keep for 2 to 4 more years.

Hogue Cellars   *1993 Reserve Chardonnay*

Region: USA—Washington   **Suggested Retail: $14.99**
Availability: Good   **Golds: PR**

Gleaning from various rave reviewers, this seems to be the consensus: rich citrusy fruit, honey, and caramel flavors; aromas of mangoes and pineapples; medium to full bodied, smooth and enticing; elegant and creamy. Need we say more? Hogue is turning out some magnificent gold-medal whites—and they aren't all Chardonnays—so check them out.

Special Awards: *Best of Class (PR); Trophy for Best Pacific Rim Chardonnay (PR)*

Did You Know ... ?

What does a Syrian-born heart surgeon who served time in Vietnam and is now chief surgeon at a major California hospital do in his spare time? Why, make wines, of course, or at least that's what Elias Hanna does, of Hanna Winery. Perhaps Dr. Hanna knows a bit about the health benefits of drinking wine. He says in winemaking he "finds balance, genuine peace, and a wonderful sense of completion."

Hunters Wines *1992 Marlborough Chardonnay*
Region: New Zealand   **Suggested Retail: $17.00**
Availability: Good   **Golds: IV**

A complex wine that shows floral and ripe lime fruit characters on the nose. On the palate the lime flavors persist with a creamy hazelnut and oaky lingering finish. This wine needs 3 to 4 years to achieve its full potential, and it is available in the United States.

J. Fritz Winery *1993 Sonoma County Chardonnay*
Region: USA—California   **Suggested Retail: $10.00**
Availability: Very Good   **Golds: PR**

This wine exhibits the entire gamut of aromas: apple, citrus, grapefruit, and tropical fruit, as well as coconut, peach, apricot, and nectarine. It has appealing hints of vanilla and butter on the middle palate and its pleasing crispness complements the fruity richness. The final pear, apple, and toasty highlights linger on the palate. We're talking superb balance. Serve it with pasta primavera, broiled salmon, fried calamari, or Cornish game hen.

Kendall-Jackson *1993 Camelot Vineyard Chardonnay*
Region: USA—California   **Suggested Retail: $16.00**
Availability: Limited   **Golds: OC, IV**

This wine is medium bodied with intense aromas and flavors of pears, pineapple, butter, and toasty oak. It has a round, luscious mouth feel and a long, lingering finish. By the way, the 1994 vintage is also a gold medalist.

Kendall-Jackson *1993 Late Harvest Select Chardonnay*
Region: USA—California   **Suggested Retail: $15.00**
Availability: Limited   **Golds: OC, IV, NW**

This inaugural vintage reveals complex flavors of peach and pear in perfect balance with its delicate floral aromas. It is rich and luscious in the mouth with a long, silky, smooth finish that lingers with a note of sweetness.

Kendall-Jackson *1993 Vintner's Reserve Chardonnay*
Region: USA—California   **Suggested Retail: $14.00**
Availability: Limited   **Golds: SF, LA, PR**

This wine combines full fruit flavors of peach and pineapple with a broad, buttery-vanilla character. Notes of toasty oak are also present. This is a full-bodied wine with a long, lingering finish. Because there are lots and lots of gold medal Chardonnays by the world-famous Kendall-Jackson, watch for the best price values. This one has a great price-to-value ratio—and look at all those golds!
Special Award: *Best of Show, White Wine (SF)*

Did You Know...?
The United Kingdom imports almost two-thirds of all wine produced in New Zealand.

Kendall-Jackson *1994 Camelot Vineyard Napa Chardonnay*

Region: USA—California   **Suggested Retail: $16.00**
Availability: NP   **Golds: SY**

This wine went all the way to Australia to win a gold in that country's very prestigious Sydney International Wine Competition. The judges loved it, and some of their comments were: "buttery, sweet nose with a popcornlike character"; "on the palate smooth, rich, subtly wooded, with a touch of sweetness"; "good acidity on the finish that seemed to hold the food quite well." (At Sydney, wines are judged alongside food. This one was served with Prawn and Leek Timbales on Crab Beurre Blanc.)

Kingston Estate *1991 Reserve Chardonnay*

Region: Australia   **Suggested Retail: $14.95**
Availability: NP   **Golds: AU**

Bright gold in color, this Chardonnay has a bouquet of rich, complex, developed fruit with underlying hints of oak. The palate shows developed fruit complexity with hints of peaches and well-integrated oak. Great weight and intensity of flavor combine with a long finish. Winner of numerous other national and international awards, this wine created a benchmark for Chardonnay from Australia's Riverland region. It is available in the United States.

Konzelmann Vineyards *1993 Chardonnay Reserve*

Region: Canada   **Suggested Retail: $16.25 CAN**
Availability: Outside USA   **Golds: CI**

Here's a very dry Chardonnay with excellent oak/fruit balance. It is lemony, with a hint of grapefruit and Granny Smith apples. Solidly balanced, it has a pleasant acid flip. This wine is available in Canada in limited quantities.

Lamoreaux Landing Wine Cellars *1993 Estate Bottled Chardonnay*

Region: USA—New York   **Suggested Retail: $15.00**
Availability: Limited   **Golds: LA, NW, IE, NY**

Lively and exotic with vibrant acidity, this wine has profound depth and complexity, displaying tiers of ripe pineapple, coconut, and pear flavors melded with a frame of vanilla-laced oak. Elegant and full bodied, it expands on the palate and finishes with a long, intense aftertaste. Here's a wine from New York State that was competing with wines from more traditionally revered regions—and won big. Try it!
Special Awards: *Best of Class (LA); Best of Class (NW); Trophy for Best New World Chardonnay (NW)*

Did You Know . . . ?

New York State grows more grape varieties than any other U.S. state. The reason is because New York has a long tradition of growing native American varieties, as well as French-American hybrids, along with the more commonly grown *Vitis vinifera* varieties planted in most fine-wine-producing regions.

Lockwood Vineyards   *1992 Partners' Reserve Chardonnay*
Region: USA—California   Suggested Retail: $17.00
Availability: Limited   Golds: LA, SD
According to the winemaker, "This wine reflects the highest quality, selectively hand-crafted Chardonnay we have to offer." Tropical fruit aromas dominate the nose.

Lockwood Vineyards   *1992 Monterey County Chardonnay*
Region: USA—California   Suggested Retail: $14.25
Availability: Good   Golds: PR, SD, MO, TG
Aromas of pineapple and banana waft from the glass. This wine is fashioned to balance the high varietal fruitiness with the rich, caramel character of French oak barrels.

Madrona Vineyards   *1993 Estate Bottled Chardonnay*
Region: USA—California   Suggested Retail: $11.00
Availability: Limited   Golds: CA, EL
Aromas of pear, lemon custard, hazelnuts, and vanilla leap from the glass. The palate is rich and smooth with notes of toasty oak in the lingering finish. This wine should continue to develop nicely over the next 2 to 3 years.
Special Award: *Best Chardonnay of Appellation (CA)*

McIlroy Family Wines   *1993 Aquarius Ranch Chardonnay*
Region: USA—California   Suggested Retail: $15.00
Availability: Limited   Golds: OC, PR, RE
Expect a wine of medium-light golden yellow with moderate body and acid. It has rich flavors of citrus, green apple, and buttered popcorn with toasty aromas of fruit, earth, and vanilla. The wine will expand with airing and has a long, attractive aftertaste.

Mill Creek Vineyards   *1993 Estate Grown Chardonnay*
Region: USA—California   Suggested Retail: $12.00
Availability: Limited   Golds: LA
Here you'll find aromas of vanilla and nutmeg, sweet pea, and piña colada. Flavors of coconut, citrus, and honeydew melon combine beautifully in a silky-textured mouth feel. An intense and complex wine, with lovely balance between fruit and oak.

Did You Know ... ?

Throughout history, wine has played a role in medicine and health. It was widely used as the medium for the infusion of medicinal herbs and many wine-based remedies back in the sixteenth century, according to the book *The Secrets of Alexis*, published in 1555.

Mission Hill Vineyards *1993 Grand Reserve Chardonnay*

Region: Canada   **Suggested Retail: $15.95 CAN**
Availability: Outside USA   **Golds: IW**

A rich and complex wine showing lemon butter, tropical fruit, and vanilla oak character that finishes clean and long. This wine has excellent cellaring potential, and is available in Canada, but not the United States.

Mitchelton Wines *1993 Victoria Chardonnay*

Region: Australia   **Suggested Retail: $16.99**
Availability: Good   **Golds: RM**

This high-quality winery wins golds left and right, and their wines are available in the United States. Unfortunately, the "tasting notes" supplied by the winery are very technical—having to do with specific gravity, volatile acid, cold stability, and so on. We suggest you skip the oenology lesson and go out and buy a bottle instead.

Montinore *1992 Willamette Valley Chardonnay Reserve*

Region: USA—Oregon   **Suggested Retail: $14.99**
Availability: NP   **Golds: RE, NW, TG**

This Chardonnay is rich and forward, loaded with fruit flavors as well as crisp, nutty-oaky flavor. The wine is well balanced with a good acidity and a creamy mouth feel. The bouquet displays butterscotch, light honey, vanilla, light pineapple-tropical fruit, and spices. A taste of this wine fills your mouth with tropical fruits, vanilla, pear-apple fruits, and an array of spices including white pepper and nutmeg. In addition to all of the golds it won in 1995, this wine also brought in a gold in 1994 from the Beverage Tasting Institute.
Special Awards: *Finalist for Sweepstakes Award (RE); Best of Price Class (NW)*

Napa Ridge Winery *1993 Napa Valley Reserve Chardonnay*

Region: USA—California   **Suggested Retail: $13.00**
Availability: Limited   **Golds: LA, MO, BT**

Barrel fermentation, aging, and lees stirring was used to bring out the richness and complexity of the Chardonnay grape in this wine.

Navarro *1993 Premier Reserve Chardonnay*

Region: USA—California   **Suggested Retail: $15.00**
Availability: Good   **Golds: OC, LA, NW, ME, TG**

This is a classic cold-weather Chardonnay with long and lingering flavor sensations. Look for apple, citrus, melon fruit, toasty French oak, and some delicate yeast-butter tones, with balanced alcohol and acidity.
Special Award: *Best of Price Class (NW)*

Did You Know ... ?

Do Old Worlders drink New World wines? Apparently they do, since in 1995 over $2 million worth of California wine was sold overseas.

Palliser Estate　*1994 Chardonnay*
Region: New Zealand　　　Suggested Retail: $16.65
Availability: NP　　　Golds: AI
You'll find this and other wines by this New Zealand producer in the United States. This one has fine structure with nice length and balance. Its ripe Chardonnay fruit characters are supported by high-quality French oak with complexity coming from the winemaking techniques employed.

Pine Ridge　*1993 Knollside Cuvée Estate Bottled Chardonnay*
Region: USA—California　　　Suggested Retail: $14.00
Availability: NP　　　Golds: OC
A generously endowed, medium- to full-bodied wine with layers of sweet, ripe, tropical fruit judiciously infused with new oak. Soft, richly fruity, as well as complex, this is a wine to drink over the next 2 to 3 years.

Plum Creek Cellars　*1993 Grand Valley Chardonnay*
Region: USA—Colorado　　　Suggested Retail: $10.00
Availability: Limited　　　Golds: NW
This one was aged primarily in French oak with a small percentage of new American oak. Smooth and mellow, with a hint of apple, this is a clear, crispy-style Chardonnay. Those who live in Denver will have the easiest time finding this Colorado beauty.

Richard Hamilton Winery　*1994 Chardonnay*
Region: Australia　　　Suggested Retail: $14.30 CAN
Availability: Outside USA　　　Golds: SY
One of the judges at Sydney called this wine "an orator rather than a pugilist." Some of the other comments from them were: "pale green/yellow in color"; "light to medium intensity on the nose"; "a Granny Smith apple nose"; "very good fruit"; "gently honeyed apple and melon flavor"; "a 'drink now' kind of wine"; "understated, delicate, harmonious, crisp, and fine." This one is available in Canada, as well as the UK, Denmark, Hong Kong, and New Zealand.

Robert Mondavi　*1993 Napa Valley Chardonnay Unfiltered*
Region: USA—California　　　Suggested Retail: $16.50
Availability: Very Good　　　Golds: IV
A naturally balanced, rich, flavorful wine. Slightly spicy aromas and flavors complement the crisp apple fruit flavors. The round, full texture is a great counterpoint to the bright fruit flavors.

Did You Know . . . ?

Plum Creek Cellars was founded back in the early eighties by six Denver wine enthusiasts into home-wine making. Former geologist Erik Bruner decided to become the full-time winemaker when their Colorado grape harvest yielded more than the six of them could drink.

Rodney Strong   *1993 Chalk Hill Vineyard Chardonnay*

Region: USA—California	Suggested Retail: $14.00
Availability: NP	Golds: RE

Extensive barrel fermentation, sur lie aging, and malolactic fermentation resulted in a boldly elegant Chardonnay with layers of complexity. Look for rich tropical pineapple and crisp apple flavors, hints of vanilla and nutmeg spice, and just the right amount of toasty oak.

Rosemount Estate   *1994 Hunter Valley Reserve Chardonnay*

Region: Australia	Suggested Retail: $13.40
Availability: Very Good	Golds: QU

On the palate this wine is soft and elegantly flavored with abundant, complex peach varietal fruit flavors and finely tuned oak, creating a wine with great length of fruit complexity and a solid texture. This wine has won over 66 golds and trophies since its first vintage in 1979. It will develop over the next 7 to 10 years in a cool cellar, and is available in the United States.

Rothbury Vineyards   *1994 Estate Reserve Chardonnay*

Region: Australia	Suggested Retail: $10.99
Availability: Good	Golds: HU

Each vintage, a small number of barriques *(small Voges barrels) are selected from Rothbury's barrel store for separate bottling. These* barriques *represent the best barrels of wine from the grapes grown on the estate. This wine comprises very ripe fruit and luscious oak. Best of all, it is available in the United States at an excellent price. (Also available in Europe and Japan.)*

Rothbury Vineyards   *1994 Barrel Fermented Chardonnay*

Region: Australia	Suggested Retail: $10.99
Availability: Good	Golds: RM

Barrel fermentation has produced an array of flavors with rich nutty characteristics underlying the dominant fruit. The fruit came from different vineyards with different terroirs, *which adds to the wine's complexity. Expect a sophisticated style of Chardonnay with an enormous mouth feel that still retains elegance. This wine is available in the United States as well as Europe and Japan.*

Did You Know . . . ?

Rodney Strong Vineyards was the first winery to identify Sonoma County's Chalk Hill appellation on its bottlings. The soil in this vineyard is *white,* and reflects the sun up and under the canopy as well as naturally down through it. The vines must struggle to survive in the poor calcareous soil, and in doing so produce fruit of great intensity with good natural acids and a distinctive flintiness.

Schug Carneros Estate *1993 Carneros Chardonnay*
Region: USA—California   Suggested Retail: $16.00
Availability: Limited   Golds: IV
This wine has a lovely, delicate bouquet filled with ripe pears, toasty overtones, and a hint of spice. Elegant fruit flavors of citrus, pineapple, and pear are framed by well-balanced acidity and a long, creamy yet clean finish. Reminiscent of a French white burgundy, it makes an exceptional accompaniment to fine cuisine, and pairs well with cream soups, seafood, and rich pasta dishes.

Sebastiani Vineyards *1993 Sonoma County Chardonnay*
Region: USA—California   Suggested Retail: $11.00
Availability: Very Good   Golds: RE, NW
Straw to gold in color, this wine has citrus and green apple aromas with hints of caramel, vanilla, and toasty oak. It's medium bodied, with tropical fruit and pear-apple flavors. The smooth finish is enhanced by butterscotch and lemon zest notes.

Sebastiani Vineyards *1994 Sonoma County Chardonnay*
Region: USA—California   Suggested Retail: $11.00
Availability: Very Good   Golds: LA
Light gold in color, this vintage has peach, pear, and Meyers lemon aromas with hints of caramel, vanilla, and toasty oak. Full bodied, it has citrus and Golden Delicious apple flavors. The finish is smooth, enhanced by notes of butterscotch and smoky oak. An excellent companion to regional favorites such as Dungeness crab and Atlantic salmon, and also wonderful with shellfish and cream-sauced dishes.

Simi Winery *1992 Chardonnay*
Region: USA—California   Suggested Retail: $13.00
Availability: NP   Golds: OC, FF
This wine is characterized in every vintage by its silky textures and well-balanced concentration of fruit and oak that follow through for a long, smooth finish. It has lush, tropical fruit notes in its aroma, and vanilla, citrus, pear, and honeyed fig notes in its flavors.

Vichon Winery *1993 Napa Valley Chardonnay*
Region: USA—California   Suggested Retail: $16.00
Availability: Very Good   Golds: LA
Look for tropical fruit aromas and flavors complemented by a creamy, rich mouth feel in this elegant Chardonnay. This is a bright wine with crisp acidity, pineapple and apple notes, and excellent balance. The winemaker suggests trying it with angel hair pasta tossed with garlic-and-oil-sautéed prawns. Yum!

Did You Know . . . ?

The standard mark-up for wine in restaurants is two to three times the suggested retail price for that bottle, yet restaurants often buy their wines at less than retail price.

Villa Mt. Eden   *1993 Grand Reserve Carneros Chardonnay*

Region: USA—California   **Suggested Retail: $16.00**
Availability: Limited   **Golds: RE, LA, CI**

Rich butterscotch, cream, and oak aromas comprise this three-dimensional tapestry. Abundant flavors, including warm spiced pear and toasted grain, add to the wine's depth. The finish is impressive and lingering.

Westport Rivers Vineyard   *1992 Gold Label Chardonnay*

Region: USA—Massachusetts   **Suggested Retail: $16.00**
Availability: Limited   **Golds: IV**

This wine has yellow-gold hues and a slight oaklike bouquet with heaps of apple tones. There's more apple, with citrus and vanilla in the mouth. It has a very smooth finish, with citric-lemony tones lingering. Although only a tiny amount of this wine was made (204 cases), we wanted to include it because New England is beginning to produce some wonderful wines that are standing up against top-class offerings from more well-known winemaking regions of the New World. The New York Times said that this one is not unlike decent wines from Burgundy—but the modest price tag makes the story even more interesting. Watch for these wines to start occupying more of your corner wine shop's shelves.

Yalumba   *1992 Show Reserve Chardonnay*

Region: Australia   **Suggested Retail: $15.00**
Availability: Limited   **Golds: IW**

This is a traditional style of Chardonnay that exhibits great fruit strength on the nose and a palate with a noticeable influence of assertive oak. The color is green-yellow and the nose conjures up melon and butterscotch entwined with nutty oak aromas. On the palate you'll find melon, coconut, and butterscotch flavors over a medium-weight palate, with tight acid and a mildly alcoholic finish. If correctly cellared it will continue to integrate and mature for 1 to 2 years. This wine is, happily, available in the United States, as well as in Canada, the UK, and New Zealand.

Did You Know . . . ?

Massachusetts's Westport Rivers Vineyard is an hour away from Boston. Situated on a seventeeth-century farm, it is the largest *Vitis vinifera* vineyard in New England. The concept of Massachusetts wine is not as strange as it might sound. It so happens that the climate there is almost identical to France's Burgundy region, except that February is colder.

Byron Vineyard *1992 Santa Maria Valley Estate Chardonnay*
Region: USA—California   Suggested Retail: $25.00
Availability: Good   Golds: OC
The 1992 displays intense aromas of honey, green apples, and luscious floral components with a hint of hazelnut. The wine reveals layer upon layer of rich, full flavors that are balanced by a firm acid structure. Complex and full bodied, this is a regal wine with excellent aging potential.

Cambria Winery *1993 Santa Maria Valley Reserve Chardonnay*
Region: USA—California   Suggested Retail: $25.00
Availability: NP   Golds: OC, CA, PR, FF
The golds this wine won tell it all. This one displays mouth-filling fruit, smooth texture, and a beautiful balance. Aromas of tropical fruit, sweet butterscotch, and toasty oak carry through on the palate and persist through the lingering finish.
Special Awards: Best Chardonnay of California (CA); Best Chardonnay of Appellation (CA)

Cambria Winery *1993 Katherine's Vineyard Chardonnay*
Region: USA—California   Suggested Retail: $18.00
Availability: NP   Golds: IV
The 1993 Katherine's Vineyard Chardonnay is a fruit-intense wine with layers of pineapple, papaya, and citrus fruit balanced by notes of vanillin oak and toast. It is a rich, luscious wine that is full in the mouth and long in the finish.

Charles Krug Winery *1992 Chardonnay Reserve*
Region: USA—California   Suggested Retail: $18.00
Availability: Limited   Golds: OC
Brilliant, green-gold in color, this wine has a lush bouquet of apple, pineapple, and tropical fruit melded with a soft vanilla character from the oak. The richness and complexity added by barrel fermentation are beautifully balanced by crisp acidity. The wine has a long and elegant finish, and was one of only 8 awarded a gold medal out of its field of 103 at Orange County.

Château Ste. Michelle *1993 Canoe Ridge Chardonnay*
Region: USA—Washington   Suggested Retail: $26.00
Availability: NP   Golds: RE
Ripe pineapple, apple, and pear aromas are evident in this debut Chardonnay from the winery. Sweet toasty oak, vanilla, and a slight spiciness are also detectable. Here's a creamy wine with abundant extract and structure. Try it with cracked crab.
Special Award: Finalist for Sweepstakes Award, White Wine (RE)

Did You Know ... ?
Founded way back in 1867, Charles Krug is the oldest winery in Napa Valley.

Château Ste. Michelle *1993 Columbia Valley Reserve Chardonnay*
Region: USA—Washington   **Suggested Retail: $30.00**
Availability: Limited   **Golds: DA**

This is a very expressive Chardonnay with pear, pineapple, apple, and melon. Oak aging contributes toast, spice, and smoke. Rich and creamy, it should grow gracefully and deliver even more complexity with cellar aging. This Washington winery has a portfolio full of gold medal winners, so if you can't find this Chardonnay, try another one. They tend to sell out quickly, so don't pass one up. Try this one with creamy seafood dishes.

Clos du Bois *1993 Calcaire Vineyard Chardonnay*
Region: USA—California   **Suggested Retail: $18.00**
Availability: NP   **Golds: RE, OC**

At Orange County this Chardonnay won one of only 8 golds awarded out of a field of 103. This is a major winery that makes serious, top-class wines. Buy a bottle and savor it on a romantic summer evening.

Clos du Bois *1992 Alexander Valley Calcaire Chardonnay*
Region: USA—California   **Suggested Retail: $18.00**
Availability: Very Good   **Golds: IV**

Here's another gold medal Clos du Bois Chardonnay, which was also named one of the Top 10 Chardonnays of the Year (1995) by Wine & Spirits *magazine. One reviewer calls it elegant. It has clear fruit on the palate, with just a hint of oak on the finish. This is an open and accessible wine—very user-friendly while young.*

Coldstream Hills *1993 Reserve Chardonnay*
Region: Australia   **Suggested Retail: $22.50 CAN**
Availability: Outside USA   **Golds: AD**

This wine is available in Canada, as well as the UK, the Far East, Europe, and New Zealand. It is bright yellow-green in color, and the bouquet is very fragrant, with melon and citrus fruit, spicy oak, and a hint of nuttiness. On the palate it is both very powerful and very long, with refreshing acidity. Cellar it up to 6 years.
***Special Award:** Trophy for Best White Wine Export (AD)*

De Loach *1993 O.F.S. Chardonnay*
Region: USA—California   **Suggested Retail: $25.00**
Availability: Good   **Golds: RE, LA**

Here's a Chardonnay full of tropical fruit aromas with elements of oak. It has deep layers of pineapple and apple flavors, a smooth, toasty richness in the mouth, and a lingering finish. The richness of the wine will deepen with 1 to 3 years of bottle age.

Did You Know . . . ?

Although Australia has achieved great success with it, Aussie Chardonnay was virtually *nonexistent* until twenty-some years ago, when world wine fashion incited a Chardonnay planting frenzy there.

E. & J. Gallo Winery   *1993 Estate Bottled Chardonnay*
Region: USA—California   Suggested Retail: $30.00
Availability: Good   Golds: OC, SF
This wine was bottled unfined and with minimal filtration in order to preserve its full character. It has richly flavored fruit; complex, rich, full texture; and natural high acidity. The final cuvée included only the "best of the best."

Fess Parker Winery   *1993 American Tradition Reserve Chardonnay*
Region: USA—California   Suggested Retail: $22.00
Availability: Good   Golds: PR, DA, LA
This is a richly textured wine with tremendous depth. From their lots of Chardonnay, select cuvées of superlative character were isolated to create a reserve wine, and then finessed to emphasize the character of the grape.

Gary Farrell Wines   *1993 Allen Vineyard Chardonnay*
Region: USA—California   Suggested Retail: $18.00
Availability: Limited   Golds: SF
A tight, compact Chardonnay offering nice, toasty oak blending with spice, pear, and apple. It expands on the complex finish, where butterscotch flavors add richness. Incidentally, of 500 Chardonnays tasted for the July 31, 1995, issue, this one was ranked highest by Wine Spectator.

Geyser Peak Winery   *1993 Alexander Valley Reserve Chardonnay*
Region: USA—California   Suggested Retail: $20.00
Availability: NP   Golds: LA, NW, FL, TG, LJ
Most of the information the winery provided about this wine is technical—malolactic fermentation (85%), 100% barrel fermented, sur lie *process, etc. We'd go by the number of golds it won, and also by the fact that Geyser Peak's Chardonnays win stacks of golds each year.*
Special Award: *Best of Price Class (NW)*

Guenoc Estate   *1993 Genevieve Magoon Reserve Chardonnay*
Region: USA—California   Suggested Retail: $22.50
Availability: Good   Golds: CA, AT, MO, TG, BT
This wine was 100% barrel fermented in pure Burgundian oak barrels similar to those used for the famous Montrachet wines. The full Genevieve fruit is etched in a creamy butter smoothness from 65% malolactic fermentation. Its rich butter and spice qualities beg for foods with varietal complexity and depth, such as lobster, wild mushrooms, and poultry with fresh herbs.
Special Award: *Best Chardonnay of Appellation (CA)*

Did You Know . . . ?
Cork is the only solid that can be compressed to half its dimension without losing any flexibility.

Guenoc Estate *1992 Genevieve Magoon Reserve Chardonnay*
Region: USA—California　　　**Suggested Retail: $22.50**
Availability: Good　　　**Golds: FF, FL**
Its opening bouquet of butter, apples, and melon develops into mouth-filling flavors of butterscotch, pears, and spice, enhanced by the subtle fragrance of orange blossoms. This wine was aged sur lie *in new Burgundian oak normally reserved for premier and grand cru Chardonnays of Burgundy. This wine will sing next to creamy soups with shiitake and chanterelle mushrooms.*

Jarvis Winery *1992 Estate Grown Napa Valley Chardonnay*
Region: USA—California　　　**Suggested Retail: $34.00**
Availability: NP　　　**Golds: LA**
The 1992 Chardonnay marks the debut of this varietal from Jarvis. It has a clean, complex white burgundy–style nose with good fruit and hints of oak and hazelnuts. The rich, deep, luxuriant flavors carry through to a long, lingering finish. No fining and minimal filtration were employed. You can order directly from the winery at (800) 255-5280.

Kendall-Jackson *1993 Grand Reserve Chardonnay*
Region: USA—California　　　**Suggested Retail: $24.00**
Availability: NP　　　**Golds: RE, OC, CI, IV**
Barrel fermentation and extended aging in small French oak barrels coupled with a secondary malolactic fermentation has added flavors of spice, smoke, vanilla, and butter to the apple, pear, and pineapple flavors from the grapes. The result is a luscious wine with a silky mouth feel.
Special Award: *Finalist for Sweepstakes Award, White Wine (RE)*

La Crema *1993 Grand Cuvée Chardonnay*
Region: USA—California　　　**Suggested Retail: $20.00**
Availability: NP　　　**Golds: LA, NW**
This is a wine marked by complexity and layers of tropical flavors (mango and papaya) blended seamlessly with ripe peach and pear, green apple, and citrus. It is rich, round, complex, and lush in the mouth and lingering in the finish. Its solid acid balance will assure long-term ageability.

Did You Know . . . ?
Jarvis, a relatively new name in Napa Valley, is located 1,000 feet up and has a 45,000-square-foot circular cave on a single level drilled into the Vacas Mountains. One writer described the cave as "other-worldly," with its design concept based on the parabolic arch, bisected by an interior babbling brook to keep the cave at a constant 80 percent humidity, spooky wall sconces, and color-changing fiber optics overhead. Wow! No photos are allowed in Jarvis's deluxe and mysterious wine cave.

Landmark Vineyards *1993 Damaris Reserve Chardonnay*
Region: USA—California   **Suggested Retail: $18.00**
Availability: Limited   **Golds: RE**
With rich apricot and pear nectar flavors, and light hints of vanilla and toast, this is a full-bodied wine of golden color that's smooth and silky on the finish. Wine Spectator *gave it a 90 rating, and Robert Parker's* Wine Advocate *rated it 88.*

Michel-Schlumberger *1992 Dry Creek Valley Chardonnay*
Region: USA—California   **Suggested Retail: $18.00**
Availability: Limited   **Golds: PR**
Uncommon in its depth of fruit, this wine flaunts flavors of citrus, apricot, and persimmon; a rich and creamy body and mouth feel; and a tart, minerally finish.

Morton Estate *1994 Hawkes Bay Black Label Chardonnay*
Region: New Zealand   **Suggested Retail: $18.35**
Availability: Limited   **Golds: NZ, ZE**
Look for nutty complexity and middle-palate weight. Typical grapefruit and melon fruit characters are balanced with biscuity barrel aromas and flavors, giving good aging potential. Do not serve chilled, says the winemaker. This wine can handle full-flavored foods, and will be at its best between 1996 and 1999. This wine is available in the United States in very limited quantities.

Rombauer Vineyards *1993 Carneros Chardonnay*
Region: USA—California   **Suggested Retail: $18.00**
Availability: NP   **Golds: DA**
Concentrated citrus fruit aromas with toasty oak suggestions; textured, ripe-apple flavors with subtle oak; and good length characterize this wine.

Sequoia Grove Vineyards *1992 Estate Bottled Chardonnay*
Region: USA—California   **Suggested Retail: $18.00**
Availability: Limited   **Golds: CI**
This Chardonnay is rich, fruity, up front, and firm, yet has a smooth body and structure.

Stag's Leap Wine Cellars *1993 Chardonnay*
Region: USA—California   **Suggested Retail: $19.00**
Availability: Limited   **Golds: OC**
Complex aromas of tropical fruit, apples, and spicy oak arise from the glass, with full-textured flavors, creaminess, and lots of oak on the mouth. This wine has a full finish and is perfect with grilled vegetables, according to one reviewer.

Did You Know . . . ?
It was the newly sophisticated servicemen returning from World War I who provided the crucial votes needed to overturn New Zealand's Prohibition in 1919.

Stonestreet Winery *1993 Sonoma County Chardonnay*
Region: USA—California   Suggested Retail: $22.00
Availability: NP   Golds: IV
This rich, round wine has flavors of apple, pear, and cinnamon with a hint of smoke in the long finish.

Stonestreet Winery *1992 Sonoma County Chardonnay*
Region: USA—California   Suggested Retail: $20.00
Availability: NP   Golds: SD
The wine is delicate in mouth feel yet packed with attractive aromas and flavors that invite retasting. It is rich, round, and supple with complex aromas of apple, cinnamon, and butter.

Stonestreet Winery *1993 Sonoma County Reserve Chardonnay*
Region: USA—California   Suggested Retail: $30.00
Availability: NP   Golds: CA
This is a daring, showy, Meursault-like wine that has intriguing aromas of honey, peaches, apples, butter, and smoke. Look for a rich, mouth-filling, full-bodied beauty with lots of concentration.

Swanson Vineyards *1993 Carneros Estate Chardonnay*
Region: USA—California   Suggested Retail: $20.00
Availability: Good   Golds: OC, LA, IW
Wow! The critics raved about this wine, which is medium straw in color and has intense floral, peach, pear, lemon drop, and vanilla scents. The flavors are firm and expansive, crisp and rich, with toasty oak and creamy tones followed by a long and lasting finish.

V. Sattui Winery *1993 Estate Bottled Carsi Vineyard Chardonnay*
Region: USA—California   Suggested Retail: $19.00
Availability: Limited   Golds: DA, MO, BT
This Chardonnay, barrel fermented in French oak, has distinctive oak and tropical fruit flavors. The winery says it is perhaps the finest Chardonnay they've ever produced. It's going fast, so order a bottle today from the winery (the only place V. Sattui's wines are sold) at (707) 973-7774, or by fax at (707) 963-4324.

Did You Know . . . ?

Archaeologists examining residues in an old clay jar from the Zagros Mountains of present-day Iran have found chemical traces of a Neolithic-vintage wine from a time long before anyone could ride a horse, make a wheel, or write. It is the earliest known evidence for winemaking, giving wine an extra 1,500 to 2,000 years of history. Tests revealed chemical proof that the vessel contained wine and traces of resin as a preservative, and scientists thus speculate that the wine probably tasted like today's Greek retsina.

ZD Wines   *1993 California Chardonnay*

Region: USA—California   **Suggested Retail: $22.00**

Availability: Good   **Golds: RE, PR, NW**

A superb example of ZD's style, this Chardonnay has richness and depth, complex tropical layers of pineapple, coconut, apricot, pear, and ripe grapefruit, and a toasty finish. The winery says this one is sold out, although they made 18,500 cases! We've found that "sold out" at the winery does not mean consumers won't find the wine in stores and on restaurant wine lists. But just in case, ZD will be rereleasing 500 cases in September 1996, with a $30 price tag to go with it. By the way, Robert Parker gave this one a 90.

Special Award: *Best of Class (PR)*

Did You Know . . . ?

Chardonnay is hands down the world's most popular varietal. During the 1980s, world wine production of Chardonnay *quadrupled.*

Baron Herzog *1994 Clarksburg Chenin Blanc*
Region: USA—California   **Suggested Retail: $5.99**
Availability: Very Good   **Golds: PR**

This is an intensely fruity, semidry Chenin Blanc with pear, melon, and subtle orange notes. It has good acidity and finishes a little dry. Here's a wine that's not made to age, so you should enjoy it right away while it's young. By the way, this Chenin Blanc has won more awards for quality than any other produced in the United States—2 years in a row.

Callaway Vineyard *1994 Morning Harvest Chenin Blanc*
Region: USA—California   **Suggested Retail: $6.00**
Availability: Very Good   **Golds: PR**

You'll find delicate aromas of peaches, pears, and tropical fruit in this Chenin Blanc, which has a rich fruit flavor and a fresh, crisp taste. It will sing and dance next to spicy foods.

Château Ste. Michelle *1994 Columbia Valley Chenin Blanc*
Region: USA—Washington   **Suggested Retail: $7.00**
Availability: Limited   **Golds: RE**

Here's a delicate, appealing Washington State wine, with a taste of ripe melons and undertones of citrus. It is off-dry and slightly spicy on the palate, with a long, lingering finish. Château Ste. Michelle has a culinary director who tastes their wines and recommends ideal foods to serve with them. He says this one will beautifully complement Asian dishes.

Dry Creek Vineyard *1994 Dry Chenin Blanc*
Region: USA—California   **Suggested Retail: $7.00**
Availability: Very Good   **Golds: CA, WC**

The lively bouquet bursts with tropical fruit aromas of grapefruit, citrus, and honeydew melon. Smooth and lush, this Chenin Blanc is packed with intense varietal fruit flavors, with a hint of flowers and honey. The finish is dry, crisp, and exceptionally well balanced.
***Special Awards:** Double Gold (CA); Best Chenin Blanc of Appellation (CA); Best Wine of Region (CA)*

Did You Know . . . ?

At the end of the nineteenth century, when Jews began to return to the Holy Land from the Diaspora, Baron Edmond de Rothschild's benefaction of 60 million gold francs made viticulture possible in Israel. Chenin Blanc cuttings imported from France were among the first vines planted there to establish what became a thriving wine industry until the 1948 War of Independence.

Dry Creek Vineyard   *1993 Dry Chenin Blanc*
Region: USA—California   Suggested Retail: $7.00
Availability: Very Good   Golds: PR, NW, HH, TN
Parading a succession of gold medals, the 1993 Dry Chenin Blanc continues the prototypical style of this varietal. It is packed with floral, honeysuckle aromas and notes of fresh citrus, pineapple, and grapefruit. Papaya and tropical fruit flavors predominate, with subtle notes of pears and honeydew melons. Extremely well balanced, this wine is smooth, soft, and lush, with a crisp, defined finish.
Special Awards: *Best of Class (PR); Best of Price Class (NW)*

Granite Springs Winery   *1994 Sierra Foothills Chenin Blanc*
Region: USA—California   Suggested Retail: $5.50
Availability: Limited   Golds: LA
This wine possesses a very floral, fruity aroma. Some residual sugar (1 1/2%) makes it slightly sweet and a good sipping wine. The Chenin Blanc is Granite Springs' "most popular wine."

Hogue Cellars   *1994 Chenin Blanc*
Region: USA—Washington   Suggested Retail: $6.99
Availability: Very Good   Golds: WW
Fresh, fruity, and appealing, this Chenin Blanc has peach and melon flavors with floral notes. Chill it well, and drink it over the next 8 to 14 months.

Hogue Cellars   *1994 Dry Chenin Blanc*
Region: USA—Washington   Suggested Retail: $6.99
Availability: Very Good   Golds: WW, CW
A textbook Chenin Blanc, this one has flowery aromas, delicate fruit flavors, light body, a slight spritziness, and admirable purity and freshness. Drink it while it's young.
Special Award: *Governor's Trophy, White Wine (CW)*

Husch Vineyards   *1994 La Ribera Vineyards Chenin Blanc*
Region: USA—California   Suggested Retail: $8.00
Availability: Good   Golds: RE, OC, FF
Enticing aromas of night-blooming jasmine and vanilla complement this wine's solid varietal core. Crisp and slightly sweet, the flavors are of tropical fruit, clover honey, green melon, and peaches. This Chenin Blanc is an ideal accompaniment to eggs Benedict, fresh crab or sole, pesto sauce, cheese and crackers. Or have it as dessert with poached pears.

Did You Know ... ?
The human brain via the olfactory receptors is capable of recognizing and remembering around 10,000 distinct aromas.

Llano Estacado Winery   *1994 Chenin Blanc*
Region: USA—Texas   **Suggested Retail: $6.99**
Availability: Good   **Golds: NW**
The aromatics offer a distinct, pleasant bouquet of tropical fruit. In the mouth the palate is treated to a combination of slightly sweet pineapple, honeydew melon, and apple flavors. The winemaker suggests serving it slightly chilled with barbecued prawns.
Special Award: *Best of Price Class (NW)*

Wente Bros.   *1993 Le Blanc de Blancs Special Selection*
Region: USA—California   **Suggested Retail: $5.00**
Availability: NP   **Golds: CA**
This is a blend of mostly Chenin Blanc with some Riesling and Gewürztraminer added for more complexity and focus. It is fragrant and fruity, and goes well with shrimp salads, light curry dishes, and Chinese cuisine.
Special Award: *Best Chenin Blanc of Appellation (CA)*

Did You Know . . . ?
Texas governor Ann Richards served Texan wine to Queen Elizabeth at a state reception in 1991. Another royal, Prince Felipe of Spain, was served Llano Estacado at the Houston Space Center, and gave it rave reviews.

Adler Fels Winery *1994 Sonoma County Gewürztraminer*
Region: USA—California   Suggested Retail: $10.00
Availability: Limited   Golds: RE, CA, SF, SD
Adler Fels's floral and spicy Gewürztraminers have won gold medals and other special awards 4 years in a row. The judges went over the top for this one, which will stand up well to spicy foods with its refreshing and cooling finish.
Special Awards: *Tie for Best Gewürztraminer of Appellation (CA); Best of Class (SD); Best White Wine (SD)*

Alderbrook *1994 Russian River Valley Gewürztraminer*
Region: USA—California   Suggested Retail: $8.00
Availability: Good   Golds: OC
The delicate nose of spice and apricots with a hint of sweet vanilla makes this wine indistinguishably Gewürztraminer. Flavors of grapefruit and pears complement the crisp, mouth-watering acidity.

Bargetto's Winery *1994 Monterey County Gewürztraminer*
Region: USA—California   Suggested Retail: $9.00
Availability: Good   Golds: RE
This medium-dry Gewürz also won a slew of silvers at major competitions, which is nothing to sneeze at. Additionally, Bargetto's Gewürztraminers have won gold medals 8 years in a row. This one has floral aromas with hints of grapefruit that entice the adventurous taster to flavors of spice and citrus. It finishes clean and crisp, complemented by the balance of the acid and residual sugar. If you like fruit wine, Bargetto's raspberry and olalliberry wines are also gold medal winners.

Cosentino *1994 Napa Valley Estate Gewürztraminer*
Region: USA—California   Suggested Retail: $12.00
Availability: Limited   Golds: FF
Explosively floral and fruity in the nose and on the palate, this wine is considered dry for this varietal. Give it a try.

Fetzer *1994 California Gewürztraminer*
Region: USA—California   Suggested Retail: $6.99
Availability: NP   Golds: CA
Delicate aromas of peach and citrus are accented with floral notes of honeysuckle and jasmine. The mouth feel is soft and elegant, with pineapple and ginger-spice flavors and a long, clean finish.
Special Award: *Best Gewürztraminer of Appellation (CA)*

Did You Know . . . ?
Yet another amazing fact about cork: it is the only solid that can be compressed in diameter without expanding in length.

Forestville Vineyards *1994 California Gewürztraminer*
Region: USA—California   Suggested Retail: $5.50
Availability: NP   Golds: FF
This wine has a spicy, ripe pear nose. It is full bodied and nicely balanced with lots of apricot and spice flavors.

Geyser Peak Winery *1994 North Coast Gewürztraminer*
Region: USA—California   Suggested Retail: $7.00
Availability: NP   Golds: OC, PR, SD, FF, TN
"Lovely," "delicate," and "clean" are the words the winemaker uses to describe this one. The palate is soft and sweet, balanced by good natural acidity. With slightly detectable urgency, the winemaker advises that this one is for immediate consumption. Please try to get home from the wine shop before you quaff this delicious stuff!

Handley Cellars *1994 Anderson Valley Gewürztraminer*
Region: USA—California   Suggested Retail: $10.00
Availability: Limited   Golds: RE
Drier and richer than previous vintages, this Gewürztraminer has an outstanding perfume in the nose. The aromas are spicy, floral, and citric, with depth and complexity. The flavors are well balanced and the wine has a luxurious weight in the mouth. The winemaker suggests serving this with Curried Parsnip Latkes (you were planning to, weren't you?), a "Culinary Adventure" recipe offered by the vintner. Call them at (707) 545-0992 for the recipe.

Hinman Vineyards *1993 Gewürztraminer*
Region: USA—Oregon   Suggested Retail: $7.00
Availability: Limited   Golds: OR
This wine displays classical Gewürz aromas of sweet spice, rose petal, walnut oil, and coconut. The palate is full and mouth filling with a perception of sweetness from the fruit and richness of extract. It should age well and continue to improve for 4 to 6 years. Drink it chilled with such foods as pork dishes, mushroom soup, and Oriental cuisine.
Special Award: *Best of Show, White Wine (OR)*

Did You Know . . . ?

Wine lovers who live in Kentucky are steaming because of a new law passed by the state legislature that makes shipping wine to that state a felony. Folks who live in rural areas are out of luck if they want to purchase hard-to-find wines from small producers whose case productions are so tiny that they only sell out of state by mail order. The new law was supposedly enacted to prevent minors from receiving mail-order alcoholic beverages, but consumers believe that's just a smokescreen for the state, which wants the lost tax revenues.

Louis M. Martini *1993 Russian River Valley Gewürztraminer*
Region: USA—California   Suggested Retail: $8.50
Availability: Limited   Golds: NW, FF
Here's a winery with a history. Winemaker Michael Martini follows his grandfather (Louis M.) and father (Louis P.) in a tradition of great winemaking that goes back to 1922. This wine's intense nose opens up to deep lychee nut and cinnamon aromas. It follows in the mouth beautifully, viscous and rich, with a strong fruity flavor. Serve it chilled or at cellar temperature.
Special Awards: *Best of Price Class (NW); Trophy for Best New World Gewürztraminer (NW)*

Madrona Vineyards *1994 El Dorado Gewürztraminer*
Region: USA—California   Suggested Retail: $8.50
Availability: Limited   Golds: SF
The usual rose petal aroma is joined by notes of grapefruit and spice. The mouth feel is smooth and rich, yet retains a crisp, refreshing finish. Great with ethnic cuisines, sausages, or lighter pork dishes.
Special Award: *Double Gold (SF)*

Napa Ridge Winery *1994 Central Coast Gewürztraminer*
Region: USA—California   Suggested Retail: $5.00
Availability: Limited   Golds: LA, IN
Robert Parker exclaims: "It's time to get on the Napa Ridge bandwagon!" This winery is making reasonably priced, delicious wines, and the Gewürztraminer is no exception.

Did You Know . . . ?
Lead, a deadly poison, has been part of winemaking since its origins. The Romans added lead to their wines to prevent them from spoiling. They also heated wine in lead vessels to produce a sweet wine called *sapa*. In the nineteenth century bottles were cleaned with lead shot, contaminating the wine. And roadside vineyards even today have problems with lead particles from car exhaust settling on both the grapes and the soil.

Augusta Winery *1994 Vignoles Missouri*
Region: USA—Missouri   **Suggested Retail: $7.99**
Availability: Limited   **Golds: SD**

This Missouri (!) white is semidry with crisp acidity. Wild strawberry and melon aromas dominate the bouquet. You'll also find fresh fruit flavors and a lingering finish. Vignoles, also known as Ravat, is a cross between a (French) vinifera grape and a native American variety.
Special Award: *Best of Class (SD)*

Ca' Del Solo *1994 Malvasia Bianca*
Region: USA—California   **Suggested Retail: $8.50**
Availability: Good   **Golds: OC**

Produced by Bonny Doon and a talented, quirky winemaker, this Malvasia Bianca, a little-produced wine, is aromatic and slightly ripe, but still bone-dry. It offers up lychee, grapefruit, and jasmine in abundance. It has good depth, firm acidity, and a long, crisp, fruit finish. By the way, Bonny Doon's press kit is wildly funny and entertaining; we applaud both their literary and winemaking originality.

Domaine de Chaberton *1993 Madeleine Sylvaner*
Region: Canada   **Suggested Retail: $10.00 CAN**
Availability: Outside USA   **Golds: PR**

A distinct off-dry Canadian white wine with charming and delightful qualities, this one is finished in a traditional French method. It goes well with seafood, pasta with cream sauce, chicken dishes, and salads. It is not yet available in the United States.

Gehringer Brothers Estate Winery *1994 Dry-Sec Pinot Gris*
Region: Canada   **Suggested Retail: $9.50**
Availability: Limited   **Golds: LA**

This wine's mellow bouquet is followed by a complexity of subtle fruit flavors, finishing in earthy tones. It has a crisp, palate-cleansing finish. Serve it slightly chilled as an alternative to Chardonnay.
Special Awards: *Best of Class (LA); Division Sweepstakes Awards (LA)*

Geyser Peak Winery *NV Premium White*
Region: USA—California   **Suggested Retail: $5.99**
Availability: NP   **Golds: PR**

"Enjoyable and easy to drink." That's all this high-quality winery sent us about this wine, but for the price, who could argue? It sounds like a good one to smuggle into the Shakespeare in the Park Festival this summer—good and chilled, that is.

Did You Know . . . ?

Right after the harvesting of Bonny Doon's 1994 Malvasia Bianca, the fire department rushed to the scene. It was a false alarm: the tremendous volume of "smoke" was caused by massive amounts of dry ice used to cool down the must.

Grant Burge *1991 Lilifarm Frontignac*
Region: Australia   **Suggested Retail: $9.95**
Availability: Limited   **Golds: PE**

This wine has a spicy fresh fruit character—the hallmark of this style. The wine finishes fresh and clean, and is crisp but not cloying. You'll find it in the United States, as well as in Europe.

Gray Monk Cellars *1993 Ehrenfelser*
Region: Canada   **Suggested Retail: $9.75 CAN**
Availability: Outside USA   **Golds: PR, CI**

This harvest produced an elegantly honeyed, orange peel, floral nose wine with fresh citrus and pepper spice flavors—surprisingly assertive with a crispy, dry finish. Perhaps more than any other grape variety, Ehrenfelser is characterized by extreme purity, a cleanliness and freshness that can be experienced on the tongue. P.S. This revered Canadian winery has been winning golds for a variety of wines consistently since 1983. This one is not available in the United States, but lucky Canadians can enjoy it.

Hagafen Cellars *1994 Napa Valley Harmonia White*
Region: USA—California   **Suggested Retail: $8.00**
Availability: NP   **Golds: NW, FF**

A fresh and fruity wine with an impression of sweetness conveyed in its flowery aroma. Chill it well to show off its flavor best.

Hunt Country Vineyards *1992 Finger Lakes Cayuga White*
Region: USA—New York   **Suggested Retail: $5.99**
Availability: Limited   **Golds: FF**

A semidry, very distinct, clear white wine with a bouquet of peaches. This is one of the winemaker's favorites because it grows consistently well and produces a fine, high-quality wine, great as an appetizer wine. The grape was developed by Cornell University. This winery is increasingly becoming known for its award-winning icewine as well.
Special Award: *Chairman's Award (FF)*

Meier's Wine Cellars *NV Haute Sauterne*
Region: USA—Ohio   **Suggested Retail: $3.69**
Availability: Good   **Golds: PR**

A full-bodied, semisweet blend of Catawba, Delaware, and mixed vinifera.

Did You Know . . . ?
Volcanoes are good for winemaking. New York's Finger Lakes district has rich, stony soil derived from volcanic rocks, so that the vine roots penetrate far below winter frost levels, and can obtain soil water easily even during dry summers.

Mirassou Vineyards   *1993 Fifth Generation Family Pinot Blanc*
Region: USA—California   **Suggested Retail: $6.99**
Availability: Very Good   **Golds: OC**

This is a dry, medium-bodied wine with inviting pear and pineapple fruit and hints of vanilla and French oak. It has a soft and creamy texture and its tropical fruit flavors meld nicely with French oak. Added to that are vanilla background notes and a clean, lingering finish.

Montelle at Osage Ridge   *1993 Virant Vineyard Stone House White*
Region: USA—Missouri   **Suggested Retail: $5.99**
Availability: Limited   **Golds: PR**

A native American wine with rich body, a touch of sweetness, and pears and apples in the nose. As a young wine it's somewhat acidic, but rich in finish.

Montinore   *1994 Willamette Valley Müller-Thurgau*
Region: USA—Oregon   **Suggested Retail: $6.00**
Availability: Limited   **Golds: LA, FF**

Müller-Thurgau is a result of the cross hybridization of Riesling and Sylvaner. The vines are prolific, the wine finished off-dry. This one is bursting with grapefruit flavors. Montinore sells out quickly, so if you chance upon a bottle on a wine list or in a wine shop, by all means snatch it up.
Special Award: *Chairman's Award (FF)*

Nichelini   *1994 Joseph A. Nichelini Vineyard Sauvignon Vert*
Region: USA—California   **Suggested Retail: $9.00**
Availability: Limited   **Golds: SF**

In California there are less than 60 acres of Sauvignon Vert. The grapes for this wine are 49 years old. The wine has complex yet delicate fruit aromas and a crisp clean finish.

St. James Winery   *NV Missouri Velvet White*
Region: USA—Missouri   **Suggested Retail: $5.49**
Availability: Limited   **Golds: FF**

A sweet wine made from the Niagara grape (a native American variety) that is very fruity in the mouth, with a delicate aroma and a smooth finish. An all-American wine from an all-American state!

Did You Know . . . ?

Getting bored with Chardonnay? According to *Investor's Business Daily,* choosing Chardonnay for a business dinner these days is almost passé. One expert suggests Müller-Thurgau to go with spicy foods of the Pacific Rim. Another recommends Viognier, great with Indian dishes. If you hail from the Midwest, as one of us does, we encourage you to have on hand a local native American white, and serve it up with fresh roast pork and garden baby potatoes with peas.

St. James Winery *NV Missouri Country White*
Region: USA—Missouri   **Suggested Retail: $5.99**
Availability: Limited   **Golds: NW**
This is a semidry white wine made from the Catawba grape, which is pink, but produces a free-run white juice before it is pressed. The wine is best when served chilled with light meat and fish. (By the way, Catawba is a native American variety, and since Missouri is about as middle American as you can get, we think patriotic Americans should try this one.)

Stone Hill Wine Co. *1993 Missouri Seyval*
Region: USA—Missouri   **Suggested Retail: $8.99**
Availability: NP   **Golds: FF**
A fresh, fruity, off-dry white with about 1% residual sugar contributing to its soft mouth feel. Melon, grapefruit, and floral notes are emphasized through cool fermentation without oak aging.
Special Award: *Chairman's Award (FF)*

Swedish Hill Vineyard *1994 Cayuga White*
Region: USA—New York   **Suggested Retail: $5.99**
Availability: Limited   **Golds: LA, NY**
This all-American white is crisp and semidry, with luscious floral and appley aromas. The Cayuga White grape was developed especially for the Finger Lakes region by Cornell University at the New York State Agricultural Station in Geneva, New York.
Special Award: *Double Gold (NY)*

Swedish Hill Vineyard *1993 Vignoles*
Region: USA—New York   **Suggested Retail: $6.99**
Availability: Limited   **Golds: NW, FF, TG, FL**
This distinctive varietal wine exudes aromas of fresh pears and peaches. The crisp acidity perfectly balances the semisweet citrusy finish, and makes this wine a great accompaniment to sweet-and-sour dishes, fresh fruits, or even light desserts.

Wollersheim Winery *1994 Prairie Fumé*
Region: USA—Wisconsin   **Suggested Retail: $7.00**
Availability: Good   **Golds: PR**
A semidry, crisp, brilliant white wine made from Seyval Blanc that is fresh, fruity, and citrusy and is considered "the best wine in Wisconsin." This winery was founded way back in 1857, and most of Wollersheim's wines are sold regionally.

Did You Know . . . ?
Stone Hill is Missouri's oldest winery, established in 1847. Their wines won medals in the 1900 Paris Exposition. During Prohibition, the winery was forced to shut down, so the vaulted stone cellars were transformed into mushroom-growing caves.

Callaway Vineyard *1994 Temecula Viognier*
Region: USA—California   Suggested Retail: $14.00
Availability: Good   Golds: FF, LB

Viognier is one of the rarest white varieties in the world, producing a wine that's most often described as melonlike, aromatic, and spicy. Without the influence of oak aging, the wine retains its delicate floral character and tropical fruit flavors. A perfect aperitif, Viognier is also well paired with salmon and fresh trout.
Special Award: *Sweepstakes Award (LB)*

Caymus Vineyards *1993 Conundrum*
Region: USA—California   Suggested Retail: $18.00
Availability: NP   Golds: OC

Caymus does not "believe" in wine competitions, and therefore would not provide us with any information about their gold medal winner. However, at the prestigious Orange County Fair competition all California wines available in Orange County are entered by the competition board, not by the winery. This way, every wine will be judged against all of its peers. Caymus's 1993 white table wine won in its category, which is quite an honor even if the winery doesn't think so. Consumers will want to know about this excellent wine. Robert Parker says of Caymus that few wineries in the world can "boast such an enviable record of consistent excellence."

Cooper Mountain Vineyards *1994 Estate Bottled Pinot Gris*
Region: USA—Oregon   Suggested Retail: $11.99
Availability: Limited   Golds: OR

We had a chance to visit this winery when we were in Portland last February on business. It's a beautiful area, balmy from the Pacific, which surprised us East Coasters. We had a lovely, spontaneous visit with Bob Gross, the owner, who chatted with us in his kitchen like an old friend. This winery produces fine wines in small quantities, so you'll be lucky to find a bottle. If you do, pick it up. This straw/pale copper–colored Pinot Gris, an out-of-the-mainstream varietal, has forward and inviting aromas with hints of orange peel, flowers, ripe pears, and spices. The wine has a luscious texture and the flavors are extremely deep, bright, and clean with citrus and pear notes. It has a lovely balance and a lingering finish. This was the only Pinot Gris awarded at Oregon State Fair among many entries.

Eberle Winery *1994 Fralich Vineyard Viognier*
Region: USA—California   Suggested Retail: $18.00
Availability: Limited   Golds: RE, OC, CA

Head-pruned, stressed vines provided an intensity of fruit that is unsurpassed in this appellation. California Grapevine named this Viognier "Best Other White Wine" in a final report for the top-medal-winning wines of 1995.
Special Award: *Best Viognier of Appellation (CA)*

Did You Know . . . ?
Viognier is becoming fashionable. We can look forward to seeing more of it toward the end of this decade, since two-thirds of California's new acreage has just now matured enough to bear fruit.

J. Fritz Winery   *1994 Melon*
Region: USA—California   **Suggested Retail: $12.00**
Availability: Limited   **Golds: LA**

Lemon, tangerine, and lime with a hint of nostalgic green apples distinguish this pleasing white wine. You'll find tons of fruit, and only a nuance of spicy oak in the finish, with a crisp, delicious spritziness that the French call pétilance. *Another winner for those who dare to stray off the well-beaten white wine path. Try it with seafood and extra spicy dishes. "It will make your oysters sing!" says the winery.*

Knudsen-Erath Winery   *1994 Willamette Valley Pinot Gris*
Region: USA—Oregon   **Suggested Retail: $11.00**
Availability: Limited   **Golds: RE**

This Pinot Gris offers lively, complex fruit flavors with subtle vanilla accents and a smooth, medium-bodied texture. The color is a lovely bright straw. The problem with Oregon wines is that they're generally made in small quantities (1,488 cases of this golden stuff was produced, so there's a decent chance that you'll find it). This well-known winery has changed their label and is now known as Erath Vineyard.
Special Award: *Sweepstakes Award, White Wine (RE)*

Mount Palomar Winery   *1993 Castelletto Cortese*
Region: USA—California   **Suggested Retail: $16.00**
Availability: NP   **Golds: PR**

This is said to be the first Cortese bottled in America, a variety that hails from northern Italy's Piedmont region. The flavors are dry, and the wine is aromatic. Look for soft gentle flavor with slightly tropical nuances and a hint of minerals. Old oak contributes round, smooth fruit flavors without a heavy oak presence.

Murphy-Goode Estate Winery   *1993 Pinot Blanc*
Region: USA—California   **Suggested Retail: $12.50**
Availability: Limited   **Golds: OC**

Melon de Bourgogne, often called Pinot Blanc, is a softer, gentler "cousin" of Chardonnay in both its flavor and structure. Smooth and creamy flavors of melon, toasty oak, and citrus envelop the palate in a silky mouthful.

Rabbit Ridge Vineyards   *1994 Heartbreak Hill Viognier*
Region: USA—California   **Suggested Retail: $15.00**
Availability: Limited   **Golds: OC**

Apricot, pear, and slightly tropical mango flavors characterize this wine. It is extremely floral in the nose with a dry but soft finish. Very round and balanced in comparison to other Viogniers.

Did You Know . . . ?
Oregon is notoriously wet, which is bad for grape growing. The good news is that the majority of rainfall happens during the months of November and April, not during the main growing season.

St. James Winery   *1993 Semi Dry Missouri Vignoles*
Region: USA—Missouri   **Suggested Retail: $10.99**
Availability: Limited   **Golds: PR, NW**
This semidry Riesling-style wine is very aromatic and full bodied. It has a fruity taste with hints of honey and apricot. Incidentally, the 1994 vintage of this wine won a gold in 1996.

Stone Hill Wine Co.   *1993 Vignoles*
Region: USA—Missouri   **Suggested Retail: $10.99**
Availability: NP   **Golds: PR**
Although we did not get any information on this particular wine from Stone Hill, it's notable for two reasons. First, because it's from Missouri, and second, because Vignoles is an unusual varietal, a French/American hybrid that does well in climates that normally cannot sustain fine-wine making. This grape produces crisp white wines that are usually mildly or very sweet but have a nice balance of acidity.

Stone Hill Wine Co.   *1994 Vignoles*
Region: USA—Missouri   **Suggested Retail: $10.99**
Availability: NP   **Golds: FF, LA, IE, MS**
One of the most unique and highly awarded wine varieties east of the Rocky Mountains. The Vignoles grape produces full-bodied wines with a lovely golden color and rich varietal flavors and aromas. It has good acidity and brings to mind peach, pineapple, and kiwi in the flavor and aroma.
Special Awards: *Best of Category (FF); Missouri State Champion Wine (IE)*

Sumac Ridge Estate Winery   *1993 Private Reserve Pinot Blanc*
Region: Canada   **Suggested Retail: $10.30**
Availability: NP   **Golds: LA**
Pinot Blanc is a dry white wine of great finesse, with fresh, crisp fruit and subtle undertones of oak. This elegant wine is well suited to salmon and other seafood dishes.
Special Award: *Best of Class (LA)*

Wild Horse Winery   *1994 Monterey Pinot Blanc*
Region: USA—California   **Suggested Retail: $12.00**
Availability: Very Good   **Golds: OC, SD, FF**
This wine has forward fruit aromas of pear, nectarine, Golden Delicious apple, and toasted grain. The flavors are of apple and citrus with a distinct flinty mineral finish. Try it with delicately seasoned pastas.
Special Award: *Best of Class (SD)*

Did You Know . . . ?
Two decades ago work started at Sumac Ridge to convert a golf course into vineyards, the clubhouse into a winery. Grape workers still find an occasional golf ball among the vines.

Château Ste. Michelle *1994 Columbia Valley Johannisberg Riesling*
Region: USA—Washington   Suggested Retail: $7.00
Availability: Limited   Golds: RE, WW
This Riesling offers floral as well as peach and citrus aromas. Classic peach and apricot flavors complement the silky, viscous mouth feel. Not one but two white wines from this winery entered at Reno were finalists for the Sweepstakes Award (the other is the 1993 Chardonnay). This Washington State winery tends to sell out quickly, so grab a bottle—any bottle—you can find.
Special Award: Finalist for Sweepstakes Award, White Wine (RE)

Columbia Winery *1994 Columbia Valley Johannisberg Riesling*
Region: USA—Washington   Suggested Retail: $6.00
Availability: Good   Golds: PR
Of pale straw color, this Riesling has a fragrant floral aroma with notes of fresh apricot, peach, and pear, and is medium-dry on the palate with a crisp, clean finish.

Columbia Winery *1994 Cellarmaster's Reserve Johannisberg Riesling*
Region: USA—Washington   Suggested Retail: $6.50
Availability: Very Good   Golds: PR
This Johannisberg Riesling is characterized by a floral honeyed aroma with notes of pear, peach, and apricot. It is full flavored with fine racy acidity and a touch of spritz from the early bottling.

Covey Run Vintners *1994 Yakima Valley Johannisberg Riesling*
Region: USA—Washington   Suggested Retail: $5.99
Availability: NP   Golds: SD
The first experimental vinifera plantings in Washington State included Johannisberg Riesling, which thrives in cool climates like those found in Germany and the Pacific Northwest. The 1994 is a true example of the variety. Flavors of peach and apricots are matched with ripe fruit aromas. Its refreshing acidity makes the wine an appealing complement to delicately flavored foods.

Fetzer *1994 Johannisberg Riesling*
Region: USA—California   Suggested Retail: $6.99
Availability: NP   Golds: OC
Fresh and fruity, this fine Riesling has floral aromas with notes of apricot and peach. Its appealing, mildly sweet flavors of apricot and ripe pear finish with a balancing lemony crispness.

Did You Know . . . ?

"Corkiness," a condition that exists when a compound called TCI is present in the cork, can ruin even the best bottle of wine. Unfortunately, the human nose can detect this chemical at *4 parts per trillion!* Lightly corked wine may simply smell like cork, but a badly corked wine smells musty, like damp cardboard or newspapers.

Geyser Peak Winery *1994 Soft Johannisberg Riesling*

Region: USA—California   **Suggested Retail: $7.00**
Availability: NP   **Golds: OC, FF, MO, CL**

A lovely, soft, delicate wine with distinct floral characters and some spicy overtones, this one is relatively sweet but well balanced by high natural acidity.
Special Awards: *Chairman's Award (FF); Best of Show (MO); Best of Class (CL)*

Gray Monk Cellars *1993 Johannisberg Riesling*

Region: Canada   **Suggested Retail: $7.35 CAN**
Availability: Outside USA   **Golds: PR**

Look for complex, floral, fresh fruit flavors dominated by tangy apple, balanced by pronounced acidity, finishing up crisp, clear, and dry. This Riesling is highly aromatic and unashamedly distinctive, with a singular intensity that is underpinned by the sweet-and-sour piquancy of its quite remarkable acidity balance. It pairs well with a variety of foods, and is excellent for special events or with Japanese cuisine. (These winemaker notes made our short list for most creative and fun to read. Gray Monk has been winning golds consistently for many of their wines since 1983, so give them a try.) By the way, if you live in Canada you can find this wine, but you won't be able to get it in the United States, unless you go border shopping.

Perry Creek Vineyards *1994 El Dorado Johannisberg Riesling*

Region: USA—California   **Suggested Retail: $7.50**
Availability: Limited   **Golds: LA**

A burst of spice and flavor highlight this vintage. You'll find hints of pears and apples with a decidedly off-dry finish.

Did You Know . . . ?

Canada's wine industry is doing a remarkable job attracting tourists by developing "farmgate wineries"—bed and breakfasts located on vineyards, where fine dining and of course fine wine are part of the package.

Colorado Cellars   *1993 Alpenglo Riesling*
Region: USA—Colorado   **Suggested Retail: $8.50**
Availability: Limited   **Golds: TG**

Here's an extremely lush, fruity wine with a hint of peach on the nose and palate. Floral notes predominate in the bouquet, and the wine is semisweet with a light golden hue. Hey, it's from Colorado!

Corbans Wines   *1991 Stoneleigh Vineyard Marlborough Riesling*
Region: New Zealand   **Suggested Retail: $8.85**
Availability: Very Good   **Golds: NZ**

Delicious, fresh, off-dry, stone-fruit flavors combine with natural acid, resulting in an elegant, crisp Riesling. This one is available in the United States, so pick up a bottle of this New Zealand delight.
Special Award: *Trophy for Champion Riesling (NZ)*

Greenwood Ridge   *1993 Estate Bottled White Riesling*
Region: USA—California   **Suggested Retail: $8.50**
Availability: Limited   **Golds: RE**

The unique coastal climate enables the White Riesling grape to maintain exceptional acidity while reaching full ripeness. The wine is tangy yet slightly sweet, with a light, crisp finish. It can be enjoyed with chicken, Oriental dishes, fruit and cheese, or by itself as a sipping wine.

Hagafen Cellars   *1994 Napa Valley Riesling*
Region: USA—California   **Suggested Retail: $9.00**
Availability: NP   **Golds: RE**

This is a crowd pleaser, both for its marvelous taste and because it goes well with many different foods. This wine is "off-dry," which means that it has a slight sweetness to it. Try it with Thai or Chinese foods, or with salads or dessert.

Did You Know . . . ?

If you keep kosher, but you like *fine* wine, you don't have to worry anymore. The word *hagafen* means "the vine" in Hebrew. All wines made at Hagafen Cellars, from vintage 1993 forward, are certified kosher by the Union of Orthodox Congregations of America and bear the OU-P. All wines except their Cabernet Sauvignon are yayin mevushal. These wines are made according to Jewish dietary laws, which prevent the use of any leavening grain or animal-based ingredients in the winemaking process. In addition, all cleansing of winemaking equipment must be done according to ritual. All vinification steps, harvest to bottling, must be performed by a knowledgeable observer in order to certify the authenticity of the product. If you want to order directly from the winery for your next holiday gathering, call them at (800) 456-VINO.

Kendall-Jackson *1994 Vintner's Reserve Johannisberg Riesling*
Region: USA—California   **Suggested Retail:** $9.50
Availability: NP   **Golds:** OC, CA

Look for a bold, complex nose of fruit and flowers with notes of mint and fig. A clean, crisp, well-balanced wine that pairs well with Oriental foods, smoked fish, or summer salads.
Special Awards: *Best Johannisberg Riesling of California (CA); Best Johannisberg Riesling of Appellation (CA)*

Kendall-Jackson *1993 Select Late Harvest Riesling*
Region: USA—California   **Suggested Retail:** $15.00
Availability: NP   **Golds:** RE, SF, IV, FF

This wine reveals flavors of jasmine and honeysuckle traditional to Sonoma grapes, and notes of melon and pear found in fruit from Santa Barbara County.

Lamoreaux Landing Wine Cellars *1994 Semi-Dry Riesling*
Region: USA—New York   **Suggested Retail:** $8.00
Availability: Limited   **Golds:** LA

Rich and complex, this full-bodied Riesling displays ripe apricot and mango flavors with just the right balance of sweetness and acidity. Serve it with spicy cuisines such as Thai, Indian, and Mexican dishes.
Special Award: *Best of Class (LA)*

Palliser Estate *1994 Riesling*
Region: New Zealand   **Suggested Retail:** $11.25
Availability: NP   **Golds:** ZE

The wine exhibits aromas of stone fruits with hints of marmalade, marzipan, and ripe apricots. Quite rich and full on the palate, it shows excellent balance with lingering flavors and a hint of residual sugar on the finish. One of the world's classic wines, Rieslings are gaining more recognition in New Zealand. The wine will age well to produce toasty, honeyed characters in 2 to 3 years. It is available in the United States.

Standing Stone Vineyards *1994 Finger Lakes Riesling*
Region: USA—New York   **Suggested Retail:** $8.50
Availability: Limited   **Golds:** SF, NY

A semidry Riesling, full of ripe apricot flavors and a nice crisp acidity. The wine has a full mouth feel, rich structure, and a long finish.

Did You Know . . . ?

In areas such as New York State, where even the climate-moderating Finger Lakes cannot entirely protect vines from freeze, vigorous techniques are used to shelter the vines from the cold. One of these involves maximizing carbohydrate levels in the vines. Why? Because the vine's reserves of carbohydrates act as natural antifreeze.

Swedish Hill Vineyard *1994 Finger Lakes Dry Riesling*
Region: USA—New York   Suggested Retail: $8.99
Availability: Limited   Golds: SF, NY
Experience this drier style of Riesling that is loaded with flowery aromas and fruity flavors.

V. Sattui Winery *1994 Dry Napa Valley Johannisberg Riesling*
Region: USA—California   Suggested Retail: $10.25
Availability: Good   Golds: SF, LA
This Riesling is fruity, floral, and light. At San Francisco, all four judges awarded it a gold in a blind taste test, so it must be delicious. The wines of V. Sattui are sold exclusively at the winery. To reach them, call (707) 963-7774, or fax them at (707) 963-4324.
Special Award: *Double Gold (SF)*

Willamette Valley Vineyards *1994 Oregon Johannisberg Riesling*
Region: USA—Oregon   Suggested Retail: $8.00
Availability: Good   Golds: LA
The color of this dry Riesling is pale straw, and the aromas conjure up floral peach and pineapple. In the mouth, apple and peach flavors emerge. The wine has a nice dry finish and medium to delicate body.

Did You Know ... ?

We were surprised and impressed on a recent trip to Oregon—our first ever—to find that every little corner dive and roadside hole-in-the-wall has an *extensive and impressive* wine list from top Northwest wineries. We sipped our way through the streets of Portland and surrounding wilderness areas, and one day struck the worst traffic jam we've ever been in (that's saying something coming from ex-New Yorkers). But we didn't let our spirits drop, because we were in the middle of an unbelievable stretch of two-lane road flanked by old-growth forest tall as skyscrapers. When we finally got to the inn overlooking the Pacific four hours later, where whales were making their spring run north, we celebrated with a bottle of Oregonian Riesling. Heaven!

Arbor Crest *1993 Bacchus Vineyard Sauvignon Blanc*
Region: USA—Washington   **Suggested Retail: $7.00**
Availability: Good   **Golds: SD**
This wine also won a truckload of silvers at major national competitions in 1995. Very accessible, it is bright, fruity, and features grapefruit, pear, and vanilla flavors and aromas. It is tremendously versatile and charming, and Northwest Palate *recommends having it with grilled salmon slathered with jalapeño butter. Yum!*
Special Award: *Best of Class (SD)*

Bandiera Winery *1994 Napa Valley Sauvignon Blanc*
Region: USA—California   **Suggested Retail: $5.50**
Availability: Very Good   **Golds: NW**
Citrus and melon background notes characterize this Sauvignon Blanc, along with a hint of grassiness typical of this varietal. The oak overtones add to the complexity and impart a long finish.

Beaulieu *1993 Napa Valley Sauvignon Blanc*
Region: USA—California   **Suggested Retail: $9.99**
Availability: NP   **Golds: RE**
This wine has a beautiful fruit aroma of citrus and melons with the distinct grassy character of Sauvignon Blanc. On the palate the wine is very crisp and refreshing with a clean, lingering finish.

Beringer Vineyards *1992 Napa Valley Sauvignon Blanc*
Region: USA—California   **Suggested Retail: $8.50**
Availability: NP   **Golds: NW**
Look for a concentrated, well-focused wine with herbal notes and lots of honeyed, smoky fruit. This dry white wine has good body, nice crispness, and elegance.

Callaway Vineyard *1994 Sauvignon Blanc*
Region: USA—California   **Suggested Retail: $8.00**
Availability: Very Good   **Golds: OC**
This wine exhibits a fresh and fruity style with lush grapefruit and grassy characteristics. Aging without oak emphasizes the wine's delicate fruit flavors, making this a classic example of the Sauvignon Blanc varietal. It is wonderful served as an aperitif and beautifully complements fish and seafood, salads, pasta, and cheese.

Did You Know . . . ?
The Musée des Arts et Traditions Populaires in Paris has a hilarious photo of three naked men in Burgundy standing thigh-high in a vat of grapes, breaking up the grape "caps" with their feet. Surprisingly, it was taken in the 1950s, and in fact the practice of foot-stomping grapes lives on today in some of the smaller wineries in Europe, although 1990s workers usually wear clothes!

Canyon Road   *1994 California Sauvignon Blanc*
Region: USA—California   Suggested Retail: $6.00
Availability: Very Good   Golds: PR, SD, NW
We didn't get a lot of information on this one, and wish we had had more time to go out and buy and try it. But here's what we can say. It's inexpensive, it won three golds and four special awards in prestigious competitions, so our advice is to pick up a bottle right away and find out what all the fuss is about. Plus it's a great deal.
***Special Awards:** Best of Class (SD); Trophy for Best New World Sauvignon Blanc (NW); Trophy for Best New World White Wine (NW); Best of Price Class (NW)*

Carmen Vineyards   *1995 Reserve Sauvignon Blanc*
Region: Chile   Suggested Retail: $9.99
Availability: Good   Golds: CI
Like its sibling, the 1994 vintage, this Chilean Sauvignon Blanc won a gold at the 1995 Vinexpo in France. It's hard to argue with world wine experts, who awarded it top honors without knowing who made it or how much it cost. We think you'll love either vintage of this wine. Both are available in the United States.

Carmen Vineyards   *1994 Reserve Sauvignon Blanc*
Region: Chile   Suggested Retail: $9.99
Availability: Very Good   Golds: CI
This wine has a light brilliant color, with intense aromas of fruit reminiscent of grapefruit, melons, and maracuya. On the palate it has good structure, with nice acidity and a long finish. This Chilean beauty, which is available in the United States, competed side by side with the world's great wines—and won the gold.

Château Souverain   *1994 Alexander Valley Sauvignon Blanc*
Region: USA—California   Suggested Retail: $8.00
Availability: NP   Golds: SD
This one is balanced toward a crisp, refreshing style with clean, light floral and melon aromas. The flavors are of honeydew and pear, with a slight herbal note. The addition of Sémillon (13%) contributes depth, texture, and a mellow fig note to the middle, and a bit of fresh yeastiness and oak toast lend complexity to the finish.

Château Ste. Michelle   *1993 Columbia Valley Sauvignon Blanc*
Region: USA—Washington   Suggested Retail: $9.00
Availability: Limited   Golds: SD, NW
This wine exhibits citrus, melon, fig, and a slight hint of vanilla in the nose and mouth. On the palate, the rich flavors have substantial depth and length. The winery's culinary director recommends, among other foods, clams oreganato as a dish this would nicely complement.

Did You Know . . . ?
The Incas built a fantastic network of canals and gullies to flood *over 3 million acres* of Chilean land that's virtually rainless in summer. This is the very irrigation system the wine growers in Chile use today!

Corbans Wines *1994 Stoneleigh Vineyard Sauvignon Blanc*
Region: New Zealand   **Suggested Retail: $8.85**
Availability: Very Good   **Golds: SY**
This classic-style Sauvignon Blanc has pale green hues and offers up a bouquet of fresh gooseberries and herbs. It has a racy, crisp, zingy nettle and herbal character and a clean, refreshing finish. Some of the judges' comments: "floral citrus bouquet"; "very clean and aromatic"; "passionfruit aroma." The winemakers made plenty of this wine, so American consumers should have no problem finding it.

Davis Bynum Winery *1994 Fumé Blanc*
Region: USA—California   **Suggested Retail: $8.50**
Availability: Very Good   **Golds: PR, FF**
Rush out and buy this wine while you can. It has lively fruit flavors, and great balance and intensity from its aroma to its long, generous finish. They call it the best Fumé Blanc they've produced to date. The wine writers went nuts over this one.
***Special Awards:** Best Pacific Rim Sauvignon Blanc (PR); Chairman's Award (FF)*

Ehlers Grove *1994 Napa Valley Sauvignon Blanc*
Region: USA—California   **Suggested Retail: $9.50**
Availability: Limited   **Golds: FF**
This wine has a creamy, lush texture animated by highlights of fresh melon and ripe grapefruit, and herbal suggestions of thyme and lemongrass.

Errazuriz Panquehue *1995 Maule Valley Sauvignon Blanc*
Region: Chile   **Suggested Retail: $6.00**
Availability: NP   **Golds: IV**
A lively, zingy wine that has excellent grapefruit character on the palate. Like most Chilean wines, this one is a wonderful value, and it is available in the United States.

Fetzer *1993 Sauvignon Blanc Barrel Select*
Region: USA—California   **Suggested Retail: $9.99**
Availability: NP   **Golds: RE, OC**
The nose is inviting with fresh honeydew melon aromas, subtle floral scents, and bright lemon-citrus notes. These fresh flavors are enhanced by light oak-spice and vanilla in a creamy smooth finish.

Fetzer *1993 Mendocino County Fumé Blanc*
Region: USA—California   **Suggested Retail: $6.99**
Availability: NP   **Golds: RE, NW**
This wine has subtle hints of tarragon and fresh grass in perfect balance with the fruit components of ripe melon and lemon-citrus.

Did You Know . . . ?
So vigorous do grapevines grow in New Zealand's rainy climate that viticulturalists there have become sought after worldwide as experts with unique knowledge of innovative ways to control overgrowth.

Geyser Peak Winery *1994 Sauvignon Blanc*
Region: USA—California   Suggested Retail: $8.00
Availability: NP   Golds: RE, OC, CA, CL, SO, LJ
The nose displays the typical asparagus, grassy, green olive, apple characteristics of Sauvignon Blanc. The palate is crisp and balanced. Look at that stash of golds!
Special Awards: Finalist for Sweepstakes Award (RE); White Sweepstakes (CL)

Greenwood Ridge *1993 Sauvignon Blanc*
Region: USA—California   Suggested Retail: $9.00
Availability: Limited   Golds: SD
Aging in French oak barrels imparts a lightly toasted oak bouquet to this wine, and lends a creamy texture. The flavors are distinctly varietal without herbal excess, and lead to a clear crisp finish. This wine is a nice accompaniment to grilled or lightly sauced poultry and fish entrees.

Guenoc Estate *1994 California Sauvignon Blanc*
Region: USA—California   Suggested Retail: $8.00
Availability: Good   Golds: OC
There is a very pleasant fruitiness to this wine. The light yellow color and fruity bouquet precede the light herbaceous characteristic of this varietal.

Handley Cellars *1993 Dry Creek Valley Sauvignon Blanc*
Region: USA—California   Suggested Retail: $9.00
Availability: Good   Golds: OC, NW
This wine has intriguing aromas of melons, herbs, grapefruit, and a touch of sweet dry straw. The clean flavors echo the aromas, with an excellent mouth feel and texture, and good length in the finish.

Hogue Cellars *1994 Columbia Valley Fumé Blanc*
Region: USA—Washington   Suggested Retail: $8.99
Availability: Very Good   Golds: FF
The dominant flavors of this wine are ripe pear, melon, and herbs, with hints of American oak spice, vanilla, and clove. The fragrance matches the flavors, with additional notes of citrus and Granny Smith apples.

J. Fritz Winery *1993 Dry Creek Valley Sauvignon Blanc*
Region: USA—California   Suggested Retail: $9.00
Availability: Good   Golds: NW
Look for full varietal aromas, lime and kiwi flavors, a lush and full mouth feel, subtle oak nuances, creamy texture, and gracefulness. It is perfectly balanced between creaminess and crispness. Spicy Szechuan or Thai will make it sing.
Special Award: Best of Price Class (NW)

Did You Know . . . ?
J. Fritz's humble winemaker, David Hastings, "believes in healthy amounts of inspiration and perspiration. Each year we learn a little more."

Kenwood Vineyards *1994 Sonoma Sauvignon Blanc*
Region: USA—California   Suggested Retail: $9.50
Availability: Very Good   Golds: SF
This wine is loaded with melony fruit components with a hint of grassiness.

Mill Creek Vineyards *1994 Dry Creek Valley Sauvignon Blanc*
Region: USA—California   Suggested Retail: $8.95
Availability: Good   Golds: LA
Aromas of grapefruit and pear with a touch of vanilla and toast will greet the nose. The flavors follow the aromas with an added hint of grassiness, and are powerful yet gentle. The wine's texture is silky in the mouth with generous amounts of fruit.
Special Awards: *Best of Class (LA); Sweepstakes Award (LA)*

Mirassou Vineyards *1993 Sauvignon Blanc*
Region: USA—California   Suggested Retail: $5.99
Availability: Good   Golds: RE
A crisp, medium-bodied wine with bright grapefruit, ripe melon, nettles, and elderflower aromas. It has a zesty melon, apricot taste backed by hints of orange peel, with a very crisp and refreshing finish.

Mission View Vineyards *1994 Estate Bottled Fumé Blanc*
Region: USA—California   Suggested Retail: $9.00
Availability: Limited   Golds: CA
Look for fresh meadow flowers with crisp honeydew melon and a touch of vanilla and honeysuckle.
Special Award: *Best Sauvignon Blanc of Appellation (CA)*

Montevina Winery *1993 California Fumé Blanc*
Region: USA—California   Suggested Retail: $7.00
Availability: Very Good   Golds: NW
Engaging, fresh, complex aromas suggesting cut melon, black olive, pimento, and bell pepper, overlaid by intriguing smoky tones. This is a medium- to full-bodied wine with brisk, richly fruited melon and citrus flavors enhanced by zesty, herbal spice notes. It has an excellent acid balance lending a crisp, refreshing finish; it's delightful now, but will gain roundness and further richness with some cellaring.

Navarro *1993 Cuvée 128 Sauvignon Blanc*
Region: USA—California   Suggested Retail: $9.75
Availability: Limited   Golds: NW, MO
Look for Sauvignon flavors that hint of grass, fennel, mint, and asparagus. Sémillon (20%) adds figlike flavors while Chardonnay (5%) adds an appley character.
Special Award: *Best of Price Class (NW)*

Did You Know . . . ?
Two silver wine coasters made between 1809 and 1819, and actually worth about $1,500, were auctioned off for an amazing $21,850. Their previous owner? Jackie Kennedy Onassis.

Perry Creek Vineyards *1994 El Dorado Sauvignon Blanc*
Region: USA—California   **Suggested Retail: $7.50**
Availability: Limited   **Golds: SF**
This one is fruity, nicely balanced, with a bit of citrus tanginess in the finish.

Simi Winery *1993 Sonoma County Sauvignon Blanc*
Region: USA—California   **Suggested Retail: $8.50**
Availability: NP   **Golds: OC**
This vintage has aromas of apple and honeysuckle, followed by layers of melon, guava, and fig. The rich fruit is combined with subtle hints of grass, which is one of the distinguishing characteristics of Sauvignon Blanc. The wine has a fine crispness and a satisfying, silky finish. The 5% Sémillon adds a delicate spicy note to the aroma and a roundness to the finish.

Simi Winery *1992 Sonoma County Sauvignon Blanc*
Region: USA—California   **Suggested Retail: $8.50**
Availability: NP   **Golds: PR**
Look for grapefruit flavors and aromas with hints of ripe melon and figs, and nice touches of oak. Big fruit and a lingering oaky finish top it off.

Washington Hills Cellars *1993 Sauvignon Blanc*
Region: USA—Washington   **Suggested Retail: $7.49**
Availability: Limited   **Golds: WW**
A beautiful golden hue is visible, while an unusual perfume of rose petals, honeydew melons, and a hint of bay leaf titillates the nose. The palate is in harmony with the aroma, showing lots of fruit and a refreshing finish. A great match for Northwest seafood, from halibut to scallops, or try it with risotto and wild mushrooms.

Zellerbach Winery *1993 Sonoma County Sauvignon Blanc*
Region: USA—California   **Suggested Retail: $6.99**
Availability: Good   **Golds: LA**
This wine has smooth, ripe, sharply focused varietal fruit, yet is not too grassy. With its slightly sweet finish and good balance, it is drinkable now, but will improve with additional cellaring.

Did You Know . . . ?
If you're a label buff, and it's the fast-glued type, here's a suggestion from William F. Doering in an open letter to *Wine Spectator* about how to get those labels off: (1) Place the bottle in a pan of hot water. (2) Add 2 to 3 capfuls of drain opener (such as Drano, which contains lye). (3) Let soak for 3 to 4 hours or overnight. (4) Drain and rinse, placing label on a dry cotton towel to dry. Hint: Wear rubber gloves. The lye burns!

Adler Fels Winery   *1992 Fumé Blanc*
Region: USA—California   **Suggested Retail: $10.00**
Availability: Good   **Golds: SF**

This dry-style Sauvignon Blanc—also sometimes called Fumé Blanc—continues Adler Fels's record streak. Since 1982, when this wine was first produced by them, they have received more gold and silver medals for it than any other American Sauvignon Blanc. Don't believe us—believe the experts at San Francisco, who loved the 1992 bottling.

Château St. Jean   *1993 La Petite Etoile Sauvignon Blanc*
Region: USA—California   **Suggested Retail: $11.50**
Availability: NP   **Golds: NW**

This wine shows a lovely herbal varietal nose with aromas of fresh peaches and a hint of grapefruit in the background. On the mouth the wine offers silky textures, flavors of peach, melon, lemongrass, and a delightful suggestion of anise on the long, complex finish.

De Loach   *1994 Estate Bottled Sauvignon Blanc*
Region: USA—California   **Suggested Retail: $10.00**
Availability: Good   **Golds: RE, OC**

At Orange County this was one of only three Sauvignon Blancs awarded a gold out of a field of 92. This two-time gold medal winner has a price that can't be beat, and it is light straw colored with full floral fruit and citrusy notes running to grapefruit and light herbal tones. The wine is well balanced and crisp in the mouth. Its rich ripe fruit and citrus follow through in the long lingering finish. Raw oysters, according to the winemaker, will go nicely with this one, as well as other seafood dishes.

Grgich Hills   *1993 Fumé Blanc*
Region: USA—California   **Suggested Retail: $13.00**
Availability: NP   **Golds: OC**

This wine, which also won 7 silvers in 1995, has crisp acidity that refreshes and activates your taste buds, and stimulates your appetite. It is tangy and bright with spice and citrusy fruit, round and complex with lovely flavors.

Did You Know . . . ?

Some might say that California's stellar international reputation can be traced to a single event twenty-some years ago in Paris, where two California wines took first place in the red and white categories in a prominent blind tasting, against such stars as France's Mouton-Rothschild and Haut-Brion. So shocked was the wine world that the press still recalls that judging today. Mike Grgich, one of the winner's winemakers at the time, founded Grgich Hills in the wake of all the publicity, and has been soaring since.

Hanna Winery   *1994 Sauvignon Blanc*
Region: USA—California   Suggested Retail: $10.00
Availability: Very Good   Golds: OC
A supple, medium-full, distinctive wine, with floral, herbal, melon, and grape flavors and aromas with a hint of oak. A long finish tops off this excellent Sauvignon Blanc. You can get this wine at an even better price by the case if you order it from the winery, at (800) 854-3987.

J. Rochioli Vineyards   *1994 Estate Bottled Sauvignon Blanc*
Region: USA—California   Suggested Retail: $13.00
Availability: Good   Golds: CA, SF
Ripe melon and grapefruit aromas with a crisp and refreshing finish are what you'll find when you pop the cork on this one.
Special Award: Double Gold (SF)

Murphy-Goode Estate Winery   *1994 Alexander Valley Fumé Blanc*
Region: USA—California   Suggested Retail: $10.00
Availability: Very Good   Golds: CA
This wine offers a profusion of citrus, pear, and pineapple aromas. The honeyed, up-front flavors are round and full on the palate, continuing through the lengthy finish.

Nautilus Estate   *1994 Marlborough Sauvignon Blanc*
Region: New Zealand   Suggested Retail: $13.40
Availability: Very Good   Golds: IW, SY, WC
Aromas of smoky gunflint and light asparagus will greet your nose. On the palate the wine has bean and asparagus flavors that dominate, showing good flavor "weight." Soft green-apple acid adds a crisp finish to the flavorsome midpalate. Best of all, it is available in the United States.
Special Awards: Trophy for Best Sauvignon Blanc (IW); Best World Sauvignon Blanc (WC)

Navarro   *1994 Cuvée 128 Sauvignon Blanc*
Region: USA—California   Suggested Retail: $11.00
Availability: Good   Golds: CA, ME
This wine has lovely figgy fruit. Its refreshing herbal character is supported with a nice oak background and a long finish.
Special Awards: Tie for Best Sauvignon Blanc of California (CA); Best Sauvignon Blanc of Appellation (CA)

Did You Know . . . ?

Some trace the start of the world's serious interest in New Zealand's wines to a single tasting in London in 1983, when judges' mouths dropped open upon sampling a New Zealand Sauvignon Blanc that captured and enraptured all the qualities of that varietal.

Palliser Estate *1995 Sauvignon Blanc*
Region: New Zealand   **Suggested Retail: $12.25**
Availability: NP   **Golds: SY, ZE**

A long warm summer resulted in a wine exhibiting fragrant gooseberry, passion-fruit, and herbal characters. The wine shows a good breadth of flavor with a lingering aftertaste. An excellent example of New Zealand's now internationally acclaimed grape variety. This wine is available in the United States.

Quivira Vineyards *1993 Reserve Sauvignon Blanc*
Region: USA—California   **Suggested Retail: $14.00**
Availability: Good   **Golds: LA**

Toasty oak, floral, citrus, and pear aromas foretell the richness and depth of this wine. Sauvignon Blanc fruit is supported and complemented by French oak in a silky, seamless mouthful. A long flavorful finish displays good acidity while showcasing the wine's finesse.

Rothbury Vineyards *1994 Marlborough NZ Sauvignon Blanc*
Region: Australia   **Suggested Retail: $12.99**
Availability: Very Good   **Golds: WC**

This cool-climate variety typifies the high-standard Sauvignon Blanc for which Marlborough is world renowned. Fine, elegant gooseberry flavors with a clean, sweet acid length give this wine vitality and freshness. Available in the United States, Japan, and Europe.

Seifried Estate *1994 Estate Sauvignon Blanc*
Region: New Zealand   **Suggested Retail: $10.20**
Availability: Good   **Golds: IV**

Bright, rich, green-gold in color, this wine is fleshy and lush. It has intense, ripe, gooseberry and melonlike flavors and an appetizing, crisp, zingy finish. It is available in the United States.

Voss Vineyards *1994 Napa Valley Sauvignon Blanc*
Region: USA—California   **Suggested Retail: $16.95**
Availability: Good   **Golds: CA**

This is an intensely aromatic wine driven by lively citrus and herbal notes. The palate has sweet, melonlike, almost tropical fruit with a vibrancy not often found in Sauvignon Blanc, and the finish is crisp and refreshing. A perfect complement to a warm, lazy afternoon.
Special Award: *Tie for Best Sauvignon Blanc of Appellation (CA)*

Did You Know . . . ?
Russian soldiers occupying the region of Champagne in 1814 wreaked havoc on those famous cellars, popping more than a few corks. As a result, however, Russians became Champagne's most devoted peacetime consumers until 1917.

Arbor Crest   *1994 Columbia Valley Sémillon*
Region: USA—Washington   **Suggested Retail: $6.50**
Availability: Limited   **Golds: RE**

An immensely pleasing wine, this one has fresh citrus scents that are repeated on the palate with tangy grapefruit and twists of lemon, while the background tantalizes with hints of mint and green herbs. The nice, bright acidity gives a clean, lip-smacking finish. Robert Parker calls it a noteworthy value, and we agree. Chill out with it and some raw oysters.

Canyon Road   *1993 Barrel Fermented Sémillon*
Region: USA—California   **Suggested Retail: $8.99**
Availability: Limited   **Golds: DA, FF**

Produced from old Sémillon vines grown in Alexander Valley, the vines are head trained and dry grown, producing grapes of low yield and maximum flavor intensity.

Concannon   *1993 Livermore Valley Sémillon*
Region: USA—California   **Suggested Retail: $12.95**
Availability: Limited   **Golds: RE**

One reviewer exclaimed that if you were to serve only one wine at your meal, this should be it; another called it one of the best. Don't forget Sémillon—it's often overlooked in the Chardonnay-versus-other-whites popularity contest. This one is lush and ripe, with honey and fresh fig aromas and flavors. It was made in a limited quantity, so keep your eyes out for other Concannon gold medal whites if you can't find this one, or call the winery directly at (510) 447-3760.

Hogue Cellars   *1994 Columbia Valley Sémillon*
Region: USA—Washington   **Suggested Retail: $8.99**
Availability: Good   **Golds: RE**

Aromas of honey, melon, ripe pear, and anise emerge from the glass. The wine has good structure and a ripe, full mouth feel with vanilla, spice, oak, and honey flavors. **Special Award:** *Finalist for Sweepstakes Award, White Wine (RE)*

Hogue Cellars   *1993 Columbia Sémillon*
Region: USA—Washington   **Suggested Retail: $5.99**
Availability: NP   **Golds: PR**

Although we had trouble getting information on this wine, you need to know only two things. First, the price is right, and second, Hogue has consistently turned out a portfolio of various gold-medal whites, so we think this one must be great as well. Besides, it's a Washington winery, and we like to root for this up-and-coming world-class winemaking region.

Did You Know . . . ?
The 1995 Pacific Coast Oyster Competition judged 141 American wines to determine which ten were most "oyster-friendly." Arbor Crest's 1994 Sémillon received one of these coveted "Oyster Awards."

Hoodsport Winery *1993 Washington State Sémillon*
Region: USA—Washington   **Suggested Retail: $7.99**
Availability: Limited   **Golds: RE**
Delicious and mostly dry with a fresh citrus bouquet and rich apricot flavors. A scent of herbs and a crisp clean finish make it a perfect complement to seafood. This wine was vinted from select Sémillon grapes and harvested from the Pleasant Vineyards in eastern Washington.

Lakewood Winery *1993 Clear Lake Sémillon*
Region: USA—California   **Suggested Retail: $12.00**
Availability: NP   **Golds: RE, PR**
Here's a personality-filled white with a full, honeyed, assertive style. This Sémillon is dry, has gobs of mouth-filling fruit, and has a good balance of crisp acids on the finish.

Paul Thomas Winery *1993 Columbia Valley Sémillon*
Region: USA—Washington   **Suggested Retail: $6.00**
Availability: Good   **Golds: NW, WW**
Sémillon has emerged as one of Washington's most successful white varietal wines. Crisp acidity and subtle flavors of melons and figs blend together in this wine. Look at those trophies! Look at that price!
Special Awards: *Trophy for Best New World Sémillon (NW); Best of Price Class (NW)*

Did You Know . . . ?
We wooed our book distributor reps with Paul Thomas Sémillon at the Cornell Club in New York in May. After we plugged *BEST WINES!* we offered "tastes" of two gold medal winners, this being one. The reps loved it, us, the book, everything. They were especially pleased that they were tasting a Washington State wine, which many had never experienced before.

Columbia Crest   *1993 Sémillon-Chardonnay*

Region: USA—Washington   **Suggested Retail: $7.00**
Availability: Limited   **Golds: NW**

This blend of 70% Sémillon and 30% Chardonnay reflects the traditional character-istics of each varietal. Citrus and pineapple flavors attributable to the Sémillon give the wine zest, but it's the Chardonnay influence that provides for a toasted, round finish.

Special Awards: *Trophy for Best New World Sémillon/Chardonnay (NW); Best of Price Class (NW)*

Concannon   *1993 California Reserve Assemblage*

Region: USA—California   **Suggested Retail: $14.95**
Availability: Good   **Golds: NW, FL**

This blend of 51% Sauvignon Blanc and 49% Sémillon got rave reviews from the wine press. It is described as clean, with fresh melon and figs and a splendidly rich mouth feel (from the Sémillon), and grassy/citrus notes (from the Sauvignon Blanc), beautiful structure, superb balance, with a nearly dry palate and a pleasant hint of oak. "Classy" is what one writer called it. Contact the winery directly if you have trouble finding it, at (510) 447-3760.

Special Awards: *Best of Price Class (NW); Trophy for Best New World Meritage-Type White Wine (NW)*

Geyser Peak Winery   *1994 California Semchard*

Region: USA—California   **Suggested Retail: $7.00**
Availability: NP   **Golds: PR, MO**

We're disappointed that two lovely French words got blended into a word that hurts our ears. "Semchard" is a blend of Sémillon and Chardonnay, in this case 75% and 25%, respectively. Oh well, at least the wine won't disappoint. It is a lovely blend of the two grapes, and displays melon fruit aromas enhanced with oak. A rich wine with great aging potential, it's an alternative to 100 percent Chardonnay wines, with their often overwhelming oakiness. Try it! The price is definitely right, and Geyser Peak is a multigold winner every year.

Grant Burge   *1994 Oakland White*

Region: Australia   **Suggested Retail: $9.95**
Availability: Very Good   **Golds: AU**

60% Sémillon provides the full flavors and roundness that form the backbone of this wine, while 40% Sauvignon Blanc provides the blend with lifted fruit and spiciness. This one is available in the United States as well as Europe.

Special Award: *Trophy for Best Dry White Table Wine, Current Vintage (AU)*

Did You Know . . . ?

Columbia Crest became the first U.S. winery to make Semchard, which is American slang for Sémillon-Chardonnay. Since then its popularity has steadily grown.

Langtry *1993 Guenoc Valley White Meritage*
Region: USA—California   **Suggested Retail: $19.00**
Availability: Good   **Golds: LA, IV**

Intense aromas of melons, apples, nutmeg, cloves, and toasted caramel and cream create a delightful style. Try this one with salmon, goat cheese, scallops, or duck. Note that the 1994 is also a gold medal winner, a good thing to know if one is looking for an interesting and consistently good alternative to Chardonnay. By the way, the blend is 85% Sauvignon Blanc and 15% Sémillon.

Langtry *1994 Guenoc Valley White Meritage*
Region: USA—California   **Suggested Retail: $19.00**
Availability: Good   **Golds: LA, IM**

Surprisingly rich accents of spice and vanilla etch a brilliant fruit bouquet in this wine. The plumpness of Sémillon is mouth filling and adds rich overtones to the crisp citrus and apple qualities in the finish. An elegant alternative to Chardonnay, try this one with ginger- or sorrel-flavored dishes to match its unique character. Incidentally, this one is a blend of 73% Sauvignon Blanc and 27% Sémillon.
Special Award: *Best White (IM)*

Llano Estacado Winery *1994 Texas Signature White*
Region: USA—Texas   **Suggested Retail: $8.49**
Availability: Good   **Golds: NW**

A blend of Chardonnay, Chenin Blanc, and Sauvignon Blanc, this prizewinner offers up pear, apple, and a touch of citrus on the nose. On the palate the wine is soft and full with ripe fruit flavors and crisp acidity. Serve it slightly chilled.

Rosenblum Cellars *1994 Sonoma Valley Sémillon/Chardonnay*
Region: USA—California   **Suggested Retail: $9.00**
Availability: Good   **Golds: RE, FF**

Fresh apple and cinnamon notes blend nicely with the fig and pear aromas in this blend of two classic grapes, Sémillon (73%) and Chardonnay (27%). It will age well for 1 to 2 years.

Tabor Hill *NV Classic Demi-Sec Special Select*
Region: USA—Michigan   **Suggested Retail: $9.95**
Availability: Limited   **Golds: PR**

This slightly sweet wine is a blend of 30% Riesling, 30% Vidal, 25% Gewürztraminer, and 15% Vignoles. It has golden color, with essences of apples, pears, apricots, and peaches. It is full bodied and the finish is semisweet.

Did You Know . . . ?
Small vineyards in isolated regions have to deal with a formidable pest: birds. Especially in the case of early ripening varieties, birds can easily destroy (i.e., eat!) an entire year's crop with no problem.

Venezia   *1994 Bianco Nuovo Mondo*

Region: USA—California   **Suggested Retail: $18.00**
Availability: Good   **Golds: OC**

Here's an extremely complex wine with an array of exotic tropical fruits, slight nutmeg, and smoky barrel fermentation characters, all in complete harmony. Rich tropical fruit follows through onto the palate with lively acidity and great length of flavor. The blend is 45% Sauvignon Blanc and 46% Sémillon (or "Semchard," as some insist on calling it).

Yalumba   *1994 Christobel's Classic Dry White*

Region: Australia   **Suggested Retail: $9.95 CAN**
Availability: Outside USA   **Golds: SY, BR**

This blend of 66% Sémillon, 29% Sauvignon Blanc, and 5% Marsanne shows intense green tints. Its nose is fresh tropical lemon with smoky tones that dominate the riper honey/butter Sémillon aromas. The palate is full bodied with fresh lemon and gooseberry flavors and a long green apple finish. You can drink the wine now, although bottle age will soften it. This wine is not available in the United States, but you can enjoy it in Canada.

Did You Know . . . ?

With its exceedingly hot climate, New South Wales in Australia produces some of the longest-lived dry Sémillons on the planet, some of them peaking 10 to 20 years after they're bottled, and developing into honeyed, nutty-flavored, buttery beauties.

Arciero Winery *1993 Estate Bottled White Zinfandel*
Region: USA—California   **Suggested Retail: $5.50**
Availability: Good   **Golds: NW**
This wine also won 2 golds and 3 silvers in 1994. Fresh fruit flavors with a touch of sweetness make this refreshing wine perfect at picnics and barbecues.

Baron Herzog *1994 California White Zinfandel*
Region: USA—California   **Suggested Retail: $5.99**
Availability: Very Good   **Golds: OC**
Made from old vines yielding intense fruit and structure, this White Zin has fresh fruit flavors and aromas with a slightly piquant finish.

Bel Arbors *1994 California White Zinfandel*
Region: USA—California   **Suggested Retail: $6.99**
Availability: NP   **Golds: OC, RE, NW**
A lovely opalescent salmon-pink color, this wine has charming aromas of fresh raspberries and sweet spice. Its flavors are filled with fruit, redolent of cranberries, strawberries, and raspberries. Mildly sweet in the mouth, its finish is crisp and refreshing. Serve this wine chilled at picnics, brunch, and for summer evening picnics. Its fresh and fruity character goes well with lighter fare.
Special Awards: *Trophy for Best New World White Zinfandel (NW); Best of Price Class (NW)*

Beringer Vineyards *1994 California White Zinfandel*
Region: USA—California   **Suggested Retail: $5.50**
Availability: NP   **Golds: OC, LA**
Although we didn't hear back from the winemaker on this wine, it has several things going for it. First of all, look at that price! Second, it's a 1994 so you shouldn't have much trouble finding it stocked at your corner wine shop. Third, it won not one but two golds, so several independent judges agreed on its excellent character. Finally, White Zin is a fun alternative to the Chardonnay-as-the-king-of-the-whites rut that many of us get in to. Try this one with spicy cuisine and you'll be in for a treat.

Fetzer *1994 California White Zinfandel*
Region: USA—California   **Suggested Retail: $6.99**
Availability: NP   **Golds: RE, SD, NW, FF**
Coral pink in color, this lively White Zinfandel has fresh strawberry fruit aromas and smooth, mildly sweet ripe cherry flavors. It has a perfect, crisp balance of natural sweetness and acidity.

Did You Know . . . ?

Most trees will die if you strip off their bark. But cork trees have two layers of · bark, an inner living layer, and an outer layer composed of dead layers as it moves outward, providing the tree with insulation against hot arid winds. The outer layer is where cork comes from.

Glen Ellen Winery *1994 Proprietor's Reserve White Zinfandel*
Region: USA—California   **Suggested Retail: $4.00**
Availability: Very Good   **Golds: NW**
A fruity wine with aromas of orange blossoms and fresh strawberries. The flavors echo the aromas with essences of juicy cherry, strawberry, and cranberry. The crisp acidity of this wine is balanced by just the right amount of sweetness. Buy a case and throw a garden party.

Ste. Genevieve *NV Texas White Zinfandel*
Region: USA—Texas   **Suggested Retail: $7.99**
Availability: NP   **Golds: NW**
Here's a wine just right for any occasion. With its light touch of sweetness and pale pink color, this wine is best chilled and served with good food and conversation.

V. Sattui Winery *1994 California White Zinfandel*
Region: USA—California   **Suggested Retail: $7.95**
Availability: Good   **Golds: NW, FF, MO**
This White Zin is delicate, with hints of cherries and watermelon. All of V. Sattui's wines are available only from the winery, which you can reach by calling (707) 963-7774 or by faxing (707) 963-4324.
Special Award: *Best of Price Class (NW)*

Weinstock Cellars *1994 White Zinfandel*
Region: USA—California   **Suggested Retail: $6.99**
Availability: Very Good   **Golds: OC, CA**
This Zin is from Lodi, the Zinfandel capital of California. It is produced almost entirely from older vines yielding more intense fruit and overall structure. Look for fresh fruit flavors and aromas and a slight piquant finish.
Special Awards: *Tie for Best White Zinfandel of California (CA); Tie for Best White Zinfandel of Appellation (CA)*

Did You Know . . . ?
What happens when a Frenchman gets transplanted in Texas? The same thing that happens when you plant French grape varieties (*Vitis vinifera*) there: success. Ste. Genevieve is that state's largest winery, and it's French owned. Half of the wine is sold in bulk to Canada, but we're lucky that the other half gets bottled under the Ste. Genevieve label. Try some Texas wine with a French accent for a total change of pace.

Chapter 12

ROSÉS

Botham Vineyards *NV Emberlight Blush*

Region: USA—Wisconsin   Suggested Retail: $7.50
Availability: Limited   Golds: PR

We are always happy when a midwestern winery wins a gold. This wine is young, fresh, and clean with citrus notes on the nose and palate. It has a perfect balance between residual sugar and acidity, with a beautiful ruby color. We imagine this could go well with some classic Wisconsin cheese and crusty homemade bread on a grassy hillside under an apple tree. A perfect summer/picnic wine.
Special Award: *Best of Class (PR)*

Chautauqua Vineyards *NV Blush*

Region: USA—Florida   Suggested Retail: $5.50
Availability: Limited   Golds: PR

Light blush color with beautiful clarity and brilliance, this wine possesses an aroma that is both floral and tropical. It has rich fruit and crisp, lively acidity, with balancing sugar and a clean finish. The flavors are round with hints of peach and pear. Try a Floridian gold medal winner for a change.

Colorado Cellars *1993 Alpenrose*

Region: USA—Colorado   Suggested Retail: $7.00
Availability: Limited   Golds: NW

If you like rosé, why not try one from Colorado? This one is a semidry, fruity, darker-hued rosé with a raspberry nose and flavor. Crisp and full bodied, it has a slight spritz apparent upon first opening.
Special Award: *Best of Price Class (NW)*

Hagafen Cellars *1994 Harmonia*

Region: USA—California   Suggested Retail: $6.00
Availability: Good   Golds: CA

Voted best blush of Napa Valley two years in a row, this wine is made from 100% Pinot Noir grapes. It is light and fruity with tropical fruit flavors. A hint of sweetness in the finish makes this a lively wine to drink with everything from appetizers to desserts.
Special Award: *Best Other Varietal Blushes of Appellation (CA)*

Did You Know . . . ?

According to the *Pensacola News Journal*, about 90 percent of new wineries fail, many because of diseases that strike the fragile grapes and vines. It's not surprising, then, that the humidity of Florida that causes so many diseases and breeds fungus has thwarted all but a few serious winemakers. However, Chautauqua Vineyards figured out, as did many backyard Florida grape growers, that the best way to make wine in that state is to use native grapes, namely the Muscadine varieties known as Carlos and Noble. With Florida third in state wine consumption, it seems they've got the right idea.

<u>Swedish Hill Vineyard</u> *NV Finger Lakes Svenska Blush*
Region: USA—New York   **Suggested Retail: $5.49**
Availability: Good   **Golds: FF**
This light and fruity wine made from native American grapes is a more refreshing alternative to White Zinfandel. This is a great picnic wine, party wine, and "hot tub wine," according to the winemaker.
Special Awards: *Best of Category (FF); Double Gold (FF)*

<u>Temecula Crest Winery</u> *1994 Cabernet Sauvignon Blanc*
Region: USA—California   **Suggested Retail: $6.95**
Availability: Limited   **Golds: NW**
This is a slightly sweet (1.5% residual sugar), very distinct blush with herbaceous aromas.

<u>V. Sattui Winery</u> *1994 Gamay Rouge*
Region: USA—California   **Suggested Retail: $12.75**
Availability: Very Good   **Golds: CA, PR, SD**
If you like rosé, it would be hard to find one that so many judges deemed "best." For the last three years V. Sattui's Gamay Rouge has won 12 gold medals. This rosé is clear, with lush fruit evocative of spring strawberries. Only available from the winery, call them at (707) 963-7774 or fax them at (707) 963-4324.
Special Awards: *Best Varietal Rosé of Appellation (CA); Best of Class (PR)*

Did You Know ... ?
Imagine driving over the George Washington Bridge and rather than wall-to-wall Manhattan skyscrapers, you're greeted by an island vineyard that stretches from the East River to the Hudson. That was the idea when settlers first came to Manhattan in the early days. But they were frustrated in their attempts to grow the finicky vinifera varieties from Europe, and soon gave up.

Chapter 13

SPARKLING WINES

Blanc de Noirs
Brut
Other Sparkling Wines

Gruet Winery *NV Blanc de Noirs*
Region: USA—New Mexico   **Suggested Retail: $12.00**
Availability: Good   **Golds: PR**
This sparkler displays a delicate, pale salmon color. The richness and superb aromas that emanate from this sparkling wine are very specific to the dominant amount of Pinot Noir (75%), the rest being Chardonnay.

Korbel Winery *1990 Blanc de Noirs Champagne*
Region: USA—California   **Suggested Retail: $13.99**
Availability: Limited   **Golds: LA**
Here's a rich and elegant champagne made from select premium 100% Pinot Noir grapes. Salmon in color, with pleasant raspberry and cherry flavors, this champagne has a crisp, delicate finish. It wonderfully suits entrees such as seafood, poultry, veal, or filet of beef. Try it with apple crisp or even fortune cookies.

Mumm Napa Valley *NV Cuvée Napa Valley Blanc de Noirs*
Region: USA—California   **Suggested Retail: $13.95**
Availability: Very Good   **Golds: LA, IW, PR, NW**
Look at all those golds! This Blanc de Noirs has a pale salmon color and a fruity character not unlike a good Beaujolais Nouveau. The bouquet of ripe Pinot Noir gives this wine a more direct, soft character that "isn't at all coy," while a small percentage of Chardonnay (15%) gives the wine power and structure. Try it with Thai or Italian food, mild chicken and mushroom dishes, even fresh berry sorbets.

Piper Sonoma *NV Sonoma County Blanc de Noir*
Region: USA—California   **Suggested Retail: $13.50**
Availability: Very Good   **Golds: LA, LB**
This wine is full and round in the mouth, has flavors and aromas of strawberry, cherry, and red berry, with hints of citrus and spice, and a crisp, smooth finish.
Special Award: *Best of Class (LA)*

Tribaut *NV Blanc de Noirs*
Region: USA—California   **Suggested Retail: $9.99**
Availability: Very Good   **Golds: OC, CA, NW**
The judges were dazzled by this one! It has medium-light body and moderate acid and fruit. Scents and flavors of hay, lemons, minerals, and nectarines pop from the glass. The wine is clean, straightforward, and slightly tart with an interesting mineral edge and elegant finish. Fine pinpoint carbonation lasts for a considerable time in the glass.
Special Award: *Best Natural of Appellation (CA)*

Did You Know ... ?
Some would be surprised to learn that New Mexico is the oldest wine-growing region of the United States, since sixteenth-century Franciscan priests first produced sacramental wines there.

Gloria Ferrer   *NV Blanc de Noirs*
Region: USA—California   **Suggested Retail: $15.00**
Availability: Very Good   **Golds: OC, RE, TN, MO, TG**

This wine's enticing salmon pink hue and lush fruitiness (apples, berries, peaches) are the result of a special pressing technique that extracts an extra bit of color and character from the predominant Pinot Noir fruit.
Special Award: *Best of Show (MO)*

Iron Horse   *1992 Wedding Cuvée Sparkling Blanc de Noirs*
Region: USA—California   **Suggested Retail: $22.00**
Availability: Good   **Golds: OC**

This estate-bottled wine has a pale salmon color, a light fruity aroma, and toasty accents. Persistent sparkles and floral suggestions add to its appeal. One writer recommended it with grilled tuna, but we suggest having some before the ceremony!

Maison Deutz Winery   *NV San Luis Obispo Blanc de Noirs*
Region: USA—California   **Suggested Retail: $16.50**
Availability: NP   **Golds: IV**

This delicate sparkling wine has wonderful floral and berry aromas, tiny, uniform bubbles, and long effervescence. It is medium bodied, rich, with elegant and graceful flavors. Robert Parker says this one can "compete with French champagnes," something he "rarely" says about California sparkling wines.

Schramsberg   *1987 Napa Valley Blanc de Noirs*
Region: USA—California   **Suggested Retail: $24.50**
Availability: Good   **Golds: NW**

Generous aromas of coffee and toast combine with a hint of watermelon to give this wine generous complexity. The Blanc de Noirs displays beautiful balance as the flavors are fresh and appealing, yet the yeast aging process has contributed great richness and depth. It will age well for many years to come. It's especially appealing with lighter meals such as veal, pork tenderloin, light pasta dishes, and wild fowl.
Special Award: *Tie for Best of Price Class (NW)*

V. Sattui Winery   *1992 Carsi Vineyard Estate Champagne*
Region: USA—California   **Suggested Retail: $16.50**
Availability: Good   **Golds: CA, LA, TG**

This triple-gold-winning sparkling Blanc de Noirs (voted best in the Napa Valley) is refreshing, creamy, light, and dry, and has flavors and aromas reminiscent of fresh cherries. But you can only get V. Sattui wines from the winery, so order a few bottles while they last by calling (707) 963-7774 or by faxing (707) 963-4324.
Special Award: *Best Natural of Appellation (CA)*

Did You Know . . . ?

Flowers are weeds to the wine grower—except roses, often planted alongside grapevines to act as canaries in a cave. Susceptible to powdery mildew, they alert the wine grower when it's time to spray.

Codorniu Napa *NV Napa Valley Brut*
Region: USA—California   **Suggested Retail: $11.00**
Availability: Very Good   **Golds: RE, CA, NW, FF**
This stylish méthode champenoise *sparkling wine has delicate nuances of pears, apples, and citrus aromas and follows with notes of vanilla, lemon, and lightly toasted nuts on the palate. It is distinguished by a liberal amount of small, extremely fine, steadily rising bubbles.*
Special Award: *Chairman's Award (FF)*

Culbertson *NV California Brut*
Region: USA—California   **Suggested Retail: $10.00**
Availability: Very Good   **Golds: NW**
You'll have no problem finding this one; 10,000 cases of this liquid gold were produced. With lots of fruit and clean, fresh yeast aromas, this Brut reflects the traditional grape varieties (70% Pinot Noir, 20% Chardonnay, 10% Pinot Blanc), each contributing wonderful characteristics: the Chardonnay and Pinot Blanc create a base that has finesse and great potential to age, while the Pinot Noir provides fruit and brings the blend together. A delightfully complex champagne.
Special Award: *Best of Price Class (NW)*

Gruet Winery *NV New Mexico Brut*
Region: USA—New Mexico   **Suggested Retail: $12.00**
Availability: Good   **Golds: PR**
Look for a remarkable and intense bouquet, with toasty crispness and finesse contributed by the Chardonnay (75%). The other 25% is Pinot Noir.

Meier's Wine Cellars *NV Brut Champagne*
Region: USA—Ohio   **Suggested Retail: $4.19**
Availability: Good   **Golds: NW**
This sparkler is very light and clean with a slight fruitiness. The varietals are mixed vinifera and labruscas.

Mirabelle Cellars *NV North Coast Brut*
Region: USA—California   **Suggested Retail: $10.00**
Availability: Very Good   **Golds: NW**
Stylistically, this sparkling wine resembles some of its French cousins with its elegant, toasty aroma that leads into crisp and complex flavors on the palate. Freshness on the midpalate continues through to the finish, beckoning for another sip. It finishes with a chorus of exotic fruit and buttery undertones and yearns to be paired with shellfish, light appetizers, or hearty vegetable-based soups.

Did You Know . . . ?
Thornton Winery (formerly Brindiamo), who also produces under the Culbertson label, has won more awards and medals for its bottled effervescence in the last five years than any other *méthode champenoise* producer in America.

Mirassou Vineyards *1991 Monterey County Brut*

Region: USA—California   **Suggested Retail: $11.99**
Availability: Good   **Golds: LA**

This is a dry, full-bodied wine with enticing "French bakery" style aromas and complex, smoky-toasty components. It is crisp and clean, well balanced, and has a full, lingering finish.

Mumm Napa Valley *1989 Winery Lake Cuvée*

Region: USA—California   **Suggested Retail: $14.00**
Availability: Good   **Golds: CA, PR, AT**

The Pinot Noir (80%) in this vintage provides the body and typical flavor of that varietal, while the Chardonnay firms the acid backbone and accents the tropical nose. This cuvée is big, brawny, and elegant.
Special Award: *Best Brut of Appellation (CA)*

Mumm Napa Valley *NV Napa Valley Brut Prestige*

Region: USA—California   **Suggested Retail: $13.95**
Availability: Very Good   **Golds: FF**

If winemaker Greg Fowler had to pick one wine above all others to represent the Napa Valley, it would be this one. Ripened fruit from more than fifty vineyards was used to produce this gold medal sparkler. The wine has a beautiful rose petal aroma and a wonderful layering component that is crisp yet creamy, rich and lingering. Try it with grilled salmon.
Special Award: *Best of Category (FF)*

Tribaut *Brut Méthode Champenoise*

Region: USA—California   **Suggested Retail: $9.99**
Availability: Very Good   **Golds: NW**

Produced from a blend of Pinot Noir and Chardonnay, this sparkling wine is made with the traditional méthode champenoise *and given a special French dosage that adds complexity and freshness to the rich, elegant finish. It has medium-light body and medium acid and fruit. Flowers, minerals, lemons, and pineapples emerge from the glass. Pleasantly tart and aromatic with straightforward fruit and fine length, the wine has fine pinpoint carbonation that lasts for a considerable time in the glass.*

Did You Know ... ?

The size and shape of a glass may play a large role in your ability to fully appreciate the wine you're drinking. Some connoisseurs insist on drinking their wine only in special glasses created for specific varietals, designed to channel that type of wine to the part of your tongue that can pick up the wine's most important palate sensations.

Culbertson   *1988 Brut Reserve*
Region: USA—California   **Suggested Retail: $18.00**
Availability: Good   **Golds: NW, TG**
The cuvée selection and assemblage for this wine reflect the richness and quality of the finest lots of Chardonnay, Pinot Blanc, and Pinot Noir. Extraordinary richness, depth, and complexity are what characterize this sparkler. The aroma is both up front and perfumed, marrying yeast and toasty undertones with an array of fruits: apple, figs, strawberry, and light citrus.
Special Award: *Double Gold (TG)*

Gloria Ferrer   *1988 Royal Cuvée Brut*
Region: USA—California   **Suggested Retail: $18.00**
Availability: Very Good   **Golds: OC, SF, PR, CL, TG, AT**
This vintage exhibits many complexities of bouquet and flavor. Aromas of strawberry, cherry, ripe apple, lime, and spice combine with bottle bouquets of toasted yeasty bread and toasted almonds. The creamy smooth mousse explodes into bright, fruity, citrus flavors. Firm acidity balances the full, rich body leading to a long, crisp finish.
Special Awards: *Best of Class (PR); Trophy for Best Pacific Rim Sparkling Wine (PR); Best of Class (CL)*

Gloria Ferrer   *1987 Carneros Cuvée Late Disgorged Brut*
Region: USA—California   **Suggested Retail: $25.00**
Availability: Limited   **Golds: OC, LA**
Disgorged after more than five years on the yeast, this fine sparkling wine has flavors and aromas of black cherries, strawberries, toasted almonds, and hints of smoke. Pale yellow-gold, it is rich and creamy. With its remarkable intensity of fruit it can be enjoyed like champagne.
Special Award: *Best of Class (LA)*

Handley Cellars   *1989 Anderson Valley Brut Sparkling Wine*
Region: USA—California   **Suggested Retail: $16.00**
Availability: Limited   **Golds: RE, LA, PR**
The 1989 is full bodied and complex, yet reflects the elegance and delicacy of a cool vintage, with a classic yeasty, toasty character. Its vibrant acidity and subtle spiciness make it a wonderful partner for the traditional champagne fare of oysters, caviar, and smoked salmon. The winemaker also adds that it will go well with Curried Mussels Appetizers (recipe is available from the winery, at 707-545-0992): the citric fruity mousse and yeasty aroma of the bubbly complement lively chiles amidst cool coconut milk and fleshy mussels in this recipe. Yum!

Did You Know . . . ?
What is so impermeable to moisture that it is used for life jackets? What retains its properties at both high and low temperature extremes and will age almost indefinitely without deterioration? Amazing cork!

J. Schram by Schramsberg   *Napa Valley Champagne*
Region: USA—California   **Suggested Retail: $50.00**
Availability: Good   **Golds: NW, AT**
This wine shows complexity, balance, and elegance and has fresh aromas of apple, pear, and tropical fruit in the nose. Subtle nuances of vanilla and butterscotch complement the toasted, nutty character, and the flavors are long, giving way to a soft, creamy finish. This wine should age beautifully. Try it as an aperitif or enjoy it with veal piccata, filet mignon, foie gras, seafood brochettes, or courses featuring wild mushrooms.

Jordan Sparkling Wine Company   *1990 "J" Sonoma County Brut*
Region: USA—California   **Suggested Retail: $23.00**
Availability: NP   **Golds: RE, LA, IW, SD, NW, BT, AT**
This, the most award-winning sparkler of 1995, displays an array of delicate fruit aromas and flavors complemented by full and round sensations on the palate. The initial aromas, reminiscent of figs, grape blossoms, pippin apples, and fresh melon, blend elegantly with the nutty aromas arising from prolonged yeast aging. The finish is long, clean, and slightly nutty. Its broad flavor profile and unique softness make it an attractive aperitif and a delicious companion to lighter dishes. If you can't find this gem, look for the 1991 J, released March 1996. It seems worth the gamble. P.S. We celebrated the finishing of our book with this one. What a delight!
Special Awards: Trophy for Best Bottle Fermented Sparkling Wine (IW); Best of Class (SD); Best Sparkling Wine (SD); Trophy for Best New World Champagne/Sparkling Wine (NW); Tie for Best of Class (NW)

Piper Sonoma   *1985 "Tete de Cuvée" Sparkling Wine*
Region: USA—California   **Suggested Retail: $28.00**
Availability: Limited   **Golds: OC, BT**
The wine's creamy texture is accompanied by its aromas and flavors of berry, lemon, and green apple. Its flavors are balanced with yeast and a faint floral background. The finish is pleasantly crisp.
Special Award: Tie for Vintage Sparkling Wine National Champion (BT)

RainSong Vineyard   *NV Oregon Sparkling Wine*
Region: USA—Oregon   **Suggested Retail: $15.00**
Availability: Limited   **Golds: OR**
This wine is made "naturel," with no sugar at all. It has a very dry, fruity style and is fruitier in the nose than most. It is essentially white, but has a faint hint of salmon color.

Did You Know . . . ?
Grapes that have to struggle to ripen achieve the greatest complexity, or so say many experts. Therefore, some argue that Oregon will be producing better wines than either California or Washington in the coming decades, since Oregon's grape-growing conditions are more challenging to the grape.

Robert Hunter Winery   *1991 Sonoma Valley Brut de Noirs*
Region: USA—California   **Suggested Retail: $25.00**
Availability: NP   **Golds: NW**
This one has a toasty/yeasty nose underlaid by ripe peach aromas. Rich, ripe fruit flavors, nice effervescence, lovely balance, and a fruity finish round it out. One reviewer suggests sipping this bubbly alongside vegetable pâté.

Tabor Hill   *NV Grand Mark Brut*
Region: USA—Michigan   **Suggested Retail: $19.95**
Availability: Limited   **Golds: PR**
Here's a midwestern winery that competed side by side with the more well-known California sparklers—and won! This Brut is slightly fruity with the essence of apples. It is light golden in color and has a finish that's very clean and crisp. The southwestern corner of Michigan has great growing conditions for champagne-producing grapes.

Wente Bros.   *NV Grande Brut*
Region: USA—California   **Suggested Retail: $15.00**
Availability: NP   **Golds: LA**
In the tradition of the finest champagnes, the wine has been aged more than 5 years in Wente Bros.' century-old sandstone caves, thus enhancing the yeast character and giving the three classic grapes (Chardonnay, Pinot Noir, Pinot Blanc) in the cuvée a chance to marry into a harmony of flavors. Look for varietal character and fine acid balance, delicate color and subtle flavors.

Did You Know ... ?
Michigan has a surprising number of wineries. Lake Michigan is so deep that it rarely freezes, and creates an almost maritime climate that's favorable to several grape varieties.

Culbertson *1993 Cuvée Rouge Artist Series*
Region: USA—California   **Suggested Retail: $12.00**
Availability: Good   **Golds: NW, AT**
Culbertson's Artist Series labels win awards left and right, but more important—for the wine lover—is that what's inside the bottles also wins golds. This wine has a full, rich Pinot Noir character (100% Pinot Noir), beautiful ruby color, and a bouquet packed with fresh strawberries and raspberries. It is finished slightly younger to keep the fruit balance more forward than the yeast.
Special Award: *Best of Price Class (NW)*

Domaine Ste. Michelle *NV Columbia Valley Sparkling Wine*
Region: USA—Washington   **Suggested Retail: $9.00**
Availability: NP   **Golds: CI**
Imagine the Old World French champagnes this wine was competing against in France at Challenge International du Vin and you'll know that this was a gold well deserved. The wine exhibits floral, fruity, and toasty characteristics in both the nose and mouth. The dosage balances the acidity, resulting in a clean, crisp méthode champenoise character with just a hint of sweetness in the finish. Now, check out that price! Is this the perfect sparkling wine, or what?

Grant Burge *NV Pinot Noir/Chardonnay Méthode Traditionale*
Region: Australia   **Suggested Retail: $15.95**
Availability: Very Good   **Golds: AD**
This sparkling wine has creamy elegance and finesse, and a wonderful balance with loads of flavor and drinkability. It is available in the United States and Europe too.

Handley Cellars *1991 Anderson Valley Brut Rosé*
Region: USA—California   **Suggested Retail: $19.00**
Availability: Limited   **Golds: LA, ME**
Displaying very fine bubbles and a lovely, pale rosy sunset color, this sparkling wine is a classic. Delicate berry aromas precede dry, elegant, tangy flavors and a creamy texture. This is a sparkler that can be matched with an astounding variety of menus; the depth of flavors and the excellent acidity make it a particularly excellent partner with spicy foods.
Special Award: *Sweepstakes White (ME)*

Did You Know . . . ?
The first American sparkling wine ever to be awarded a gold medal at Challenge International du Vin in Blaye-Bourg, France, was from Washington State: Domaine Ste. Michelle, the label of Château Ste. Michelle, founded way back in 1934.

Handley Cellars *1989 Blanc de Blancs*
Region: USA—California **Suggested Retail: $19.00**
Availability: Limited **Golds: NW**
This 100% Chardonnay sparkler is rich and lively with wonderful balance. The flavors have a creamy, lemony note with a subtle yeasty, toasty character. Firm acidity and a very lengthy finish indicate that this wine should age well.

Jepson Vineyards *1989 Blanc de Blanc*
Region: USA—California **Suggested Retail: $16.00**
Availability: Good **Golds: SF**
This sparkling wine has a wonderfully elegant aroma of Chardonnay fruit, toasty yeast, hints of spice, with a dry and pleasing finish.

Korbel Winery *1991 Master's Reserve Sparkling Blanc de Blancs*
Region: USA—California **Suggested Retail: $13.99**
Availability: Good **Golds: OC**
A full-bodied, elegant champagne that is delicate and creamy in texture with hints of vanilla, honey, and apple. It has a clean, crisp finish.

Korbel Winery *Natural Champagne*
Region: USA—California **Suggested Retail: $11.99**
Availability: NP **Golds: RE**
This is a light, dry champagne produced from the classic champagne blend of Pinot Noir and Chardonnay grapes. It possesses flawless balance and a satin finish, and pairs beautifully with most appetizers, seafood, and any dish featuring citrus or apples.

Korbel Winery *NV California Rouge*
Region: USA—California **Suggested Retail: $11.99**
Availability: Good **Golds: NW**
A medium-dry champagne with a distinctive red color and intense black cherry and strawberry-plum aromas and flavors. It has a moderately crisp balance with hints of vanilla spice, and very light oak suggestions. Have it at your next Thanksgiving turkey feast.

Did You Know . . . ?

If you're looking for just the right food to go with a delicious wine, Handley Cellars offers recipes that are part of their Culinary Adventure series. Some of the recipes include Avocado, Tomato, and White Corn Salsa (best served with their Sauvignon Blanc), Rachel's Salmon Mousse (to go with their Brut Rosé), and Oysters with Scallions and Ginger (with their Blanc de Blancs). Call them at (707) 545-0992 for a copy of these and other recipes.

Maison Deutz Winery   *NV Brut Rosé*

Region: USA—California   Suggested Retail: $20.00
Availability: NP   Golds: LA

Elegance is the featured characteristic of this sparkling rosé, with its raspberry nose and hints of nuttiness. It is rich in texture, with concentrated fruit flavors and spice. Great length finishes it off. One reviewer thinks it would go well with braised vegetables and grilled seafood.

Schramsberg   *1991 Cuvée de Pinot Sparkling Brut Rosé*

Region: USA—California   Suggested Retail: $22.75
Availability: Limited   Golds: OC

This wine has wonderfully complex fruit characters. The aromas are reminiscent of raspberries and strawberries, complemented by a subtle toasty nuance. On the palate the flavors are round and luscious, leading to a refreshing, crisp finish. Delicious with mild cheese, fruit platters, pasta putanesca, and spicy Asian cuisine.

Schramsberg   *1990 Cuvée de Pinot Brut Rosé*

Region: USA—California   Suggested Retail: $22.75
Availability: Limited   Golds: NW

Bright cherry and watermelon aromas abound, followed by a hint of toasty complexity. The fruit flavors are fresh and lively, giving way to a round finish. This wine is delicious now, but will gain additional complexity with further aging. Try it with prosciutto and melon, rabbit, pâté, grilled meat, and fresh or poached fruits.

Ste. Chapelle Vineyards   *NV Special Harvest Riesling Champagne*

Region: USA—Idaho   Suggested Retail: $7.99
Availability: Good   Golds: RE, PR, GH

Look for a beautiful dessert-style champagne that is lush, fruity, with crisp acidity. This sparkler is made from 100% Johannisberg Riesling. The critics raved about this wine, and several well-known publications tagged it a "Best Buy." Ste. Chapelle also makes a triple-gold-winning late harvest Johannisberg Riesling if you're looking for a delicious dessert wine at a very reasonable price ($10).
Special Awards: *Sweepstakes Finalist, White Wine (RE); Best of Class (PR)*

Stone Hill Wine Co.   *NV Missouri Golden Spumante*

Region: USA—Missouri   Suggested Retail: $7.99
Availability: NP   Golds: FF, MS

A festive sparkler emphasizing fresh fruity aromas and flavors. It has pale straw color, lively acidity, and a medium, sweet finish.
Special Award: *Chairman's Award (FF)*

Did You Know . . . ?

Idaho's largest winery, Ste. Chapelle, is also the fourth largest winery in the Northwest, situated east of the beautiful Snake River Valley.

Chapter 14

SWEET/DESSERT/FORTIFIED WINES

Icewine
Muscat
Other Sweet Wines
Port
Sherry

Gehringer Brothers Estate Winery　*1994 Riesling Ice Wine*
Region: Canada　　　　　　　**Suggested Retail: $38.00**
Availability: Limited　　　　　**Golds: LA, IV, IE**

The grapes for this wine were picked at -12 degrees Celsius—cold enough to freeze the berries into solid marbles. During pressing, all the sugars, acids, and flavor components slowly dripped out, leaving behind the berries' water content as ice crystals in the press. Like a liqueur in concentration, but with an alcohol level similar to wine, this icewine has with a sweetness balanced by a proportionately concentrated acidity. With its delicate fruit flavors, it is meant to be sipped as a dessert or after-dessert wine, served slightly chilled. According to the winemaker, icewine is "nature's gift to mankind."

Henry of Pelham Estates　*1993 Niagara Peninsula Ice Wine*
Region: Canada　　　　　　　**Suggested Retail: $46.00 CAN**
Availability: Outside USA　　　**Golds: IV**

The aromas range from apple and pear to apricot, which also come through on the palate. Of rich, golden color, this icewine provides steely mineral qualities and acidity that enhance the structure of the wine. A rich, full-bodied texture in the mouth is enhanced by a long finish supported by good acidity. The best and most simple enjoyment of this wine is on its own as the conclusion to a meal, but it will lend itself to careful pairing with fresh fruit desserts—not overly sweet. It is available in Canada, but not the United States.

Hillebrand Estates Winery　*1993 Ice Wine*
Region: Canada　　　　　　　**Suggested Retail: $44.95**
Availability: Good　　　　　　**Golds: IV**

This golden-colored wine has complex aromas of orange blossoms, tropical fruit, hazelnut, peach, quince, mango, honey, apricot, and caramel. It is well balanced in the mouth with lots of finesse and complexity. With a touch of oakiness, and crystallized fruits and ginger in the finish, it has a very long and intense aftertaste. Excellent as an aperitif or with dried fruits or fine desserts.

Inniskillin Wines　*1993 Vidal Ice Wine VQA*
Region: Canada　　　　　　　**Suggested Retail: $47.00 CAN**
Availability: Outside USA　　　**Golds: IV**

Luscious and concentrated, vivid and intensely aromatic with a myriad of tropical fruits, this wine is long on the finish, and has excellent balance of natural residual sugar and naturally concentrated acidity. It was harvested frozen on the vine in December 1993. Look for this one in Canada if you're driving across the border. It's not available in the United States.

Did You Know . . . ?
Canada produces more icewine than any other country in the world, and is universally recognized for these unusual and precious wines.

Magnotta Winery   *1993 Riesling Ice Wine Limited Edition*
Region: Canada   **Suggested Retail: $29.50**
Availability: Limited   **Golds: IV, AC, BT**
This icewine is amber gold in color with a spicy, tropical fruit, and lychee bouquet. It has a honeyed orange and toffee flavor and is rich, well balanced, with good acidity, and a lingering aftertaste. Serve it well chilled.
Special Award: *Black Diamond Award (IV)*

Reif Estate Winery   *1993 Niagara Peninsula Vidal Ice Wine*
Region: Canada   **Suggested Retail: $33.00**
Availability: Good   **Golds: VI, WC**
This wine was produced by time-honored German tradition, requiring that grapes actually be harvested by hand while frozen on the vines. Reif's winemaker prefers temperatures between -10 and -13 degrees C, usually requiring pickers to be out in the vineyards in the middle of the night. Their efforts yielded a wine with warm, golden color and rich, concentrated aromas. It is full bodied, perfectly balanced, with nuances of apricot, peaches, and sweet, ripe honey melon. The substantial mouth feel is followed by a long finish. One bottle will serve up to 12 people. Serve it chilled in small tulip-shaped liqueur glasses. By the way, this one is available in the United States.
Special Award: *Grand Gold Medal (VI)*

Reif Estate Winery   *1987 Vidal Ice Wine*
Region: Canada   **Suggested Retail: $71.00**
Availability: Limited   **Golds: IV**
An excellent example of the aging potential of icewine, this wine has a dark golden color and shows beautiful overtones of chocolate and toffee on the nose. Nice acidity keeps it fresh, and the typical fruits of apricots and peaches still dominate the flavor. It has only won gold medals! From Intervin it won golds in 1988, 1991, and 1995, and Robert Parker called it one of the 10 best wines of the year in 1989. Although the case production was tiny (400 cases), some of them are being released in 1996, so search high and low until you find one, although your best bet is to visit the winery near Niagara-on-the-Lake, Canada.

Did You Know . . . ?

The Reif family began their own tradition of winemaking in Germany's Rhine region over 100 years ago. Emigrating to Canada in 1977, the family selected the beautiful and historic Niagara-on-the-Lake to pursue their trade. In order to use as few chemicals as possible, they use pheromone discs in their vineyards, which seduce male berry moths away from fertile females, thus preventing reproduction. They also opt for chicken and cow manure instead of synthetic fertilizers. Hooray!

Stoney Ridge Cellars *1994 Puddicombe/Smith Vidal Ice Wine*
Region: Canada   **Suggested Retail: $41.95**
Availability: Good   **Golds: IV, WC**

Look for flavors and aromas of honey and peaches, lingering rich flavor, an inviting nose, and a delicious aftertaste. This wine hit the shelves in summer 1996, so you should be able to find a bottle, even though the quantity produced of this liquid gold was relatively small (450 cases). By the way, the 1993 vintage of this wine was also a gold medal winner, so Stoney Ridge has obviously mastered the secret of making superior icewine year after year.

Vineland Estates Winery *1993 Vidal Ice Wine*
Region: Canada   **Suggested Retail: $44.50**
Availability: Good   **Golds: IV, AC**

The result of 6 months of slow, cool fermentation turned this nectar into a luscious and golden dessert wine. The wine has a rich amber color, an intense, apricot, honey nose, and exotic flavors of kiwi, papaya, and mangoes.

Wagner Vineyards *1991 Ravat Blanc Ice Wine*
Region: USA—New York   **Suggested Retail: $9.99**
Availability: Limited   **Golds: NW, TG, NY**

A concentrated dessert wine abundant in the aromas of exotic, tropical fruits. Pineapple and papaya fill the mouth and culminate in an expansive, lingering finish. You'll find slight undertones of mint and caramel in the nose.
Special Award: *Best of Price Class (NW)*

Did You Know . . . ?
Besides Canada, New York's Finger Lakes region is one of the few places in the world where weather conditions are perfect for the production of icewines.

Alderbrook   *1994 Late Harvest Muscat de Frontignan*
Region: USA—California   **Suggested Retail: $20.00**
Availability: Limited   **Golds: CA, LA, IV, FF, TG, EL, CO**
Golds, golds, and more golds, plus special honors aplenty. Aromas of apricots, honey, and overripe pineapple enhance the rich, full texture of this wine.
Special Awards: *Double Gold (CA); Best Muscat of Appellation (CA); Best of Class (LA); Division Sweepstakes (LA); Best of Five (FF)*

Brindiamo   *1994 Moscato Aromatico Muscat of Alexandria*
Region: USA—California   **Suggested Retail: $6.00**
Availability: Good   **Golds: OC**
As the name indicates, this is a very aromatic and intensely rich wine. At one time, Muscat of Alexandria was widely planted in California and used primarily for raisins. The vines used for this beauty date back to the 1890s, and produce low yields and intensely flavored grapes. The varietal's spicy, fruity aromas leap from the glass, and this wine is finished off-dry and balanced with crisp acidity.

Lava Cap   *1994 Muscat Canelli*
Region: USA—California   **Suggested Retail: $15.00**
Availability: Limited   **Golds: OC**
Look for intense fruity flavors and Muscat aromas. This is a delightful, semisweet aperitif, or try it with fruit and cheese.

Quady Winery   *1994 Electra*
Region: USA—California   **Suggested Retail: $6.99**
Availability: Limited   **Golds: CA**
Short cold fermentation, light alcohol (only 4%), high acidity, and slight effervescence create a refreshing soft sweet taste in this Muscat—perfect for brunches and picnics. Although it will be close to miraculous if you can find a bottle of this in stores, we include it because Quady's dessert wines win golds every year, no matter the vintage. We think it's a sure thing, so pick up a bottle of the latest release and get ready to smack your lips—but do it soon because their wonderful wines sell out lightning fast.

Did You Know . . . ?
It takes 25 years before a cork tree is ready to yield its first bark for cork. (Cork comes from the outermost layer of bark from the cork oak.) However, the first harvest will be irregular in size and density, great for floor tiles or insulation material, but not refined enough for wine stoppers. The next harvest can't take place for 9 more years. But even then the cork can't be used for stoppers. Only on the third harvest, when the tree is about 53 years old, can wine-bottle corks be made.

Quady Winery   *1994 Elysium Black Muscat*
Region: USA—California   Suggested Retail: $12.50
Availability: Limited   Golds: OC, EL
Black Muscat is a black-skinned Muscat grape that can offer up "haunting roselike aromas." The only problem with this and other Quady dessert wines is that they're too darned good! They're made in tiny quantities and go fast. We list this one in the hopes that some lucky reader will find a bottle and grab it off the shelf.
Special Award: *Double Gold (EL)*

Quady Winery   *1993 Elysium Black Muscat*
Region: USA—California   Suggested Retail: $12.50
Availability: Limited   Golds: LA, PR, NW
You probably won't find this beauty in your wine shop, so why are we including it? Because the Elysium wins golds consistently, and sells out quickly, year after year. If you're into Black Muscat, we don't think you'll go wrong with Quady's—no matter the vintage.
Special Awards: *Best of Class (PR); Best of Price Class (NW)*

Quady Winery   *1994 Essensia Orange Muscat*
Region: USA—California   Suggested Retail: $12.50
Availability: Good   Golds: OC, EL
The aroma shows a full, rich, melon-apricot character with subtle hints of orange blossom. In the mouth, considerable richness and body are apparent. The wine shows excellent tartness and finishes clean. It has a perfect balance of sweetness and fruit acidity. Quady only produces dessert wines, and wins golds in top international competitions every year. We can't wait to try it.

St. Supery Vineyards   *1993 Dollarhide Ranch Moscato*
Region: USA—California   Suggested Retail: $13.00
Availability: NP   Golds: PR
A light, sweet wine with the fruitiness of ripe melons, wildflowers, and apricots. The fruitiness is enhanced by the intense, crisp, clean finish. This wine should be served well chilled by itself or with fresh strawberries, peaches, or nectarines.
Special Award: *Best of Class (PR)*

Tucker Cellars   *1993 Muscat Canelli*
Region: USA—Washington   Suggested Retail: $5.99
Availability: Limited   Golds: RE, WW
Here's a fragrant Muscat with a nice touch of sweetness. Muscat character with fresh tangerine delivers a nice balance.

Did You Know . . . ?

Bees *love* Muscat grapes. Pliny the Elder referred to Muscat as *uva apiana,* or "grape of the bees."

V. Sattui Winery *1994 California Muscat*
Region: USA—California   **Suggested Retail: $12.00**
Availability: Good   **Golds: LA, IV**

Rich and intense with nuances of peaches and orange blossoms, this winning dessert wine can be purchased directly from the winery. Call them at (707) 963-7774 or fax them at (707) 963-4324.

Windsor Vineyards *1994 Late Harvest Muscat Canelli*
Region: USA—California   **Suggested Retail: $12.17**
Availability: Good   **Golds: FF**

This Muscat is full bodied and very aromatic with hints of gardenias and lemons in the nose. It has abundant fruit flavors with a well-balanced finish. It is smooth and not very sweet.

Yalumba *Museum Release Old Show Reserve Muscat*
Region: Australia   **Suggested Retail: $22.90**
Availability: Limited   **Golds: WC, BT**

A tiny quantity of this 10-year-old Muscat was produced, but it is available in the United States, as well as Canada, the UK, and New Zealand. If you can find some, expect a luscious dessert wine that has flavors reminiscent of raisined fruits, with a complex aged character. The color is deep tawny with faint copper-green tints. In the bouquet you'll find raisined fruits with spicy gingerlike complexity. On the palate it has subtle wood-aged complexity that is well integrated. The spicy Muscat flavors linger on.
Special Award: *Best Fortified Wine in Show (WC)*

Did You Know . . . ?

Ever heard of Flying Winemakers? No, they're not a circus act, but they do perform great feats. The term was coined in the late eighties when an English wine merchant by the name of Tony Laithwaite paired talented Australian winemakers, virtually idle during harvest time in the Northern Hemisphere (since Australia's winters are our summers), with wine producers who had a lot of grapes and juice, but not much expertise. The idea caught on, and by the early 1990s Australian or Australian-trained winemakers were flying all over the world, notably South America, where they often have to bring in their own materials and mobile equipment to produce extremely fine wine where it otherwise would not have happened.

Breitenbach Wine Cellars *1994 Ohio Frost Fire Niagara*
Region: USA—Ohio   Suggested Retail: $6.11
Availability: Good   Golds: FF
This one is very fresh and fruity, like "plucking a grape off of the vine." Light and sweet, this wine has a light amber color and is light bodied—a great dessert wine.

Caterina Winery *1994 Late Harvest Johannisberg Riesling*
Region: USA—Washington   Suggested Retail: $9.00
Availability: Limited   Golds: TC
This luscious wine shows typical Washington State Riesling characteristics. The emphasis is on pineapple, pear, and apricot.

Concannon *1992 Late Harvest Johannisberg Riesling*
Region: USA—California   Suggested Retail: $9.50
Availability: Limited   Golds: OC
Here's what you'll find in a glass of this dessert wine: gorgeous honey and dried apple fruit, a highly extracted mango, honey, and caramelized butterscotch nose, and subtle undertones of nutmeg and cinnamon. One reviewer called it a "hedonistic roller coaster." Call the winery if you have difficulty finding it, at (510) 447-3760.

Covey Run Vintners *1993 Late Harvest Johannisberg Riesling*
Region: USA—Washington   Suggested Retail: $8.99
Availability: NP   Golds: DA
This is a rich and sweet wine with perfumed aromas and a viscous mouth feel. Its peach, apricot, nectarine, and honey/spice character is well balanced with fresh acidity. According to the winemaker, it is "Yakima Valley's signature white wine."

Fetzer *1993 Late Harvest Reserve Johannisberg Riesling*
Region: USA—California   Suggested Retail: $6.49
Availability: NP   Golds: DA
Attractive Riesling qualities of clean, fresh floral aromas are accented by apricot and peach fruit notes. Appealing flavors of apricot and ripe pears are balanced by crisp lemon notes in this delightful wine.

Hogue Cellars *1994 Late Harvest White Riesling*
Region: USA—Washington   Suggested Retail: $6.45
Availability: NP   Golds: SD
A Wine Spectator *Best Buy, this one is fairly sweet, but has enough crispness to balance the ripe apricot, citrus, honey flavors. It has a flowery, long, lingering finish that will go well with your apple pie.*

Did You Know . . . ?
Riesling is the most widely planted grape in Washington State and the second most planted grape in Oregon. Australia has more acreage of it than any other white wine variety.

Montinore *1993 Late Harvest Riesling*
Region: USA—Oregon   Suggested Retail: $5.99
Availability: NP   Golds: RE

The wine has a rich bouquet of quince, peach, and apricot with notes of roses and honey, and a nice acid-sugar balance with apricot and quince flavors, followed by an earthy aftertaste.

Montinore *1993 Late Harvest Estate Bottled Gewürztraminer*
Region: USA—Oregon   Suggested Retail: $5.99
Availability: NP   Golds: SD, FF, OR

Peaches, apples, and cloves make up the bouquet of this wine, which has the classic spiciness of European Gewürztraminers. Firm acids and light sweetness showcase the baked apples and citrus aromas.

Palmer Vineyards *1993 Select Harvest Gewürztraminer*
Region: USA—New York   Suggested Retail: $9.99
Availability: Limited   Golds: LA

Ideal late-season sunshine in the vineyards allowed Palmer to carry this variety to ultimate ripeness. Such rare concentration of flavor and sugar, coupled with selective harvesting, creates a wine of lavish flavor intensity and sweetness. It is rich and has exotic aromas and concentrated flavors. A perfect ending to any meal.

St. James Winery *NV Missouri Velvet Red Sweet Concord*
Region: USA—Missouri   Suggested Retail: $5.49
Availability: Limited   Golds: FF, MS

One of their most popular sweet wines, this one has been winning awards for years. It is sweet and fruity, made from the Concord grape, grown here since the 1800s.

Stone Hill Wine Co. *American Steinberg*
Region: USA—Missouri   Suggested Retail: $7.99
Availability: NP   Golds: PR, FF

Look for a delicate, floral aroma, rich fruity flavor, and crisp acidity balanced by a nice touch of sweetness. Very Germanic in style.
Special Awards: *Best of Class (PR); Best Pacific Rim Dessert Wine (PR)*

Yalumba *1994 Family Reserve Botrytis Sémillon/Sauvignon Blanc*
Region: Australia   Suggested Retail: $8.65
Availability: Good   Golds: SY

Look for a rich yellow-gold color and tropical honeyed aromas evident on the nose from the pungent, sun-concentrated Sauvignon Blanc. The palate is rich, full, and luscious. Flavors of apricot and peach with a hint of oak are balanced with a drying alcohol and acid finish. The patient cellarer will be rewarded in 10 to 15 years, but it can be consumed now. This wine can be found in the United States and Canada.

Did You Know . . . ?
A *Wine Spectator* survey found that wine drinkers who drink more than five glasses per week are mostly female (58 percent).

Arrowfield Wines *1993 Show Reserve Late Harvest Rhine Riesling*

Region: Australia   Suggested Retail: $15.50
Availability: Limited   Golds: RM, PE

The fruit used for this wine was full flavored and luscious. The resultant wine has a delicate floral bouquet with rich mellow flavors, balanced by crisp acidity on the finish. This is a truly outstanding dessert wine that will benefit from cellaring. Rich, smooth, and sweet, this one teams well with chocolate desserts. By the way, this wine has won 5 gold medals to date, in 1994 and 1995 wine shows. It must be amazing, and it's available in the United States, Europe, New Zealand, and Japan.

Arrowfield Wines *1993 Cowra Late Harvest Gewürztraminer*

Region: Australia   Suggested Retail: $12.50
Availability: Limited   Golds: PE, RM

The fruit used for this wine was full, concentrated in flavor, and luscious. The resultant wine has an intense golden color, a lifted floral varietal bouquet, and long sumptuous flavor balanced by crisp acidity. This unique dessert wine will benefit from cellaring. Drink it at the end of any meal. Its rich, smooth sweetness makes it a must with rich caramel desserts, and it also teams well with stone fruits and cheese. It is available in the United States as well as New Zealand, Europe, and Japan.

Concannon *1993 Monterey Late Harvest Sémillon*

Region: USA—California   Suggested Retail: $11.95
Availability: NP   Golds: RE

If you love dessert wine, this heavily botrytized wine has lots of fig, apricot, honey flavors, a silky and viscous mouth feel, and a long lingering finish. It will sing for you after your meal. If you have trouble finding a bottle, call the winery directly at (510) 447-3760.

De Loach *1994 Estate Bottled Late Harvest Gewürztraminer*

Region: USA—California   Suggested Retail: $14.00
Availability: Good   Golds: CA

This dessert wine has an intriguing aroma of ripe pears followed by flavors of apricot, spice, and rich honey with a touch of citrus. The winemaker and his family enjoy this luscious wine poured over fresh raspberries, strawberries, or blueberries, with a small glass to enjoy on the side.
***Special Awards:** Best Gewürztraminer of California (CA); Tie for Best Gewürztraminer of Appellation (CA)*

Did You Know . . . ?

In the 1630s in post-Roman Britain, a law was passed that made it illegal to sell wine in glass bottles. The reason was because unscrupulous wine merchants took advantage of the fact that no two bottles held the same amount, and thus profited whenever they could. For the next 230 years, people purchased wine by measure, then poured it into their own personally stamped bottles.

Geyser Peak Winery *1994 Late Harvest Riesling*
Region: USA—California   Suggested Retail: $16.00
Availability: NP   Golds: SF, LA, PR, FF, AT
*This one from Geyser Peak is available in their tasting room only. Call them at
(800) 945-4447 if you're in the Sonoma County area. We're sure that the judges
who didn't get to swallow this very sweet dessert-style wine with strong honey,
raisiny, and botrytis characters were wishing they were on the other side of the
panelists' table.*
Special Awards: *Double Gold (SF); Best Dessert Wine (SD)*

Geyser Peak Winery *1993 Late Harvest Riesling*
Region: USA—California   Suggested Retail: $16.00
Availability: NP   Golds: PR, SD, FF, LJ
*This one is only available in the Peak's tasting room, so call them at (800) 945-4447
if you're bicycling the back roads of Sonoma County and need something sweet after
your cheese and crusty French bread roadside picnic.*
Special Awards: *Best of Class (PR); Best of Class (SD)*

Hermann J. Wiemer *1994 Late Harvest Johannisberg Riesling*
Region: USA—New York   Suggested Retail: $10.00
Availability: Good   Golds: LA
*Here's an Alsatian-style, late harvest wine exhibiting the apricots and honey flavors
of botrytized fruit. The wine is rich and full bodied with delicately balanced sugar
and acid. Though perceptibly sweet, it is a beautiful companion to food. Serve it
with lobster, heavy cream–sauced dishes, fresh fruit, and Swiss or sharp cheddar
cheese.*

Herzog Wine Cellars *1994 Monterey County Johannisberg Riesling*
Region: USA—California   Suggested Retail: $13.99
Availability: Good   Golds: LA, TG, IE
*The distinctive dried apricot, pineapple, and apple aromas will remain with this
wine for many years. The low pH and structured acidity balance the very high level
of sugar and will, as well, provide the framework for long aging potential. It pairs
well with desserts, as well as fruit, pâté, soft cheeses, or by itself.*

Did You Know . . . ?

What's my line? I closely examine the color and hairiness of a grapevine's
shoot, shoot tip, petiole, and young and mature leaves; the contour, texture,
shape, and indentations of grape leaves; the shape of the flowers; compact-
ness and shape of grape bunches; the color, shape, and number of grapes.
I'm an ampelographer, among a group of elite, obscure, highly trained
individuals whose job it has been since the beginning of this century to
identify and classify grape varieties. DNA "fingerprinting" may put these few
out of business.

Husch Vineyards *1993 Estate Bottled Late Harvest Gewürztraminer*
Region: USA—California   **Suggested Retail: $14.00**
Availability: Limited   **Golds: DA**

This is a sweet wine with classic late-picked aromas of honey and apricots combined with the spicy varietal character of Gewürz, producing a wine of extraordinary richness and appeal. Firm acidity keeps the flavors crisp and lively. It is great by itself or will complement many lighter desserts, and can be cellared for a long time.

J. Lohr *1993 Late Harvest "Bay Mist" Johannisberg Riesling*
Region: USA—California   **Suggested Retail: $10.00**
Availability: Limited   **Golds: RE, OC, SF**

The color of the wine is deep, golden straw, characteristic of wine produced from botrytis-infected grapes. The aromas are of apricot and honey with hints of hazelnut and orange blossom. The sweet flavors of honey and dried fruit are carried on a thick rich texture. This wine is wonderful paired with desserts like cheesecake or fruit-based dishes, and makes a great marinade for strawberries.
Special Award: *Double Gold (SF)*

Konzelmann Vineyards *1993 Select Late Harvest Vidal*
Region: Canada   **Suggested Retail: $16.25 CAN**
Availability: Outside USA   **Golds: IW, IV**

Here's a full-bodied dessert-style wine with good acid balance and incredible tropical fruit flavors. It is available in Canada in limited quantities.

Les Côteaux Kefraya *1993 Château Kefraya Lacrima d'Oro*
Region: Lebanon   **Suggested Retail: $12.30**
Availability: Limited   **Golds: CI, BR**

This elegant and distinctive wine, with the golden yellow color of its name, is produced from late harvests. The nose captures the scents of aniseed and licorice. It is round and harmonious on the palate. Drink it as an aperitif or instead of dessert. Kefraya's wonderful gold-medal wines are a tribute to the tenacity of the human spirit, and are available in Europe. However, if you are an American who is interested in buying or distributing these wines, please call them at 96 11 494171, or fax them at 96 11 494820.
Special Awards: *Grand Prix d'Honneur (CI); Honorary Mention (BR)*

Did You Know . . . ?

Some of Lebanon's Châteaux Kefraya wines have been compared to the greatest Côtes du Rhônes from France. Situated in the Bekaa Valley, this vineyard enjoys 240 days of almost unbroken sunshine a year. During 1982, the year Israel invaded Lebanon, the valley was under siege, and Israel set up a checkpoint outside the newly built château and slapped a night curfew on the area. During harvest season, workers toiled from seven at night until five in the morning without being able to leave. The wine produced that year by Kefraya won a silver medal at Concours International du Vin.

London Winery *1993 Late Harvest Vidal*
Region: Canada   **Suggested Retail: $17.55**
Availability: NP   **Golds: CI**
*This wine features a deep golden color with brilliant clarity. The bouquet wafts forth
with essences of green apples and fresh apricots. The palate features honeyed raisin
nuances with a pleasant, smooth finish. Icewine was blended into this late harvest
Vidal, giving it tremendous depth and full body. Serve as an aperitif or for dessert.*

Madrona Vineyards *1993 Select Late Harvest Riesling*
Region: USA—California   **Suggested Retail: $16.50**
Availability: Limited   **Golds: CA, EL**
*Intense aromas of dried apricots, peach preserves, honey, vanilla, and orange peel
carry over into the palate and linger into the finish. The exceptional acid structure
balances the sweetness, resulting in a rich sensation.*
***Special Awards:** Best Wine of Region (CA); Best Johannisberg Riesling of Appella-
tion (CA); Runner Up for Best of Show (CA)*

Navarro *1993 Mélange à Trois Late Harvest Johannisberg Riesling*
Region: USA—California   **Suggested Retail: $14.00**
Availability: Limited   **Golds: NW**
*This wine has exotic flavors of mandarin orange and tropical fruits. The Riesling
(30%) tastes of ripe apricots and peaches. The Chardonnay (21%) tastes like
buttered and caramelized apples. All of the flavors are wrapped in a honey blanket
of botrytis.*

Pillitteri Estates *1993 Ontario Select Late Harvest Vidal*
Region: Canada   **Suggested Retail: $15.00 CAN**
Availability: Outside USA   **Golds: VI**
*This wine has aromas of apricot and orange marmalade that carry over to the
palate. The wine's moderate sweetness and full mouth feel are matched by a crisp
acidity and the warmth of alcohol. It is only available in Canada.*

Santa Barbara Winery *1993 Late Harvest Sauvignon Blanc*
Region: USA—California   **Suggested Retail: $16.00**
Availability: Good   **Golds: OC, WC, BT**
*This was one of only two wines at Orange County to receive a gold star from all
four judges. It was made from heavily botrytized grapes of the aromatic Musque
clone of Sauvignon Blanc. It has delicious tropical fruit flavors and aromas
enhanced by the spicy characteristics coming from oak barrel fermentation. A
delicious alternative to desserts, this one will also complement pear and peach tarts
or bread pudding.*

Did You Know . . . ?
France's announcement in June 1995 of its nuclear tests in the South Pacific
launched a worldwide boycott of French products, wine among them. One
French wine exporter noted a 20% drop in sales.

Santino Wines *1989 Dry Berry Select Harvest Riesling*
Region: USA—California **Suggested Retail: $10.95**
Availability: NP **Golds: OC**

It all started in 1982 when a grape grower in El Dorado County called winemaker Scott Harvey to say that his Riesling crop was infested with mold. He was hoping that Harvey, with his German training, could do something with the frightful-looking grapes. That mold turned out to be 100% Botrytis cinerea *(so-called noble rot) and resulted in a delicious, fabulously rich and concentrated sweet wine. This 1989 gold medal winner has a classic bouquet that is rich and honeyed, concentrated, but still delicate and fresh. Exotic fruit flavors explode across the palate and the rich texture is finely balanced by acidity. Serve it as a dessert by itself. Kudos to the crazy guy in Amador County who buys moldy grapes!*
Special Award: *Best of Class (LA)*

Santino Wines *1989 Dry Berry Select Zinfandel*
Region: USA—California **Suggested Retail: $10.95**
Availability: Limited **Golds: LA**

What do you do with a crop of moldy-looking grapes? German-trained winemaker Scott Harvey jumps up and down, because if that mold is Botrytis cinerea, *the results can be a remarkable wine that is a dessert in itself, as this one is. The high residual sugar and high acidity blend together well, giving the ultimate taste sensation of plum pudding.*
Special Award: *Best of Class (LA)*

Stone Hill Wine Co. *1994 Late Harvest Vignoles*
Region: USA—Missouri **Suggested Retail: $15.99**
Availability: NP **Golds: SF, MS**

This is a sweet, rich, late harvest, dessert-style wine that is deep golden in color with concentrated aromas of apricot and honey.
Special Awards: *Governor's Cup (MS); Best of Show (MS)*

Swedish Hill Vineyard *1994 Late Harvest Vignoles*
Region: USA—New York **Suggested Retail: $11.99**
Availability: Limited **Golds: SF**

Here's a classic dessert wine produced by leaving the grapes on the vine until the first freeze. Honey, pineapple, and melons highlight the aromas. Try it with cheesecake or by itself after dinner.

Did You Know . . . ?
Which plant is mentioned in the Bible more than any other? The answer is the grapevine, of course (remember that ancient viticulturalist Noah, for example?), as well as its product, wine.

Brindiamo   *1994 Aleatico*
Region: USA—California   **Suggested Retail: $18.00**
Availability: Limited   **Golds: FF, RE, PR**

Aleatico is an obscure and lesser known red Muscat variety of central and southern Italy. Traditionally made as a dry red or slightly sweet rosé, this particular vintage is done in a fortified style known as Aleatico Liquoroso. It has a rich, spicy, floral character with a hint of cherries, strawberries, and chocolate balanced with the silky feel of sweetness and the mellow warmth of brandy. Time in the bottle will bring the tannins and the overall body into harmonious balance as the fruit aromas develop richness and complexity.

Château St. Jean   *1992 Select Late Harvest Gewürztraminer*
Region: USA—California   **Suggested Retail: $22.50**
Availability: NP   **Golds: NW**

Aromas of apricots, honey, varietal spice, and a pleasant nuttiness fill the nose of this Botrytis-affected late harvest Gewürztraminer. On the palate the wine is viscous and forward, yet fresh with intense flavors of peach, honey, apricot, and baked apple spice persisting throughout the long, rich finish.

Lynfred Winery   *1992 Late Harvest Private Reserve Zinfandel*
Region: USA—Illinois   **Suggested Retail: $20.00**
Availability: Limited   **Golds: SF, BT**

Illinois, our editor's home state, is not just the land of corn and hogs. We were thrilled to see that this Illinois wine was awarded golds from all four judges at San Francisco (known as a "double gold,"). It has deep garnet color and a rich plum aroma loaded with layers of oak spices, vanilla, and nuances of chocolate. It is mouth filling, rich, and full of long, ripe plum flavor. High-extract fruit is balanced with lingering acidity for a long, rich finish. The winemaker suggests serving it like port with English Stilton or—what else?—Illinois Nauvoo Blue or Iowa Matag Blue cheese, ripe figs, or poached pears.
***Special Award:** Double Gold (SF)*

Navarro   *1993 Cluster Select Late Harvest Johannisberg Riesling*
Region: USA—California   **Suggested Retail: $19.50**
Availability: Limited   **Golds: OC, LA, PR, IV, NW, CO, ME**

A wonderful dessert wine, this wine is loaded with sweet, luscious honey and apricot flavors. It has great acid and a lengthy finish. We barely have room to list all the golds! You'd better try this one.

Did You Know . . . ?
Brindiamo wines are a label of Thornton Winery, whose Champagne Jazz Series, now in its seventh year, features nationally renowned contemporary jazz artists, stupendous cuisine, and an outdoor setting in their acoustically superb patio to indulge every sense. Oh yes, there's wine too!

R.L. Buller & Son   *Museum Release Very Old Rutherglen Tokay*
Region: Australia   **Suggested Retail: $64.00 CAN**
Availability: Outside USA   **Golds: SY**

Made from 20-year-old vines and over 50 years old, this Tokay is made from the Flame Tokay clone, also known as Muscadelle. Here are one judge's tasting notes from the Sydney competition: "Deep brown ochre color with a yellow edge. Very positive Tokay nose, quite classic, and I'm sure this will develop a lot further. An outstanding wine, even majestic. Intensely rich, very fresh, in relative terms, and it will keep for years. Very fine depth and length. This was a great wine." By the way, you can buy this very rare wine in Canada or New Zealand.
Special Award: *Trophy for Best Fortified Wine (SY)*

River Run Vintners   *1993 Late Harvest Zinfandel*
Region: USA—California   **Suggested Retail: $18.00**
Availability: Limited   **Golds: OC**

Here's a very sweet but not cloying wine with flavors and aromas of rich, ripe blackberries.

Silverado Vineyards   *NV Late Harvest Limited Reserve*
Region: USA—California   **Suggested Retail: $25.00**
Availability: Limited   **Golds: IW**

This is Silverado's first late-harvest wine, made in the style of classic Sauternes, but with Chardonnay taking the place of Muscadelle de Bordelais. It is brilliant golden yellow; has pungent aromas of honey, peach, spice, and earth; tart and sweet flavors; hints of spice, dried fruit, and tobacco; and a long, toasty finish. The blend is 49% Sauvignon Blanc, 34% Chardonnay, and 17% Sémillon.

Stoney Ridge Cellars   *1994 Botrytis Gold*
Region: Canada   **Suggested Retail: $19.95**
Availability: Limited   **Golds: IV**

This blend of botrytis Sauvignon, Sémillon, and late harvest Gewürztraminer delivers exotic honey, melon, and apricot flavors and aromas. It is very rich, but not cloying.

Did You Know . . . ?

In order to get botrytis, or the noble rot, grapes have to be subjected to a magical set of conditions, among them foggy mornings and warm afternoons at just the right time of the season. Producers face the agonizing decision: to wait or not to wait. Harvest the grapes too late for regular wine and they'll be overripe. Wait for the fungus to appear, and pray that the limited amount of the resulting botrytized wine will be great, or even good. Some California wine producers can't stand the gamble, and so have experimented with spraying laboratory-grown fungus spores on already-picked, healthy wine grapes to force the rot to happen under controlled conditions.

Château Reynella   *1994 Vintage Port*
Region: Australia   **Suggested Retail: $14.99**
Availability: Good   **Golds: RM**
Purple-red in color, this port made with 100% Shiraz has a bouquet of ripe berry fruit that melds beautifully with the young brandy spirit. The palate possesses generous spicy fruit flavors. Cellar this gem for 20 years or more. It is available in the United States.

Château Reynella   *1988 Vintage Port*
Region: Australia   **Suggested Retail: $14.99**
Availability: Limited   **Golds: MC**
This fortified sweet Shiraz port is deep red and offers a nose of blackberries, spirit, and spice. The rich palate has delicious ripe blackberry flavors balanced by fine tannins and warm spirit. It is available in the United States.

Château Reynella   *1993 Vintage Port*
Region: Australia   **Suggested Retail: $14.99**
Availability: Limited   **Golds: AU**
This 100% Shiraz port is deep red with purple hues, and possesses a nose that exhibits spicy Shiraz fruit. The palate displays concentrated blackberry fruit with a fine tannin finish. It will benefit from 20 years of cellaring, and is available in the United States.
Special Award: *Top Gold (AU)*

Ficklin Vineyards   *1986 Vintage Port*
Region: USA—California   **Suggested Retail: $24.00**
Availability: Limited   **Golds: LA**
The grapes used to produce this wine consist of the four Portuguese varieties that were planted in the family vineyards in 1945. Look for a very full grape, ripe plum nose, leading into a prune, earthy character. It has hints of cognac, and a subtle floral aroma. Upon opening, this wine will develop a smoky, chocolate aroma. It is well balanced without overpowering tannins, with rich fruit flavors and underlying tones of chocolate and spicy flavors. A pleasant finish, some lingering tannin, and a full velvety texture round out the whole experience.

Did You Know . . . ?
Classical and Medieval winemakers were not above duping their customers. Recipes from that time include tricks to disguise "sick" wines that had turned sour, suggesting the addition of milk, ashes, mustard, nettles, and even lead! A disgusted Pliny the Elder, whose important works include his surviving book that sheds light on the history of viticulture in Ancient Rome, commented: "Not even our nobility ever enjoys wines that are genuine."

Guenoc Estate   *1992 Vintage Port*

Region: USA—California   **Suggested Retail: $15.00**
Availability: Good   **Golds:** OC, IV, PR, SD, FL, IN, HH

An elegant vintage of Zinfandel fruit from vines nearly a century old is blended with a touch of Petite Sirah to add complexity and depth to the ripe flavors of cassis, chocolate, and almonds. Touches of tobacco and leather promise to develop in the years ahead.
Special Awards: *Best of Class (PR); Best of Class (SD); Best of Show (FL)*

Joseph Filippi Vintage Co.   *NV Ruby Port Reserve*

Region: USA—California   **Suggested Retail: $8.50**
Availability: Limited   **Golds:** OC

From a winery founded in 1922, this special-aged port offers the fruit and ruby color of young wine and the maturity of aging. Harvested late for maximum sweetness, it has a smooth creaminess associated with higher-pH- and low-acid-type vintages. It is light bodied and sweet with a lovely finish. Best served at room temperature before or after dinner, this one is wonderful with nuts, fruit, cheeses, and rich desserts.

Konrad Estate Winery   *1991 Admiral's Quinta Petite Sirah Port*

Region: USA—California   **Suggested Retail: $18.00**
Availability: Limited   **Golds:** NW

Made of 100 percent Petite Sirah grapes and fortified with alembic brandy, this port is organically grown and has aromas of lilacs, blueberries, and plums complemented by rich, full-bodied flavors. Great with chocolate truffles or Stilton cheese. The winery bottled this port in 500 ml green French glass with a 22-karat gold labels fused onto the bottle. Wow!

Quady Winery   *NV Starboard Batch 88 Port*

Region: USA—California   **Suggested Retail: $15.00**
Availability: Good   **Golds:** DA

Very rich and spicy, this portlike wine is well crafted and has character and concentration. The brilliant berry flavor stretches clear through the finish, overlayed with hints of smoke and spice. By the way, Quady calls this "vintage character port," which is made from lighter wines than traditional ports and is kept in cask for 3 to 5 years (as opposed to 2, for port), which means it can be consumed immediately upon release. (Vintage ports need several years to develop in the bottle.)

Did You Know . . . ?

That port, particularly a decanter of vintage port, must be passed from the right to the left of diners is a time-honored tradition. Yet no one seems to know where it all started. At New College Oxford, in the Senior Common Room, they went so far as to build a miniature custom railway to transport port decanters across an inconvenient fireplace so that the tradition could be upheld.

Santa Ynez Winery   *1994 Cabernet Port*
Region: USA—California   **Suggested Retail: $20.00**
Availability: Very Good   **Golds: OC**
This is a dark, ruby red wine with big, rich, ripe blackberry and cassis fruit and a background of toasty oak. Ripe blackberry fruit flavor is buttressed with sweet oak flavors. This Port of Cabernet Sauvignon should improve in the bottle for 6 to 8 years.

Trentadue Winery   *1993 Petite Sirah Port*
Region: USA—California   **Suggested Retail: $16.00**
Availability: Limited   **Golds: FF**
This port has a deep, dark purple color with rich spice and plum aromas. Having a good structure and balance of residual sugar and tannins, it will last and age well for 8 to 10 years.

Wiederkehr Wine Cellars   *1985 Cabernet Sauvignon Port*
Region: USA—Arkansas   **Suggested Retail: $25.00**
Availability: Limited   **Golds: DA**
A port wine aged in American oak, this one is very mellow and possesses distinct Cabernet characteristics (made with 100% Cabernet Sauvignon). Since this is the only Arkansas wine in our book, we urge you to try it. Being adventurous has many rewards!

Windsor Vineyards   *NV Rare Port*
Region: USA—California   **Suggested Retail: $11.67**
Availability: Good   **Golds: PR, NW, WC, CL**
This Port has rich ruby color, sumptuous raisin and honey flavors, and is aged in oak. One wine writer said it conjured up butter pecans, bittersweet chocolate, and tea, among other things. All of the judges loved it.
Special Awards: *National Champion and Best Buy (WC); Best of Class (CL)*

Did You Know . . . ?
Arkansas is the only U.S. state to commercially produce all five species of wine grapes: vinifera, rotundifolia, labrusca, aestivalis, and French hybrids. All five are produced by Wiederkehr Wine Cellars as well.

Louis M. Martini   *NV Cream Sherry*
Region: USA—California   **Suggested Retail: $6.00**
Availability: Good   **Golds: OC**
"In a class by itself," this wine is produced from Palomino grapes and its smooth, agreeable, caramellike flavor and fine texture win awards in sherry tastings year after year. After fermenting small batches of wine to the proper sweetness and then stopping fermentation by the addition of brandy (hence, "fortifying the wine"), the wines are then aged and blended to make this luscious cream sherry.

Louis M. Martini   *NV Dry Sherry*
Region: USA—California   **Suggested Retail: $6.00**
Availability: Good   **Golds: OC**
Very pale and very dry, this sherry has a nutty flavor and fine texture. Each bottle of Dry Sherry has a weighted average age of about 14 years.

Louis M. Martini   *NV California Dessert Sherry*
Region: USA—California   **Suggested Retail: $6.00**
Availability: NP   **Golds: FF**
We didn't get much information about this wine from the winery, but we do know this: an Italian immigrant, Louis M. Martini founded the winery in Kingsburg, California, in 1922, and was among the first vintners in that state to release vintage-dated varietal wines. Obviously this winery has experience, and the golds they win can attest to the quality. Try this sherry for a change of pace after your favorite meal.

Windsor Vineyards   *California Cream Sherry*
Region: USA—California   **Suggested Retail: $6.67**
Availability: Good   **Golds: OC**
This wine is amber colored with a smooth texture and an intense nutty flavor.

York Mountain Winery   *Dry Sherry*
Region: USA—California   **Suggested Retail: $6.00**
Availability: Limited   **Golds: OC**
Here's a sherry with a dry, nutty character and amber color that is medium bodied, smooth, and has a complex finish. The sherry comprises a blend of 1974 wine that has had 15 years barrel aging.

Did You Know ... ?
Louis Pasteur was the first scientist to understand and explain the process of alcoholic fermentation. Before he discovered that living cells in the form of yeast fed on the sugar and transformed it into alcohol and carbon dioxide, the world thought that fermentation was a spontaneous act or accident of nature.

Appendix 1

KEY TO COMPETITION ABBREVIATIONS

*As we explained in Chapter 2, in order to be featured in this book each winning wine had to be awarded a gold medal from at least one of the Top 24 Competitions (in **boldface** below). If a winery informed us that their winning wine also received a gold from a competition other than one of our Top 24, we included that gold as well in the Part III listings. (Note, however, that we were unable to verify all of these claims, and can only assume that the wineries were being honest!) Below is an abbreviation key to all of the wine competitions and blind tastings listed in Part III.*

AA	**Ansett Australia Sydney Royal Wine Show**
AC	All Canada Wine Championships (Windsor, Canada)
AD	Adelaide Wine Show (Australia)
AI	Asian International Wine Classic
AL	Alameda County Fair Wine Competition
AM	Amador County Fair Wine Competition
AR	**Vinandino, Mendoza (Argentina)**
AT	Atlanta Wine Summit
AU	**National Wine Show of Australia (Canberra, Australia)**
BA	Barossa Wine Show (Australia)
BL	Bullarat Wine Show (Australia)
BR	Brisbane Wine Show (Australia)
BT	Beverage Tasting Institute (Chicago)
BU	Concours Mondiale (Brussels)
CA	**California State Fair Wine Competition**
CE	Clare Wine Show (Australia)
CI	**Challenge International du Vin (Vinexpo, Blaye-Bourg, France)**
CL	Cloverdale Citrus Fair Wine Competition
CN	Cincinnati International Wine Festival
CO	Colorado State Fair Wine Competition
CR	Cairns Wine Show (Australia)
CW	Central Washington State Fair Wine Competition
DA	**Dallas Morning News Wine Competition**
EL	El Dorado County Fair Wine Competition
FF	**Farmers Fair of Riverside Wine Competition**
FL	Florida State Fair Wine Competition

FW	Torrance Gourmet Food and Wine Show
GH	Grand Harvest Awards (New York)
GR	Griffith Wine Show (Australia)
HH	Hilton Head Wine Competition
HO	Hobart Wine Competition (Australia)
HU	Hunter Valley Wine Show (Australia)
IE	International Eastern Wine Competition
IM	Independent Meritage Competition
IN	Indiana State Fair Wine Competition
IT	Expo Food, Milano (Italy)
IV	**Intervin International**
IW	**International Wine and Spirit Competition**
LA	**Los Angeles County Fair Wine Competition**
LB	Long Beach Grand Cru Wine Competition
LJ	Vino Ljubljana (former Yugoslavia)
LS	Lone Star State Wine Competition
MB	Mount Bark Wine Show (Australia)
MC	McLaren Vale Wine Show (Australia)
ME	Mendocino County Fair Wine Competition
ML	Mother Lode Fair Wine Competition
MO	Monterey Wine Competition
MS	Missouri State Fair Wine Competition
NE	**Northwest Enographic Wine Festival Awards**
NF	New York Wine and Food Classic
NW	**New World International Wine Competition**
NY	New York State Fair Wine Competition
NZ	**Air New Zealand Wine Awards**
OC	**Orange County Fair Wine Competition**
OR	**Oregon State Fair Professional Wine Awards**
PE	Perth Wine Show (Australia)
PR	**Pacific Rim International Wine Competition**
QU	Queensland Royal Wine Show (Australia)
RE	**Reno West Coast Wine Competition**
RM	**Royal Melbourne Wine Show (Australia)**
RU	Rutherglen Wine Show (Australia)
SC	Santa Cruz County Fair Wine Competition
SD	**San Diego National Wine Competition**
SE	Southeastern International Wine Competition
SF	**San Francisco Fair International Wine Competition**
SM	**Selections Mondiales**
SO	Sonoma Harvest Fair
ST	Stanthorpe Wine Show (Australia)
SW	Expovina (Switzerland)

SY	**Sydney International Wine Competition**
TA	Tacoma Community College Wine Competition
TC	**Tri-Cities Northwest Wine Festival**
TG	Tasters Guild Wine Competition
TN	Tennessee International Wine Festival
TX	Houston Club Best of Texas
VE	Vernon Winter Carnival
VI	**Vinitaly**
WC	International Wine Challenge (London)
WR	Cowra Wine Competition (Australia)
WW	**Western Washington Fair Wine Judging**
ZE	New Zealand Liquorland Royal Easter Show
ZU	Zurich International Wine Awards

THE BEST OF *BEST WINES!*

Line up two hundred wines of the same type in identical, unmarked glasses, place a panel of top wine experts behind the table, people whose knowledge and experience in the field have earned them stature as the most qualified wine judges in the world, and let them have at it. Every wine in this book, as we've mentioned numerous times, was subjected to just such a test, and won big. Winning a gold medal under such conditions, where the wines are judged blind, is a high honor.

Now consider a wine undergoing such a trial several times, in different blind tastings, with different judges and competitors, and still winning the top prize, in some cases three, four, or more times. These are truly the "best of the best" wines, and one would be hard pressed to find an ordinary wine enthusiast who didn't love every one of these multiple-gold-medal wines.

Below are wines that won three or more gold medals from our Top 24 Competitions (for an explanation of the Top 24, see Chapter 2). We think this list is as close to a guarantee of total wine-drinking satisfaction as you're ever likely to find. Stock up your cellar with these and enjoy! By the way, the wines whose page numbers appear in **boldface** *are also great bargains: $15 and under!*

A. Rafanelli Winery   1992 Cabernet Sauvignon Unfiltered, 83
Adler Fels Winery   1994 Sonoma County Gewürztraminer, **200**
Alderbrook   1994 Late Harvest Muscat de Frontignan, 252
Atlas Peak Vineyards   1992 Napa Valley Sangiovese Reserve, 100
Bel Arbors   1994 California White Zinfandel, **229**
Brindiamo   1994 Aleatico, 262
C. A. Henschke   1992 Mount Edelstone, 149
C. A. Henschke   1993 Cabernet Sauvignon, 87
Cambria Winery   1992 Tepusquet Vineyard Estate Bottled Syrah, 149
Cambria Winery   1993 Santa Maria Valley Reserve Chardonnay, 190
Camelot Winery   1993 Central Coast Pinot Noir, **127**
Camelot Winery   1993 Santa Barbara County Chardonnay, 176
Canyon Road   1994 California Sauvignon Blanc, **216**
Château Julien   1991 Cabernet Sauvignon Private Reserve, 88
Château Souverain   1992 Alexander Valley Cabernet Sauvignon, **77**
Château St. Jean   1989 Reserve Cabernet Sauvignon, 88
Codorniu Napa   NV Napa Valley Brut, **239**

Page numbers in **boldface** indicate wines that are $15 or under.

De Loach   1992 O.F.S. Estate Bottled Pinot Noir, 132
Eberle Winery   1993 Fralich Vineyard Syrah, 150
Eberle Winery   1993 Norman Vineyard Barbera, 100
Eberle Winery   1994 Fralich Vineyard Viognier, 207
Fess Parker Winery   1993 American Tradition Reserve Chardonnay, 192
Fetzer   1994 California White Zinfandel, **229**
Gainey Vineyard   1994 Santa Ynez Valley Johannisberg Riesling, 281
Gary Farrell Wines   1992 Ladi's Vineyard Merlot, 113
Geyser Peak Winery   1992 Reserve Cabernet Sauvignon, 90
Geyser Peak Winery   1993 Late Harvest Riesling, 258
Geyser Peak Winery   1993 Sonoma County Chardonnay, **179**
Geyser Peak Winery   1993 Winemaker's Selection Malbec, 121
Geyser Peak Winery   1994 Late Harvest Riesling, 258
Geyser Peak Winery   1994 Sauvignon Blanc, **218**
Geyser Peak Winery   1994 North Coast Gewürztraminer, **201**
Gloria Ferrer   1988 Royal Cuvée Brut, 241
Greenwood Ridge   1992 Estate Bottled Cabernet Sauvignon, 90
Greenwood Ridge   1993 Scherrer Vineyards Zinfandel, **159**
Guenoc Estate   1991 North Coast Petite Sirah, **123**
Guenoc Estate   1992 Bella Vista Reserve Cabernet Sauvignon, 91
Guenoc Estate   1992 North Coast Petite Sirah, **123**
Guenoc Estate   1992 Vintage Port, **265**
Handley Cellars   1989 Anderson Valley Brut Sparkling Wine, 241
Hess Collection Winery   1991 Napa Valley Cabernet Sauvignon, 92
Husch Vineyards   1994 La Ribera Vineyards Chenin Blanc, **198**
Indian Springs Vineyards   1993 Cabernet Sauvignon, **79**
J. Fritz Winery   1993 80 Year Old Vines Zinfandel, **160**
J. Lohr   1993 Late Harvest, **259**
Jordan Sparkling Wine Company   1990 "J" Sonoma County Brut, 242
Joseph Phelps Vineyards   1991 Napa Valley Insignia, 145
Kendall-Jackson   1993 Grand Reserve Chardonnay, 193
Kendall-Jackson   1993 Late Harvest Select Chardonnay, **182**
Kendall-Jackson   1993 Select Late Harvest Riesling, **213**
Kendall-Jackson   1993 Vintner's Reserve Chardonnay, **182**
McIlroy Family Wines   1993 Aquarius Ranch Chardonnay, **184**
McIlroy Family Wines   1993 Porter-Bass Vineyard Zinfandel, **160**
Montinore   1993 Late Harvest Estate Bottled Gewürztraminer, **256**
Mumm Napa Valley   NV Cuvée Napa Valley Blanc de Noirs, **237**
Napa Ridge Winery   1993 North Coast Pinot Noir, **125**
Navarro   1993 Cluster Select Late Harvest Johannisberg Riesling, 262
Navarro   1993 Premier Reserve Chardonnay, **185**
Quady Winery   1993 Elysium Black Muscat, **253**
Rabbit Ridge Vineyards   1993 Dry Creek Valley Zinfandel, **162**

Page numbers in **boldface** indicate wines that are $15 or under.

Raymond Vineyard 1992 Napa Valley Merlot, 282
Rosenblum Cellars 1993 TLK Ranch Carignane, **120**
Shafer Vineyards 1993 Napa Valley Merlot, 114
St. James Winery 1993 Missouri Norton, **116**
Swanson Vineyards 1993 Carneros Estate Chardonnay, 195
Tribaut NV Blanc de Noirs, **237**
V. Sattui Winery 1991 Howell Mountain Zinfandel, 165
V. Sattui Winery 1991 Mario's Reserve Cabernet Sauvignon, 96
V. Sattui Winery 1994 Gamay Rouge, **234**
Villa Mt. Eden 1993 Grand Reserve Carneros Chardonnay, 189
Villa Mt. Eden 1993 Grand Reserve Carneros Pinot Noir, 130
Wild Horse Winery 1994 Monterey Pinot Blanc, **209**
William Hill Winery 1993 Napa Valley Chardonnay, 283
ZD Wines 1993 California Chardonnay, 196

Page numbers in **boldface** indicate wines that are $15 or under.

Appendix 3

MAIL-ORDER WINE SHOPPING

If you can't find gold-medal-winning wines in your local shop (don't forget, most shops will custom order for you if you ask), or you're just too busy to get out, don't despair. You can have your choices shipped right to your door by a number of mail-order vendors. Nearly all have "800" numbers, and most will ship overnight, so you're giving up very little if anything in the realm of convenience to get a virtually unlimited selection and often outstanding prices.

Most of the vendors listed below put out regular catalogues. You can get on their mailing lists for updates on new inventory, specials, and news you can use. The Wine Exchange, in particular, does a great job of seeking out gold medal wines, and provides lots of down-to-earth commentary and educational material in their newsletter as well.

You'll typically need to order by credit card, and you'll have to check with each vendor regarding guarantees or returns policies. Since wine is hard to return, and a disagreement over taste is hard enough to propose at a restaurant much less across the country, we suggest you start by ordering small until you feel comfortable with the reliability and service of a particular vendor.

A few things to bear in mind about wine, as opposed to other mail-order purchases:

1. Don't forget to add shipping to your costs (figure about $2.00 per bottle when buying a case). Still, you'll often avoid sales tax and you'll often get better pricing, so the net cost of purchasing by mail shouldn't be any greater than buying in person.
2. Broken bottles are the responsibility of the shipper and/or the carrier. You don't have to take the risk of an accident—so check your shipment immediately (wiping your finger on the underside of the crate ought to give you a clue!). Seriously, we raise this issue but it's not likely you'll confront it in reality. Wines are shipped all over the country and all over the world. Those involved have learned how to move those bottles around competently.
3. Receiving wine in certain states is problematic from a legal standpoint (your vendor will definitely know if you're in a difficult location). Partly under pressure from local distributors, and partly in quest of ever-greater tax revenues, some states have made a major effort to collect sales tax on wines shipped into their state from other jurisdictions. It's unclear

whether a customer receiving wine would ever have any legal liability, but various states have made noises about prosecuting shippers, and some have actually seized shipments as the prelude to legal battles. So, you get not only the pleasure of drinking excellent wine without having to brave the traffic on the way to the wine shop, but the pleasure of the forbidden as well. It's just like Prohibition! But not if you live in Florida, Kentucky, or Pennsylvania. Mail-order vendors won't ship to those states, where the D.A.'s are like Dobermans.

4. Summer's not the greatest time to order wine safely. Every effort will be made to get you a great bottle intact, but you must bear in mind that wine does not like heat, and heat is what you have in summer. There could be some damage to the character of a bottle during the hot months—though many will pass through a night on the overnight courier plane just fine.

5. The FTC Mail or Telephone Order Rule: goods must be shipped to you within thirty days of your order unless the firm asks for more time in its catalogue or sales materials. With the vendors in this book you're not likely to experience any delays, but you should know that beyond the thirty-day-to-ship rule you may cancel your order and you're entitled to a refund.

6. Some vendors have minimum orders; find out ahead of time so you're not frustrated when you call for that one special bottle.

7. If you have a problem—or an especially good experience—we want to know about it. You can contact us at: THE PRINT PROJECT, P.O. Box 703, Bearsville, NY 12409.

The following are vendors we've identified as those who may be useful to readers of this book. *We have accepted no advertising or promotional fees for listing these vendors,* and you should not assume that we recommend all or any of these firms.

Brown Derby International Wine Center, 2023 South Glenstone, Springfield, MO 65804, (417) 883-4066. They've been around since 1937 and take pride in their in-depth selection of wines from all over, including some of the uncommon wines from their region. All wines are shipped in pre-approved boxes and go second-day air to anywhere except Kentucky. Also, they're one of one of the top retailers of Riedel crystal from Austria, which is rapidly catching on all over the world. The deeper into good wine you get, the more you want good crystal (although we found it quite charming recently when served a great vintage in a jam-sized Ball jar by a blushing, apologetic hostess).

Central Liquor 726 Ninth Street, N.W., Washington, DC 20001, (202) 737-2800 or (800) 835-7928. Central stocks over 4,000 different wines and has most of the California wines, although they don't focus that much on the small producers. They ship anywhere but Hawaii and Kentucky.

Duke of Bourbon 20908 Roscoe Boulevard, Canoga Park, CA 91304, (800) 4-FINE-WINE, (818) 341-1234, or fax (818) 341-9232. "The Duke" has a full-service retail and mail-order business carrying a full line of wines, spirits, gourmet foods, accessories, books, microbrewery beers, and cigars. It was chosen by Zagat's as one of the top five wine marketplaces in LA and has been top-rated by various industry associations. The Duke features the best wines from California and around the world, with an emphasis on top-quality producers. Prices range from retail to interesting special discounts—you can get on their mailing list just by calling. They ship everywhere that's legal in the United States, and will ship anywhere in the world. As Ron noted to us (and as most vendors have said), summertime shipping is dicey. If wine is shipped via overnight or two-day air, the chances of spoilage are limited. But if you order by UPS, the risk will be on you. You can also get special orders accomplished here, as well as obtaining gift baskets and personalized gifts. If you want to buy Bordeaux futures, they will be happy to oblige.

The Internet Wine people love the Internet, and the information super-highway is literally littered with wine-related sites. There are chat groups that taste and quibble, sites sponsored by magazines, "expert" sites, home pages from wineries, and of course, areas for shopping for wine and accessories. You can even order wines directly from the wineries in many cases. We'd need another book to detail all the possible places you can go and areas you can shop on the Internet—and it would be out of date almost as soon as compiled—so our best advice is to use a browser and search under "wine" or "wineries." It will keep you busy for hours and hours.

Mr. Liquor 250 Taraval Street, San Francisco, CA 94116, (800) 681-WINE, or fax (415) 731-0155. If it were up to us, we'd go with something a bit Frenchier, like "Monsieur Liqueur." Nevertheless, Mr. Liquor carries hard-to-find California wines and imports, focusing on wines of the sort covered in this book—prizewinners and wines rated 90 or better by leading magazines and experts. Even though it may be hard for them to find these wines, they discount prices across the board. They ship anywhere in the United States second-day air, door to door, and regularly ship to many foreign countries. Bear in mind that the kinds of wines they carry don't just sit on the shelves. Their inventory of over 2,500 outstanding labels turns over quickly. Call the 800 number for their free eight-page brochure, which comes out every couple of months.

Red Carpet Wines Their toll-free number is (800) 339-0609 and they ship anywhere in the United States, except Florida or Kentucky. This firm specializes in California wineries. Their hedge against the other discounters is that they shy away from the "big guys" like Kendall-Jackson or Mondavi. They deal with wineries whose case productions are from 100 to 1,000 (in other words, many of the wines in Part III with "Limited" availability). If your local shop comes back with the news from his distributor that your dream wine is "sold out," try Red Carpet.

Sam's 100 West North Avenue, Chicago IL 60622, (800) 777-9137. Sam's is as big as they get in the wine business, the Wally's of the Midwest as much as Wally's is the Sam's of the West. Their stock is broad and deep, with, typically, over 9,000 wines in stock. They carry most California wineries, as well as Oregon, Washington, South America, Australia, New Zealand, and South Africa—all the countries covered in our book! Sam's will special order for you if they don't have what you request. They put out a regular catalog with inventory and specials every two or three months, which is free: just call to get your name on the list. Sam's also trades in Bordeaux futures (it's Chicago, after all).

Wally's (800) 8-WALLYS, 2107 Westwood Boulevard, Los Angeles, CA 90025. This is a huge wine store rated Number One Wine Store in LA by Zagat's guide. It's also consistently rated number one in all the local papers and magazines. In addition to carrying a huge selection of wines, they carry spirits, beers, and do a huge cigar business. They have a deli, do catering, and offer classes. They do business all over the world and stock a broad selection of gold medal winners. If you need pros to help you with a big order, better call Wally's.

Wine Cask 813 Anacapa Street, Santa Barbara, CA 93101, (805) 966-9463 or (800) 436-9463. They can ship anywhere and can get most hard-to-find wines, with an emphasis on imports. They also have a retail store (including books), full bar and restaurant, and do catering.

The Wine Club 953 Harrison Street, San Francisco, CA 94107, (415) 512-9086, (800) 966-7835, (800) 966-5432, or (800) 678-5044. The Wine Club is not actually a club, but a discount merchandiser of wine. You can call one of the "800" numbers and get on their mailing list for free, where savings of up to 60 percent are possible in special cases. You can also get books, truffles, caviar, and, as they say, much more.

The Wine Country 2301 Redondo Avenue, Signal Hill, CA 90806, (800) 505-5564. Not only are they a mail-order source, but also a retail store with a very artsy, homey feeling. They have several murals of various wine regions, such as a 30-by-50-foot mural of the Alsace region, and a 3-D replica of the Mondavi arch. With Spanish tiles and murals, this is a great place to visit if you're in the area. There's no minimum order.

The Wine Exchange 2368 North Orange Mall, Orange, CA 92665, (714) 974-1454. The owner/buyer, Steve, is very friendly and helpful—and this attitude permeates their entire business. We can hardly wait from issue to issue for their fascinating newsletter. They are also a high-volume discounter carrying a complete line of alcoholic beverages, microbrewery boutique beers, single malt scotches, and even cigars. They have over 2,000 wines in stock and ship anywhere except Kentucky, Pennsylvania, and Florida. Even though they deal in high volume they "haven't forgotten what it's like to be a wine merchant," because in Steve's words, "it's still fun for us." Locally, The Wine Exchange puts on a steady stream of tastings and educational seminars. Get hold of their list if you live in southern California or are contemplating a trip.

The Wine Messenger 371 North Avenue, New Rochelle, NY 10801, (800) 760-3960. This is a new business and currently only ships to New York and Conneticut, but is working on New Jersey next. They carry a lot of hard-to-find wines, but nothing Canadian. Their focus is on education—with every wine shipped they send a full page of information.

The Wine Stop 1300–1304 Burlingame Avenue, Burlingame, CA 94010, (800) 283-WINE. They handle everything from everyday wines to first groves. They have a very diverse selection, including first-level boutique California wines and second-level Oregon and Washington State wines. So some unusual items will turn up in their inventory. They also have a retail store and put out a newsletter every two months.

Appendix 4

THE OTHER GOLD MEDAL WINNERS

When we first began contacting wineries, requesting tasting notes and other information on their gold medal wines for this book, the responses were slow to come. No one had heard of us and it seemed like a lot of trouble to them. But fortunately most of the wineries eventually responded, although in some cases it took a letter, then a fax, then a follow-up phone call before they believed we were legit.

But in dealing with so many wines and wineries, there are bound to be ones that slip through the cracks. In some cases, wineries just wouldn't take the time to send the information we required, in spite of sweet cajoling on our part. In other cases, wineries sent information on the wrong wines, or sent the wrong type of information on the right wines, and no amount of pestering would get them to provide us with what we required.

Alas, the wines listed below became lost causes, insofar as earning full-feature treatment in the book with all the information we felt consumers deserve. However, don't let that bias you. They are every bit as excellent as the other wines in Part III. Some of them are triple gold winners (also listed in Appendix 2, The Best of BEST WINES!), and many merited special awards from the judges above and beyond their golds.

By the way, only Canadian and U.S. gold medal wines are listed here, since availability in North America is one of the criteria for inclusion in our book, and that's a piece of information we could not confirm.

Canada	Golds
Cedar Creek Estate Winery 1993 Reserve Merlot	IW
Cedar Creek Estate Winery 1994 Okanagan Valley Ehrenfelser	LA
Château des Charmes Wines 1991 Paul Bosc Estate Cabernet Franc	CI
Colio Wines of Canada 1994 Riesling Traminer	CI
Jackson Triggs Vintners 1993 Proprietor's Selection Ice Wine VQA	IW, IV
Konzelmann Vineyards 1993 Riesling Traminer Ice Wine	IV
Marynissen Estates 1993 Vidal Ice Wine VQA	IV
Pillitteri Estates 1993 Icewine	IW
Stonechurch Vineyards 1993 Vidal Ice Wine	IV
Stoney Ridge Cellars 1992 Chardonnay Reserve VQA	IW
Stoney Ridge Cellars 1993 Puddicombe/Smith Vidal Ice Wine	IV
Vinoteca 1990 Cabernet Sauvignon	IW

USA—California	Golds
Alto Vineyards 1987 Cabernet Sauvignon	CI
Baily Vineyard 1993 TV Red	PR

USA—California (continued)   **Golds**

Benziger Family Winery 1990 Estate Tribute   CA, PR
   Special Awards: Double Gold (CA); Best Bordeaux Varietal Blend
   of Appellation (CA); Runner Up for Best of Show (CA); Best of
   Class (PR)
Benziger Family Winery 1990 Sonoma Mountain Cabernet Sauvignon   LA
Benziger Family Winery 1991 Estate Bottled Sonoma Mountain Merlot   OC
Benziger Family Winery 1991 Sonoma County Cabernet Sauvignon   DA
Benziger Family Winery 1992 Cabernet Sauvignon   CA
Benziger Family Winery 1992 Estate Tribute White Table Wine   FF
Benziger Family Winery 1993 Carneros Chardonnay   CA
   Special Awards: Best Chardonnay of Appellation (CA)
Benziger Imagery Series 1992 Blue Rock Vineyard WOW Cabernet Franc   OC
Benziger Imagery Series 1992 Dry Creek Valley Sangiovese   DA
Benziger Imagery Series 1992 Paso Robles Petite Sirah   DA
Benziger Imagery Series 1993 Skinner Vineyard Pinot Blanc   OC
Beringer Vineyards 1988 Port of Cabernet Sauvignon   IV
Beringer Vineyards 1993 Napa Valley Chenin Blanc   FF
Beringer Vineyards 1994 California Johannisberg Riesling   SD
   Special Awards: Best of Class (SD)
Bettinelli 1993 Napa Valley Chardonnay   OC
Blackstone 1993 Napa County Merlot Reserve   OC
Boeger Winery 1993 Walker Vineyard Zinfandel   CA
   Special Awards: Double Gold (CA); Tie for Best Zinfandel
   of Appellation (CA)
Château De Baun 1993 Finale Late Harvest Symphony   SD, FF
Château Potelle 1993 Napa Valley Sauvignon Blanc   FF
Château St. Jean NV Sonoma County Blanc de Blancs   RE, LA
   Special Awards: Best of Class (LA)
Château St. Jean NV Sonoma County Brut, Méthode Champenoise   LA
Cheval Sauvage 1993 Paso Robles Pinot Noir   OC, FF
   Special Awards: Chairman's Award (FF)
Christian Bros. NV Meloso Cream Sherry   OC
Clos du Bois 1991 Alexander Valley Briarcrest Cabernet Sauvignon   IV
Clos du Bois 1991 Marlstone   CA
Clos du Bois 1993 Sonoma Zinfandel   SF, LA
   Special Awards: Double Gold (SF)
Côtes de Sonoma 1994 Sonoma County Sauvignon Blanc   CA, SF
   Special Awards: Best Sauvignon Blanc of Appellation (CA)
Cypress 1992 Cabernet Sauvignon   OC
Cypress 1994 California White Zinfandel   NW
   Special Awards: Best of Price Class (NW)
De Lorimier Winery 1991 "Lace" Estate Bottled Sauvignon Blanc   OC
De Lorimier Winery 1991 Late Harvest Sauvignon Blanc   NW
De Rose 1992 Pinot St. George   OC
Deer Springs 1992 Michael Pozzan Cabernet Sauvignon   PR
Delicato Vineyards 1993 California Sauvignon Blanc   RE
Delicato Vineyards 1994 California White Zinfandel   NW
   Special Awards: Best of Price Class (NW)

Dolce   1991 Late Harvest Sémillon   OC
Domaine Carneros   1990 Sparkling Blanc de Blancs   OC
Domaine Carneros   1991 Sparkling Brut, Méthode Champenoise   OC
Fallenleaf   1994 Sonoma Valley Sauvignon Blanc   CA
Fess Parker Winery   1994 Muscat Canelli   NW
  Special Awards: Best of Price Class (NW)
Fieldbrook Valley Winery   1992 Pacini Vineyard Petite Sirah   OC
Fieldbrook Valley Winery   1993 Pacini Vineyard Zinfandel   SF
  Special Awards: Double Gold (SF)
Fieldbrook Valley Winery   1994 Webb Vineyard Sauvignon Blanc   OC
Franciscan Oakville Estate   1990 Magnificat   DA
Franciscan Oakville Estate   1991 Cabernet Sauvignon   OC
Franciscan Oakville Estate   1991 Magnificat   IW
Franciscan Oakville Estate   1991 Napa Valley Red Meritage   RE
Franciscan Oakville Estate   1993 Barrel Fermented Chardonnay   NW
Franciscan Oakville Estate   1993 Napa Valley Zinfandel   SD
Fratelli Perata Winery   1993 Estate Bottled Merlot   SD, FF
Gainey Vineyard   1993 Santa Ynez Valley Sauvignon Blanc   NW
Gainey Vineyard   1994 Santa Ynez Valley Johannisberg Riesling SD, NW, FF
  Special Awards: Trophy for Best New World Riesling (NW);
  Best of Price Class (NW)
Galleano Winery   NV Cucamonga Valley Medium Sherry   SF
  Special Awards: Best of Class (SF); Best Dessert Wine (SF)
Galleano Winery   NV Three Friends Port   NW
  Special Awards: Trophy for Best New World Dessert Wine (NW);
  Best of Price Class (NW)
Gan Eden Wines   1993 Black Muscat   DA
Gan Eden Wines   1993 Muscat Canelli   NW
Glen Ellen Winery   1993 Proprietor's Reserve Merlot   CA, NW
  Special Awards: Best of Price Class (NW)
Hop Kiln Winery   1992 Russian River Valley Zinfandel   NW
Husch Vineyards   1991 La Ribera Vineyards Cabernet Sauvignon   FF
Husch Vineyards   1992 Mendocino La Ribera Red   FF
Husch Vineyards   1993 Mendocino Chardonnay   FF
Jepson Vineyards   1993 Mendocino Estate Chardonnay   NW
Lang Wines   1992 Twin Rivers Vineyards Zinfandel   CA
Les Vieux Cepages   1993 North Coast Limited Release White   FF
  Special Awards: Chairman's Award (FF)
M.G. Vallejo   1993 California White Zinfandel   NW
M.G. Vallejo   1993 Merlot   OC
M.G. Vallejo   1994 White Zinfandel   CA
  Special Awards: Tie for Best White Zinfandel of California (CA);
  Tie for Best White Zinfandel of Appellation (CA)
Maacama Creek   1992 Estate Bottled Cabernet Sauvignon Reserve   OC
Maison Deutz Winery   1990 Blanc de Noirs Reserve   LA, NW
  Special Awards: Best of Class (LA); Best of Price Class (NW)
Martini and Prati Wines   1991 Sonoma County Zinfandel   LA
Maurice Carrie Winery   1992 Temecula Nebbiolo   FF

USA—California (continued)   **Golds**

	Golds
Meeker Vineyard 1991 Scharf Family Vineyard Cabernet Sauvignon	NW
Meridian Vineyards 1993 Edna Valley Chardonnay	CA
Meridian Vineyards 1993 Pinot Noir Reserve	SF
Monterra 1992 Sand Hill Merlot	CA
Special Awards: Best Wine of Region (CA); Best Merlot	
of Appellation (CA)	
Orfila Vineyards NV Tawny Port	SD
Special Awards: Best of Class (SD); Best Dessert Wine (SD)	
Pepperwood Grove 1992 Cask Lot 2 Cabernet Franc	NW
Pepperwood Grove 1994 Gamay Beaujolais Nouveau	CA, NW
Special Awards: Best Nouveau of Appellation (CA);	
Double Gold (CA)	
Prager Winery and Port Works 1985 "Noble Companion" Old Tawny Port	OC
Prager Winery and Port Works 1993 Sweet Madeline	NW
R.H. Phillips Vineyard 1993 Barrel Cuvée Chardonnay	NW
Rabbit Ridge Vineyards 1992 Sonoma County Syrah	CA
Special Awards: Best Syrah/Shiraz of Appellation (CA)	
Rancho de Philo NV Triple Cream Sherry	PR, NW
Raymond Vineyard 1990 Private Reserve Cabernet Sauvignon	NW
Raymond Vineyard 1991 Amberhill Cabernet Sauvignon	NW
Raymond Vineyard 1991 Napa Valley Cabernet Sauvignon	RE
Special Awards: Finalist for Sweepstakes Award, Red Wine (RE)	
Raymond Vineyard 1992 Napa Valley Merlot	OC, CA, IV
Richardson Vineyards 1993 Sangiocomo Vineyard Merlot	RE, SF
Rosenblum Cellars 1992 Napa Valley Port	PR
Rutherford Estate Cellars 1991 Napa Valley Cabernet Sauvignon	NW
Rutherford Estate Cellars 1992 Cabernet Sauvignon	SD, FF
Rutherford Estate Cellars 1992 Napa Valley Chardonnay	NW
Rutherford Estate Cellars 1992 Napa Valley Merlot	SD
Special Awards: Best of Class (SD)	
Rutherford Estate Cellars 1994 White Zinfandel	OC
S. Anderson Vineyard 1989 Napa Valley Brut	LA, NW
S. Anderson Vineyard 1990 Napa Valley Blanc de Noirs	NW
Sanford Winery 1992 Benedict Vineyard Barrel Select Pinot Noir	IW
Shenandoah Vineyards 1994 Amador County Orange Muscat	OC, CA
Special Awards: Best Muscatel-type Fortified Wine	
of Appellation (CA)	
Single Leaf Vineyards 1994 El Dorado White Zinfandel	CA
Special Awards: Best White Zinfandel of Appellation (CA)	
Sonoma Creek Winery 1992 Cabernet Sauvignon Reserve	OC
Sonoma Creek Winery 1993 Sonoma County Old Vine Zinfandel	CA, SD
Special Awards: Best of Class (SD); Best Red Wine (SD)	
St. Clement Vineyards 1992 Napa Valley Cabernet Sauvignon	NW
St. Clement Vineyards 1992 Napa Valley Merlot	CA
Ste. Claire Winery 1992 California Cabernet Sauvignon	DA
Thomas Coyne Wines 1993 "Amarone" Late Harvest Zinfandel	OC
Thomas Fogarty Winery 1992 Estate Reserve Chardonnay	SF
Thomas Fogarty Winery 1994 Ventana Vineyards Gewürztraminer	RE
Special Awards: Finalist for Sweepstakes Award, White Wine (RE)	

USA—California (continued)

	Golds
Van Roekel Vineyards 1993 Temecula Sauvignon Blanc	RE, DA
Van Roekel Vineyards 1993 Temecula Sweet Salud	NW
Vigil Vineyard 1992 Château Margarite Cabernet Sauvignon	RE, LA
Vigil Vineyard NV Terra Vin Red Table Wine	IV
Voss Vineyards 1992 Chardonnay	OC
Wheeler Winery 1991 Norse Vineyard Reserve Cabernet Sauvignon	DA
Wild Horse Winery 1991 Cabernet Franc	SD
William Hill Winery 1990 Reserve Cabernet Sauvignon	IW
William Hill Winery 1992 Napa Valley Merlot	NW
William Hill Winery 1993 Napa Valley Chardonnay	SD, NW, FF
Windsor Vineyards 1988 Sonoma County Blanc de Noirs	OC, LA
Windsor Vineyards 1993 California Grenache Rosé	NW
Windsor Vineyards 1994 Sonoma County Gamay Beaujolais	NW

USA—Colorado

	Golds
Columbine Cellars 1993 Chardonnay	IV

USA—Illinois

	Golds
Alto Vineyards 1993 Rosso Classico	LA
Alto Vineyards 1994 Illinois Vidal Blanc	LA

USA—Indiana

	Golds
Huber Orchard Winery 1994 Indiana Seyval Blanc	LA

USA—Michigan

	Golds
Fenn Valley Wines NV Classic Reserve	LA

USA—Missouri

	Golds
Blumenhof Vineyards 1994 Missouri Vignoles	PR, NW
Special Awards: Best of Class (PR); Best of Price Class (NW)	
Mount Pleasant Winery 1993 Jour de la Victoire Vidal Blanc	PR
Mount Pleasant Winery 1994 Augusta Village	SF

USA—New York

	Golds
Hermann J. Weimer 1994 Semi-Dry Johannisberg Riesling	LA

USA—Ohio

	Golds
Chalet Debonne Vineyards 1994 Reserve Johannisberg Riesling	LA
Lonz Winery NV American Madeira	PR
Lonz Winery NV Ruby Port	PR

USA—Oregon

	Golds
Montinore 1992 Willamette Valley Reserve Chardonnay	RE
Pioneer Hopyard Winery 1993 Oregon Chardonnay	OR
Tyee Wine Cellars 1993 Willamette Valley Gewürztraminer	SD

USA—Region Unknown

	Golds
Chestnut Hill Winery 1991 Old Vines Cuvée Zinfandel	SD
Kalyra 1991 Vintage Port	OC

USA—Region Unknown (continued)   **Golds**
Poalillo Vineyards   1992 Zinfandel   OC
Stony Ridge Winery   1993 Sauvignon Blanc   NW

USA—Virginia   **Golds**
Piedmont Vineyards   1993 Virginia Special Reserve Chardonnay   NW
Prince Michel Vineyard   1993 Barrel Select Chardonnay   SD
Prince Michel Vineyard   1993 Virginia Chardonnay   NW

USA—Washington   **Golds**
Barnard Griffin   1991 Columbia Valley Cabernet Sauvignon   NE
Covey Run Vintners   1993 Yakima Valley Reserve Chardonnay   LA
Thurston Wolfe Winery   1992 JTW's Port   TC
Whidbey's   1990 Washington Vintage Port   FF
    Special Awards: Chairman's Award (FF)
Zillah Oaks Winery   1994 Yakima Valley Muscat Canelli   WW

Indices

We've organized the indices in a way that we hope will be most useful to wine lovers. Index 1 is a reference to gold medal wines by type and by region; Index 2 lists the corresponding winning wineries and their region. You can use these indices in a number of ways to expand and enrich your wine-buying habits and knowledge.

Let's say that you love Chardonnay, but want to try one that's not Californian. Index 1 will help you there. It's enlightening and fun to compare an Australian Chardonnay, say, with a Canadian one.

*If you love Pinot Noir, but don't want to pay more than $15 dollars a bottle, check out the Pinots listed in Index 1 in **boldface**. (All page numbers in boldface, in both indices, indicate wines that are $15 or under.)*

To take another example, if you loved a certain gold medal winner, there's a good chance the winery that produced it will have other gold medal wines in the book. Index 2 will help you find all the gold medal wines in Part III produced by that winery. Trying different wines from a single producer is a great way to acquaint yourself with a winery's "style." You may find yourself becoming a loyal follower. Most wineries, by the way, have 800 numbers, mail-order offers at special prices, newsletters, and special events.

1. WINES BY TYPE AND REGION

RED WINES
Baco Noir
  CAN Lakeview Cellars, **118**
Barbera
  CA Eberle Winery, 100
  CA Montevina Winery, **98**
  CA Preston Vineyards, **98**
  CA Renwood Winery, 100
  CA Sebastiani Vineyards, **102**
Cabernet Franc
  CA Cosentino, 71
  CA Gold Hill Vineyard, **71**
  CA Guenoc Estate, **71**
  CA Gundlach-Bundschu, **71**
  CA Kendall-Jackson, 71
  CA Latcham Vineyards, **72**
  CA Madrona Vineyards, **72**
  CA Mount Konocti, **72**
  CA Nevada City Winery, 72
Cabernet Sauvignon
  CA A. Rafanelli Winery, 83
  CA Altamura Winery, 86

  WA Apex, 86
  CA Bandiera Winery, **73**
  CA Barefoot Cellars, **73**
  CA Beaulieu, 86
  CA Bel Arbors, **73**
  CA Beringer Vineyards, 76, 86
  AUS BRL Hardy Wine Company, 86, 87
  CA Brutocao Cellars, **76**
  CA Buena Vista Carneros, **76**, 87
  AUS C. A. Henschke, 87
  CHI Canepa Winery, 87
  CA Canyon Road, **73**
  CHI Carmen Vineyards, **88**
  AUS Chapel Hill Winery, **76**
  CA Château Julien, 88
  CA Château Souverain, 77
  CA Château St. Jean, 88
  AUS Coldstream Hills, 89
  CA Corbett Canyon Vineyards, **73**
  CA Creston Vineyard, 77
  CA De Loach, 77, **78**, 89

Page numbers in **boldface** indicate wines that are $15 or under.

Cabernet Sauvignon *(continued)*

CA   Douglas Hill Winery, **78**
CA   Dry Creek Vineyard, 89
CA   E. & J. Gallo Winery, 89
CHI Errazuriz Panquehue, **74**
CA   Fetzer, **74**
CA   Filsinger Vineyards, **78**
CA   Forestville Vineyards, **74**
CA   Freemark Abbey, 90
CA   Geyser Peak Winery, **78**, 90
AUS Grant Burge, 78
CA   Greenwood Ridge, 90
CA   Grgich Hills, 91
CA   Guenoc Estate, 91
CA   Gundlach-Bundschu, **79**
CA   Hanna Winery, 79
AUS Hardy Wine Company, 91
CA   Heitz Cellar, 91
CA   Herzog Wine Cellars, **79**
CA   Hess Collection Winery, 92
CA   Hop Kiln Winery, **79**
CA   Indian Springs Vineyards, **79**
CA   J. Lohr, **81**
CA   Joullian Vineyards, **80**
CA   Justin Vineyards, 92
CA   Kendall-Jackson, **80**, 92
CA   Lambert Bridge, **80**
CA   Lava Cap, **80**
AUS Leasingham Wines, **81**
CA   Louis M. Martini, 92
CA   Madrona Vineyards, **81**
CAN Magnotta Winery, **81**
CA   Mario Perelli-Minetti Winery, **82**
CA   Markham Vineyards, 93
NZ   Matua Valley Wines, 82
CA   Mazzocco Vineyards, 93
AUS McGuigan Brothers, **74**
CA   Meeker Vineyard, **82**
CA   Merryvale Vineyards, 93
TX   Messina Hof Wine Cellars, **82**
CA   Michel-Schlumberger, 93
AUS Mitchelton Wines, 93
CA   Mont St. John, 94
CA   Napa Ridge Winery, **74, 82**
CA   Navarro, 82
CA   Newlan Vineyards, 94
CA   Peju Province, 94
AUS Penley Estate, 94
CA   Perry Creek Vineyards, **83**
WA   Preston Vineyards, 94
CA   Renaissance Vineyard & Winery, **83**

CA   Richard L. Graeser Winery, **83**
CA   Robert Mondavi, 95
CA   Rodney Strong, 95
CA   Sebastiani Vineyards, **83**
CA   Sequoia Grove Vineyards, 95
WA   Seven Hills Winery, 95
CA   Shafer Vineyards, 95, 96
CA   Sierra Vista Winery, **84**
CA   Silverado Vineyards, 96
CA   St. Supery Vineyards, **84**
TX   Ste. Genevieve, **75**
CA   Stone Creek, **75**
CA   Stonestreet Winery, 96
AUS Stonier's Winery, **84**
WA   Tefft Cellars, 96
ARG Trapiche, 84
CA   V. Sattui Winery, 96, 97
CHI Vina Domaine Oriental, **75**
WA   W.B. Bridgman, **85**
CA   Weinstock Cellars, 75
CA   Wente Bros., **75, 85**
CA   Wild Horse Winery, **85**
OR   Willamette Valley Vineyards, 97
CA   Windsor Vineyards, **85**
AUS Yalumba, **85**
CA   ZD Wines, 97

Carignane
CA   Audubon Collection, **119**
CA   Rabbit Ridge Vineyards, **120**
CA   Rosenblum Cellars, **120**

Charbono
CA   Parducci Winery, **118**

Concord
OH   Meier's Wine Cellars, **116**

Cynthiana
MO   Augusta Winery, **116**

Gamay Beaujolais
CA   Beringer Vineyards, **117**
CA   Fetzer, **117**
CA   Geyser Peak Winery, **117**
CA   Glen Ellen Winery, **117**
CA   Pedroncelli Winery, **118**
CA   Preston Vineyards, **118**

Generic and Proprietary Reds
SAF La Motte, **119**
VA   Prince Michel Vineyard, 121
CA   Rabbit Ridge Vineyards, **118**
NY   Swedish Hill Vineyard, **116**

Grignolino
CA   Emilio Guglielmo Winery, **98**

Lemberger
WA   Covey Run Vintners, **117**

Page numbers in **boldface** indicate wines that are $15 or under.

Malbec
 CA Geyser Peak Winery, 121
 CA Jekel Vineyards, 121

Merlot
 WA Andrew Will Winery, 112
 CA Belvedere Winery, **105**
 CA Beringer Vineyards, 112
 CA Buena Vista Carneros, **105**
 CHI Carmen Vineyards, **103**
 WA Caterina Winery, **105**
 CA Château St. Jean, **105**
 WA Château Ste. Michelle, 105, 112
 WA Columbia Crest, **106**
 WA Covey Run Vintners, **106**
 CA Creston Vineyard, **106**
 CA De Loach, **106**
 CA Dry Creek Vineyard, 112
 CA Fetzer, **106**
 CA Firestone, **107**
 CA Forest Glen Winery, **107**
 CA Freemark Abbey, 107
 CA Gary Farrell Wines, 113
 CA Grand Cru Vineyards, **103**
 AUS Grant Burge, **107**
 WA Hogue Cellars, **107**
 CA Indian Springs Vineyards, **107**
 CA Kendall-Jackson, 113
 CA Kenwood Vineyards, 108
 CA Konocti Winery, **108**
 CA Lambert Bridge, **108**
 CA Leeward Winery, **108**
 CA Louis M. Martini, **103**
 CAN Magnotta Winery, **108**
 CA Matanzas Creek Winery, 113
 SAF Meerlust, 109
 CA Merryvale Vineyards, 113
 TX Messina Hof Wine Cellars, **103**
 CA Mill Creek Vineyards, **109**
 CA Napa Ridge Winery, **109**
 WA Paul Thomas Winery, **104**
 CA Pedroncelli Winery, **109**
 CA Pine Ridge, 114
 CA Rabbit Ridge Vineyards, 109
 CA Rodney Strong, **110**
 CA Round Hill Vineyards, **104**
 WA Seven Hills Winery, 114
 CA Shafer Vineyards, 114
 CA Smith & Hook Winery, 114
 CA St. Francis Vineyards, 114
 CA Sterling Vineyards, 115
 CA Stevenot Winery, **110**
 CA Stonestreet Winery, 115
 CA Storrs Winery, 110
 CA Swanson Vineyards, 115
 CA Truchard Vineyards, 115
 WA W.B. Bridgman, **110**
 WA Washington Hills Cellars, **104**
 CA Wellington Vineyards, **110**
 CA Whitehall Lane Winery, 111, 115
 CA Wild Horse Winery, **111**

Mourvèdre
 CA Château Julien, **119**
 CA Cline Cellars, **119**
 CA Hart Winery, **119**
 CA Ridge Vineyards and Winery, **120**
 CA Sebastiani Vineyards, **120**

Napa Gamay
 CA Weinstock Cellars, 120

Nebbiolo
 CA Brindiamo, **98**

Noble
 FL Chautauqua Vineyards, **116**

Norton
 MO St. James Winery, **116**
 MO Stone Hill Wine Co., 116

Petit Verdot
 CA Geyser Peak Winery, 121
 CA Jekel Vineyards, 121

Petite Sirah
 CA Bogle Vineyard, **122**
 CO Colorado Cellars, **122**
 CA Concannon, **122**
 CA Deer Park Winery, 123
 CA Fetzer, **123**
 CA Foppiano Vineyards, 123
 CA Guenoc Estate, **123**
 CA Latcham Vineyards, **124**
 CA Lolonis Wine Cellars, 124
 CA Mirassou Vineyards, **124**
 CA Parducci Winery, **122**
 CA Storrs Winery, 124
 CA Windsor Vineyards, **124**

Pinot Noir
 CA Acacia Winery, **126**
 NZ Ata Rangi Vineyard, 131
 CA Beaulieu, **126**
 CA Brindiamo, **126**
 CA Byron Vineyard, 126
 CA Camelot Winery, **127**
 CA Cartlidge & Browne, **125**
 CA Château Souverain, 127
 CA Château St. Jean, **127**
 AUS Coldstream Hills, 127, 128, 131
 CA Cosentino, 131

Page numbers in **boldface** indicate wines that are $15 or under.

Pinot Noir *(continued)*

CA   Creston Vineyard, **128**
CA   David Bruce Winery, **128**, 132
CA   Davis Bynum Winery, 132
CA   De Loach, 132
CA   Edna Valley Vineyard, **128**
CA   Elkhorn Peak, 133
CA   Fess Parker Winery, **129**
CA   Fetzer, **129**
CA   Gary Farrell Wines, 133
CA   Greenwood Ridge, **129**
CA   J. Rochioli Vineyards, 133
CA   La Crema, 133
CAN Magnotta Winery, **129**
CA   Napa Ridge Winery, **125**
CA   Navarro, **130**
CA   Robert Mondavi, **130**
CA   Rodney Strong, 130
CA   Sanford Winery, 134
CA   Schug Carneros Estate, 130
CA   Sterling Vineyards, 134
CA   Stonestreet Winery, 134
CA   Trout Gulch Vineyard, 134
OR   Tualatin, 134
CA   Villa Mt. Eden, **125**, 130
OR   Willamette Valley Vineyards, **125**, **130**
CA   York Mountain Winery, **125**

Red Blends

CA   Beringer Vineyards, **137**
CA   Bonny Doon Vineyard, 142
CA   Brindiamo, **137**
AUS C. A. Henschke, 142
CA   Carmenet Vineyard, 143
CA   Castoro Cellars, **137**
AUS Château Reynella, **138**
CA   Cline Cellars, **135**, **138**
CA   Concannon, 138
CA   Cosentino, 143
CA   Firestone, 143
CA   Flora Springs Wine Company, 144
CA   Geyser Peak Winery, 144
CA   Golden Creek Vineyard, **139**
WA   Hedges Cellars, 144
CAN Hillebrand Estates Winery, 145
AUS Hillstowe, 139
CA   Joseph Phelps Vineyards, **139**, 145
CA   Justin Vineyards, 145
CA   Langtry, 145
AUS Leasingham Wines, **135**

LEB Les Côteaux Kefraya, **139**
CA   Madrona Vineyards, **135**
NZ   Matua Valley Wines, 140
CA   Mount Veeder Winery, 146
CA   Pedroncelli Winery, **135**
AUS Penley Estate, 146
CA   Quivira Vineyards, 140
AUS Richard Hamilton Winery, 146
CA   River Run Vintners, **140**
AUS Rosemount Estate, **136**
CA   Santino Wines, **140**
CA   Stonestreet Winery, 146
CA   Trentadue Winery, **141**
AUS Yalumba, **136**
CA   Zaca Mesa Winery, **141**

Sangiovese

CA   Atlas Peak Vineyards, 100
CA   Mosby Winery, 100
CA   Mount Palomar Winery, 100
CA   Renwood Winery, 101
CA   Robert Pepi Winery, 101
CA   Swanson Vineyards, 102
CA   Vino Noceto, **99**

Syrah/Shiraz

AUS Arrowfield Wines, 149
AUS Ashwood Grove, **149**
AUS BRL Hardy Wine Company, **149**
AUS C. A. Henschke, 149
CA   Cambria Winery, 149
AUS Chapel Hill Winery, **150**
AUS Château Reynella, **150**
WA   Columbia Winery, 150
CA   Eberle Winery, 150
CA   Geyser Peak Winery, **151**
AUS Hardy Wine Company, **151**
AUS Kingston Estate, **152**
AUS Leasingham Wines, **147**, **152**
AUS McGuigan Brothers, **147**
AUS Merrivale Wines, **152**
AUS Miranda Wines, **153**
AUS Normans Wines, 153
AUS Rosemount Estate, 153
AUS Rothbury Vineyards, **147**
CA   Swanson Vineyards, 153
CA   Truchard Vineyards, 154
AUS Yalumba, **148**, 154
CA   Zaca Mesa Winery, **154**

Zinfandel

CA   A. Rafanelli Winery, **162**
CA   Adelaida Cellars, **157**
CA   Alderbrook, **157**
CA   Baron Herzog, **157**

Page numbers in **boldface** indicate wines that are $15 or under.

Zinfandel *(continued)*
- *CA* Belvedere Winery, **157**
- *CA* Castoro Cellars, **155**
- *CA* Cline Cellars, **157**
- *CA* Davis Bynum Winery, **158**
- *CA* Dry Creek Vineyard, **158**
- *CA* E. & J. Gallo Winery, **158**
- *CA* Eberle Winery, **158**
- *CA* Edmeades Estate, 158, **159**
- *CA* Estrella River Winery, **155**
- *CA* Fetzer, **155**
- *CA* Gary Farrell Wines, **159**
- *CA* Granite Springs Winery, **155**
- *CA* Greenwood Ridge, **159**
- *CA* Haywood Estate, 159
- *CA* Hop Kiln Winery, 159
- *CA* J. Fritz Winery, **160**
- *CA* Jankris Vineyards, 160
- *CA* Kendall-Jackson, 160
- *CA* Lava Cap, 160
- *CA* McIlroy Family Wines, **160**
- *CA* Meeker Vineyard, **161**
- *CA* Mission View Vineyards, **161**
- *CA* Montevina Winery, **155**
- *CA* Nichelini, **161**
- *CA* Peachy Canyon Winery, 161
- *CA* Preston Vineyards, **161**
- *CA* Rabbit Ridge Vineyards, **162**
- *CA* River Run Vintners, **162**
- *CA* Rodney Strong, **163**
- *CA* Rombauer Vineyards, 163
- *CA* Rosenblum Cellars, **156**, 163
- *CA* Sausal Winery, **156**
- *CA* Sierra Vista Winery, **164**
- *CA* Silver Horse Vineyards, **164**
- *CA* St. Francis Vineyards, 164
- *CA* Storrs Winery, 164
- *CA* Storybook Mountain Vineyards, 165
- *CA* Topolos at Russian River, 165
- *CA* V. Sattui Winery, 165
- *CA* Villa Mt. Eden, **156**
- *CA* Whaler Vineyard, **165**
- *CA* Windsor Vineyards, **166**

ROSÉ WINES

All Varietals
- *WI* Botham Vineyards, **233**
- *FL* Chautauqua Vineyards, **233**
- *CA* Hagafen Cellars, **233**
- *NY* Swedish Hill Vineyard, **234**

- *CA* Temecula Crest Winery, **234**

Gamay Rouge
- *CA* V. Sattui Winery, **234**

Lemberger
- *CO* Colorado Cellars, **234**

SPARKLING WINES

Blanc de Noirs
- *CA* Gloria Ferrer, **238**
- *NM* Gruet Winery, **237**
- *CA* Iron Horse, 238
- *CA* Korbel Winery, **237**
- *CA* Maison Deutz Winery, 238
- *CA* Mumm Napa Valley, **237**
- *CA* Piper Sonoma, **237**
- *CA* Schramsberg, 238
- *CA* Tribaut, **237**
- *CA* V. Sattui Winery, 238

Brut
- *CA* Codorniu Napa, **239**
- *CA* Culbertson, **239**, 241
- *CA* Gloria Ferrer, 241
- *NM* Gruet Winery, **239**
- *CA* Handley Cellars, 241
- *CA* J. Schram by Schramsberg, 242
- *CA* Jordan Sparkling Wine Company, 242
- *OH* Meier's Wine Cellars, **239**
- *CA* Mirabelle Cellars, **239**
- *CA* Mirassou Vineyards, **240**
- *CA* Mumm Napa Valley, **240**
- *CA* Piper Sonoma, 242
- *OR* RainSong Vineyard, **242**
- *CA* Robert Hunter Winery, 243
- *MI* Tabor Hill, 243
- *CA* Tribaut, **240**
- *CA* Wente Bros., **243**

Other Sparkling Wines
- *WA* Domaine Ste. Michelle, **244**
- *AUS* Grant Burge, 244
- *CA* Handley Cellars, 244, 245
- *CA* Jepson Vineyards, 245
- *CA* Korbel Winery, **245**
- *ID* Ste. Chapelle Vineyards, **246**
- *MO* Stone Hill Wine Co., **246**

Sparkling Red
- *CA* Culbertson, **244**
- *CA* Korbel Winery, **245**

Sparkling Rosé
- *CA* Maison Deutz Winery, 246
- *CA* Schramsberg, 246

Page numbers in **boldface** indicate wines that are $15 or under.

SWEET/DESSERT/FORTIFIED WINES

Aleatico
CA   Brindiamo, 262

Concord
NY   Palmer Vineyards, **256**
MO   St. James Winery, **256**

Generic and Proprietary Dessert Wines
LEB   Les Côteaux Kefraya, **259**
CA   Silverado Vineyards, 263
CAN   Stoney Ridge Cellars, 263

Gewürztraminer, Late Harvest
AUS   Arrowfield Wines, **257**
CA   Château St. Jean, 262
CA   De Loach, **257**
OR   Montinore, **256**

Icewine
CAN   Gehringer Bros. Estate Winery, 249
CAN   Hillebrand Estates Winery, 249
CAN   Inniskillin Wines, 249
CAN   Magnotta Winery, 250
CAN   Reif Estate Winery, 250
CAN   Stoney Ridge Cellars, 251
CAN   Vineland Estates Winery, 251
NY   Wagner Vineyards, **251**

Late Harvest Riesling
CA   Geyser Peak Winery, 258

Muscadelle
AUS   R.L. Buller & Son, 263

Muscat
CA   Alderbrook, 252
CA   Brindiamo, **252**
CA   Lava Cap, **252**
CA   Quady Winery, **252, 253**
CA   St. Supery Vineyards, **253**
WA   Tucker Cellars, **253**
CA   V. Sattui Winery, **254**
CA   Windsor Vineyards, **254**
AUS   Yalumba, 254

Niagara
OH   Breitenbach Wine Cellars, **255**

Port
AUS   Château Reynella, **264**
CA   Ficklin Vineyards, 264
CA   Guenoc Estate, **265**
CA   Joseph Filippi Vintage Co., **265**
CA   Konrad Estate Winery, 265
CA   Quady Winery, **265**
CA   Santa Ynez Winery, 266
CA   Trentadue Winery, 266
AR   Wiederkehr Wine Cellars, 266
CA   Windsor Vineyards, **266**

Riesling, Late Harvest
AUS   Arrowfield Wines, 257
WA   Caterina Winery, **255**
CA   Concannon, **255**
WA   Covey Run Vintners, **255**
CA   Fetzer, **255**
CA   Geyser Peak Winery, 258
NY   Hermann J. Wiemer, **258**
CA   Herzog Wine Cellars, **258**
WA   Hogue Cellars, **255**
CA   Husch Vineyards, **259**
CA   J. Lohr, **259**
CA   Madrona Vineyards, 260
OR   Montinore, **256**
CA   Navarro, **260**, 262
CA   Santino Wines, **261**

Sauvignon Blanc, Late Harvest
CA   Santa Barbara Winery, 260

Sémillon, Late Harvest
CA   Concannon, **257**
AUS   Yalumba, **256**

Sherry
CA   Louis M. Martini, **267**
CA   Windsor Vineyards, **267**
CA   York Mountain Winery, **267**

Steinberg
MO   Stone Hill Wine Co., **256**

Vidal, Late Harvest
CAN   Konzelmann Vineyards, 259
CAN   London Winery, 260
CAN   Pillitteri Estates, 260

Vignoles, Late Harvest
MO   Stone Hill Wine Co., **261**
NY   Swedish Hill Vineyard, **261**

Zinfandel, Late Harvest
IL   Lynfred Winery, 262
CA   River Run Vintners, 263
CA   Santino Wines, **261**

WHITE WINES

Catawba
MO   St. James Winery, **206**

Cayuga
NY   Hunt Country Vineyards, **204**
NY   Swedish Hill Vineyard, **206**

Chardonnay
CAN   Andres Wines, **169**
WA   Arbor Crest, **169**
CA   Atlas Peak Vineyards, 175
CA   Baileyana, **175**
CA   Baron Herzog, **175**
CA   Beaulieu, **169, 175**
CA   Belvedere Winery, **169, 175**

Page numbers in **boldface** indicate wines that are $15 or under.

Chardonnay *(continued)*

CA Beringer Vineyards, **175**
AUS BRL Hardy Wine Company, **176**
CA Byron Vineyard, 176, 190
CA Callaway Vineyard, **176**
CA Cambria Winery, 190
CA Camelot Winery, 176
CA Canyon Road, **169**
CHI Carmen Vineyards, **170**
CA Cartlidge & Browne, **170**
AUS Chapel Hill Winery, **177**
CA Charles Krug Winery, 190
CA Château Souverain, 177
CA Château St. Jean, 177
WA Château Ste. Michelle, 190, 191
CA Clos du Bois, 178, 191
AUS Coldstream Hills, 191
WA Columbia Crest, **170** .
WA Columbia Winery, 178
CA Concannon, **170, 178**
CA De Loach, 191
CA E. & J. Gallo Winery, 192
CA Edmeades Estate, **178**
CA Edna Valley Vineyard, **178**
OR Eola Hills Wine Cellars, **179**
CHI Errazuriz Panquehue, **171**
CA Estrella River Winery, **171**
CA Fess Parker Winery, 192
CA Fetzer, **171, 179**
CA Franciscan Oakville Estate, **179**
CA Gary Farrell Wines, 192
CA Geyser Peak Winery, **179, 180,** 192
CA Gloria Ferrer, 180
AUS Goundrey Wines, **171, 180**
CA Guenoc Estate, **180,** 192, 193
CA Hanna Winery, **181**
CAN Henry of Pelham Estates, 181
CAN Hillebrand Estates Winery, **181**
WA Hogue Cellars, **181**
CA Hope Farms Winery, **171**
NZ Hunters Wines, 182
CA Indian Creek, **172**
CA J. Fritz Winery, **182**
NY J. Furst Winery, **172**
CA Jarvis Winery, 193
CA Kendall-Jackson, 182, 183, 193
AUS Kingston Estate, **183**
CAN Konzelmann Vineyards, 183
CA La Crema, 193
NY Lamoreaux Landing Wine Cellars, **183**
CA Landmark Vineyards, 194

CA Lockwood Vineyards, 184
CA Madrona Vineyards, **184**
CA McIlroy Family Wines, **184**
CA Michel-Schlumberger, 194
CA Mill Creek Vineyards, **184**
AUS Miranda Wines, **172**
CAN Mission Hill Vineyards, **185**
AUS Mitchelton Wines, 185
OR Montinore, **185**
NZ Morton Estate, 194
CA Napa Ridge Winery, **185**
CA Navarro, **185**
NZ Palliser Estate, 186
CA Parducci Winery, **172**
CAN Pillitteri Estates, 172
CA Pine Ridge, **186**
CO Plum Creek Cellars, **186**
CA R.H. Phillips Vineyard, **173**
AUS Richard Hamilton Winery, 186
CA Robert Alison Winery, **173**
CA Robert Mondavi, **173,** 186
CA Rodney Strong, **187**
CA Rombauer Vineyards, 194
AUS Rosemount Estate, **187**
AUS Rothbury Vineyards, **187**
CA Schug Carneros Estate, 188
CA Sebastiani Vineyards, **188**
CA Sequoia Grove Vineyards, 194
WA Silver Lake Winery, **173**
CA Simi Winery, **188**
CA Stag's Leap Wine Cellars, 194
CA Stonestreet Winery, 195
CA Swanson Vineyards, 195
ARG Trapiche, **173**
CA V. Sattui Winery, 195
OR Valley View Winery, **174**
CA Vichon Winery, **174,** 188
CA Villa Mt. Eden, **174,** 189
MA Westport Rivers Vineyard, 189
AUS Yalumba, **189**
CA ZD Wines, 196
CA Zellerbach Winery, **174**

Chenin Blanc
CA Baron Herzog, **197**
CA Callaway Vineyard, **197**
WA Château Ste. Michelle, **197**
CA Dry Creek Vineyard, **197, 198**
CA Granite Springs Winery, **198**
WA Hogue Cellars, **198**
CA Husch Vineyards, **198**
TX Llano Estacado Winery, **199**
CA Wente Bros., **199**

Page numbers in **boldface** indicate wines that are $15 or under.

Cortese
CA   Mount Palomar Winery, 208
Ehrenfelser
CAN Gray Monk Cellars, 204
Frontignac
AUS Grant Burge, 204
Generic and Proprietary Whites
CA   Caymus Vineyards, 207
CA   Geyser Peak Winery, **203**
CA   Hagafen Cellars, **204**
OH   Meier's Wine Cellars, **204**
MO   Montelle at Osage Ridge, **205**
Gewürztraminer
CA   Adler Fels Winery, **200**
CA   Alderbrook, **200**
CA   Bargetto's Winery, **200**
CA   Cosentino, **200**
CA   Fetzer, **200**
CA   Forestville Vineyards, **201**
CA   Geyser Peak Winery, **201**
CA   Handley Cellars, **201**
OR   Hinman Vineyards, **201**
CA   Louis M. Martini, **202**
CA   Madrona Vineyards, **202**
CA   Napa Ridge Winery, **202**
Malvasia Bianca
CA   Ca' Del Solo, **203**
Melon
CA   J. Fritz Winery, **208**
CA   Murphy-Goode Estate Winery, **208**
Müller-Thurgau
OR   Montinore, **205**
Niagara
MO   St. James Winery, **205**
Pinot Blanc
CA   Mirassou Vineyards, **205**
CAN Sumac Ridge Estate Winery, **209**
CA   Wild Horse Winery, **209**
Pinot Gris
OR   Cooper Mountain Vineyards, **207**
CAN Gehringer Bros. Estate Winery, **203**
OR   Knudsen-Erath Winery, **208**
Riesling
WA   Château Ste. Michelle, **210**
CO   Colorado Cellars, **212**
WA   Columbia Winery, **210**
NZ   Corbans Wines, **212**
WA   Covey Run Vintners, **210**
CA   Fetzer, **210**
CA   Geyser Peak Winery, **211**

CAN Gray Monk Cellars, 211
CA   Greenwood Ridge, **212**
CA   Hagafen Cellars, **212**
CA   Kendall-Jackson, **213**
NY   Lamoreaux Landing Wine Cellars, **213**
NZ   Palliser Estate, **213**
CA   Perry Creek Vineyards, **211**
NY   Standing Stone Vineyards, **213**
NY   Swedish Hill Vineyard, **214**
CA   V. Sattui Winery, **214**
OR   Willamette Valley Vineyards, **214**
Sauvignon Blanc
CA   Adler Fels Winery, **221**
WA   Arbor Crest, **215**
CA   Bandiera Winery, **215**
CA   Beaulieu, **215**
CA   Beringer Vineyards, **215**
CA   Callaway Vineyard, **215**
CA   Canyon Road, **216**
CHI Carmen Vineyards, **216**
CA   Château Souverain, **216**
CA   Château St. Jean, **221**
WA   Château Ste. Michelle, **216**
NZ   Corbans Wines, **217**
CA   Davis Bynum Winery, **217**
CA   De Loach, **221**
CA   Ehlers Grove, **217**
CHI Errazuriz Panquehue, **217**
CA   Fetzer, **217**
CA   Geyser Peak Winery, **218**
CA   Greenwood Ridge, **218**
CA   Grgich Hills, **221**
CA   Guenoc Estate, **218**
CA   Handley Cellars, **218**
CA   Hanna Winery, **222**
WA   Hogue Cellars, **218**
CA   J. Fritz Winery, **218**
CA   J. Rochioli Vineyards, **222**
CA   Kenwood Vineyards, **219**
CA   Mill Creek Vineyards, **219**
CA   Mirassou Vineyards, **219**
CA   Mission View Vineyards, **219**
CA   Montevina Winery, **219**
CA   Murphy-Goode Estate Winery, **222**
NZ   Nautilus Estate, **222**
CA   Navarro, **219, 222**
NZ   Palliser Estate, **223**
CA   Perry Creek Vineyards, **220**
CA   Quivira Vineyards, **223**
AUS Rothbury Vineyards, **223**

Page numbers in **boldface** indicate wines that are $15 or under.

Sauvignon Blanc *(continued)*
- *NZ* Seifried Estate, **223**
- *CA* Simi Winery, **220**
- *CA* Voss Vineyards, 223
- *WA* Washington Hills Cellars, **220**
- *CA* Zellerbach Winery, **220**

Sauvignon Vert
- *CA* Nichelini, **205**

Sémillon
- *WA* Arbor Crest, **224**
- *CA* Canyon Road, **224**
- *CA* Concannon, **224**
- *WA* Hogue Cellars, **224**
- *WA* Hoodsport Winery, **225**
- *CA* Lakewood Winery, **225**
- *WA* Paul Thomas Winery, **225**

Seyval
- *MO* Stone Hill Wine Co., **206**
- *WI* Wollersheim Winery, **206**

Sylvaner
- *CAN* Domaine de Chaberton, **203**

Vignoles
- *MO* Augusta Winery, **203**
- *MO* St. James Winery, **209**
- *MO* Stone Hill Wine Co., **209**
- *NY* Swedish Hill Vineyard, **206**

Viognier
- *CA* Callaway Vineyard, **207**
- *CA* Eberle Winery, 207
- *CA* Rabbit Ridge Vineyards, **208**

White Blends
- *WA* Columbia Crest, **226**
- *CA* Concannon, **226**
- *CA* Geyser Peak Winery, **226**
- *AUS* Grant Burge, **226**
- *CA* Langtry, 227
- *TX* Llano Estacado Winery, **227**
- *CA* Rosenblum Cellars, **227**
- *MI* Tabor Hill, **227**
- *CA* Venezia, 228
- *AUS* Yalumba, **228**

White Zinfandel
- *CA* Arciero Winery, **229**
- *CA* Baron Herzog, **229**
- *CA* Bel Arbors, **229**
- *CA* Beringer Vineyards, **229**
- *CA* Fetzer, **229**
- *CA* Glen Ellen Winery, **230**
- *TX* Ste. Genevieve, **230**
- *CA* V. Sattui Winery, **230**
- *CA* Weinstock Cellars, **230**

Page numbers in **boldface** indicate wines that are $15 or under.

2. WINES BY WINERY AND REGION

ARGENTINA
  Trapiche, 84, **173**
AUSTRALIA
  Arrowfield Wines, 149, 257
  Ashwood Grove, **149**
  BRL Hardy Wine Company, 86, 87, **149, 176**
  C. A. Henschke, 87, 142, 149
  Chapel Hill Winery, **76, 150, 177**
  Château Reynella, **138, 150, 264**
  Coldstream Hills, 89, 127, 128, 131, 191
  Goundrey Wines, **171, 180**
  Grant Burge, 78, **107, 204, 226,** 244
  Hardy Wine Company, 91, **151**
  Hillstowe, 139
  Kingston Estate, **152, 183**
  Leasingham Wines, **81, 135, 147, 152**
  McGuigan Brothers, **74, 147**
  Merrivale Wines, **152**
  Miranda Wines, **153, 172**
  Mitchelton Wines, 93, 185
  Normans Wines, 153
  Penley Estate, 94, 146
  R.L. Buller & Son, 263
  Richard Hamilton Winery, 146, 186
  Rosemount Estate, **136,** 153, **187**
  Rothbury Vineyards, **147, 187, 223**
  Stonier's Winery, **84**
  Yalumba, **85, 136, 148,** 154, **189,** 228, 254, **256**
CANADA
  Andres Wines, **169**
  Cedar Creek Estate Winery, 278
  Château des Charmes Wines, 278
  Colio Wines of Canada, 278
  Domaine de Chaberton, 203
  Gehringer Brothers Estate Winery, **203,** 249
  Gray Monk Cellars, 204, 211
  Henry of Pelham Estates, 181, 249
  Hillebrand Estates Winery, 145, **181,** 249
  Inniskillin Wines, 249
  Jackson Triggs Vintners, 278
  Konzelmann Vineyards, 183, 259, 278
  Lakeview Cellars, **118**
  London Winery, 260
  Magnotta Winery, **81, 108, 129,** 250

Marynissen Estates, 278
Mission Hill Vineyards, 185
Pillitteri Estates, 172, 260, 278
Reif Estate Winery, 250
Stonechurch Vineyards, 278
Stoney Ridge Cellars, 251, 263, 278
Sumac Ridge Estate Winery, **209**
Vineland Estates Winery, 251
Vinoteca, 278
CHILE
  Canepa Winery, 87
  Carmen Vineyards, 88, **103, 170, 216**
  Errazuriz Panquehue, **74, 171, 217**
  Vina Domaine Oriental, **75**
LEBANON
  Les Côteaux Kefraya, **139, 259**
NEW ZEALAND
  Ata Rangi Vineyard, 131
  Corbans Wines, **212, 217**
  Hunters Wines, 182
  Matua Valley Wines, 82, 140
  Morton Estate, 194
  Nautilus Estate, **222**
  Palliser Estate, 186, **213, 223**
  Seifried Estate, **223**
SOUTH AFRICA
  La Motte, **119**
  Meerlust, 109
USA—ARKANSAS
  Wiederkehr Wine Cellars, 266
USA—CALIFORNIA
  A. Rafanelli Winery, 83, **162**
  Acacia Winery, **126**
  Adelaida Cellars, **157**
  Adler Fels Winery, **200, 221**
  Alderbrook, **157, 200,** 252
  Altamura Winery, 86
  Alto Vineyards, 278
  Arciero Winery, **229**
  Atlas Peak Vineyards, 100, 175
  Audubon Collection, **119**
  Baileyana, **175**
  Baily Vineyard, 278
  Bandiera Winery, **73, 215**
  Barefoot Cellars, **73**
  Bargetto's Winery, **200**
  Baron Herzog, **157, 175, 197, 229**
  Beaulieu, 86, **126, 169, 175, 215**

Page numbers in **boldface** indicate wines that are $15 or under.

USA—CALIFORNIA *(continued)*

Bel Arbors, **73, 229**
Belvedere Winery, **105, 157, 169, 175**
Benziger Family Winery, 279
Benziger Imagery Series, 279
Beringer Vineyards, 76, 86, 112, **117, 137, 175, 215, 229,** 279
Bettinelli, 279
Blackstone, 279
Boeger Winery, 279
Bogle Vineyard, **122**
Bonny Doon Vineyard, 142
Brindiamo, **98, 126, 137, 252,** 262
Brutocao Cellars, **76**
Buena Vista Carneros, **76,** 87, **105**
Byron Vineyard, 126, 176, 190
Ca' Del Solo, **203**
Callaway Vineyard, **176, 197, 207, 215**
Cambria Winery, 149, 190
Camelot Winery, **127,** 176
Canyon Road, **73, 169, 216, 224**
Carmenet Vineyard, 143
Cartlidge & Browne, **125, 170**
Castoro Cellars, 137, **155**
Caymus Vineyards, 207
Charles Krug Winery, 190
Château De Baun, 279
Château Julien, 88, **119**
Château Potelle, 279
Château Souverain, 77, 127, 177, **216**
Château St. Jean, 88, **105, 127,** 177, **221,** 262, 279
Cheval Sauvage, 279
Christian Bros., 279
Cline Cellars, **119, 135, 138, 157**
Clos du Bois, 178, 191, 279
Codorniu Napa, **239**
Concannon, **122,** 138, **170, 178, 224, 226, 255, 257**
Corbett Canyon Vineyards, **73**
Cosentino, 71, 131, 143, **200**
Côtes de Sonoma, 279
Creston Vineyard, 77, **106, 128**
Culbertson, **239,** 241, **244**
Cypress, 279
David Bruce Winery, **128,** 132
Davis Bynum Winery, 132, **158, 217**
De Loach, 77, **78,** 89, **106,** 132, 191, **221, 257**
De Lorimier Winery, 279
De Rose, 279
Deer Park Winery, 123

Deer Springs, 279
Delicato Vineyards, 279
Dolce, 280
Domaine Carneros, 280
Douglas Hill Winery, **78**
Dry Creek Vineyard, 89, 112, **158, 197, 198**
E. & J. Gallo Winery, 89, **158,** 192
Eberle Winery, 100, 150, **158,** 207
Edmeades Estate, 158, **159, 178**
Edna Valley Vineyard, **128, 178**
Ehlers Grove, **217**
Elkhorn Peak, 133
Emilio Guglielmo Winery, **98**
Estrella River Winery, **155, 171**
Fallenleaf, 280
Fess Parker Winery, **129,** 192, 280
Fetzer, **74, 106, 117, 123, 129, 155, 171, 179, 200, 210, 217, 229, 255**
Ficklin Vineyards, 264
Fieldbrook Valley Winery, 280
Filsinger Vineyards, **78**
Firestone, **107,** 143
Flora Springs Wine Company, 144
Foppiano Vineyards, 123
Forest Glen Winery, **107**
Forestville Vineyards, **74, 201**
Franciscan Oakville Estate, **179,** 280
Fratelli Perata Winery, 280
Freemark Abbey, 90, 107
Gainey Vineyard, 280
Galleano Winery, 280
Gan Eden Wines, 280
Gary Farrell Wines, 113, 133, **159,** 192
Geyser Peak Winery, **78,** 90, **117,** 121, 144, **151, 179, 180,** 192, **201, 203, 211, 218, 226,** 258
Glen Ellen Winery, **117, 230,** 280
Gloria Ferrer, 180, **238,** 241
Gold Hill Vineyard, **71**
Golden Creek Vineyard, **139**
Grand Cru Vineyards, **103**
Granite Springs Winery, **155, 198**
Greenwood Ridge, 90, **129, 159, 212, 218**
Grgich Hills, 91, **221**
Guenoc Estate, **71,** 91, **123, 180,** 192, 193, **218, 265**
Gundlach-Bundschu, **71, 79**
Hagafen Cellars, **204, 212, 233**
Handley Cellars, **201, 218,** 241, 244, 245

Page numbers in **boldface** indicate wines that are $15 or under.

USA—CALIFORNIA *(continued)*

Hanna Winery, 79, **181, 222**
Hart Winery, **119**
Haywood Estate, 159
Heitz Cellar, 91
Herzog Wine Cellars, **79, 258**
Hess Collection Winery, 92
Hop Kiln Winery, **79**, 159, 281
Hope Farms Winery, **171**
Husch Vineyards, **198, 259**, 280
Indian Creek, **172**
Indian Springs Vineyards, **79, 107**
Iron Horse, 238
J. Fritz Winery, **160, 182, 208, 218**
J. Lohr, **81, 259**
J. Rochioli Vineyards, 133, **222**
J. Schram by Schramsberg, 242
Jankris Vineyards, 160
Jarvis Winery, 193
Jekel Vineyards, 121
Jepson Vineyards, 245, 280
Jordan Sparkling Wine Company, 242
Joseph Filippi Vintage Co., **265**
Joseph Phelps Vineyards, **139**, 145
Joullian Vineyards, **80**
Justin Vineyards, 92, 145
Kendall-Jackson, 71, **80**, 92, 113, 160, 182, 183, 193, **213**
Kenwood Vineyards, 108, **219**
Konocti Winery, **108**
Konrad Estate Winery, 265
Korbel Winery, **237, 245**
La Crema, 133, 193
Lakewood Winery, **225**
Lambert Bridge, **80, 108**
Landmark Vineyards, 194
Lang Wines, 280
Langtry, 145, 227
Latcham Vineyards, **72, 124**
Lava Cap, **80**, 160, **252**
Leeward Winery, **108**
Les Vieux Cepages, 280
Lockwood Vineyards, 184
Lolonis Wine Cellars, 124
Louis M. Martini, 92, **103, 202, 267**
M.G. Vallejo, 280
Maacama Creek, 280
Madrona Vineyards, **72, 81, 135, 184, 202**, 260
Maison Deutz Winery, 238, 246, 280
Mario Perelli-Minetti Winery, **82**
Markham Vineyards, 93

Martini and Prati Wines, 280
Matanzas Creek Winery, 113
Maurice Carrie Winery, 280
Mazzocco Vineyards, 93
McIlroy Family Wines, **160, 184**
Meeker Vineyard, **82, 161**, 281
Meridian Vineyards, 281
Merryvale Vineyards, 93, 113
Michel-Schlumberger, 93, 194
Mill Creek Vineyards, **109, 184, 219**
Mirabelle Cellars, **239**
Mirassou Vineyards, **124, 205, 219, 240**
Mission View Vineyards, **161, 219**
Mont St. John, 94
Monterra, 281
Montevina Winery, **98, 155, 219**
Mosby Winery, 100
Mount Konocti, **72**
Mount Palomar Winery, 100, 208
Mount Veeder Winery, 146
Mumm Napa Valley, **237, 240**
Murphy-Goode Estate Winery, **208, 222**
Napa Ridge Winery, **74, 82, 109, 125, 185, 202**
Navarro, 82, **130, 185, 219, 222, 260**, 262
Nevada City Winery, 72
Newlan Vineyards, 94
Nichelini, **161, 205**
Orfila Vineyards, 281
Parducci Winery, **118, 122, 172**
Peachy Canyon Winery, 161
Pedroncelli Winery, **109, 118, 135**
Peju Province, 94
Pepperwood Grove, 281
Perry Creek Vineyards, **83, 211, 220**
Pine Ridge, 114, **186**
Piper Sonoma, **237**, 242
Prager Winery and Port Works, 281
Preston Vineyards, **98, 118, 161**
Quady Winery, **252, 253, 265**
Quivira Vineyards, **223**
R.H. Phillips Vineyard, **173**, 281
Rabbit Ridge Vineyards, 109, **118, 120, 162, 208**, 281
Rancho de Philo, 281
Raymond Vineyard, 281
Renaissance Vineyard and Winery, **83**
Renwood Winery, 100, 101
Richard L. Graeser Winery, **83**
Richardson Vineyards, 281
Ridge Vineyards and Winery, 120

Page numbers in **boldface** indicate wines that are $15 or under.

USA—CALIFORNIA (continued)
River Run Vintners, **140, 162**, 263
Robert Alison Winery, **173**
Robert Hunter Winery, 243
Robert Mondavi, 95, **130, 173**, 186
Robert Pepi Winery, 101
Rodney Strong, 95, **110**, 130, **163, 187**
Rombauer Vineyards, 163, 194
Rosenblum Cellars, **120, 156**, 163, **227**, 281
Round Hill Vineyards, **104**
Rutherford Estate Cellars, 281
S. Anderson Vineyard, 281
Sanford Winery, 134, 281
Santa Barbara Winery, 260
Santa Ynez Winery, 266
Santino Wines, **140, 261**
Sausal Winery, **156**
Schramsberg, 238, 246
Schug Carneros Estate, 130, 188
Sebastiani Vineyards, **83, 102, 120, 188**
Sequoia Grove Vineyards, 95, 194
Shafer Vineyards, 95, 96, 114
Shenandoah Vineyards, 281
Sierra Vista Winery, **84, 164**
Silver Horse Vineyards, **164**
Silverado Vineyards, 96, 263
Simi Winery, **188, 220**
Single Leaf Vineyards, 281
Smith & Hook Winery, 114
Sonoma Creek Winery, 281
St. Clement Vineyards, 281
St. Francis Vineyards, 114, 164
St. Supery Vineyards, **84, 253**
Stag's Leap Wine Cellars, 194
Ste. Claire Winery, **281**
Sterling Vineyards, 115, 134
Stevenot Winery, **110**
Stone Creek, **75**
Stonestreet Winery, 96, 115, 134, 146, 195
Storrs Winery, 110, 124, 164
Storybook Mountain Vineyards, 165
Swanson Vineyards, 102, 115, 153, 195
Temecula Crest Winery, **234**
Thomas Coyne Wines, 281
Thomas Fogarty Winery, 281
Topolos at Russian River, 165
Trentadue Winery, **141**, 266
Tribaut, **237, 240**
Trout Gulch Vineyard, 134
Truchard Vineyards, 115, 154

V. Sattui Winery, 96, 97, 165, 195, **214, 230, 234**, 238, **254**
Van Roekel Vineyards, 282
Venezia, 228
Vichon Winery, **174**, 188
Vigil Vineyard, 282
Villa Mt. Eden, **125**, 130, **156, 174**, 189
Vino Noceto, **99**
Voss Vineyards, 223, 282
Weinstock Cellars, **75**, 120, **230**
Wellington Vineyards, **110**
Wente Bros., **75**, 85, **199, 243**
Whaler Vineyard, **165**
Wheeler Winery, 282
Whitehall Lane Winery, 111, 115
Wild Horse Winery, **85, 111, 209**, 282
William Hill Winery, 282
Windsor Vineyards, **85, 124, 166, 254, 266, 267**, 282
York Mountain Winery, **125, 267**
Zaca Mesa Winery, **141, 154**
ZD Wines, 97, 196
Zellerbach Winery, **174, 220**
USA—COLORADO
Colorado Cellars, **122, 212, 234**
Columbine Cellars, 282
Plum Creek Cellars, **186**
USA—FLORIDA
Chautauqua Vineyards, **116, 233**
USA—IDAHO
Ste. Chapelle Vineyards, **246**
USA—ILLINOIS
Alto Vineyards, 282
Lynfred Winery, 262
USA—INDIANA
Huber Orchard Winery, 282
USA—MASSACHUSETTS
Westport Rivers Vineyard, 189
USA—MICHIGAN
Fenn Valley Wines, 282
Tabor Hill, **227**, 243
USA—MISSOURI
Augusta Winery, **116, 203**
Blumenhof Vineyards, 282
Montelle at Osage Ridge, **205**
Mount Pleasant Winery, 282
St. James Winery, **116, 205, 206, 209, 256**
Stone Hill Wine Co., 116, **206, 209, 246, 256**, 261
USA—NEW MEXICO
Gruet Winery, **237, 239**

Page numbers in **boldface** indicate wines that are $15 or under.

USA—NEW YORK
Hermann J. Weimer, 282
Hermann J. Wiemer, **258**
Hunt Country Vineyards, **204**
J. Furst Winery, **172**
Lamoreaux Landing Wine Cellars, **183,
213**
Palmer Vineyards, **256**
Standing Stone Vineyards, **213**
Swedish Hill Vineyard, **116, 206, 214,
234, 261**
Wagner Vineyards, **251**
USA—OHIO
Breitenbach Wine Cellars, **255**
Chalet Debonne Vineyards, 282
Lonz Winery, 282
Meier's Wine Cellars, **116, 204, 239**
USA—OREGON
Cooper Mountain Vineyards, **207**
Eola Hills Wine Cellars, **179**
Hinman Vineyards, **201**
Knudsen-Erath Winery, **208**
Montinore, **185, 205, 256,** 282
Pioneer Hopyard Winery, 282
RainSong Vineyard, **242**
Tualatin, 134
Tyee Wine Cellars, 282
Valley View Winery, **174**
Willamette Valley Vineyards, 97, **125,
130, 214**
USA—REGION UNKNOWN
Chestnut Hill Winery, 282
Kalyra, 282
Poalillo Vineyards, 283
Stony Ridge Winery, 283
USA—TEXAS
Llano Estacado Winery, **199, 227**

Messina Hof Wine Cellars, **82, 103**
Ste. Genevieve, **75, 230**
USA—VIRGINIA
Piedmont Vineyards, 283
Prince Michel Vineyard, 121, 283
USA—WASHINGTON
Andrew Will Winery, 112
Apex, 86
Arbor Crest, **169, 215, 224**
Barnard Griffin, 283
Caterina Winery, **105, 255**
Château Ste. Michelle, 105, 112, 190,
191, **197, 210, 216**
Columbia Crest, **106, 170, 226**
Columbia Winery, 150, **178, 210**
Covey Run Vintners, **106, 117, 210,
255,** 283
Domaine Ste. Michelle, **244**
Hedges Cellars, 144
Hogue Cellars, **107, 181, 198, 218, 224,
255**
Hoodsport Winery, **225**
Paul Thomas Winery, **104, 225**
Preston Vineyards, 94
Seven Hills Winery, 95, 114
Silver Lake Winery, **173**
Tefft Cellars, 96
Thurston Wolfe Winery, 283
Tucker Cellars, **253**
W.B. Bridgman, **85, 110**
Washington Hills Cellars, **104, 220**
Whidbey's, 283
Zillah Oaks Winery, 283
USA—WISCONSIN
Botham Vineyards, **233**
Wollersheim Winery, **206**

Page numbers in **boldface** indicate wines that are $15 or under.

Tasting Notes

Tasting Notes

Tasting Notes

Tasting Notes

Tasting Notes